THE RAINBOW BRIDGE

Also available in the Plant Hunters series
with introductions by Geoffrey Smith:

THE DOLOMITES by Reginald Farrer

THE VALLEY OF FLOWERS by F. S. Smythe

PLANT HUNTING ON THE EDGE OF THE WORLD
by E. Kingdon Ward

THE MYSTERY RIVERS OF TIBET by E. Kingdon Ward

A NATURALIST IN WESTERN CHINA by E. H. Wilson

THE
RAINBOW
BRIDGE

BY REGINALD FARRER
INTRODUCTION BY
GEOFFREY SMITH

CADOGAN BOOKS
LONDON

First published in Great Britain in 1921
by Edward Arnold & Co.

This edition (reprint of third impression, 1926)
published in 1986 by Cadogan Books Ltd,
16 Lower Marsh, London SE1 7RJ

ISBN 0–946313–48–2

Printed and bound in Great Britain by
Redwood Burn Ltd, Trowbridge, Wilts.

INTRODUCTION TO THIS EDITION

There is a map in the back of the copy of 'The Rainbow Bridge' which after reading the book repays careful study. There, clearly defined, is the route followed across the Kansu Province of China by Reginald Farrer and his close friend and companion, William Purdom, on expeditions during the early months of the 1914–18 war.

To share company with someone over weeks of near isolation, under conditions both primitive and extremely dangerous, puts a strain on any relationship. How then did the character of Purdom and Farrer compare? My own assessment can only be arrived at from reading biographical accounts of the two men, and considering the evaluations made by those with the benefit of personal contact and conversation.

It is very obvious that it would have been difficult to select two people so different in character to share the hazards of plant hunting in one of the most dangerously unsettled regions of the world at that time, the Southern border of Kansu Tibet. Purdom, tall, athletic in build, a trained horticulturalist, had worked in the famous nurseries of James Veitch, and for several years at Kew Gardens. Quiet, unassuming and something of an introvert, Purdom undertook his first plant hunting expedition to China in 1908. This extended expedition took him to Kansu and the Tibetan borderland where, no doubt, he noted the diversity and richness of the local flora.

Farrer was, both in appearance and manner, the complete antithesis of Purdom. Stocky, heavily-built, with dark hair and moustache, he was often brusque even rude in manner,

and, at times, venomously sarcastic. For all the obvious con-
tradictions, Farrer writes of Purdom as his beloved companion, and as an absolutely perfect friend and helper.

They both shared, however, a love of flowers and a delight
in the raw, unspoiled mountainous terrain in which the new,
marvellous species were to be found. Possibly Farrer, the enthusiastic amateur with an artist's eye and the romanticism of
a poet, provided just the right counterbalance to the profess-
ionalism of Purdom. What is indisputable is that the end
product of their combined plant collecting efforts has permanently enriched British gardens.

The first season, which concluded in Lanchow on a grey,
rain-drenched November day in 1914, is recorded in two
volumes, very aptly titled 'On The Eaves of the World'. In
this book, which describes the second Purdom/Farrer season,
I believe the author reveals more of his inner character than
even his letters disclose. Were I pressed into choosing just one
of Farrer's books as an example of his penmanship, then this
would be the one. Having read 'On The Eaves of the World'
and the descriptions of revolution, brigandry, looting and
murder, I am surprised that they should have had any desire
to remain in China. Eventually, the situation became so vola-
tile and dangerous the partners were forced to move back
over the border into Tibet. The murderous intent of a
brigand whom Farrer calls the 'White Wolf', Tepos 'black of
heart as of head', unco-operative monks, and lamas added a
most unprecedented threat to the whole enterprise. Eventually, the outbreak of World War I brought the expedition to a
premature close.

In the preface written on May 19th, 1918, Farrer gives expression to some of the frustration, sadness, and distress
engendered by the turmoil and senseless destruction of war.
He writes: "Across the distress of the present I wonder if I
shall be able to escape into the sunshine of the past". Escap-
ism, some might say, yet surely anyone would wish to
exchange the violence of war for a recollection of mountains
filled with quiet and tapestried with flowers. I think the

'Rainbow Bridge' was written not so much as a yearning for things past, more as a hope for the future, the promise of a world again at peace with time to consider the beauty of flowers, and the pleasure to be derived from their cultivation. When botanising, Farrer escaped so completely, became so totally absorbed in the plants around him that he was oblivious even to the perils of avalanche, flood or precipice. To be incarcerated in an office after experiencing the luxurious quiet and immense vistas of mountain landscape around Wolvesden must have been a difficult transition and who could blame him for wishing to relive the experience in writing of the adventure.

I wonder also if it were not in some way a spiritual cleansing of the foul vapours of war. It is enough for me that he wrote it all down so that I can read and re-read of Bill Purdom, "the ferocious frightfulness of Mafu, the goggle eyed Go-go of the drooping lips, and the undauntable endurance." Two years later Farrer died during the course of another journey far away from his beloved Ingleborough in the wilds of Upper Burma.

GEOFFREY SMITH

THE RAINBOW BRIDGE

BY

REGINALD FARRER

Author of
"On the Eaves of the World"

Third Impression

LONDON
EDWARD ARNOLD & CO.
1926

Dedication

Still
To Bill
It is my will
This Book be dedicated.

Although
I know
The Press will go
And say it's overstated.

PREFACE *

Across the distress of the present I wonder if I shall be able to escape successfully into the sunshine of the past ? The attempt is worth making, and, as the crowded months of anxiety flock past, it will grow more and more desperate, as further and further the sunshine recedes, crowded into the background of recollection by multitudinous darkness. Already very far away behind me lie Tien Tang and Chebson, and the huge harsh glory of their desolate land : if I let them slip further they may escape me altogether, or be of no profit to anyone but myself. Let us go, then, for a while out of storm into calm, out of the clamour of guns into the radiant stillness that fills the remote heart of Asia. For, after all, the guns may roar for their time, and lay a world in ruins round us ; but now the irises are blooming again at the Halls of Heaven. And when the guns are broken and silent once more, the irises will still go on blooming year by year. But the Halls of Heaven are a long way hence !

R. F.

May 19, 1918.

* *Mr. Reginald Farrer died far away in the wilds of Upper Burmah, in the course of another adventurous journey, on October 16, 1920 In these circumstances it has been thought best to print his original Preface unaltered.*

CONTENTS

THE RAINBOW BRIDGE

CHAPTER I

LANCHOW

I took a temporary leave of you, reader, in Lanchow, you remember, in November of 1914, after my first season of adventures up the Southern border of Kansu-Tibet. For the tale of those, the Siege of Siku, the Wars of the Wolves, the Murderous Monks and the Tepos black of heart as of head, you must wander *On the Eaves of the World*. I take it for granted, in fact, that that succinct and laconic work is by now so deeply embedded in all your memories that I need not explain to you myself, nor my objects, nor my party : nor introduce to you again my beloved companion, Purdom, whom we will henceforth allow ourselves the freedom of knowing as Bill, and the ferocious frightfulness of Mafu ; and goggle-eyed Go-go of the drooping lip and undauntable endurance. This small caravan it was that, after many perils and triumphs, at last came drifting weary into Lanchow in the frozen dead of the year, to rest for the winter of 1914, until the heart of Asia should once more melt into spring and flowers.

For the time we alighted in the chief inn, described as " semi-foreign." This means no more than that it has panes of glass in its windows as well as paper. Otherwise it was merely the typical inn of a big Chinese capital. Up a narrow little long dark alley you go, hedged in closely on either side by dark little rooms like hutches, to where at the end, behind a painted wooden screen (on which is

1   B

depicted a very stout and very *décolletée* lady), the main
building stands, with three rooms of honour on the ground
floor, and three more rooms of honour above, and then
another line of hutches on either side at right angles, running
back above the lower ones.   Of the state apartments in
the upper story we took possession while the servants
unfolded in the darker set beneath, and considered ourselves
very lucky to have secured such accommodation, though it
was obvious that we could not long endure to retain it.
Both feelings sprang from the same cause.   Lanchow,
being a capital, and the seat of a Viceroy, is always densely
crowded with officials in Esse or in Posse, men out of a job,
or hoping for a better one.   So that every inn in the town
is perpetually occupied by office-seekers, awaiting from
day to day, often for many months on end, the moment
that shall at last call them to audience of His Excellency,
or of some minion of His Excellency's who may be able
to open a backdoor to prosperity, in consideration of proper
presents bestowed.   And, as hope deferred maketh the
heart sick, stimulant is clearly indicated for those awaiting
jobs, heavy-handed as they are with idleness and expectation.
All day and most of the night they sit on their kangs and
play the morra-game for thimblesful of warm spirit, until
the noise of their revelry grows deafening, and their shouts
reverberate in the close dark channel of the courtyard.
Accordingly we very soon concluded that, for peace and
quietness, we must remove into more secluded quarters and
take a house of our own.

It became a matter of making acquaintances.   Lanchow
has no European residents at all (not being a treaty town)
except a knot of Missionaries outside the city.   The Postal
Commissioner—call him Postmaster for short—happened in
1914 to be a Yorkshireman of that true-blue brand which
only Lincolnshire produces.   And with this jovial soul
we had gladly foregathered, in mutual satisfaction at
finding a fellow human being who read real books and had
real interests.   When the need of a house grew plain we

repaired to him, and found that he and his sparkling little
wife had a ramification of acquaintance among the citizens
exactly of the sort we wanted to help us to our object.
Negotiations were soon set going, and we embarked on
the tortuous currents of Ma-y's friendship. Ma-y was a
crony of the Postmaster, but not a person of any social
standing : being a man of nothing, who by mule-contracting
on a grand scale had raised himself rapidly to affluence. He
was—as his name declares, Ma being Mahomed—one of the
Mahomedans with whom North Kansu so ominously
swarms—a round comfortable person with a comfortable
round red face, twinkling undecipherable little eyes like
blobs of darkness, and a geniality sinister, enveloping and
unescapable. In every pie he had a finger, and in each
transaction an interest. Despite the protests of the Post
Office that Ma had a soul of lily-pure disinterestedness, the
truth of things could not be hidden. There was nothing
we wanted that Ma could not procure, not a wish that he
did not anticipate, but always at an excessive price, benignly
stated and inexorably maintained. Out of his vast circles
he collected pictures, bronzes and china. Mafu grew
every day more dour and furious at seeing my avidity and
innocence being so beguiled. But there was no help for it :
sustained by scoldings from Bill and Mafu I might indeed
learn to be adamant against pictures that I didn't want, at
prices that I didn't wish to pay : but it was inevitable,
on the impulsion of the Post Office, that Ma should have
the privilege of getting us a house.

Meanwhile the social aspects were developing. We
dined with our friends of the Post Office, and began to
meditate official calls, learning that the Viceroy hoped to
see me. To my experience and exalted rank, City Governors
were by now no more accounted of than silver in the days
of Solomon, but Viceroys, it was felt, were fish of a larger
fry, and needed more stately approach. Accordingly
a go-between was found to arrange the protocols of a meeting
between two such potentates. And the next morning, as I

sat in a red impotent fret of worry over long-dead happenings in the war, there entered to me Mr. Li, a radiant little vision of elegance pale and dainty and smiling, sumptuous in fur-lined coat and skirt of brocaded silks. It was my first sight of a Southern Chinese, of that delicate, small-boned, small-made pussyfoot type, quick-witted as a needle, and supple, sinewy, and nervous as the small cat that it irresistibly suggests ; wide poles asunder from the large and solid-minded carthorse type of Northern China.

Mr. Li and Mr. Lo—for I cannot ever think of them apart —were a brace of strayed swallows from Canton, young gentlemen of wealth and quality, dispatched for family reasons into an Ovidian exile in the remote and inexpensive North. For about these reasons, Mr. Lo made no disguise. " In Canton," he said, " plen'y dlink, plen'y ho'house, plen'y money lose. My Fam. think go way more better." And accordingly here were these two little frail birds— it is so I always think of them, as a pair of lovebirds together on a perch—enduring the rigours and deprivations of hard work and scant diversions in Lanchow, serving in the Post Office. Probation, not pay, was their object : each day they appeared in fresh furs and satins, always glittering with neat elegance. Amid the dust and damnations of the Post Office they daily shivered and shone : and when work was over, retired to shift their silks again in the many-yarded house where they lived together and collected bronzes and pictures. Mr. Li had little English and Mr. Lo had less : but they became to me very real people, for they were so much gentlemen, and of so genuine a charm. They had wide ideas too, and made me parties at which Mrs. Lo and charming Mrs. Li played an unabashed part impossible in any really provincial family of North China.

However, this is for the future. Mr. Li first dawned on me as my medium for approaching the Viceroy. He announced that His Excellency hoped to see me in the very near future, but would I, in the meantime, go and pay a call on

General Wu ? Mr. Li would be my escort : a day was duly appointed. But now as these splendours surged over our social horizon, the heart of Mafu grew troubled with the problem of presenting Great Lord Law-and-order (which is the Chinese for Me) in adequate style. Unassuming dignity had been all very well in Jo-ni and Siku ; but Viceroys and Generals I must meet on a more ostentatious footing. Mafu besought me, through Bill, to remember hard what other honorifics, or titles of nobility I might possess. I ransacked my memory, and ran down a mental list of the various Clubs and Learned Societies that I adorn. But nothing suited : and unfortunately this all happened long before these latter days when initials of honour rain so copiously that few can hope to escape. However, at last it came upon me that I was indeed a Justice of the Peace : to Mafu I tried to explain the rather misty majesty of a Great Unpaid, and he went away in apparent satisfaction. To return in triumph a few days later, with a brand-new visiting card of scarlet, a foot long by six inches wide, on which enormous black characters announced the " Great Man Law-and-order, Lord High Keeper of the King's Peace." On contemplating which I felt that even Viceroys must now assuredly bite the dust, and that China in general, considering the European war, would certainly feel how properly the Lord High Keeper of the King's Peace was here in Lanchow, his functions at home being so lamentably in abeyance. Surely never yet have Peace and Justice (excellent humdrum inevitabilities of life as we used to think them) been expanded into so majestic a mantle for the draping of a mere everyday J.P.

Arrayed then in my new majesty, and trying to live up to it in stateliness of demeanour, I accompanied Mr. Li to call on General Wu. Down the long main East-West street we proceeded, stiltedly conversing across smiles, till we reached the big Yamen half-way towards the main market-place on which the huge outer gate of the Viceregal palace directly fronts. Salutations and presenting of arms. Up and up through successive courtyards we passed, all of them as neat and clean as a packet of new pins : till, after waiting a moment in the room of an A.D.C., we were shown on into the innermost sanctum, and there received, with significant courtesy, on the very threshold, by the General. Few people have more charm of courtesy and dignified cordiality than a cultivated Chinese official of high standing, and General Wu was no exception—a singularly attractive, pleasant-smiling man of about forty, slim and elegant in his uniform. You will often see his portrait in French Galleries, but there he is called Cardinal Richelieu, and has nothing of the geniality and less of the refinement that he shows in China. In a high and stately flow of courtesies, with assiduous swimmings and floatings and bowings on my part, we were conducted in, through apartment after apartment, each presenting the aspect of a railway refreshment-room with a long white-clad table down the middle and white-clad chairs set round, and the whole place done with white, spacious and clean in the mellow glow of the sunlight pouring in through the pane of glass that made the centre of each paper-latticed window down one side of the wall. Tea, too, was served in European coffee-cups : we sat and chatted of *la haute politique* with that *au bout des lèvres* effusiveness which is the rule in China, revealing nothing at all under an appearance of ebullient ingenuousness. Mr. Li interpreted, and I can but hope that Law-and-order lived up to his visiting-card. I think he must have : the General expressed himself much gratified with our talk, and congratulated the city on now holding within its walls a man of such high erudition and breadth of view. Not only this, but when—having sipped, as etiquette bids, the valedictory tea which is always the Chinese tag for ending an interview, the Yours Sincerely of conversation which we unfortunately have only for the written word—we rose to go, the General persisted in seeing us through all the many courtyards down to the street-gate itself.

This, you must know, if you have not already learned,

is the crucial point of decorum in a Chinese leave-taking.
Down through the various courts the host must personally
escort the guest : and at each gate the guest must pat him
back and protest against his coming any farther, while the
host must insist on being allowed to do so. But all the
time both parties know perfectly well the precise point
to which the host must advance without showing either too
much honour or too little, and the precise point at which
the guest can let himself be abandoned without losing face.
Codes, both subtle and rigid, govern each step of welcome
and farewell, and the possibilities of insult are infinite,
though both insult and the possibility of it are alike invisible
to the innocent stranger who does not know his claims in
honour, nor how minutely the lookers-on are noting the
degree of respect he is receiving from his host. If a new-
comer is escorted to the outermost gate, the news is all over
the city in an hour, and his status is secure. So that Mr.
Li grew discreetly enthusiastic over the success of our visit
to the General.

But Viceroys tower, in China, far higher than Generals :
and not even Lords Keepers of a King's Peace can expect
more than three or four gateways'worth of farewell from
Eminences so August. A few days passed—days of dancing
diamond deliciousness in the hard brilliant clearness of the
Northern winter, and then, after inquiring if I wished to
talk politics or merely to pay a call, the Viceroy made an
appointment to receive me. This time there was no question
of going a-foot. Mr. Li, more splendid than ever, called
for me in a Peking cart, and together we jolted awfully up
the cobbles of the lane, and along the main street. The
scene and the ceremonial were similar to those of my last
visit ; but the ceremonial was more brief and stately, the
scene a great deal ampler. For the Viceregal Palace at
Lanchow is an enormous place, huge open expanse behind
expanse, with living-courts for the family tucked away in
lateral labyrinths. At various of the vast gates we waited,
and attendants hurried forward with our cards, and then

came back to call us on. Then there were sittings about in *salles d'attente*, the walls of which were hung with scrolls that in the floweriest of involved language gave hints on the advantages of brevity in speech when dealing with Viceroys. And finally a railway restaurant-room like that of the other day, but larger : a solemn pause—and then in loomed the Viceroy, the most complete contrast to General Wu—a great stout heavy man, with immense bullet-head and solid jowl, tightly bound in dull black satin, and looking the very image of a reformed dissenting burglar, buttoned up in his Sunday blacks for Chapel. He was stout and solid in manner too : not easily genial like General Wu, but ponderous and searching in his questions. I twittered inside my cloudy grandeurs, and gradually as he talked I felt him growing larger and larger upon me in every way, like a thing in a nightmare, until the Viceroy of Kansu[1] came to remain in my mind as one of the biggest men I have ever confronted. All went well, however ; Mr. Li congratulated me afterwards, and said that His Excellency was really anxious to be all that was cordial, and promised an invitation to a banquet at an early date. So homeward we came, and by way of a bathos proceeded to call on the City Governor. I had meant only to leave cards, but finding he would like to see me, in I went, and found him a kindly old black-satin gentleman in a bowler hat, but without very much to say. And thus finished the round of dissipation for the day.

House-hunting now filled our thoughts in the intervals of getting the season's store of seeds duly cleaned, sorted, packed and dispatched. But incidentally there were strolls through the streets, and idle chafferings for the few poor *objets d'art* that are all Lanchow has to offer the

---

[1] I call him the Viceroy : under the then-moribund republic his title changed from day to day, and one never knew for long which to call him—Changchun or Dudu or something else. But Dudu I always wanted to avoid : it sounded such a silly name, like some extinct bird.

collector (and that at preposterous prices) unless he has the entrée to private collections, and can purchase quietly. This was the secret of Mr. Lo and Mr. Li, knowing, as they did, all " the best circles, spheres, lines, ranks, everything " in Lanchow. We had a notable lunch-party in their house one day to inspect their treasures. We went, and Mr. and Mrs. Post Office went, and charmingly pretty little Mrs. Li was hostess, and beside her Mrs. Lo in her tight silk trousers, and between them a tiny solemn Japanese dolly girl-child, in whom a very un-Chinese amount of pleasure was obviously taken. The meal was very merry, and a happy hybrid between Chinese and European styles, with soup, sharks' fins, pigeons' eggs in a soft sop, duck, fried mutton, chicken and bamboo shoots, beef rissoles, and many another delicacy served in Chinese fashion, and without forks, so that the knives were useless, and it became a case of bravely plying chopsticks. And in the middle of the banquet, served in a round copper bowl on a flaming Etna, appeared the delicious stewing lotus seeds (like little sweet chestnuts) which are essential to every Chinese feast, as they are held to keep off the ravages of the hot spirit which is perpetually being poured out of little kettles into elfin cups no bigger than thimbles. On this occasion, though, beer was the beverage : no doubt it was this fatal Boche drink that inspired Mr. Lo with the typical Boche remark that women ought not to be taught too much.

But by this time the house was found, and taken, through Ma-y, and at Ma-y's price—a combination that made Mafu as glum as a dyspeptic gorilla. It was a stately place, though, and I was in no heart to cavil at terms, tired as I was by this time of the roars and stinks of the inn. My house was in the roughly cobbled street that goes straight to the North Gate. It had the advantage of having Mr. and Mrs. Post Office living only a dozen or so doors down in the main street, so that we could mutually dine and play bridge without having to rush home early for fear of being cut off from one's home by the wooden gates like

cages that stand at all the important intersections of streets
in Lanchow, and after 9 at night are shut and locked.
And in itself it was worthy even of my habitation and a
Viceregal visit. Past the gate-keeper's lodge you went
into a wide clean court : then fronted you a very long
building with carved and latticed verandahs, divided
longitudinally into one back room and one front one :
it was here that Law-and-order had his tabernacle. Behind
this there was a neat new alley-court with rooms and to
spare for the staff on either hand : and at the end of all
a block of buildings for Bill's quarters. The whole place
was solid and handsome and new : when we had evicted
some soldiers and their horses and litter, it took us little
time to put things in order, white-paper the state apartments, lay down matting, install stoves and generally
make the house shipshape for a winter residence.

We were in luck, indeed, to get it at all. We were told
it was the property of a Mahomedan noble, who, on being
suspected of complicity in some Mahomedan intrigue against
the Chinese, had been so overcome with shame as to throw
himself into the Yellow River, off the hideous iron bridge
just outside the North Gate. But the currents of Chinese
gossip are as devious and subtle as those of Chinese politics :
the real fact of the matter was that our unwitting landlord
had fled away Southward to the safe Mahomedan district
of Ho-jo, where no Chinese would ever venture, let alone
lay hands on him. Everybody knew this, and everybody
knew that every one else knew it : but the polite fiction
of his suicide in the Hwang-ho was imperturbably maintained. In no case did the question trouble us : for in
the meantime we were in possession of his house, and for a
rent of 24 taels a month. This means some £3 12s., and
is, for China, grossly excessive to the extent of surpassing
what a Chinese would have paid by about sixteen taels :
but I could not grudge it, first or last, though the Mafu's
gloomy sourness put me to confusion, as also did the cluck-
cluckings of Mr. Lo and Mr. Li when they heard the price,

and the civil snoring suppositions of Great Lord Lang as to what he thought I should be giving—as compared with the facts of what I really was giving.

For polite life was now in full flow : visits and cards were returned, and dear old Jang[1] actually turned up from Siku to hang round Lanchow drearily on his savings till the Viceroy should give him a new job. We had to increase our staff to cope adequately with our new way of living. A door-keeper was established in the gate-house, and to replace the good little Cook, whom wife-hunger now recalled to Siku, we engaged a gaptoothed Mahomedan person with a flapped fur hat, a repulsive face, and a Christian smile acquired in Missions, whence also, it is only fair to add, he had drawn the much more useful art of making scones. Our former staff seemed rather grotesque in a city. Even Mafu as major-domo was like a gorilla promoted butler ; and when one afternoon General Wu came riding up in state to return my call, there was only the Go-go to hand. Left alone to cope with such an emergency, the poor lad lost his head completely, and rushed wildly about with eyes protruding from their sockets under the impression that here was the Viceroy come in person.

Come the great man did, though, a few days later : but by the convention of etiquette we were " not at home," so that only his card adorned the room. A few days later came the announcement of his promised banquet. Law-and-order by that time lay sick of a fever : however, it was very urgently represented by Mr. and Mrs. Post Office that only death could justify the star-guest in evading His Excellency's feast. So I buckled myself into a firm deter-mination to be better : and better I promptly therefore began to be, as soon as I had signified my intention of waiting on the Great Man at dinner. In response to my acceptance there came back a lovely folded card of scarlet silk crape, on which, beneath golden headings, columns of delicate spidery characters gave a list of the

[1] For him and the good little Cook see *On the Eaves of the World*.

proposed guests. Under our own columns Bill and I made marks of acknowledgment, and returned the document, though eagerly did I long to keep it.

The next day was that of the banquet. We got ourselves into what bests we could achieve, and considered how imposing a cortège could be managed. Mafu and Go-go by this time had adapted themselves to our new social exigencies by fitting themselves out in khaki-coloured livery, copied by a Lanchow tailor from Bill's own khaki tunic and breeches, so that they now presented a much more suitable appearance. Chairs, too, were hired—not common carrying chairs, but the stately, roomy, well-upholstered ones such as important officials affect, covered in dark cloth, with glass windows and silvered top-knots and pole-knobs and fittings, and lined with soft fur. About 4 o'clock the summons came, and the procession formed. Bill went ahead of me in the first chair, and the Keeper of the King's Peace followed augustly after with Mafu and the Gate-keeper on the ponies clattering before and behind, and two enormous lanterns of scarlet with characters announcing my name and quality bobbing and floating up the December dusk of the street before me.

In due course we alighted at the outer gate of the Palace and proceeded through the courts and along labyrinths of alleys, each shabbier than the last, till we came at length into a smaller yard with rockworks like a skeleton edifice of Pulhamite preparing for a show, and a big white airy room at the end. Here were many of the guests already gathered—Mr. Post Office, and General Wu, General Lu and Mr. King (who some say is the real power in Kansu), with various others, including Mr. Li, very sumptuous but very *piano*, as neither age nor status gave him any place at such feasts, to which he was only asked as a conversational link between me and my host. We all stood about and bowed and smiled : suddenly there was a murmur of announcement, and in rolled the Viceroy with his curious smooth swift massiveness of movement. Handshakes all

round and quick bows over each : more guests arrived :
we sat down along the white-clothed table, drinking tea
and smoking and making suitable remarks while we awaited
the call to dinner. On word of this His Excellency arose :
arm in arm we led the procession out into the frosty dark,
through an *œil-de-bœuf* door in the wall, and along the
rim of a huge forested and mounded garden park (which
I hope to show you again when it is no longer all bare
dust-coloured earth) till we came to a new room lit feebly
with electric light. Here the feast was spread at a round
table, with absurdly low seats. I was duly posted in my
proper place, and the banquet began.

By this time I knew the duty of a principal guest, and
lost no time in dipping first into each dish as it was plopped
on the centre of the table, and transferring as little as I
could to my own tiny plate, or as choice a morsel as I could
find to that of any neighbour I wished to honour, with
breath-takings and smiling bows. For myself I felt in
no very fine feather for feasts, and dreaded both the good
victuals and the drink. The latter proved to be hot
Curaçao : a fearsome food at first, but practice ere long
made perfect in its consumption, and a modest joviality
began to develop. But with the food I could not cope,
except for an omelette of sharks' fins, a souse of pigeons'
eggs, and a jujube pudding. Bird's-nest soup-bouilli seemed
to me tasteless, and all the most cherished Chinese dishes
are in general glutinous, gristly, or gelatinous, invariably
sloppy in juice and dishwash, and usually of a rather nauseous
insipidity to the untrained foreign palate. However, the
feast flowed well, and His Excellency flowered into an
unbuttoned gaiety that showed him in quite a new light.
We foregathered particularly over pictures and *objets
d'art*, of which he is the chief and (naturally) most successful
collector in these parts : learning that I had enthusiasms
in the same direction he announced that he wanted to see
my acquisitions, and that I must certainly ask him to dinner
in return.

This daunted me : for who can cope, in collecting, with Chinese Viceroys ? Everything of the best goes first to them as a matter of course, and in the way of presents they do far better than the foreigner with no matter how large a power of cash. But let no one therefore think that these great and honourable persons are to be corrupted by gifts from aspirants to office, or officials under a cloud. Far from it : they are rigid in their refusal of any present of more than some half-a-crown's worth or so in value, such as is therefore a merely formal token of respect. But alas for human wickedness ! how should an innocent Viceroy guess the real worth of some masterpiece of Tang that an unscrupulous would-be Governor is offering him as a mere humble half-crown's worth ? All the world knows how ill-bred and ungracious it is to look a gift horse in the mouth : who could be so tactless then as to point out that the five-shilling scroll would really be cheap at twenty thousand dollars ? This would be to wound the aspirant unduly, to convict him brutally of either ignorance or dishonesty. Accordingly the picture goes smoothly into the Viceregal gallery : and by an odd coincidence a plump office slides ere long with equal smoothness into the hands of its former possessor.

I hope I do not detain you unduly with feasts and foods ? But the fact is that the countless cross-examinations I have undergone since my return at the hands of the more intelligent have left me with a conviction that people's prime interest in one's travel-experiences lies in learning what one had to eat and drink. So that I intend to continue unashamed, not burking the various banquets that occur in my course, on account of any craven fear of repetition or the accusation of it. And in any case remember, you who have read *On the Eaves of the World,* that there are many small points that I must needs touch on here again in order to make the details of Chinese life and ceremonial plain to those who haven't.

But on Ma-y's feasts I will not dwell : I never enjoyed

them. He made me many, and insisted on my going to all of them : and in a wish not to offend him (and still more the Post Office, which patronized him strongly) I went again and again, however reluctantly, and however clearly realizing that all this was done, neither for fun nor friendship, but simply to gain " face " by getting known as the constant dinner-host of so eminent a person as Law-and-order. From one of these parties, indeed, I returned the richer by a large orange-coloured cat : but even this, I soon learned, Ma-y had only " given " me on the hire system. I had flirted with it during the course of an interminable meal, and at the end, just as I was climbing into my cart, Ma-y, flushed with convivial generosity, but not to the extent of forgetting prudence and profit, pursued me from his house brandishing the puss by its hind leg. On to my lap he frantically compiled it, and told me how much I was to pay : and the cart set off. But this cursory treatment had, not unnaturally, discomposed the puss : and she screamed vindictively all the way home. This meant much, for the way was very long and very bumpy, Ma-y living meanly in a mud-built shack, outside the city wall, down in a desolate loess area of wide expanses and little rutty lanes.

Nor when I got her home did the cat ever develop into a comfort. She was, in fact, a stupid cat, with a great silly face like a kitchen clock. Also, she spoke, and understood, nothing but Chinese, and never made the smallest attempt to learn English. Temperamentally, too, she was unresponsive as a dead slug : passive of caresses, but never reciprocating them, and unrestrainably evasive. A dull dog : not even when Go-go pursued her about with saucers of milk and " Mao-lai, Mao-lai " did she manifest any human feelings : but perhaps her particular brand of Mahomedanism had narrower notions about milk than her original owner's about wine. In any case, back to her original owner she soon returned, packed up in a basket, with my best thanks and declared disinclination to deprive him longer of such a treasure.

Thus we settled into the jog-trot monotony of that long winter, broken only by the New Year celebrations. Those of the New Style coincide, of course, with our New Year, and were marked by a huge official banquet at the Palace, following on a general review of the Kansu troops. All the *sommités* were gathered on the verandah at the top of the parade ground, and proceedings began at an unearthly hour of the morning by no means welcome to those who had done the New Year the honour of seeing it in. Between lapses into irrepressible slumber I feebly murmured answers to the various officials who came up to me and made talk in the inner room where the more select personages awaited the arrival of the Viceroy : the one bright spot was Mr. Post Office, who had donned, by way of official attire, an unhappy-looking venerable frock-coat and an ancestral top-hat fluffy as a Georgian relic. And outside, all this time, thousands of trim khaki-uniformed soldiers were manœuvring to the braying of bands.

Then after what seemed hours of waiting came a crescendo of noise beginning from afar and swelling nearer and nearer. His Excellency was arriving : out we all went on to the verandah again, the soldiers in dense lines made a vast wide lane of emptiness down the length of the parade ground : minute at last in the distance of the vacant vista, appeared the Viceregal sedan, glittering in gold and green, advancing rapidly in magnitude up towards us at a trot with many bearers and attendants. At the foot of the stairs it was set down, and out stepped His Excellency. A most superb figure of a man this time, in full uniform of blue and gold, with blue and golden kepi, from the front of which stiffly aspired one of those foot-high blue shaving brushes which must assuredly be of such vital usefulness in war. Having saluted us and various others, the Viceroy took his stand in the middle of the verandah, and the Review proceeded. It was of interminable tediousness, as all such functions are : by hundreds the battalions and regiments defiled before us, eyes-righting abruptly to the Viceroy as they passed, and goose-stepping with a most ridiculous precision all the time. Yet an imposing sight too : and not one expected in popular conceptions of China. It went on and on till at length there came a pause, and in a series of stentorian staccato shouts the Viceroy began delivering an allocution on patriotism to a knot of officers assembled beneath the verandah. We seized the opportunity to slip unobtrusively away, with some difficulty found our carts among the assembled multitudes of others, and so returned home to rest till 3, when it was time to get up again and dress for the party.

This, as I say, was a huge gathering : dinner was half foreign, and served in foreign fashion, with me, in foreign fashion also, on my host's right hand. It turned out really, despite my leaden anticipations, very gay : I had the greatest fun with the Viceroy, who by this time seemed quite an old friend. He revealed his full skill in drink : but foreknowing his determination to triumph over mine, I was able to elude all his cunning wiles. No serious talk on this occasion : except that he had at last had news, in which he was much interested, of a big letter I had written to Yuan Shih Kai, his cousin, about the state of things on the Border (Weltpolitik up there is a small immediate thing, but it completely fills one's view, and one cannot keep one's hand from it). So we laughed and ragged together : and in the intervals I scanned the guests on either hand, down the long narrow length of the table. Some I knew and some I didn't, but all, I supposed, were important : I wondered, therefore, here and there to see a little meek person, unspeaking and unspoken-to, perfectly silent except for the sonorous gulps of deglutition with which it is Chinese etiquette to advertise your enjoyment of your dinner. This moved my curiosity, and at length I discovered that they were, indeed, " ghosts," not personally there at all, but only officially, so that they were not supposed to be noticed, or even seen.

For in China, it seems, if you have accepted an invitation to dinner, and then are unable or unwilling to go, you send your secretary or your valet to take your place. He prevents your seat from being empty by sitting in it, and your share of the food from being wasted by eating it : but otherwise, in himself, is non-existent. At least they enjoyed their dinner, these shadow-people : and a good dinner it was, and seemed to last till midnight, though eight had barely struck, in fact, when the cups of rice appeared. This is the end of a Chinese feast, and on this signal you immediately rise up and say good-bye. So out we all came, and down through the various courts, lovely in the dark with the illumination of crimson lanterns everywhere : and home along the streets now also all aglow with strings of lanterns, shining like ruby balls down the long straight perspectives.

The real Chinese New Year comes much later, in the middle of February. I found it a depressing time, as it lasts a whole fortnight, and all the shops keep shut throughout, so that one's English sense of cut-off-ness at Christmas and Easter is here multiplied to fivefold. Moreover I was now alone, for Bill, with that indefatigable kindness which reduces all I can ever say of him to a pale nothing, had gone off Southward, over the frozen world, back to Jo-ni and Ardjeï, to bargain on my behalf for various treasures of Tibetan copper : and in particular for two of those great cooking vats which you first heard of " On the Eaves of the World," and which are prizes so difficult to attain that none have as yet ever come to Europe. However, Bill had long had his mind's eye on a pair of these which, in the break-up of a family, he thought there was a chance of securing. So off he rode one afternoon on an iron-cold day of greyness with snowflakes falling drearily : with only his pack beneath him, and alone except for a brace of very smart khaki-clad mounted soldiers from the Viceroy's own bodyguard, a special tribute which I hailed with satisfaction, because it would certainly give him much higher " face " on the road than the solitary ragamuffin that he would otherwise have had from the City Governor.

Bleakly I remained behind, with only proofs and various

tedious works of the sort for sole company and occupation
till he should return. Not, indeed, that I was really quite
so solitary : for by now I was harbouring in my house a
brisk little American journalist, a born nomad, who had
drifted down into Lanchow again from Si-ning and the
remote North. But he came as the friend of the Post
Office, and with Mr. and Mrs. Post Office he fed and lived,
only returning home to sleep : so that it was little, in reality,
that I saw of his round cherubic head, bald and blue-eyed
and gold-spectacled, the image of a chubby little innocent
pink Monsignore—though with more pinkness than innocence
in his character.

Time hung heavy, and the war hung heavier. Long
since, in the common expectation that it would soon be
over, I had concluded best to stay where I was and complete
my contract—having come so far to do it, and at such a
cost of time and peril—but nothing could alleviate the
leaden oppressiveness of sitting there all that agelong
winter, in forced inactivity, the prey of fears and hopes
that one could do nothing to prevent or further, and of
anguishes long since settled and dead by the time one read
of them. The reading of six-weeks-old newspapers was a
double oppression in the winter of 1914, and even the
telegrams we received, by arrangement, up-country, only
served to keep one oscillating in an agony of impotent
anxiousness. I sank myself hard in work during the
mornings, and dutifully patrolled the shops in the afternoons,
clothed in a quilted blue gown of cotton-duvet and black
velvet Wellington boots lined with lynx : on my head a
beaver hat, and about me, when the day was extra cold,
a black satin dolman lined with soft black fur. And in the
evenings I went to bed as soon as was decent.

Not that the shops in Lanchow are of any merit : but
to wander round them and sit and bargain and joke with
their proprietors was always fun, and something to fill the
radiant winter afternoons. The only shops that interest
one are, naturally, those of *objets d'art* : these are chiefly

to be found down one side of the big open market-place in the centre of the city, immediately outside the palace. A forlorner assemblage of more wretched rubbish was seldom seen, however : though by the prices asked for each sham bronze or third-rate picture you might imagine yourself to be bargaining for pearls and diamonds. They are open to the day, these shops, without frontage or door, separated each from each by only a partition : you wander in and sit before the counter, and send your glance roving round until such time as the proprietor intrudes on you with something specially hideous that he hopes you may be got to buy. In the meantime what you see all round you crowded on the shelves is the strangest jackdaw-collection of odds and ends : the glittering brass of incense-burners, fire-pots, openwork chaufferettes for the hands : bronzes, lumbering and spurious, odds and ends of indifferent china, official necklaces and derelict official hat buttons of the dead Imperial days : terrible pictures on glass : roots of ginsing like withered tiny human atomies, framed and glazed : European handbasins of tin, painted gaudily with pansies and roses : lampglobes to match : and other flotsam and jetsam of foreign introduction higgledy-piggledied up with wild brass devils down from Tibet, and bland Bodhisats and Madonnas.

But nowhere anything of beauty or value : unless the owner, on a later day, mysteriously takes you into an inner room and there shows you a really good piece of bronze, or a picture, or a screen of panels encrusted with fruits and flowers made of precious stones, jade and jasper and topaz and cornelian and chalcedony, that he has got in from a friend to sell on commission. Or it may be, perhaps, that in the glass cases on either side the entrance, among the rubbish of lockets and buckles and old spectacles and snuff-bottles of no account, you may now and then happen on one of carved coral, a treasure of former days, such as I never saw in Peking later on, being the official present of the Sovereign to the great viceroys on the high occasion of a birthday. But in no case is the buying done then and there : nor must you even show a spark of attention for anything you want to buy. In fact, the more you mean to have it, the less must you seem to notice it at all. I am very bad, myself, at disguising appetence : so that after a few initial disasters, which had the effect of making Mafu growl like a bear, I always used to take him with me on my walks, following at my heel, to preserve me from any impetuous imprudence.

To him, then, when I had found anything I wanted, I would point it out : round to my house it would ere long be brought, and then would begin the real serious business of bargaining, often protracted over months, with feigned advances and retreats, and histrionic indignations, and the laughter of assumed derision, and hands of silent protest thrown to Heaven over the rapacity of one party or the parsimony of the other : culminating, of course, in the triumphant surrender of the merchant to a price which, however much I may have beat him down, was always at least three times as much as he would ever have got, or tried to get, from a compatriot. I used to believe that if the purchaser gave double what he offered at first, and half of what he had been asked, he would be doing none so ill : long experience in Lanchow and Peking have taught me now that even if one pays as little as a tenth of what was first demanded, one is giving the seller, by Chinese standards, nothing short of a walk-over.

All this applies to those more showy shops in the market-place, where the more important things are found. And here I always had Mafu to safeguard me. But scattered rarely in the minor streets there are other little rubbish shops where I used to poke and pry alone, secure in the knowledge that even if I did pay a dollar for some small jar or danglet that wasn't worth half, no very great harm was thereby done. And it was much more fun to roam alone. But in particular, all round the outside of the wall between the South Gate and the East Gate, above the moat, there

runs an unbroken series of wooden shops, accumulated with
the most fascinating chaos of trash and old clo'. In the
winter the moat is frozen and the clamour of its summer-
time stenches is stilled : so that in the afternoons, when the
long lane is flooded with sunshine and sheltered from cold
winds by the towering height of the city wall behind, I used
to wander very happily from shop to shop, chaffering and
laughing with their owners. One shop was my special
favourite, and indeed was the public show of a dealer who
kept a much more ambitious private store in one of the
streets beyond the South Gate : from him, the Long Brother,
I gradually made many purchases, my culminating triumphs
being four fascinating little old sages of painted stone and a
cracked powder-blue plate which after weeks of higgling I
secured at the price of two empty bottles without earning
reproaches even from Mafu.

CHAPTER II

THE NEW YEAR

And now, suddenly, all this came to an end, and every shop was shut for an interminable fortnight. Each family was keeping up its New Year's Beano, and commerce was wholly in abeyance. The only diversions of those days were the various festal ceremonies that one met in the streets. One has always, indeed, the chance of seeing an almost life-size pink paper horse and paper people, standing outside a doorway to indicate that its owner has just "mounted on high," leaving a mourning family behind : but during the New Year special festivities occur. One day it is an expulsion of evil spirits : going out into my street I found myself submerged in an excited mob, in the midst of which a gaunt painted woman, with a face grey with frenzy, surged drunkenly this way and that, while behind her followed a rhythmical chorus of some dozen long black drums. Their bearers would beat *fortissimo* in measure, *BOOM* BOOM, *BOOM* BOOM ; then swinging round, sink to a *pianissimo*, *boom boom, boom boom :* and so *da capo* and *da capo* all up the street, with the Sibyl swaying her wild course ahead. And the brisk monotonous alternation of noise, in its relentless rhythm and rise and fall, ended at last by having a quite hypnotic effect, which has haunted my memory ever since.

On another occasion I was crowded almost off my feet by another mob of enthusiasts : a parcel of bedizened painted people, in tinsel jewels and tinsel robes and crowns and flowers pranced Mænadically down the streets on stilts, and after them followed a corybantic procession, with crackers and drums and gongs in pandemonium.

23

Or yet again, a still mightier crowd, and a still louder clamouring, in attendance on a mob of many little boys caracoling down the street on paper hobby-horses, escorting an immense and wildly-agitated paper dragon with terrifying mask of papier mâché : while behind there came paper fishes flashing gilt and colour, and a great cardboard kylin of blue and gold with a body all of straw fringe, looking like a colossal poodle gone pale. But these are rare diversions of this close season, and in the meantime I turned my attention perforce to the beauties of Lanchow and its environs. Do not grumble at me if I make you linger there also, and along the preliminaries of my travel. For, if you are to share its flowers and fun, it is only fair that you should share its delays and dullnesses too, so as to gather a complete notion of what that country and that northern winter and spring are like, and how our life went by there, in long slow slabs, prefacing the hurry of the working-time.

Lanchow, among big Chinese towns, is my dream city. It is precisely what I had seen Sian-fu, in visions which Sian-fu entirely declined to fulfil. It lies in a flat plain with the Yellow River flowing round its Northern wall, at the foot of the high crumpled fells of desolation that are called the Golden Hills and dominate the city with the theatre and pagoda on one of their nearer lesser peaks. It is a very steep scramble up any of those heights, over slippery tracks of pebble and smoothworn loess hard as marble and treacherous as glass to the tread. And all this is a land of death and the dead. This country is so old that the dead are everywhere : from each bank or scarp nameless earth-coloured bones protrude from the dead ages, and in weatherworn clefts or scoops of the loess you can see skulls. There are few acts of merit higher than to re-bury these exposed indelicacies of the past, and leave them reverently covered once more : just as to the Chinese mind, there are few offences more ugly and disastrous than to remove any abandoned bone, or disturb the sleeping dead. But the valleys and dry ravines concealed among the Golden Hills have by no means even yet lost their sepulchral value : and as you go, the squeal and scurrying flight of disturbed kites will make you suddenly aware that their focus, under that bit of dull red rag among the stones, is the derelict body of some forlorn outcast child.

On a prominent brow, high, high above the river, are the pagoda and its theatre. Beneath your feet, across the Hwang Hor, the city lies mapped out completely, and in the middle the forested park of the palace, and the waterwheel outside the city wall (the Northern boundary of its precinct) which lifts a constant rill from the Yellow River for the Viceroy's electric light and the irrigation of his garden. On the far side of the city stretches a plain of orchards, and the distance beyond is closed by a long high mass of fell, on which summer-houses and pleasant pavilions perch, for the villeggiatura of Lanchow's wealthy ones during the summer heats. In summer, indeed, the scene is opulent in a surf of green, but in winter a clear cold ochre-coloured death is the universal note. Scrambling down the scarp at last, you come to a specially steep fall of the hillside to the river, and up this, like swallows' nests plastered up the face of a cliff, more summer-houses and curly-roofed pavilions lodge and cling and alight wherever foothold is possible. And in winter it is hard to imagine the delicious airiness of them in the stifling August heats, as you sit here, perched in vacancy amid a blessed concourse of draughts, open on all sides to the air, and commanding the whole enormous prospect of the orcharded landscape below you away and away to the distant dry hills, with the river down below you, and the city like an island in the ocean of green, and its gate-towers like cliffs emerging high above the surf of the trees.

But the winter here has its uncanny charm, too, when all the world is unimaginably dead and arid, a strange wonderful view of corrugated fawn-colour, with the jingling floe-ice racing down the river at your feet, and the far hills blue and filmy in haze. The Yellow River, here a mere trifle of a few hundred miles from its birth, up on the Roof of the World, between the Oring-Nor and the Tsaring-Nor, magical lakes of magic names, that few eyes have ever seen, is already as broad at Lanchow as the Thames at London. But a vast mud-coloured water it is, boiling down from the snows of Tibet ; soon after leaving Lanchow it takes its wild northward sweep up into the inhospitable deserts of the Ordes, and round the North in fierce rapids that make it untamable for traffic, before it curves South again straight along the hard line of the Shansi hills, till at length at the weak angle of their junction with the Tsin-ling Alps, advancing across Shensi, the Wei Hor and the Hwang Hor join forces to make a push for freedom, and unite in their devastating downward break to the sea. At Lanchow the Hwang Hor is smooth and swift and silent : as far as Ning-Hsia you can descend on rafts, and there are even navigable stretches : but this river is always sinister and terrible.

In winter, of course, it is in leash : the Tibetan highland is fast-bound in frost, and its rivers are starvelings accordingly. But even so, the Hwang Hor is a portent of weight and power : one never wearies standing on the European iron bridge that links Lanchow to the Golden Hills across the river, and looking down on the surreptitious velvety violence of that brown swell creaming in concentrated malignity round the piers. By mid-December the ice packs are already coming down : gradually a crust forms along either bank, and day by day encroaches on the central current, till at length there remains only quite a narrow channel of furious racing water curding up a crested hedge of ice on each side as it tears its way. And then, a few days later, there is no more water at all, and the mighty Hwang Hor, tamed by winter, is imprisoned fast under what is now a huge flat expanse of glacier, wild and tumbled and rough as an instantly frozen sea, across which you can save the troubles and tolls of the bridge by taking your strings of carts and

camels in every direction from bank to bank. For a month
or more the glittering white chaos imprisons one of Asia's
most imperious rivers, and then towards the end of February
the carts turn cautious and begin to resume the Bridge :
a streak of darkness gradually dawns and with a crash
the river is loose again. Within a few hours more channel
after channel has opened, and the broken packs of ice
and flat cruel bergs come tearing down with silvery crashes,
battering the ice-banks, and piling up over each other,
and battering and swirling again, until more bergs are
cracked off and more packs go hurtling down. And in a
few days the ice is wholly gone : though the end of February
brings an odd relapse, after all the radiance of winter, into
a strange feeling of dark ominousness, when the air seems
full of pale cries, heralds of fluttering dust-storms on the
wings of incessant flaws of wind, from which you wake one
morning to find the whole world gone dead again in cloud
and an unrelieved whiteness of snow.

But, apart from such brief relapses, and occasional
snaps of dark weather and hard steely cold, no words can
do justice to the glare and glory of midwinter in Northern
Asia ; its vast and pure serenity, its flawless light, its colour,
its feeling, its atmosphere. There is hardly a day when
it is not like champagne to take the air in Lanchow. There
are strange old temple courts to visit in the city, yards of
grey quiet filled with a moss-grown ancient silence, so
solemn under the venerable trees that the cloisters and the
dark vacant theatre seem haunted, and the towering old
bronze incense-burner to be on guard. Then there is the
Mahomedan Mosque, out near the Western Gate, with its
fantastic many-storied tower flashing with tiled roofs of
emerald and turquoise. The building is of a rich and
elaborate Chinese type, but the carved and latticed ark of
the interior, duskily fragrant, is all that is properly Islamic.
A beautiful and benevolent old greybeard presides : the
certainty that the Mahomedans would gladly murder all
the Chinese of the Inner Empire, and fully intend to do

their best at the first possible moment, only lends ironic point to the presence of this gorgeous fane in a Chinese capital, and to the large Olympian kindliness of its minister, whom, as you see him, deep in the shadow of the smooth great columns in the approach, with his hand on his little grandson's head, you would take for an Adept in some cult of pure affection. But all this country swarms with sons of the Prophet, and though the alien race has modified its lines into some vague general resemblance to the Chinese, yet you very soon learn to tell them apart, and easily recognize the heavier, dourer, more sombrely built faces and figures of the Mahomedans, even if it were not for the six-sided little silly cap of satin that here replaces the fez.

It would take long labour to explore the many corners of beauty in Lanchow : each suspect alley may lead to some vast abandoned building, derelict examination-hall, or tower of coloured tiles. The real examination-hall, though, of old Imperial days, has now entirely disappeared and nothing remains of it except the solid arch of the entrance just outside the West Gate of the city. The park-like expanse within has been swept clear of buildings and turned to the uses of the garrison. Old and new meet here ; for standing under the arch you look back out of a modern camp to the immemorial Gate Tower of Lanchow with its rows of square windows painted with sham cannon mouths : and above on the descending laps of the hill are the square guard-fortresses of former times, without any door on the ground, but you sent up your garrison by ladders to a door half-way up the wall and then took your ladders away so as to obviate any risk of your garrison following suit.

And farther yet, out beyond the little beck that comes down into the Hwang Hor from the southward hills, remote on a sloping plateau above, stands utterly deserted the big walled city where once the Manchu population of Lanchow dwelt in arrogant isolation, till the Manchurian Line came crashing to its end in 1911 and brought down the Dragon Throne in its fall. The little beck beneath is a very little beck in winter, meandering sadly among wide stretches of sand ; busy housewives beat their clothes there, and pile their stacks of carrots and melons in summer. But it is spanned by one of the sights of Lanchow—the famous Camel's Bridge—so called because no camel ever crosses it, of course, but its arcaded passage has a high hump-backed look. And on the far side round over the bend there is a specially beautiful new Taoist Temple, ample and stately amid sombre forested cloisters frescoed all round. Its sumptuous roofs gleam azure and emerald above the heavy black-dark plumage of the Cypresses that envelop them ; and here in the sunny angles of the yards *viburnum fragrans*, in enormous bushes, covers itself with blossom in spring ; and here in spring there is a famous picture-sale at which even the Viceroy condescends to bid.

But now into the laborious quiet of my days there came a diversion, for a note arrived from Bill, saying that all was well indeed with his expedition, but that those two smart soldiers of the Viceroy's guard, the loan of whom we had taken as such a compliment and comfort, had, in point of fact, turned out quite the reverse, so misbehaving to the country people and innkeepers down the road, beating them and bullying them (as soldiers have the unenviable name for doing in China, and are popular accordingly), that at last Bill had sent them back to the city with a note to their commanding officer explaining their misdeeds, but in such a way as to mitigate the affront to the Viceroy involved in returning his escort. Pondering this unpleasant news (for, quite apart from the general moral objections, it is very undesirable in China to get mixed up, however remotely, with any ill-treatment of the people), I concluded that the soldiers ought certainly to be visited for their sins, and that, as certainly, they would not have been such fools as to present that card to their officer. For though, of course, they could not read it, they would obviously have understood that it gave the reason for their dismissal. No, assuredly they would have torn it up, and given some cock-and-a-bull story instead to account for their return. And it was intolerable to me that they should so cheat justice. I consulted with Mr. Li, but found him disinclined to meddle in the matter between such eminences as myself and the Viceroy : so finally, with the most nice elaborate elegance of language, I wrote direct to His Excellency, recounting the tale. After which I sat with folded hands, complacent in the certainty that honour would be satisfied with a touch of the stick or a few days' imprisonment.

Alas for my little comprehension of the East, and my forgetfulness of China's veneration for the written word, so deep-seated that nobody will ever destroy a piece of paper with writing on it. A few days later, as I sat at work, Mr. Li came rushing in, pale with the excitement of high and urgent matters. In a voice that tottered with emotion he implored secrecy and then unfolded the matter. Those luckless soldiers, after all, it seemed had duly presented Bill's card to their commanding officer : on reading which he immediately ordered their trousers down and had them spanked within an inch of their lives. This was already much more than I had meant, of course, and had happened before any move on my part was known.

But now, hardly had they begun to congeal again, than my letter arrived (translated, too, no doubt, into much too heavy terms, as there was nobody with any command of English at court). Whereupon he towered instantly into an Imperial passion, counted the beating a mere bagatelle, and insisted that both men should be shot forthwith. Nothing else would serve him : nothing could deflect him. Glamour was general in the city, and mutinies were rumoured. I was speechless with horror when I learned what a storm I had unwillingly aroused. Quite apart from the iniquity of killing the men for so small a crime, their death would certainly get all foreigners an evil name in the province, and destroy my own chances of getting on happily, as before, with the people. A certain feeling of insecurity was already abroad anyhow : some Honan soldiers had already achieved a burglary with violence somewhere outside the city, and a few of them had been executed for it ; with the result that the troops were grumbling and fractious. It was quite on the cards (on causes so small do great events hinge, as I fancy some capacious mind may have observed before) that another execution at my behest might prove the danger spark to a general explosion that might shatter the Viceroy and me, and the foreign residents in Kansu, and the peace of the province, and the stability of its Government, all in one devastating cataclysm.

So I was fully penetrated by the alarm of Mr. Li and addressed myself instantly to the writing of another letter to the Viceroy, pleading for mercy as urgently as Portia. This I meant to go round and present in person that it might have even more weight. But appointments could not be made to fit, messengers went fruitlessly to and fro, and in a constant fret of anxiety the day was frittered away. Next morning Mr. Li returned to the charge, with Mr. Post Office, too, this time to back him. I needed no incitements : off went the letter and the Viceroy acknowledged the receipt of it immediately, as the etiquette is. And then nothing happened. More hours passed and still nothing happened : I spent the night in figuring the hapless offenders as clay-cold corpses by this time with a general insurrection brewing round their graves. Till the morning brought a little note in the oddest English from the Viceroy, announcing that he consented to let off his " humble soldiers," and how lucky they were to escape his execution. So that was all right, but *what* a comfort ! I vowed that never again would I play a lone hand in the fearful game of Chinese diplomacy, with other peoples' life and death for the stakes.

Mrs. Li, all this time, has been absent from the scene, and there were no more parties in that pleasant little semi-foreign room in the shady courtyard. Mrs. Li, in fact, was having a baby ; and when the baby appeared, it was a girl. Mr. Li must certainly be very exceptional among Chinese, and, indeed, among fathers of any nationality :

for, though he already had one daughter (and no doubt desired a son as ardently as all reasonable people must, all the world over, but in China most notoriously and especially), he yet greeted this new " guest " with such enthusiasm that he proposed to celebrate her arrival in the world with a resounding festivity.

The appointed day dawned cold and dreary. I myself felt ill and disinclined to the prospect of sloppy food and the warm nastiness of Chinese wine. All the morning I awaited my summons, but it did not come till nearly 4. Mr. Post Office and I then clambered into carts, and off we set, across the city and down towards the South Gate to where, up an alley to the left, you find the stately temple of Tseng Tso Tang. Tseng-Tso-Tang was the soldier-statesman quite unknown to Europe, whose fame in China is so illustrious that he ranks almost as a saint (though only dead within memory of man) and has temples to his glory all over Northern China. For it was he who succeeded at last in closing the bleeding wound of the Mahomedan Rebellion that was still draining inland China white when the Grand Dowager began her reign. His temple in Lanchow is one of the city's finest buildings to-day, and is the special place for giving banquets of special splendour.

Such as Mr. Li's. When I entered I found myself in an enormous room, cold and draughty, like the nave of a church, with sturdily-pillared aisles up either side to the end, where, instead of a chancel, there rose a stage, on which the most ap-palling pandemonium was proceeding, braying of gongs and crashing of cymbals, and long-drawn squawks and wailings of the bedizened actors who were performing their unending evolutions quite unheeded by the crowd of black-satin gentlemen who filled the body of the hall. For this was indeed a party—crowds and crowds of people, so that I almost got writer's cramp with handshaking. Mr. Li had cast his net far and wide. Ma-y had actually been asked—a mighty jump into social recognition : and at the other end of the scale, though Mr. Li had not aspired quite

as high as the Viceroy, his son, a pleasant slim pale boy,
Mr. Li's particular friend, was present, besides the City
Governor, and most of the other *sommités* of Lanchow,
civil and military.   But it was weary work, standing about
on our hind legs and waiting for the food.   For, to make the
probation keener, there it all was, plain to view.   Up and
down the body of the hall were a dozen large round tables,
in three ranks : while aligned up the red-pillared aisles to
right and left were rounds to fit them, already set with all
the fittings and apparatus of a Chinese feast, the tall tazzas,
and the low saucers and dishes, stacked with many-coloured
pyramids of candied fruits and sweetmeats and savouries
that make a well-set Chinese dinner-table even more fascinating to sit down to than an English one.   But still more
guests were coming, and the feast could not begin: we
circulated, and marked time, and chatted as best we could
for the devastating din on the stage.

However, at length there came a sense of imminence and
an electric pause in the buzz of talk.   From all sides attendants now came swiftly forward, carrying the round table-
tops : and in a trice the twelve tables were set with their
burdens.   Immediately the draughts seemed to diminish,
and the fire-box to give more warmth, and the huge hall
to look much brighter with its many rosy lanterns beaming
down on that triple row of opulently furnished tables.   Mr.
Li and Mr. Lo began urging us to our places, each guest
to his appointed position at the table foreordained as fitting
to his rank.   To my horror I now found that for me there
waited the foremost place of all, at the central table up at the
top, immediately under the cataclysmal cacophonies of the
stage.   However, there was nothing for it but to " suffer
in silence, with a smiling h'eye " : I took my seat, and
we all—six at each table—fell to on the dessert, browsing
from pink pyramids to green, and from green to gold,
slices of pear and stuffed jujubes, and forcemeat, and
strips of chicken mayonnaise, and ruby bars of fruit jelly,
and sugared walnuts, and slices of ancestral eggs, and the

D

gleaming little golden candied oranges that come up from Szechwan and are as delicious as anything produced in Nice. Rapidly the mounds of delight before us dwindled and crumbled : and then came the long procession of the real dinner, not necessary, by this time, to repeat to you. Piles of apricot kernels served the purposes of bread, to nibble and play with, but I cannot find a reason for the universal popularity of melon seeds in the same context —flat little hard dry ovals, which you have to split with tongue and teeth, and then spit out the two halves, keeping only the thin flake that lay between them—a very poor reward for so much trouble. However, the Chinese do not think so, and eat melon seeds at an amazing rate, and in the most amazing quantities all day, indoors and out of doors and everywhere.

This was a feast, too, served by sirens. Not only did the busy attendants run diligently round with drink, and others come and go in a pitiless procession of foods, but the tables were particularly haunted by queer little damsels, proffering love and wine as they doddered round on tiny feet—a most unappetizing pack of small drabs, curiously infantile and pudding-faced, and like Eskimos, with the brown bright eyes of baby rabbits and their front hair flopping on either side of their face. Not one of these dingy fledglings of Aphrodite seemed a day over fourteen, and their prattle had, I imagine, something of a child's soft charm, to the sophisticated, in these inappropriate circumstances. Not that I could judge of it with any equanimity : the din above me was so deafening that I could hardly hear myself think. It was always pandemonium, of course, but with periodical explosions of extra noise that made the intervening stretches seem balmy by comparison. The play interminably proceeded : the same nothingness appeared to happen again and again : the same people, archaic and rigid in their magnificent robes of tinsel, again and again to come forward and make their protracted wailing querimonies, to the accompaniment, jangled and chaotic, of all conceivable instruments of torture by sound, dominated by violent outrages on gongs, and a criminal cruelty to cymbals.

And yet, through all the anguish, there was a certain hieratic charm about the performance. The stately figures and their sumptuous slow movements got a hold of one's imagination, and so did the fantastic wonder of their vestments, and enormous crowns and head-dresses of glittering vacillating quivering tawdriness, and the stoles and long lappets of dazzling embroideries and colour, blatant all over with gold, and bedight with bits of mirror. It is curious in Chinese art, the cult of the beard, so little seen in Chinese life : these cautious-moving compilations of rickety splendour were all venerable in long beards that waggled and went up and down when they wailed. But old men, kings and sages were by no means the only persons in the play. What it was all about I could not tell you, but the leading rôle was that of a lady, nymph or fairy. She was played, inevitably, by a man : I did not need to be told that here was the central point of the whole performance, and that I was seeing the Divine Sarah of Kansu.[1]

It was an amazing performance. He was a slim thin-faced lad, painted and powdered to an almost uncanny degree of elfin moth-eyebrowed beauty : and he was a great actor. He had a square mobile mouth, made for emotion, and dark wild eyes, in which he did marvels of flashing love and fear and hate and *câlinerie*, till we were quite caught by the sinister haunt of his charm as he came and went in his many exquisite mincing feminine disguises, and postured and posed and swayed and swam and swooped and swung in time to the clashing blare of the gongs and cymbals, and the leaping of his own trilling cries and wails like a fairy bird. And finally he descended from his strange heavens, and came down among men, circulating round the tables (as the star-actor's habit is, to collect financial

---

[1] This, I am told, requires elucidation : the allusion is to a certain Madame Bernhardt, a French actress of repute.

evidence that he has pleased his audience), as elaborate still in his slender grace, and the penetrating dart of his profound liquid gaze, as the perfected Japanese Geisha whose cultivated charm he so poignantly recalled in his willowy movement, and sweetly condescending inclinations, and trailing kimono of pale colours, and high-puffed coiffure.

So the long loneliness of the winter went, and insensibly the frozen world began to stir. The Yellow River by now was once more a vast and dirt-coloured tempest of muddy water, and the North Water-gate was turned to a sop and a slough. A kindlier feeling came into the clear air : a hinted promise of green began to suffuse the black haze of the willows, and among their branches the buzzard wheeled with faint sweet whistlings, and high overhead the air was crowded with children's kites, dragons and butterflies and enormous paper ogres, but dwindled to mere gnats in the blue vault where they hung motionless, while high again above even these the cranes went honking North-westward in a V-shaped tail of black specks. Even the desolation of the hills grew tenderer : towards sunset looking up or down the Hwang-Hor from the iron bridge, the distances were very lovely in Egyptian lines and softened Egyptian colours of fawn and ochre, misty in a haze of mauve and pale blue tones, with a brighter yellow effect of fog now blurring the willow-forests along beneath the hills into the utmost distance, and above all, ghostly and diaphanous, a harvest moon mounting slowly up, as golden as a guinea, and as big as a plate behind the veiled atmosphere of blue and dun. And when one came home at night, the air was no longer cruel, and it was a joy to walk up the silent cobbled street, pale and empty beneath that same glorious full moon, now high in the zenith of a breathless cloudless vault of stars.

Work was all done, and the end of waiting was at hand. As symptoms of coming movement, fresh members swam into my staff, one by one, like the heralding swallows of spring. Out of the South from Jo-ni, came Lay-gor, the good donkey-man, and a little later my eyes were gladdened unexpectedly by the sight of Gomer, that stalwart, jolly lad of the Border whom I had last so sadly seen dwindling Southwards on the road from Taochow back to Jo-ni, and had never hoped to see again. He came, with an elder brother, a notable figure of a man, on an errand of propitiation to us, bearing a present of elk's feet from the Prince of Jo-ni, now so perturbed by the troubles raised for him by the Viceroy that he himself was now actually to come to Lanchow—and wished, therefore, to deprecate further hostilities on our part. But indeed it was time that China looked into his suspect movements with the monasteries and the Mahomedans : it was notorious how he had taken bribes from the monks of Chago, and given them to the Mahomedan general and the Chinese inspector : the winter appeared to have gone very troublously down on the Border. But I no longer had any quarrel with those storms, for I was to owe to them one of the sturdiest props of my second year's expedition. Quite suddenly there dawned on me one day the Wicked Wa-wa.

He dawned, indeed, slowly, and it was some time before I realized his qualities. When first I saw him, he was a very grubby little rosy-cheeked Tibetan-looking urchin of about twelve, in greasy old quilted breeches and jacket of Chinese blue, with a round cap on his head, and a pigtail hanging down unkempt behind. This was a chrysalis of no special promise. But at first his tender years and forlorn condition made me look on him as an injured innocent, and rejoice in the chance of shielding him. He was the son and heir of Lay-gor the donkey-man, and there was a wonderful story of a battle for a water-mill at Nalang, in the course of which it unfortunately befell that a Chinese had his head smashed in with a stone Of course the Wa-wa had had no hand in this ; oh no. But at this point the tale grew hazy, and all that clearly emerged was the fact that that spotless infant was maliciously denounced, and fled away by devious tracks into the North, to seek his father, and take shelter under my wing. I glowed with benevolence : the poor child had evidently endured much, and used to wake up in the night screaming with nerves. Food and peace and comfort restored him ; he grew plumper and redder-cheeked every day : I used to see him about the yard, but he was too abject a creature to be allowed any approach to my presence or hand in my service. He was supposed to do odd jobs for the servants, but nothing much came of it.

But with returning security the Wa-wa began to wax once more into his native wickedness. The screams in the night began to be screams of rage, not nerves. He slept on the cook's kang, and he declared, with sobs of passion, that the cook beat him, whereas I now believe it was he that beat the cook. In any case the staff developed storms, and, though it seemed ridiculous that trouble should ascend into our calm circle from so small a speck, so far beneath our notice, I at last began to wonder what to do with this useless grubby little dour Tibetan blockhead, sullen and tempestuous and stupid. And then, one night, a miracle was certainly wrought. For the American Monsignore, fired by a climax of cordiality, pursued the shrieking Wa-wa round the moonlit courtyard, seized him by the pig-tail, hauled him hither and thither by it, like Melisande, but protesting a great deal more loudly (indeed he yelled like a stuck pig in the certainty of a stuck pig's fate), and finally sawed it asunder with a Turkish carving knife. I now hold the theory that it was in his pigtail that the Wa-wa kept his stupidity.

For on the next day, surveying the mournful relic, I gave order that he was to have the rest removed and his head cropped *à l'anglaise*. And immediately on this the miracle began to happen. Dirt gave way to perfect spick-and-spanness, slouchiness to smartness, stupidity to needle-sharp intelligence, and abjectness to a most soaring insolence. He began to take charge of everything and everybody, would even lecture Mafu himself on how to do things ; and as for

poor Go-go, in quite a short time he was down and out of my
presence, completely second in command to the Wa-wa,
who by this time, having vertiginously climbed the ranks
of service by sheer audacity, was now my own particular
guardian and attendant, filled with just such a supercilious
superiority, bland and brazen, as that of some chubby little
smart buttony page at the Savoy, of whom the wicked one
was the living image.

The entire household crept in terror of his tongue : even
Mafu withdrew into silence, and poor goggling Go-go was
nowhere. And, as for his good meek father, the way that
graceless infant scolded him, and the exhaustive command
of unprintable language in which he did so, were such as to
raise the hair of the household, and cause even his masters
to meditate the propriety of a corporal protest. Only
Gomer defeated him with the radiance of his twinkle, and
the bubbling bursts of his jolly laughter, proof against the
Wa-wa's most volleying Billingsgate and shrillest, subtlest
insult : he would just smack the Wa-wa's bullety little
black head, and laugh at him. And the Wa-wa would
laugh too. But as for the Mahomedan cook with the
Christian smile, he pulled down the fur flaps over his ears,
and went.

It was time : we no longer wanted him. For the road
called. Bill had come back, laden with rich treasures out
of Tibet ; and now the house was being dismantled, and
everything being got ready for the start. Out towards
the still-frozen North the chubby little Monsignore at last
winged his forlorn way, all alone as usual, with his worldly
goods in a pack across a small white pony that went quite
loose ahead of him, and alternately bolted aside into the
inane of the desert, or ran ahead irrecoverably into distant
cities. His departure was the herald of our own. All the
loose ends were tied up, and the formal farewells accomplished.

Accompanied by Mafu in black satin and a Trilby hat,
and by Go-go in his khaki suiting, I paid my devoirs to the

Viceroy. We had a most enthusiastic interview in his private room, and he showed me some of the lovely things, pictures and china, in his collection ; we giggled and laughed a great deal, and exchanged vows for future meetings and future feastings : then he saw me ceremoniously out, conducting me down through long courtyards of hideous new blue-brick buildings in course of construction, to where, at last, he stopped and bowed good-bye on the threshold. A moment later I glanced back. He still stood there on the step, but the chuckling smile was quite gone, and he loomed more enormous than ever, in his huge habitual sternness. It was like a great grey monolith, from which the glow of sunset has abruptly faded. And so good-bye, for the time, to Lanchow : home I went again, in highest heart for the new adventure of the year, after all these months of inactivity. And two days later we were off.

CHAPTER III

THE START

The evening had closed grey and ominous, but though March 28 dawned grey, it soon cleared and grew glorious. We rose, as usual, early for the start, and as usual had a wait that seemed endless, sitting about in the stripped and littered yards, while still the string of mules contracted for with Ma-y gave no signs of arriving, till at length, in the presence of Mr. Lo and Mr. Li, and to the open satisfaction of Mafu, I diminished his great ruddy smirking face by asking if we might expect the promised animals *on the morrow*. However, at long last they did turn up and were loaded. The procession filed out of my deserted yard about 11.30.

It was a noble cavalcade, for in China the fashion is for all one's friends to speed the parting guest for some distance on his journey; and the more friends you have to swell your tail, the higher your rank and estimation in the eyes of the admiring multitude. We resorted to no illicit methods of hire, such as often increase a Chinese procession of farewell, but our cortège consisted, besides our own eight mules and two of Lay-gor's wise little asses, and Mafu and ourselves on three ponies, of Mr. Post Office and Mr. Li (very brave in silks and furs and velvet shoes) on ponies also, and Mr. Post Office's Mafu and Ma-y following behind on a cart with Mr. Lo. The high officials, of course, could not be expected to derange themselves in person, but honour was satisfied, and " face " amplified, by formal messages from the Viceroy and the City Governor regretting deeply that affairs of state prevented them from escorting me forth.

Down into the thronging crowds of the main street we
proceeded, and cut through the Western Gate and the Western suburb with its long line of grain shops and basket shops
and shops for all sorts of neat wooden implements of agricul-
ture and husbandry.   Then down across the hot dusty
beck-bed below the Camel's Bridge and up the other side,
through more seething streets.   And now we were fairly
out of Lanchow, advancing Westwards through open country
once more up the stony desolations of the Hwang-Hor vale,
towards the mysterious Alps of the North.   The procession
tailed off homeward : Mr. Lo and Mr. Li returned to their
post office duties, and soon there was only Mr. Post Office
left, of our long winter life in Lanchow.   Even he, in time,
deserted us, after some seven miles of the torrid trail, at a
point where a rib of spur descends from the fells with a
sumptuous temple clambering round its arête.   And after
this the joy of the trek was complete, the hopes and hunger
of springtime and the hills.

The way grew firmer and less dusty now, advancing up
the broad flat orcharded stretches beside the huge and
shingled Hwang-Hor.   That first day's stage is more nearly
thirty miles than twenty : endless level bay of road followed
on endless level bay interminably under the fierce glare
through which we dreamily moved between the little arid
hills that enclose the plain of the river.   Nowhere was
there any sign of green life, but there were uncounted flocks
of white woolly sheep and lambs on the stark stony downs,
where there did not look to be even as much provender as
might have provided a mouthful for a slug.   And beside
the river at intervals there rose the huge Earl's Court-like
irrigation wheels that are such a feature of this Sahara, and
indeed its one artificial means of redemption from complete
lifelessness, whirling the Yellow water up to a height of some
thirty or forty feet, and then by long troughs and channels
distributing it across the pebbly hopelessness of the plain.

Dusk of dark brought us into Newton (Hsin-Chung),
so mouldy and crumbling a little old place in the twilight

that it seemed as if many a long age must have gone by since it was first justly so called. We were a long way ahead of the caravan by this time, and had a weary hunt for an inn, which, however, at last we found in the dark out beyond the town wall, in the Western Gwan. There was trouble at first about rooms, but ere long, when night was well down, we discovered that the big raised hall at the back of the end of the yard had two fine kangs, one in each wing. So in its bare gloom we awaited the mules, and when they arrived had the usual first day's eternity of delay while the packs were taken off and the muddle of bales undone in the night, and the various necessities of life run to earth in their unsuspected corners of each bundle. After the first day, of course, every one knows where everything is, and unpacking becomes a quick light job ; but on the first stage, chaos and uncertainty prevail at the trail's end, and must be allowed to settle. However, we were very merry in the triumph of travel really begun, and so long an initial stage achieved : Mafu ceased to curse delinquents, and set to on showing how good a dinner he could cook on how short notice : and, having dined hugger-mugger, we were very glad of a hugger-mugger bed in the crowded obscurity of the barn.

The night was one of sweet short sleeps, broken by bells and packings and startings of other people's mules. We rose at length very early, to a grey cold day, and I walked out ahead of the caravan, up across the flat bare fields in the bend that the river here takes, under the enclosing fell, to where the ferry barge awaited us. And on the way I admired to see how they fertilize their fields in these unfertile parts. For in each plot they sink a well, with a windlass, and out of it, from the lower strata beneath, they pulley-hawl up supplies of shingle silt, with which they so universally mulch their ground that hereabouts the face of the earth is pocked with the little pebbly ulcers of these silt-wells.

It was still chilly, the sky flocculent and leaden : the country Arabian and colourless. Not even later would there be a difference : for all the promising-looking orchards that fill the flats are really only of thorny Zao'erh (jujube-trees), a crabbed spiteful witch-tree of desert-places. By the placid river Go-go· and I and the pony had to await the arrival of the main procession, as the ferryman not unnaturally did not want to make two traverses of it in his huge primeval barge. Very calm and vast and broad the Hwang-Hor surges along. On the near side towered great water-wheels, and on the far, above the sharp red rim of the bank, the plain was filled with a dark haze of Zao'erh, and then bounded by a line of convoluted dull grey fells, arid as dead bones, with here and there a crumbling old fortress tower on a spur, profiled pale against the pallor of the sky ; while nearer, down the right, the sun kindled to brilliant red the long battlemented wall of one of the many blind little gateless Cities of refuge that stud this region, and made it stand out vividly against the Zao'erh darkness from which its wide rectangle and fortalice towers emerged.

Now the caravan arrived, and there began much further talk and haranguing about making two trips of it instead of one, seeing what a crowd we were. But Charon was obdurate, and vowed he would get us all safe across. So in we pavidly packed, as best we could, hoping for the best, but removing coats and boots for caution as we squatted in our places, and watched the mules and ponies being got into theirs. And gradually they all were got in, and gave no trouble—except Spotted Fat, who kicked and fought like ten devils : men and beasts were tight as sardines in a tin by this time, so that now a mule could hardly have kicked if it wanted, but had any of them grown obstreperous the worst must assuredly have happened, as the barge was gunwale-laden with this unusual concourse. Smoothly and gradually she swung out, though, into the vast sinister quiet of the Hwang-Hor, now luckily low and comparatively tame, yet rolling rapidly as an express. Insensibly the paddles bore us on and the river bore us down : the near bank dwindled behind us, and the far one swelled before us. Without misadventure we made our landing-stage, and without misadventure got all the mules and all their packs ashore : disembarked even Spotted Fat without protest, and with real relief stood firm again on firm ground.

We were to cut across the angle made by the descent, higher up, of the Sining-Hor into the Hwang-Hor. So now was good-bye to the Yellow River : our way was to be straight Westward, up the Sining-Hor, while the Hwang-Hor fetches its wild backward sweep here, from out of the far South, off the Roof of the World. From the bank we began to breast a steep ascent of gullies filled with salt-pools, and thence came out on to a wide open plateau, with the Hwang-Hor curling away into the left-hand distances far below : then dipped to the level again down a crimson gulch of ruin conspicuously riven and ghastly even in this rent ghastly country, and turned up to the right at last between dull low hills, and cliffs half red, and half dead-grey in a rigid stratum-line, into the wide flat rise of the Sining River's valley, now perfectly naked and smooth and bare in its broad expanse. On and on I slowly rode, far ahead of the caravan by now, and in a huge slow rise the level of the vale ascended, more and more completely stony and arid. The sun had conquered the clouds, though, so that there was warmth and a pleasant air.

On and on still : unattainably remote, scarp after scarp came into sight ahead up the distance, and then insensibly dropped away behind, revealing more and further and further limitless stretches of plain. On the yellow despair of the downs on either hand, broad smeared streaks of smooth whiteness like high-roads indicated the marching-routes of the sheep-armies that invade them : and at length, learning that our destination was only forty li farther, fifty having been now achieved, I alighted to await Bill and the mules, on a wide torrid expanse of pebbly bareness, veiled in a peppered scrub of a tamarisk so cropped and tiny that it might have been new-burnt heather on a starveling moor. Here, stretched upon a warm hummock in the glare, I ate my luncheon of toast and honey and cold tea : and then lay out deliciously, pillowed on tamarisk, while the little green lizards frolicked about me so tame that they flirted in between my knees, and came to peer into my tumbler between sips. But oh, the utter dead immortal hopelessness of this pale shallow land : so grisly and uniformly colourless in the grey ungenial brilliance!

When Bill at length appeared with the mules, we lingered awhile to contemplate the scene : then pursued them in a pleasant leisure. Our way now made another cut : we topped another bluff at a bend, crossed another high level : and so came down to the river-flat again, by a very magnificent double cliff and undercliff of red ruin, immediately overhanging the mud-coloured brabble of the Sining-Hor far beneath, while beyond a featureless monotony of reclaimed shingle plain and jujube orchards melted flatly away to the lifeless ravinated hills.

Then came another long stretch of levels : while the day darkened awfully to storm and rain driving blue and violet across all the congregated peaks and high masses on either side, till at last, while we were resting in a sad little lorn hamlet over wooden bowls-ful of floor-sweepings tea, the anger of the gathering dark burst in a furious dust storm, with rare icy drops of rain in the squalls. After this it cleared, and the day was yet young when we rode into Blackwaters, where Mafu, riding ahead, had got us a good broad-yarded inn. It was a pleasant small place, poor and bare, on the grey plain in which these little clay-walled towns and occasional towered farms are peppered, away and away into the fading perspective, like red islets becalmed on a lifeless ocean. The people were a jolly crowd too : there was a Beano raging in the village street when we rode in, with European photographs revolving in a show. We ourselves soon became the main exhibit, however : the yard grew packed with sightseers, and there was much noise of fun and laughter, especially when a well-directed burst of the siphon sent some too inquisitive householder staggering drenched away into the crowd again, amid the delighted yells of all his friends. So the chill dusk came, with the sky threatening grimly for us ahead over the hills : in view of a dawn start on the morrow, we were glad of an early bed, and hoped the next day's stage would not prove quite so arid and Petraean.

The brewing storm erupted during the night in bucketing deluges, and when we rose it was to a cloudless day of cold, with new snow transfiguring all the scarpy hummocks of hills. But the day's journey was like its predecessors : yet longer, though, and yet duller, without any grandeurs at all. Never was there so heartless a land as this is in spring, surfaced universally in shingle—not well-drawn silt, but pulverized dead bones of bygone rivers, strewn over the face of the earth—and with the young green crops barely beginning to peer among the pebbles. But the soil begins to grow a little better here : no longer is each little rill-marsh hoar-frosted with salt, as on the preceding day. *Chortens* [1] begin to appear too, advance guards of Tibet that make one's heart gulp with sudden pleasure of anticipation. For a long time I sucked godly emotions, and a glow of pious fervour from certain big battlemented towers of loess, square and broadening to their base, that at certain intervals of the stage rise more or less proudly near the roadside, according as they are in a less or more crumbling condition of disrepair. Each of them has five baby towers on the same model, clustering at its angles or aligned in front of it : I felt certain they must be the shrines of Bodhisats or Arahats, with the ashes of their disciples in lesser shrines before them ; and rejoiced over the evident prevalence of piety in these parts. Until I ultimately discovered that these little colonies of towers only mark the stages of the road ; and are, in fact, nothing more august than milestones.

The hills, as you go, become yet more dumpish and dishcovery : and still the long ascending tracks of the sheep-

---

[1] These, it may be mentioned, are big whitewashed structures, like a reversed wine-glass, containing relics or ashes of some Saint or Bodhisat. You will see a picture of one at Tien Tang.

routes, like deep terraces, wind whitely about their flanks, and broadly sweep to their summits. These began the day by looking alpine. But as the snow melted, they all returned to their proper proportions, and their native drab and destitute dreariness. However, at last there dawned a vision of hope. From behind the dull lines of fell on the left, there slid and gradually unfolded a real alpine range, serrated, peaked and wild and high—the first genuine mountains I had seen since Lien Hwa S'an faded down the backward distances of 1914. With hat in hand I saluted the Kweite-Salar Alps and the hopes that their emergence aroused. They cheered the long last worst of the way. For the li appeared to lengthen out telescopically as I advanced, and Gomer ahead of me on Spotted Fat could hardly coax a movement out of that cosseted animal. And then, quite unexpectedly appeared our day's destination—a village hardly a mile away sitting in the plain, under a high and rather more lively-looking range of hill on the right. I congratulated myself on having reached our stage so soon in the day.

Not a bit of it, only wait. For instead of advancing placidly up the plain and into the village now immediately under our hand, we diverged unintelligibly to the right, by a shoulder with a fine colony of milestone towers, and up and up and around about among a set of ridiculous irrelevant hills and gullies. It was as maddening as the approach to Minchow. And then, when the summit of the sharp little pass was attained, the reason of these divagations became clear. For now we descended vertiginously downwards upon a quite unsuspected river, cold-looking and clear and dark, flowing down from the right in a splendid deep black gorge that clove its way through the hills and revealed, above, in the gap, a country of more hills and higher, with wintry woods and a real suggestion of heights and alpine vegetation not so very far away. Deep in the dark chasm of the gorge the river slept and rippled from pool to pool, and a wooden bridge gracefully spanned the depths with an ample high-flung arch. I did not know it, but this was our first sight of the Da-Tung-Hor, here falling to its junction with the Sining-Hor, not so many miles' journey since it received the beck of Wolfstone Dene up there in the high Alps.

But the river's lovely past was hidden from me, up ahead in our own future. We crossed the bridge and ascended again up the shaly slope of the gorge on the other side, and over the brink, and round the shoulder, and so at length into Shan Tang, which had seemed so near such a long time ago. The next day brought us into the gorges of the Sining-Hor. The early part of the stage offers no such diversity as that of the previous day, which begins, on leaving Hei Shuidz', with a long footwalk beside the river's very edge, cold under the shadow of red crumbling cliffs. Instead, it meanders up and down along the bare fell-slopes, past many a group of ruinous castellated mile-towers, with the Kweite-Salar Alps more and more magnificent on the left. Our track rounded a corner and traversed an alluvial lap, richly fertile for a change, with orchards of pear and cherry, every trunk picked glove-smooth of all old bark that could harbour noxious bugs, and looking, therefore, unnaturally neat and naked and pale. Embowered in these orchards nestled a village, which, though not as ruinous as yesterday's country-towns, all smashed and slaughtered by the last Mahomedan rebellion, was equally perking once more into prosperity to be smashed in time by the next. Ere long we turned up to the right, and the valley narrowed, after we had lost sight of another rich promontory opposite on the left. Far down beneath us lay the mapped-out plain of the river, where a tributary beck runs down into the Sining-Hor from the Kweite-Salar Alps, very splendid now to see, at the head of their country. And then, after preliminary ups and downs, we found ourselves in the famous gorges of the Sining-Hor.

These are steep and dark and granitic ; enclosing and deep ; but rarely precipitous and never magnificent. The valley of the Sining-Hor from this point is like a string of sausages : a stretch of amplitude and then a constriction, and so on repeatedly. The hills are still dry, though ; the chief

E

pleasure is to watch the big rafts come undulating down the river, each built of some twenty to thirty enormous inflated yak-skins, containing goods as well as air, and looking like a bound-up phalanx of dead bloated cattle-corpses. Down the surging rapids of the filth-coloured river they are sinuously piloted by a pair of men with big paddles and then swim easily over the swift smoothness of the pebbled expanses below. They sometimes bump and ground, but can never upset: in a trice they can be dismantled or diminished. In the gorges one of them was good enough, indeed, to stick on a rock while we were sitting to a snack of food: it was being lengthily heaved off by its men, and by chance assistants, all in waders of yakskin or sheepskin, inside out, that sagged and bellied oddly as the wearers emerged from the water.

The way through the gorge is arduous and tiresome, up and down. Though much narrower it suggests the Tao valley near Jo-ni. But the dark hot rocks yield flowers: nothing was in bloom yet, of course, but these were the first real plants of my second year—a rock lilac, the Tibetan Androsace, the sere suggestion of last year's Adenophora and Dracocephalum, and abundant in between the torrid sombre stone as we clambered in the sun-trap narrows, the fresh green sproutings marbled with milkiness, of Aquilegia viridiflora (but I always think of this fascinating elf of a perverse Columbine as a " viripeculia "). A little later the torrid inky rocks of the gully must be quite gay, but when I ascended it there was only wreckage and promise, and hard iron-coloured walls that reverberated the bleak and barren sunshine in a sweating stuffiness of heat. And all the world of the wayside in these parts is sheeted in swathes of Iris ensata, now pushing up in speary dense hassocks of greyish green.

Finally the first gorge reaches its climax in a steep, very steep, sharp climb over rocks. And on the other side we drop suddenly into a quite new world. No more pebbled wastes, no more drab desolations, or dreary simulacral orchards of Zao'erh, but a fresh wide vale of loess, filled with real orchards of fruit-trees, and densely set with poplars,

and rich with fertile fields, and studded with happy little
fat clay villages among the trees : and with the Sining hills
(or rather, the hills towards Dangar and the Koko-Nor)
very far away at the end, a serration of bare low ranges
crumpled and corrugated. And water now abounded.
Beyond the first hamlet stretched a line of small bone-dry
hummocky fells, but their base was simply oozing moisture
in a succession of green spongy slopes of marsh. Onwards
we rode, well ahead of the tired mules : and gradually the
Salar Alps came into sight again to cheer the dull billowing
lines of the pale tawny hills on our left, across the valley.
And here we were joined at last by evidences of civilization.
For round upon us from the right coiled out of the hills the
big main road (capable of carts) and escorted by a line of
telegraph poles from Lanchow to Sining—a branch of the
Great Road through Ping-fan and the sand-blown cities of
the far North, to Kashgar and Samarcand and Holy Moscow.
But ours is the road to Holy Lhasa : and down it the Lord of
Lhasa himself has come. For long you have noticed how all
the little road-arches and gates are broken along the road,
and wondered why the damage is so universal. It is because
the Dalai Lama has passed this way. The sanctity of the
pontiff is such that he must never go under an earthly gate.

Not that one would suspect the importance of this road,
or give it a better name than a cart-track. Onward we
pursued its course through village after village, while the
Salar Alps slid away out of sight. At one point we had to
weather a string of camels, nightmarishly advancing upon
us in a processional vista as interminable as that of Banquo's
descendants : I anticipated the worst, knowing how ponies
abhor camels, and bolt for miles on the sight or smell of
them. However, anticipations of ill, like watched pots,
very rarely come to the boil : and though I was on the brisk
little iron-grey beast we had bought in Jo-ni, he stood quite
sedately while the camels drifted by in their grotesque and
silent undulations. So without misadventure we came into
Go-Miaodz', and in time discovered a good inn, new and clean

and neat, pleasantly fresh, as all recent work is in this con-valescent country. And here we had a very long wait for the coming of the caravan that meant the coming of our dinner : I went up and sat on the flat mud roof, and watched the ugly greyness that was now beginning to film the distance in the direction of the Alps.

On the edge of dusk the mules trailed in, and by dusk we had dined. Suddenly, in the inn yard outside, a violent noise of smacking and hammering and wails. Amid a crowd of onlookers, the landlord of an inferior inn upstreet, which we had first looked at, but decided against, was now helplessly kneeling and being pummelled by Mafu and Go-go, who pranced passionately round him and his friend, plant-ing blows where they saw fit. It soon appeared that the pair of them had stolen, or connived at the stealing, of one of our horse-pads, and was now being practically cross-examined. The sight was too much for the wicked Wa-wa : dropping the dinner plates he bounded forth to battle, seized an enormous long-handled wooden spade of about twice his own height, and magnificently banged the criminals with resounding thwacks, in between the more methodical punches and slaps of the Mafu. All doubt as to the Wa-wa's previous career now faded completely : he clearly held no priggish scruples about murder. To prevent the worst accordingly, Bill immediately sallied out upon the scene.

In an instant all was uncanny calm ; wailings died into businesslike supplications. The occasion was considered so important as to call for my own presence : so out I haughtily stalked, deploying my fullest majesty, and stood with awful sphinx-like rigidity while the kneeling sinners beat their fore-heads in the dust before me. Ultimately things got satis-factorily settled, and we accepted a new pad in pledge for the restoration of our own, which was to be recovered by the military authority, on pain of a worse thing. But in this country of confused clamour and intricate responsibilities it is always very hard to feel sure that you have got the real facts of any story : and all I could get certain of in this case was that there had undoubtedly been a theft committed upon us, for which the landlord was properly liable.

The next day's stage for many a mile repeated yesterday's, through the wide alluvial plain, red-soiled or loessed, but always rich with poplar and willow and orchards of apricot and peach. Then out of the hills on the right, what look like titanic palaces begin to emerge—clean-cut vast cliffs, fluted and red, with double horizontal strata topping them, till they look like colonnades and architraves of porphyry, hewn in the living hill-front for the entrance to some dead king's cave-temple of Egypt or Persia. And at this point the journey traverses the one real walled town between Lanchow and Sining. This is Nien-Bi-Hsien, and quite a large place, both within the walls and outside them, though only half come to life again from the long agony of the Mahomedan rebellion. Here we waited to send in cards to the Laoyeh, and get an escort on to Sining": and when this was achieved proceeded outside the city to pause and eat toast in the sun beneath a high bank of loess from which we were watched by a gay bevy of women, smiling and comely, with hair done up behind in an upstanding oval knob, like that which prevails at Siku, though here it is more flattened out into a duck's bill shape.

They lied, however, in saying we only had another 20 li to go; but they always do. Not remembering this invariable rule, we rode on in good heart, through string after string of unregarded camels, but it was 50 li at least before we reached the end of the vale, threaded a short little dull defile, and found ourselves then in a new vale, mostly of loess, duller even than the later stretches of the last, and hedged by hills yet dumpier, drabber and uglier, with the end of the Salar range looming upon us nearer to the left, and beyond it other snow-ranges, peakier and more jurassic : and then yet more still, away and away, fading into the dull grey distance of an afternoon gone steely and filming. And even now it was still goodness know how far : a feeling of frustrate crossness began to fill me, as bay after bay of the river revealed no village. However at long last, and quite suddenly, we did discover our destination, and were blown forward on a stern gale, into a sad little squalid hamlet that squatted close under a chain of dumpling-like downs, studded copiously as a pudding with currants of black conglomerate boulders.

After the last defile, the houses begin more and more to approach the flat-roofed, box-shaped Tibetan type : but our inn was Chinese, and poor. It was long before the mules arrived, as usual : and then we settled drearily into the damp horse-puddled rooms. But then there arose a rumour of more rooms and better ones that might be had : we set out to explore, and very soon found court behind court of beautiful clean new-timbered buildings aswarm with neat wives and innumerable little gay babies playing, all apparently of the same age. I thought it must be a Chinese kindergarten ; but now we penetrated into the main room and found a noble apartment like nothing I had yet seen on the road—large and light and airy and high, of fragrant bright wood work, all hung with pictures and red-satin banners and scrolls, and with a dais of state, and big latticed paper windows, and an altar and a reredos of black and gold, and a full set of ceremonial furniture.

And there, on the dais, sat Paterfamilias himself, busily impressing a Tibetan visitor with his importance. He was a most superior person, in fact, thin and old, with a thin white beard and a narrow scholastic expression ; he treated us with the greatest discourtesy and many a dishonouring little breach of etiquette, trying to impose his rank and erudition upon us, as his excuse for fobbing our party off with an outhouse, while he himself retained these palatial quarters. But Mafu would have none of this nonsense and so yelled down his haughtiness and insolence with derision that at last his batteries were all hammered out of action, and he gave place to us in crestfallen resentment, none the less bitter for the obvious pleasure of the Tibetan friend.

So out he cleared and I was duly ensconced for the night,

amid beauties and comforts and luxuries such as never
before or after did I meet with on the road. The evening
slowly advanced : as the last slants of light began to die,
a door in the far court opened, and in trotted strings of
sheep, come home from their arduous day's pasturing ; and
then their shepherds, and then whole troops of skipping
tumbling tiny lambs. In a spate they came bucking and
bounding in, to play with the playing babies, and butt into
their supper-bowls of sop, and wrestle with them round the
yard, till babies and lambs and all were one undistinguishable scramble of fun. And so, on this Arcadian little scene,
the icy dusk closed in, and the blizzard that now shrouded all
the distant ranges in grey advanced rapidly on the wings of a
shrilling gale that augured ill for the morrow. However I gave
small thought to this as I sank to sleep, quite awed and dazzled
by the pin-new splendour of the decorations around me.

The promise of evil was fulfilled. Snow lay thickly everywhere the next morning, and all the hills were lost in darkness, and the air was grey and sullen. Gloomily we rode out,
upon· a journey even duller than its predecessors. At one
point though, we were cheered by a reminder of how near
we were getting to Tibet. On the right, almost impending
over the road, jutted ahead a mighty fluted bluff of red
precipice ; and tucked into a cranny near its base neatly
gleamed the windowed square white walls and flat dark
roof of a tiny monastery. Steeply from the foot of the cliff
a high slope of boulders fell away to the plain beneath, and
at one point of the holy path up to the shrine, a crude
colossus of the Buddha, beneath a roof and painted pale
blue on a creamy ground, was carved in relief from the face
of a rock. This is Bei Ma Ssŭ, which means White Horse
Chapel. I saw no horses there, though, white nor black,
but congregations of camels clustered at rest in the plain.

The day gradually lightened and the snow departed. At
length we crossed an unexpected bridge over the Sining-Hor,
traversed a third defile, last and least of all, and emerged into
the final plain, with the city wall of Sining in a straight low

line across the distance very far away, and crumply pale shallow fells in all quarters of the huge wide prospect, and nowhere the smallest suggestion of an Alp. My heart sank: the little American Monsignore had spoken of Sining with such a warmth of affection and longing that, taking for granted a uniformity in our tastes, I had expected a city beautiful as the home of dreams, nestling deep and pictur-esquely into the roots of enormous rugged snow mountains overshadowing it all round. On my love and longing for Siku, in between the toes of Thundercrown, I had, in fact, built up an image of Sining as even more magical, in a cirque of mountains even more overwhelming: and now here was nothing but the weariful monotony of yet another dull flat plain, with yet more corrugated dead dull hills meandering round the horizon; and ahead of us yet another dull flat grey city prone across the vast tedium of the prospect. And still so far away.

We rode and rode: and the city seemed to draw no nearer. But even the weariest cart-track winds somewhere safe to town: in due course we found ourselves advancing up the chaotic desolation of the Eastern suburb, only just beginning to revive from the ashes in which it was laid by the Mahome-dan rebellion. And so through the noble double gate into the city. Here there were ambiguities and ridings to and fro: but at length we worked our way to the best inn of the place, and found it very dark and tiny, with a tiny inner yard which we proceeded to occupy. There we unpacked and unfolded in the complete fatigue of relaxation after the strenuous and successful achievement of these first five days on trek, though, really, I must hope that my com-placency was physical, and not at all mental: for what is there so creditable in merely sitting on a horse and going steadily and uneventfully forward through five long days of placid dullness, without the slightest hardship or exertion? All the same, the arrival at Sining marked the end of the preface to our year. For now we were once more close upon the scene of work.

CHAPTER IV

SINING-FU

The inn was a dank unhealthy stinking hole. Our first care was thoroughly to clean, re-paper and whitewash our quarters, and to evict the other occupants of the yard—a rogue-faced fat bull of a doctor-man who lived in the corner room, and really was a rascal of the worst, with a comely " sewing woman " (this is the conventional name) in the opposite room, in whose company he obviously solaced himself with love, in the intervals of consultations. For it became clear that our stay in Sining would have to be a long one : no chance of getting away to the hills in a day or two, as I'd fondly hoped. There were the various high authorities, in the first place, to be visited and consulted and conciliated, the Governor of the city, the Military Governor, the Viceroy of the Koko-Nor : and then the distant ranges must be prospected, to find a likely base for the summer's work.

All this would take time : while they were white-papering the inner rooms (leaving the side cloisons of dark wood panels as they were—a most modern effect), I took refuge from the decorators up on the flat mud roof. And there indeed, there really were mountains—though very far away in the West, up towards Dangar and the Koko-Nor, a low remote ruffle of gleaming snow-peaks. And, as I scanned yet farther, from different elevations of the universal boundless mud roof that gives you a complete open walk over every house in a block of Sining between street and street, I came into view of yet other snow ranges, just appearing over the high loess crumples that fill the North.

I roamed the roofs, indeed, hither and thither, only deterred by discretion, as every now and then I would find myself looking down into some neat little deep inner house-yard, with its central well full of lilac-bushes and viburnum, and under its verandah the lady of the house unsuspiciously sewing shoes. When she glanced up to see a foreign head intruding over the skyline, her expression clearly indicated disapproval of such tactlessness, and I bashfully retired, across the undulating mud-stretches with chimney pots towering here and there, and the occasional shallow surge of what you might almost call a gable, until I reached the unquestionable territory of my own roof, fronting upon the street, with the splendid square wooden tower, and green-and-azure tiling of the Confucian Temple rising just across the way.

Sining-fu lies in an open vale, at the tie point of a cross where four valleys meet. At right angles one broad valley runs down to the Sining-Hor through the Northern hills ; and on the South confronting it, another comes straight from the South, out of the Kweite-Salar ranges. Just West of the juncture the city lies expanded, within the irregular precinct of its walls : up above on the West, several pale tower-structures on the plain commemorate the repulse of a Tibetan invasion, and the many miles of rolling slopes that ascend to the hills on the South below the city are mole-hilled universally with innumerable myriads of graves, blurred and obscured in immemorial antiquity. The reason why the city wall violates the Chinese rule of the regular rectangle is both curious and pathetic. For while the wall was building (and still, therefore, damp and malleable), it appears that there came by one day a dragon. And he was tired, and lay down along the wall, and found it comfortable to his back, and so snuggled against it as to bulge it all out of shape. So that now it has a wavy line, instead of four precise straight ones with a gate-tower in the middle of each.

Otherwise Sining is just such another town as Lanchow,

though smaller, more squalid and crumbling, more remote
and provincial. It has notable buildings, though, the Confucian Temple for one, and the Dung Ling Ssu for another,
a very spacious and stately fane, with ample expanses of
cobbles, and parcelled, pebble-hammered pavements, and
stone lions, and very solid Pailo gateways, and an elaborate
carved theatre-house, and low solemn buildings with tiled
roofs. And the whole grey quiet of the place, lions and
roofs and cobbles and all, is clothed in a lichen-like rust of
golden bronze.

Outside the Northern wall, close under its cold shadow,
there falls away a steep slope, wooded delicately with poplars
and willows, and threaded by bubbling little rills as clear
as diamond in their beds of marsh and lawn, unexpectedly
emerald in April among the sere tawny of the scene : here
there are toy-pagodas, and walks, and little pavilions for
tea. This is the Rosherville of Sining : and down below, by
stony stairways from the Northern gate, you descend into
sparse suburbs where the peach blossom is brilliantly pink
by the end of the month, and so across fields and flats of
loess, perking with drifts of Iris, you come at last to the sandy
shingles of the Sining-Hor, a very broad stretch of pebble
and strand, with silky Oxytropids flaring violet from their
silvery tuffets among the dark stones, or on the pale sand, and
in the middle the river flowing, an exiguous thread of
water in April, spanned by a wooden trestle-bridge with
quaking causeway of straw and mud compiled along the
top. But the bridge is only temporary : for that exiguous
thread of water becomes a roaring waste of waters when the
snows of Tibet are loosed in summer ; and no bridge would
have a chance of surviving.

Of all these beauties I had ample time to make the
acquaintance. For Bill declared that he must go off now
on a prospecting tour : and that, as he would want to travel
very quick and very light, and as all his toil (or much of it)
might be fruitless, it would not be worth while for me to
accompany him, with the staff and all the cumbrous para-

phernalia of the caravan. So I was to stay in Sining, under
the guardianship of Wa-wa and Gomer and Go-go, while
Bill and Mafu, saddled on their bedding, were to fare wildly
forth in pursuit of Alps. Not till his return did we mean to
begin our visits to the Mandarins, so as to have our plans
ready cut and dried to lay before them. So we rested
content with seeing the City Governor, a bead-eyed little
gentleman in furred silks and a bowler hat, with whom we
exchanged a deal of bowing and smiling. And then, on a
glorious day of sunshine, Bill went cantering out of Sining
on the bright little brown pony we had newly bought,
followed by Mafu, touching his hat as he went with the
" Good day, sir," which were his only three words of English,
and reserved for most special occasions.

The days that followed were long and empty, but nearly
always vibrant with the crystalline loveliness of the Northern
Spring. Gradually the earth began to awake, and a clean
thrill of new life flooded my veins after the Winter. Morning
by morning I used to stroll over the expanse of the roofs,
to see how the lilacs and viburnums were advancing in the
little courtyards.   On the viburnums there sat myriads of
busy sparrows : no doubt they must have been at work on
some toothsome bug in the branches, as they never seemed
to peck the young buds. And in the afternoons there were
the streets. Being a big city, and so near the border,
Sining is the special centre of the four races—Tibetans,
Mongolians, Mahomedans and Chinese. So that the flow
of street life is very varied and gay.

Not that the streets have the solid prosperous-looking
neatness of the main streets in Lanchow. On the contrary,
Sining High Street is comparable only to a minor lane in
Lanchow : its houses are low and scattered and ramshackle :
big trees overshadow the wider space in front of the decaying
entrance to the Yamen, and the little stalls of curiosities
that occur here and there offer only the saddest old trash..
But the moving crowds are more brilliant : for besides the
flow of Chinese and Mahomedans, you here have also the

musty red of monks, the rich yellow of high ecclesiastics, or magnificent strapping Mongols with peaked caps of fur and scarlet, and scarlet robes, and great square reliquaries of silver flashing on their breasts. There are numbers of miserable dusty beggars, too, whom you meet returning in a flood from the city's weekly dole of bread. Once I met a man with hair and eyebrows matted solid by that curious disease of Plica Polonica : and in particular there was a tall gaunt maniac or idiot, who always used to appal me with his resemblance to some wild prophet, some John the Baptist, stalking down the street : mere skin and bone, with swollen joints, almost naked but for a sheepskin, with face thrown up in a wild sibylline glare, and a dense shaggy mat of hair standing out in a shock all round behind, like an unkempt and clotted black fleece, all greyed with dust.

My favourite walk was to the South Gate, from which one climbs by a long stairway-slope, to the ramp of the wall. I had never managed to get on to the city wall at Lanchow, and even at Sining there were sentries on guard below, and all along the wall itself, a succession of little guard houses. But no objection was made to my afternoon strolls, in which I came to take much delight. For, from this high causeway, you have all the city and the country unrolled before you, and in the big square buttress-bays or seated between the battlements, you can sun yourself deliciously. On the inner side there are no battlements, and you look straight down into long strips of garden that flow to the very root of the wall. They are very pleasant gardens, too, with tall old trees, and dark spruces, and jungles of flowering shrubs at their feet, and sumptuous bushes of Viburnum, and winding paths, and summer-houses lurking in the shady places. And all round, in the clear distance, roll the hills, and the flat stretches of the valley : every day the peaks towards the Koko-Nor seemed to grow bluer, and the crops and orchards of the four converging alluvial plains perceptibly grew greener.

April was trailing towards its third week when Bill quite unexpectedly arrived one afternoon. He had had a very strenuous time, and returned with nerves strained by hardship, and with fear of failure for the year's work. For he had many terrible days of traversing high bare lands, and arid hills and valleys without any promise : and, when at last he had come into a big Alpine Chain, it was only to be confronted with prospects of a fresh Chago-affair at Tien Tang Ssŭ, where the monks were hostile and unapproachable. However, as usual, he had succeeded in making friends, had found a likely centre, and now had returned over a high Alpine pass, bringing with him clumps of three dormant primulas.

But now followed yet more delays before we could be off. An unprecedented snap of cold and snow shut all the country up again in winter : and Bill, too, needed rest before taking the road again. We could not even manage the three days' journey over the Southward hills to the famous Abbey of Gumbum, where lives the miraculously-charactered holy tree of Ligustrina amurensis But after all, many people had been already to Gumbum : perhaps even the Fathers Huc and Gabet, though their pictures throughout are of such pure Canton tea-tray style as to set one wondering. And in any case, one big Tibetan Abbey is very like another : I should have liked to see Labrang with its Egyptian-looking square mansions, but Gumbum offered no special attraction beyond the Holy Tree, and the tombs of eight unfortunate Buddhas who fell on an evil fate. For the Abbey was once raided by a barbarous unbeliever : he had the eight sacred bodies haled before him, and mocked them with a sinister question : "You, Blessed Ones, who know all the past and all the future, foretell me, then, the day of your own deaths." To which, with a perilous pessimism, they infelicitously answered, "To-morrow." "Quite wrong," he pounced at them, "To-day," and the eight holy heads were stricken off on the spot.

But the days dragged for me in that boring little burg.

We filled them with social activities, and on the afternoon appointed rode out in state to visit the Chang Gwan of the Koko-Nor. The Viceroy of Koko-Nor Tibet is not really supposed to have his residence in Sining at all. His proper seat is in a crumbling and utterly deserted walled town, out near the dreary borders of the Dark-Blue Sea, Ching Hai the Holy, the vast and mournful Koko-Nor that gives the name to his viceroyalty. But Koko-Nor Tibet is a wild and dangerous land : untameable nomad tribes sweep across its undulating plains of grass, and very long ago the Viceroys concluded that they would be a great deal safer and more comfortable inside the walls of Sining. So to Sining they retired, and in Sining they have stayed ever since : only going out once a year to their deserted Viceregal seat, for a fortnight or so of pomp and state, to receive China's due of homage and tribute from the Mongol and Tibetan princes. But they are not officially resident in Sining : they are officially invisible and unknown there, without standing or existence—though in practice, of course, their prestige far overtops that of the City Governor, who is actually subordinate to the Viceroy of Kansu.

Off we all rode in pomp, and round to the rather squalid-looking small Yamen in a side-street. But it proved surprisingly big : we were led along from court to court, till we came out into a very spacious garden, with tall trees, and a summer-house on a mount, and a muddy moat with a bridge and many little plots. Here in the verandah there met us the stumpy little bowlered figure of the Chang Gwan, a stout, heavy-faced gentleman, with very long drooping moustaches. For, alone among the Viceroyalties of the new Regime, that of the Koko-Nor was still in the hands of a Manchu.

Ceremoniously he conveyed us indoors, to a magnificent square stone-paved apartment of state, the finest I had yet seen—with three of its sides all light with glass panes and paper lattices. Arrayed up and down it were white-clothed tables and chairs, each table adorned with boughpots (in horrible European vases) of forced viburnum in its white form, as lovely and sweet as the best white lilac. At a table, prepared with chalky sweets, candied pear-slices, and biscuits, we sat and highly conversed : until, on a question from the Chang Gwan, Mafu let it be known that we entertained no evangelistic views about the bottle, such as are proclaimed by Protestant (but not by Catholic) missionaries. A thimbleful or so of wine all round accordingly cheered up the party considerably : the Chang Gwan blossomed into a charming and childlike joviality, putting questions of a devastating indiscretion to the missionary who on this occasion was our chaperone. He became, in fact, quite intimate : studied the cut of our hair and the make of our clothes, and came closer to me to find out how my moustache was fixed, so as not to flop forlornly like his own ; and then observed that my nose is not, unfortunately, as straight as my character. Upon which discovery he delighted the assemblage by remarking that the poor thing was " sick."

Then, when the entertainment and the catechism was done, the Chang Gwan took us out to see his garden, with rows upon rows, in successive yards, of lilacs, potentillas, viburnum, peonies and roses and jasmine in pots and vats. Evidently the Viceroy of the Koko-Nor followed the Manchu tradition, and was as keen a gardener as the Grand Dowager, his late mistress, that " worthy gentlewoman, and notable lover of these delights." He even had cold-houses, too, for his plants, to winter them ; and warmed go-downs to force them, full of jasmine and viburnum blooming softly in the soft white glow of the paper walls. He gave me a bush of the white form, seeing my enthusiasm ; and I, in return, seeing that he also had European pansies and stocks in pots, promised to get him more seeds over from England. So at length he saw us out, down through the garden ; and showed us yet another sight as we went. For there, beneath a noble tree of Ligustrina, stood a noble tame elk, with magnificent antlers, and his elegant wife close by. After which we departed, feeling we had laid good foundations for our summer, though the plan-talk had hitherto been only a vague pleasantness, the limitations of territory and authority being so very uncertain on the Border that no Chinese Mandarin will ever commit himself beforehand about letting one go to this place or that.

The very next morning we were thrown into a flurry by news that Mâ Dâ-ren the Military Governor was on his way to call. However, it was not till 11 that he arrived. He turned out to be a Mahomedan—a huge tall voluminous fellow, with a pleasant heavy smile, escorted by a whole tail of followers including some smart uniformed soldiers. He was perfectly amiable, but rather unhelpful in talk. I felt him a guarded cold personality, not in the least like the gentle little jovial Chang Gwan. But he was quite as much interested in our things, though critically and acquisitively as well. He examined the siphon, the rifle, and even the flower-sketches. But the field-glasses appealed to him most of all. Nothing would serve him but to try them. He bunched up his satin skirts and climbed up the ladder on to the roof : much to my terror, lest the yielding insecure mud-plateau should collapse beneath his weight. However it held good despite its tremblings, and with grunts of enthusiasm he viewed the prospect o'er through the glasses, highly appreciative of their military value. He sent for his own to show us, and they helped to account for his enthusiasm, being a flimsy gimcrack pair of opera glasses. I had, in fact, much ado to evade his proposals to buy mine : and only did so at last on promise to wire to England for another pair. And so at length got rid of him after a two-hours' visit that left us pale and wan.

Spring till tarried, and the winds continued glacial : I thought I saw a film of green appearing on the low range outside the city on the South : so sallied forth with Gomer across the dumplinged millions of graves up the spur, where a grand red temple sits, in which people give parties.

F

But when I got there, I found only a tight-packed carpet of Oxytropis, and the tiny gorse-like Caragana, in bushes nibbled almost flat : and there was no other sign of life whatever, except two enormous Roman-nosed old ravens on a bummock. So home I came, and on the way, by mere chance, came upon my first flower of the year. For, down in a hollow of the loess sheltered and warm, there was a small flat plot of turf, all glowing with the lovely little pale intelligent faces of Viola Patrinii.

But even this delight was ere long put out of my head by the bustle and fuss among the staff at home on news that the Chang Gwan was on his way to call. It seemed a small and squalid place in which to entertain so large a potentate as the Viceroy of Koko-Nor Tibet : however, he was perfectly happy and pleased with everything ; and though he did also stay for a couple of hours, he was always such a simple jolly old gentleman that I never found him anything like so heavy in hand as the rather malign massiveness of Mâ Dâ-ren, the Military Governor. We showed him all our tricks, the field-glasses, the siphon, the sketches : it was characteristic of the difference between the Chinese and the Mahomedan outlook that whereas Mâ had been bored by the sketches and thrilled by the glasses, the Chang Gwan was only politely interested in the latter, but became absorbed in the sketches, particularly in those of the flowers. He chortled and chuckled copiously : but was still much upset about my poor nose. It continued evidently sick, and he was anxious to know if it hurt.

But, above all, things of the toilet appealed to this vain old charmer : he was very desirous to have some turn-down linen collars like mine, and there came a quite ecstatic moment when we waxed the enormous droops of his moustache for him, and turned them up in long thin tails. A mirror was called for : into it he deeply gazed for a moment ; and then His Excellency, the Viceroy of Koko-Nor Tibet, began giggling with delight, as coyly and consciously as any schoolgirl.

A few days later Mâ gave a party for us, a vastly ceremonious Beano. We walked to it after lunch, when the
summons came ; and the horses were led in front of us in
state, so as to save our " face " from the shame of going
afoot. We found his palace a huge and solid structure, and
the decorum of our reception was to match, entirely un-
Chinese in its regulated and formal magnificence. Through
a long vista of courtyards we had to proceed as majestically
as we could, with hands at the salute, up a ranked avenue of
soldiers presenting arms : and as we crossed the threshold
of the last gate towards the verandah (where Mâ, as massive
as a mountain, stood awaiting us) the band burst suddenly
into a braying blare of music. Mâ now led us into the main
hall, and thence aside into a lateral room, all tapestried
round with scrolls of gold and scarlet-and-gold. There
were treasures of old bronze, too, and a lovely carpet,
and all the chairs and state-seats were frocked in vermilion
silk caparisons, elegantly broidered. Installed on the
main throne, I sat and nibbled the usual *zakoushka* of
nuts and sweets : gradually the select few fellow-guests
gathered : and in due course we moved out on to the
verandah again, for Bill to take a photograph of the
gathering.

In the middle of the group the General loomed gigantic,
with his scarlet umbrella of state upborne behind him.
Half-way through the proceedings, though, he must needs
go and don his uniform. This took a long while, but he
certainly looked no less magnificent when he reappeared
in it, and the state umbrella in the background, like a
deep-flounced table on a pole, pointed an effective contrast
between the old style and the new. Meanwhile the whole
household and all the hangers-on were gathered densely
in the courtyard to see the fun. And among the crowd
Mâ spied the nurse, and the hope of his house, a fascinating
little urchin in scarlet. He, too, must of course be immortalized : and this put dinner further off than ever, for
neither bribes, persuasions nor cajolements could prevail on

him to face the camera. However, at last all was accomplished, and we moved in to food.

This went by rote ; and Bill, as usual, sustained our reputation by intrepidly luxuriating on all the gristles and soused elastic of *la haute cuisine* in China. I myself acquired much credit by drinking the health of my mother, whose birthday it was : but when, on further inquiry, it appeared that she was by no means yet a centenarian, my credit correspondingly declined. There is nothing venerable in China about having sprightly parents of half a century or so : veneration dawns only upon the eighties, and increases by geometrical progression year by year. I myself felt almost reverend, in fact, with age, before the course of a First Class Chinese dinner (there are three grades, and woe betide anybody who offers you the wrong one) had unfolded its full length. It was a relief when the bowls of rice appeared and Mâ rose up and escorted us all the way down the courtyards to the outermost gate, amid awful bursts of braying from the bands, that made the ponies bound wildly about in terror.

I feared the worst, but Go-go held Big Grey tight, and I clambered up, and made my bows, and rode forth straight-backed in conscious pomp through the admiring multitudes, amid an eruption of brazen blasts like pandemonium. Then, round the corner of the street, we dismounted, to walk humbly home. And, though it was now half-past six, and the day filmed with cloud, the air was soft and balmy to breathe, as I had never felt it since leaving beloved Siku. The spring was really come at last : we dined out of doors in the yard, under a night now glorious with stars and moon, in an inexpressible tranquillity of warmth.

And the spring in Sining floods the whole city in a sudden sea of pink peach-blossom. Mâ Dâ-ren's garden is a noble sight then. It is a very big open park in the heart of the town, and now, on invitation, we went one afternoon to see it. There is no residence attached, but through the gate you find yourself entering a series of wide courtyards with weedy plots and irrigation runnels : there are complicated rockeries and pavilions and pagodas perched about, and a big high gazebo on a mount, and spacious derelict cloisters, and summer-rooms, and empty pools. And all of it enforested in the shade of huge spreading poplars, high over the tangles beneath, of peach, and plum, and lilac and rose, and barberry and viburnum, and aged masses of tree-peony.

In the end of April it is all a haze of shell-pinkness, with the blue blur of bare poplar-branches beyond, and then, in the Westward distance, bluer than all, the Alps of the Koko-Nor. It was the first time, too, that I had ever seen *Viburnum fragrans* blooming in its full magnificence out of doors—an epoch-marking instant in anyone's life. Gasping with the loveliness of that sad abandoned ground, we roamed and sauntered, climbed the outermost wall to look down alternately into the city and the garden through the veil of peach-bloom, and wandered among the desolate cloisters and corridors and grey old pleasure rooms crumbling to decay. And then, out of nowhere, as it seemed, the little Mâ's appeared, with a withered patriarch acting as nurse. Boys and girls, they were a very friendly crowd, and played with us, and escorted us round, and helped us take photographs of the viburnum, but bolted wildly, with squeaks and squawks and giggles, whenever we turned the camera in their own direction.

CHAPTER V

OVER THE ALPS

Peach-bloom in the plains ought to herald the unlocking of the hills ; so now we felt we could fairly ripen matters for the start. Everything went on oiled wheels ; mules and men and mandarins were all amenable ; we even succeeded in selling Spotted Fat, and replacing him by a sprightly little beast with a good " dzo." For Sining is a notable place for horse-coping, and here, for a price, you can get special specimens of " dzo-ma "—that is, ponies trained to a very rapid amble, quick as a smart trot, but perfectly smooth and effortless, and easy to the rider as if he were sitting in a Pullman arm-chair. Even from Peking do horse-fanciers, foreign as well as Chinese, send for amblers to Sining. As for Spotted Fat, clotted in incorrigible laziness, one-eyed, sullen and demoniacal, I was determined to have no more of him at any cost, even if I should have to give him away, or bribe somebody to accept him. So that I was agreeably surprised to find a somebody actually simple enough to purchase him for nineteen taels, which is about £2 18s.

It was, then, in sound and perfect delight that we saw the mule-packs corded and got on to their cradles and these duly lowered on the mules. In a morning of clear dazzling brilliance we rode out of Sining on the 3rd of May. At first we went back Eastward again down the valley : but soon turned leftwards to the river, and crossed by a double bridge to its far side, along which we continued among willows and poplars, now growing green, and amid orchards gone dingy by this time towards their fruit. But everywhere the double peach-bloom was still in the climax of its almost intolerable loveliness, pink as no rose is ever pink, in a furious clean glow. And now, about 10 li down the Sining-Hor, we turned at a sharp right angle up to the left, into the valley of the Wey-Yuan-Pu-Hor. The valley of Officialton River is very like that of the Sining-Hor, except that it is not so wide, running through just the same (if rather ruddier) Saharan dry ranges of hummocks.

But always, ahead of us at the top of the far distance, we now had the Da-Tung Alps to cheer us—an amazing apparition after all these miles and months of mere loess desolation. This whole country runs so high, of course, that the peaks themselves by no means have their proper height-value in the view. The wide open vale of Sining and its encompassing shallow downs suggest nothing in the world less than an Alpine country : yet Sining itself could look down on the Mont Cenis. For its elevation, though variously estimated, is about 7,000 ft., and the crumpled hills attain another 1,000 feet ; you are well up here already on your way to the Roof of the World. But here the slant of the Eaves is so enormous and so slow and smooth, that you have little sense of rising, and none at all of the height you are at : when you have reached the Koko-Nor itself you have still no realization of height, and the Sacred Sea, the highest of the world's lakes, lies so vastly expanded in so vast and dull a country of low undulations and simple-seeming shallow ranges, that you might be down on the level of the ordinary sea itself, at an uninteresting part of its shore, instead of 12,000 ft. up on the Tibetan highland, with Alpine chains all round you, camouflaged as downs and dunes.

The Da-Tung Alps belong to the Northern, not to the Southern mountain system of Asia. Round the South run the Himâlya, and thence Northward the Tibetan highland breaks down into China in a huge succession of mountain chains, roughly parallel. And up these the Himâlyan Flora continues, gradually modifying. But

the Min S'an and then Lama Ling and Lotus Mountain
are the last fading efforts of the Alps, and from Didao
North to Sining there is nothing more but fells of gravel
and loess, till North of Sining you meet the advancing
surge of that other mountain system which corresponds to
the Himâlya, sweeping in a gigantic curve round Northern
Tibet, splashing isolated ranges downwards, from the
main breakers of the Kwen Lun, the Ala S'an and the
Altai, right across Turkestan, Siberia, Mongolia to the
Long White Mountain of Manchuria, and the Yablonoi
chain right away up to Kamschatka.

And this northern sweep carries the Northern Flora,
repetitions and cousins of old Alpine friends. Diminishing
as they come South, the northern races fade out in the
downward-dying ranges above Sining, just as the ascending
Himâlyan Flora dwindles up to the Min S'an and Lotus
Mountain. So that, between the two systems of Alps and
Alpines, there here comes a real hiatus, across which some
of the races succeed in shaking hands. The Da-Tung
Alps, in fact, are a meeting-point of Northern and Southern,
both weak at the extremity of their stretch. A few ranges
higher up the world, or lower down, and you would be in
the bull's eye of either North or South : the Da-Tung gives
you neither the one thing nor the other, but a strained
attempt at combination.

This, however, is to proticipate. That May morning, in
that clear pale valley, the Da-Tung Alps ahead were the land
of promise, suggesting the Maritimes as you see them from
La Napoule—a long line of serrations and snowy pyramids,
utterly (and had I stopped to consider that difference further,
ominously) unlike the Dolomitic castellations of Thundercrown and the Min S'an ; rising from crumpled unwooded
fells of lovely mauve tones. Very gradually the valleys
mount in an ample leisure to the leisurely lines of the
foothills : the whole country forms so huge and high a
pedestal for the mountains as almost to diminish them.
From North-West to South-East descends the corrugated

complicated mountain system of the Da-Tung Alps. Behind, in the deep trough of them, runs the Da-Tung-Hor, but up their Western front the Alps decline on to a cushion of foothills, running out down the long slope of the highlands below in ribs like breakwaters, between which, from out of the Alps, descend vast fan-shaped deltas of long-dead rivers, stony moorland wastes now, with only a trickling rill and an abundance of boulders to suggest the remote ages when those mountains must have expended their substance so furiously in such furious volumes of water.

The rise of the lowland valley is very long, dull and flat (though steadily, imperceptibly ascending) over tracts of loess and levels, with irrigation runnels in the track, threading the expanses of white-stemmed poplars, now beginning to shimmer with green. But already there began to be flowers. On all the torrid downs the goat-cropped tight little dumps of Caragana were golden as gorse : densely crowded masses of Iris Ensata were spearing up in the levels, and at one point, on the edge of a kloof, a vinous flare of purple gave me my first sight of Iris tigridia : while at the very entrance to the Officialton valley a metallic yellow Adonis had paradoxically appeared in the dry lands.

And before us, and behind, the distance was filled with mountains. Higher and higher in the South-West unfold the Kweite-Salar Alps, as you advance North-East towards the developing masses of the Da-Tung Alps. Flatter and flatter goes the valley, though, less and less poplared, but advancing steadily towards the foothills, until at length it fades out into a wide irregular sea of plain, curving beneath their slopes. More often than not we were in the expanded shingles of the river, now flattened out into a convergence of many stony little becks. Officialton was very coy : long after we had divined its presence far ahead, in the upmost flat of the river-bed, in one of the many poplared divergencies towards the foothills, it eluded us steadily ; and village after village brought us no nearer, though the mountains now rose more and more immediate in front of us in a wide semicircle, very dark and wild and rugged, powdered with snow, and suggesting the Cottians without the Viso.

Ever upwards we advanced, in the indefinite valley-head, and at length, about 4.30, turned suddenly, and saw a seeming rampart of loess ahead of us, and a curly tower, ensconced beneath a little green-and-red promontory that here jutted into the highland plain.

It was Officialton at last : into it and round about and through it we rode, in search of the Yamen, and Mafu, and the inn that he had ridden on in front to secure. The smart Mahomedan soldiers whom Mâ Dâ-ren had given us for an escort secured us everywhere the most respectful salutations : but still there was no inn, and the Yamen was shut, and the Lao-yeh away. Never was there a more concealed little tumbly place, too, with complicated loess walls, and inner walls, and Gazebo-towers at their corners. But as we rode in and out it showed as a very prosperous townlet, full of fat shops, and oddly abundant in flowers and plants in pots.

But I was glad at length to discover our inn, long, and narrow-yarded, with a good gabled mud roof all round, on which I immediately climbed up, to sit and watch, over the scattered crumbling loess roofs and gables of the town, and the black poplar fog beyond, and the high purple hill behind, how the slants of sundown deepened bluely in the sharp corrugations of the Kweite-Salar chain, now pale and cold in the opalescent twilight under the arch of a grey sky, with yet another range showing dazzling white in sunshine, very far away over a low depression, against the clear gentle gold of sundown that filled the arch, while along to the right the range seemed to continue to another " massif " by a dipping bridge of lesser hills, from which one point in especial stood violently up, in a solid beak of purple all by itself.

Officialton contains many Chinese, but it has its name

from being the central borough of the aborigines. Like
pebbles scattered in a flood, there occur all over China,
here and there in the ocean of Chinese, Mahomedans,
Mongols and Tibetans, these queer little outcrops of dying
races forgotten from of old. And on this Westward fall
of the Da-Tung Alps you come on this territory of the
Tu-ren, the Children of Earth, as the Chinese call them ;
which is nothing more nor less than " Αὐτόχθονες,"
aborigines. Their central point is Officialton, and they
pervade just this one small spot on the face of China, a
curious race, wholly unlike the Chinese, the Mongols, the
Tibetans, and the Mahomedans, if only in the fact that they
are very dark, and very dense with curly black hair.

As for their women, these are in a much more magnificent
style—stalwart stately ladies, who stride over the country
in sweeping draperies of red and blue, with swinging chains
of silver, and square silver reliquaries on their bosom, and
two broad leathern stoles, before and behind, adorned
with large round plaques of white porcelain. On their
heads they wear a gigantic superstructure, exactly like that
of the Duchess in Alice in Wonderland, or the head-dress
in which Queen Isabeau de Bavière accepts the tome of
Christine de Pisan—a swelling edifice of scarlet, rounded,
with a dip in the middle, over which is draped a deep
valance of blue fringe, and a blue veil behind. One would
not think the court costume of Queen Isabeau conducive
to rural activities, but these mediæval-looking matrons
ply their businesses unimpeded, and can even show an
undesirable activity ; for while they are quite friendly and
curious, they are also incurably coy about the camera,
and the moment you switch it in their direction, take to their
heels, and become a mere blur of red and blue, flapping
across the face of the world with the agility of Atalanta.

Officialton was a friendly pleasant place too : even the
people of the town brought presents of corn and beans,
and a general amiability prevailed—perhaps because the
little town specializes on the kindly gift of Bacchus, and is

famous, far and wide, for the purity of its spirit. With this
we took steps to stock our cellar for the summer : it was
clean and dry and pure, and clear as white water and hot
as white fire, inexpressibly nasty, like quintessential paraffin,
but violently and immediately prophylactic against cold
and wet in the mountains. No wonder if Officialton is so
beautifully bonhomous : even the air of it is as if " a passing
fairy had hiccoughed, and had previously visited a wine-
vault." A deep joy pervaded me that evening, to be so
close at last to the hills, though not in sight of them, and
still with the barrens all around. For the main Alps have
long vanished behind their children before you reach
Officialton : and round behind the town the children rise
so abruptly as wholly to usurp one's attention—a sweep
of high corrugated craggy purple peaks, dark and splendid,
and, on this, their Western face, entirely bare of woodland.

But the barrens are more varied here, with stretches of
sward : the next morning Bill rode away ahead with the
Wicked Wa-wa, on some pretence that thinly veiled his
real purpose of getting things perfectly prepared for my
arrival in the mountains, and I was left to a quiet day of
sauntering in Officialton.

The morning was dark and filmy, but the afternoon
cleared to perfect glory. Into the dancing air I sallied
forth, attended by the Go-go and two of the Mahomedan
soldiers. (But the remaining seven of the dozen with which
we had been favoured we had now sent back, for want of
food for them in the Alps : taking care to keep two Mahomedans, so as not to damage the " face " of Mâ Dâ-ren.)
For hours we wandered round and about : rarely have I
known a day of such dazzling sparkle, with such wonderful
clouds and colours, and floating films of rain occasionally
drawn over the dark sapphire crags, and the air keen and
virginal with freshness as a boy's laughter, except when it
was winged with wafts of stale wine, dull and musty, from
the town. Outside the walls there are wide patches of
culture, interspersed with stretches of grave-bummock

sward as fine and green and close and springy as the most perfect tennis court, with dead walls and boundaries here and there, melted down under a lacquer of the same vivid turf.

Wide yards of it, too, are made of a tiny matted Edelweiss, serried in thousands of minute silver-grey rosettes, soft and silky, on which sits tight a stemless galaxy of fluffy silver stars. This is Leontopodium F.740, and if it will only keep its neat ways in richer soils and cooler moister climates I foresee it as a wonderful turf-plant over here also, and especially desirable if you can contrive to get the purple chalices of Crocus speciosus to come perking through its silver floor. So in a warm ecstasy I wandered, and finally lay out on the grass of a ruined tower, rapt in the marvellous rich colours of the nearer ranges, and the diaphanous blue loveliness of the far ones. The Perrier-Jouet air crowded me with beatitudes, and the mood lasted through the evening, though the night came down muggy and dark in a uniformity of cloud that promised ill for the morrow.

And handsomely was the promise fulfilled. Agog with the joy of actually going up into the mountains, I spurned my truckle-bed at 7, and leapt out into a dark chill morning, as dull and gloomy as if the world indeed were feeling last nightish from its raptures of the day before. The darkness deepened, denser grew the clouds, as packing proceeded for the culminating stage. Hope bubbles in me always irrepressible, though, and the joy of going by far outweighed the fear of pains in the process. My only worry was for nine poor white hens, tied in two pendent bunches by their collected feet, upside down on either side of a mule. I tried to urge other methods of conveyance, but Mafu was quite firm, and I had long since learned better than to interfere with things in China.

So I mounted up on to the Grey, and off the procession started. A wild flow of large raindrops immediately began driving at us on a bitter gale, and the cloud deepened towards night, and the hidden mountains bellowed afar in rolling thunders. We rode along and along for an hour or more beneath the red promontory that juts upon the town. And we rode now in the blind white obscurity of a dense snow-storm that blotted out almost everything. But I could just see that culture soon faded out off the flat vale of the beck (but not on the hill) giving place to a dark-soiled marish expanse of green, grass and sedge, on which ran strange big partridge-like birds ; while on the far side rose a range of violently red ferruginous bummocks. And ahead, dimly looming, were the mountains : as the snow gradually thinned and ceased, at last they came out profoundly dark in wet violet, almost black. But now we turned up sharply to the right, and over the promontory by a steep pull, and down as steeply on its other side, into another flat moorland stretch. Crossing the wide vale we entered a long winding ravine, where the loess expanses were clothed in Iris Ensata. The Alps were nearer now, our direction slanting towards them, over successive breakwater downs and their intervening deltas.

It was all steely and cold and dark, but soon the snow returned, and in a blinding white flurry we climbed a very steep slope of red earth, and rounded a high bare breast of down towards a col. Here, in such weather, there could be no question of riding, for the track was a mere porridge of slimy slush, some six inches wide on the brent face of the fell. So I alighted and toiled up as best I could through the blizzard ; and underneath my feet, and all about me on the slope, were carpets and cushions of Androsace tibetica, astonishingly broad in leaf, and always of a lovely pinkness, wherever I saw a rare early bud beginning to open its round fascinating face on this snowy world.

Now from the neck in dense and denser snow we descended into a bare little glen as white as midwinter, in which a tiny flat-roofed village huddled. I hoped that this might be Weston-of-the-Pass, which I knew occurred on the journey. In the desperateness of the day I almost meditated calling a halt here, instead of attempting the passage of the Alps.

But the difficulty of travelling was not so great as it might have been, for the wind and snow were driving down on us from behind. So on we went, and the place was not Weston-of-the-Pass at all. And now suddenly the darkness lessened and lightened, and in a few minutes more the snow was over, and we were debouching, under a clear sky, down into the very wide flat vale of a river. Here we turned sharply up it to the left: and there, only a mile or two in front of us at the top of the plain, rose the craggy fastnesses of the Alps, virgin in new snow, and toweringly magnificent, even though these were not really the main Alps at all, but only their foothills and buttresses still.

In quiet relaxation we moved easily forward, over the soft springy sward of the delta, strewn with many rounded boulders that spoke of bygone ages when a real river lived here, and not merely one small beck: until we were within two miles or so of where the glen of the pass came coiling out of the Alps, and widened into the plain. On the left, along beneath the projecting spur of downs, now appeared Weston-of-the-Pass, crouching and crumbling in its poverty. For all this country runs so high, and its conditions are so harsh and Alpine, that this is the very topmost limit of possible cultivation, and even so, the grain only ripens here in one season out of three. So that Weston hangs on to a bare livelihood by the skin of its teeth, the last and poorest village up towards the Alps.

We did not pass through, but kept away to the right, over the plain. By a big square grain-fortress out in the flats I got off to eat, and wait the arrival of the mules and the two poor little donkeys,[1] now labouring far behind. They were so long in coming, in fact, that at last I strolled forward again up the turfy levels that stretch two miles or so to the mouth of the gorge, with the mountains impending on either hand. Tucked into a high fold of the fell on my right, there appeared the neat church and monastic buildings of Bread Abbey—Mo-mo Ssu in Chinese, and Manto Ssu

[1] Hands off, critics; this is the spelling of the Divine Jane.

in Tibetan—but otherwise the scene was perfectly gaunt and lifeless and Alpine, with many a promise, I thought, beginning to dawn in the elastic Alpine dampness of the sward, which reminded me most vividly of those high turfy stretches below the Clear Lake on Moncenisio.

The caravan was very slow in overtaking me. I was almost in the mouth of the defile by this time : so turned to stroll back and meet it, with a wonderful new prospect now facing me, of the vast upland fall to Officialton, sombre in green and blue, and beyond it, most imperial under the wild sky, in violent purples, the long distance of foot-hills, and the crested sweep of the Kweite-Salar Alps. Hardly had we joined forces and turned back and entered the gorge, than there met us wayfarers descending. And these, though I did not recognize them, proved to be the Tibetan interpreter, lent us by the Chang Gwan, to talk straight words to the monks of Tien Tang, returning with a friend. They both produced notes from Bill, in which he advised me, if the weather promised ill, to halt for the night at Weston, as the pass was very steep and high and hard. However, the day looked as if it had now definitely broken into decency, and my own inclinations are always against leaving a job half done. I took counsel with Mafu, and found that his opinion was the same. So, as the day was still young, we concluded to proceed : with smiles and bows we parted from the interpreter, and sped him on his downward way to Weston.

Soon we were well into the throat of the defile, between steep slopes of Rose and Barberry and Daphne, all still as mere an undecipherable blur of deadness as if it were mid-December : except for the glossy dark evergreen of the Daphne, in its rather straggly little bushes. And hardly were we safe caught in the toils of the ravine than the day darkened once more, and soon a third snowstorm, even heavier than its predecessors, was softly enveloping us in its embrace, and wholly wiping out the prospect in every direction. It descended on us windless, silent, with an uncanny relentlessness of calm : we climbed and coiled in a numb lethargy, drifting through a white dream. At one point, indeed, on a scree-slope we were crossing in a gully I caught a flare of purple on the snow and the dark wet shingle ; and leapt from my saddle to the first primula of the year. This made sunshine : otherwise only dim ghosts of peaks, dolomitic and fantastic, far above me, at first suggested themselves : and soon even these faded, and all was nothing but a blind whiteness of dark, in which we perpetually toiled forward, without knowing how or where.

After a long time of this I was sensible that we were coming to the pass itself, the work growing harder, the rise of the ground, the loops of the track becoming steeper. And then, looking up through the universal snowfog, I was appalled to see that vanishing dim ladder of coils, serpentining up above me so fearfully steep and high, till it melted into the vague, with no suggestion of ever reaching an end. I got off to climb : the snow was very deep, the ascent of the severest : across the whiteness scudded whirring coveys of that big fat snow-grouse which is called the Blood Pheasant, because it is neither bloody nor a pheasant. In the obliterating silence of the dark these made the only sign of life, until far up out of sight came an elfin jangle of bells. And then, emerging like ghosts, descended on us Bill's mules returning down to Weston. We met, and passed : their men told us we were nearing the crest. And in that same moment the hopeless darkness broke, the snow ceased, the clouds ravelled out by magic, and there was the sun supreme in a Heaven of blueness and whiteness unbelievable.

In all the days of all the years you might never have the luck to be on Wolvesden Pass in such conditions. My heart thumped, agonizing with height and ecstasy, as I toiled up the remaining yards, and stood on the actual crest, some 13,600 ft. above the sea, delirious in the vista of marvellous peaks all round me, swimming among silvery vapours, and blinding in the unmitigated glory of virgin snow. Over the brink,

G

deep down below, lay the head of Wolfstone Dene, and its course was soon diverted by the whole splendid panorama of the main Da-Tung Alps, the cruel needle of Omos, and the stately gables of Achthos, Axeinos and Thanatos. To right and left, guarding the pass, soared up the peaks of Kelainô and Keraunô, the one as white now as the other : while down the way we had come lay the curves of the gorge, deep under the crags and pinnacles of wet blue and violet, gleaming in the sun ; and out beyond, beneath straight heavy layers of purple cloud and golden horizon, lay the plains and rivers, very remote and sullen. It was a vision of crystal fairyland, a transformation scene in some Olympian pantomime—cruelly vast in scale, cruelly blue above, and cruelly white all round in the glare, with only here and there rock shadows as black as jet, and dark fantastic pinnacles of dolomite jetting up from the slopes in phallic towers with streaming flanks of wetness in the sunshine.

The mountains being all new to me, were as yet, of course, nameless : now was the obvious moment to immortalize them in a photograph. But I was high ahead of the toiling caravan ; out of the white depths below, its line of minute black dots came slowly coiling. At last, after half a crowded hour of glorious but impatient waiting (for the sun was going quickly westward, and imperilling every moment the portrait of Keraunô) Go-go appeared, flopping to and fro on a mule, with those tragic hens hanging stark on either side, mere bunches by now of dead white feathers, stiff and staring. And it then came out that it was Lay-gor who that day had the privilege of carrying the camera. And Lay-gor was the very last of all, in attendance on his own two little donkeys, still far away down at the tail of the caravan. So there I still had to wait another hour, while the mules went jingling on, dropping out of sight down the Eastward wall of the pass. Every moment the light on Keraunô got more wrong, as the day began quickly dying. Warmth and radiance sank into a solemn twilight, and the snows turned coldly blue. I kept life in my feet by prospecting for plants in the reef of rocks that is the actual crest, and for seed-vessels perking from the snowfield of the slopes and arête. But there was evidently nothing new : the Poppy was the Harebell one, and the sere Primula pods were certainly Woodwardii. And now Lay-gor was really approaching, and in a few more minutes had arrived. I snatched the camera in a passion of pent-up energy. But the ardours of the journey had jangled its innards out of gear. It was useless.

In a speechless annoyance I renounced the struggle and started to run down the Eastern wall of the pass. For an actual wall it looks to be from the top, a sheer precipitous drop to the valley-head beneath, so abrupt that you cannot see, from above, how it goes. And almost a wall it really is : in very short zigzags the track winds downwards, among precipices and projecting bluffs. It was all dark and cold in shadow : the sun only lingered in the valley, where I could see Mafu and the ponies, very tiny, awaiting me. Down the coils I picked my way, and as soon as the diminishing snow allowed, pelted and tore, exhilarated as I went by lovely lavender heads of Primula that smiled at me amid the icicles, in ledges and cavities of the cliffs lower down. It is a long descent, fearsome and far : but in time I found myself at the foot of the pass, in a quite new world of cooler glens, scrubby with small Rhododendrons, and, lower yet, with coppice of a dark ugly little aromatic Cypress on their drier-hotter folds.

So here I mounted again in the last sad slants of sundown in the mountains, and we set forward down the glen, straight towards the overpowering mass of Omos-Thanatos. I had been told it was no great distance from the Valley-head to Wolvesden. On the contrary, it was the worst stretch of the day, very long, and cruelly trying. For now the dusk swooped, and it was soon dead dark. Round bay after bay of slippery little invisible track we proceeded, along the lip of dim cliffs above the beck ; or else across stretches of rounded granite boulders, overlaid by new mushy snow that concealed the cavities ; till, in the enveloping blackness of the dark, our progress was only a blind miracle, and the tired ponies were perpetually stumbling in the holes, or scrabbling for foothold on an unexpected face of rock. On and on we groped : now we were evidently deep in gorges, overwhelmed in blank midnight by mountains on either hand ; and water roared below, and wet boughs across our faces emphasized the woodland in which we were now engulfed. Apathetically we crawled through the blackness, almost too tired to speak. My heart was gnawed for those poor hens, and the two brave little donkeys, left far behind : and still we went, deeper and deeper in the bowels of the Alps : again and again we had to wrestle, saddle-high, through the brawling cold of the river ; and again and again skirt warily along the cliffs, above unplumbed abysses of night.

It seemed as if we were never to arrive : Mafu himself was hopelessly surly and monosyllabic with fatigue. Even when I did at length, round another shoulder of brushwood, catch a spark of light ahead in the gloom, I dared not give it any credit. No doubt it was a mere pixy-glimmer, luring us to doom in some deep ghyll among the rocks. But no ; gradually out of the night there dawned two of our own people with a lantern. Down by slippery coils they escorted us to the river again : one more surging plunge through its depths, and in ten minutes more I was alighting before the threshold of an invisible building. Into this I stiffly tumbled out of the blank dark, into the brilliant light of two tiny and ravishing rooms like ships' cabins, papered all over with virgin white, illuminated by a constellation of candles, the warm glow of a stove and the sizzle of sausages on a plate, with which the Wicked Wa-wa now came running. Weak with the long labours of the day, I could almost have wept with mere gratitude for the elaborate forethought of the welcome Bill had prepared me, and the apple-pie delightfulness of the summer home he had come ahead to make me. So that in the very highest feather I concluded this memorable achievement: the little donkies arrived also, in due course, and none the worse for wear, and even of those nine wretched hens it turned out that four were still alive, though not unnaturally stiff and poorly and upset.

CHAPTER VI

WOLVESDEN HOUSE AND WOLFSTONE DENE

What a thing it is to arrive in a new place after dark, so that all its actualities burst sheer upon you the next morning. Hardly had my little white room begun to glow with filterings of light than I could bear my bed no longer, slung on my gown, and was out into the yard, and out into the glen, in less time than it now takes my mind to revisit the scene.

I found myself in an open high Alpine valley, as it might have been outside the Chiabotta del Pra. The air sparkled with a cold Alpine brilliance, and over the bank of mountain across the beck in front, so high that it cricked one's neck to look up at what seemed its top, the sun was already slanting powdery shafts of gold into the blue gulfs of air that filled the valley. Wolfstone Dene coils East and West, being the bed of the mountain beck that gathers tributaries from the lateral glens all along, and ultimately descends into the Da-Tung-Hor at Bridgehead about twelve miles down from the pass. It is the main mule-track connexion between Ping-fan across the Eastern, and Sining across the Western fall of the Alps: and I do not fear blame from even the most austere for giving it the name of Wolfstone Dene (with Wolvesden House and Wolvesden Pass for variants), since Lang Shih Tang (or Lang Shih Gô) means exactly Wolf Stone Valley, neither more nor less. And having this importance as a channel of communication, its course is set with tiny mud-roofed refuge-houses or mule inns, some ten in all to the foot of the pass.

Wolvesden House is the third of these, as you descend.

On the open Western side, the Alps rise immediately from a vast sloping highland already reaching a considerable elevation : on the Eastern the Alpine valleys, amid the complications of the range, have much farther to sink, and in much less distance, to the deep hot channel of the Da-Tung. So that here the elevations run higher, in view of the swifter fall, than they do on the Western descent of the pass : my heart, my aneroid and the Rhododendrons of Wolvesden combined to assure me that Wolvesden House must indeed stand at some 11,000 feet above the sea. This, even in the Tibetan Alps, is Alpine, and if I tried to render you the rapture of that first blue-and-golden morning there under the dark mountain wall of woodland, I might this time indeed rouse the animosity of such tail-less foxes of criticism as nurse a cabbage-gardener's contempt for the more flamboyant flowers of speech that deck the mental parterres of the enthusiastic.

Let us speak of Wolvesden, then, and its flowers, in grey, dusty terms of cabbage and groundsel, rather than in the dewy radiant language of rose and lily. And, indeed, I could not well trust myself with livelier colours, for fear they should blur and overflow. The affections of one's memory move strangely ; and the scenes of life have a love-value quite different from their apparent one. Wolvesden and its dull Alps sometimes held me bored, and often disappointed : yet now it is with eyes veiled in the anguish of longing that I go back across the darkness of the years to Wolvesden and Tien Tang, and the noble tranquillity of Chebson—more often indeed, and with livelier pains of memory than even to Siku and the Gorges and the Pink Temple and the great precipice of Thunder-crown, with its snow rills wavering down in gusty golden veils of sparks from the heights above. Perhaps it is that Wolvesden was my last scene of intimacy with the Alps, while the Siku summer still saw promise of another ahead. Anyhow, Wolvesden lies very close to my heart ; I love the place, and hope never to see it again, and know I never shall.

The Dene is here about a hundred yards wide, and at this point is rounding the toe of the Omos-Thanatos mass, completely out of sight, and so very high overhead that outside the door of Wolvesden House you crane your vision arduously up a heaven-kissing wall of Rhododendron and rare fir, towards a great snowy buttress of precipice impending dizzily overhead, upon a wild torn couloir. And even this is but the merest bastion of Crest Royal, out of sight above, which itself is merely the fading spur of the Dome and Omos and Pope's Nose, which in turn are only poor cousins of Achthos, Axeinos and the culminating bulk of Thanatos.

All these, though, are unguessed and unguessable from Wolvesden House, which snuggles into the sunny slope of a much drier, lower, hotter range, inhospitable with torrid rocks, and mangy with copse of arid dusty-coloured cypresses. And the House is yet further protected by a flat high breakwater of lawn descending into the Dene from Southerly Valley, immediately behind the only considerable glen that Wolvesden beck receives from the Southward-facing range. In front of Wolvesden House stretches a flat bouldered lawn, rich, in due course, with iris and globe flower and Gentians straw-coloured and ultramarine, and the big pink faces of Pylzow's geranium. Then you arrive at the beck, brawling fiercely among the boulders of its bed. The boulder-bed is very wide, with stranded islets of soil where the little blue Rhodo lives, and Potentillas, and many another treasure ; and its stones are of all sorts you can conceive, granite (though I never found where this rolled from), shingle, shale, conglomerate, dolomite. Then you plunge through the cold clearness of the water, or pole-jump from boulder to boulder and find yourself immediately in the cool and mossy darkness of damp Alpine woodland, at the foot of the Rhododendron slope, with miniature glaciers still lingering from the winter along the shaded swirls of the river under the rocks, offering fodder, far into the summer, for the ice-cream machine that was one of our most popular magics in 1915, till the dog-star left the Siphon and the mincer in undisputed supremacy again.

Wolvesden House, as you see, is a flat-roofed, low building round four sides of a small square yard, with a little hutch built out by the door, and an additional line of stabling along its western wall. The roof was of beaten mud, a little depressed and untrustworthy in places with time : its more solid walls were of raw poles laid horizontal on each other and plastered with mud, its less important ones of mudded brushwood. On the top side of the yard ranged the kitchen and woodshed and servants' quarters : the southern side was taken up by an open arcade of mule-stabling. My own two rooms and the main gate and two black dens that were to be the dark room, made up the lower side of the square. Then came the door out into the stable annexe : then the west side of the square, where Bill had his apartment, and we also kept, like Mrs. Norris, a spare bedroom for a friend. All the rooms were floored with hard mud, and in Bill's and in both of mine (to say nothing, of course, of the servants') were mud-beaten kangs for the muleteers. It was, in fact, a most superior place, the only inn on the way to the pass that catered not only for the mules, but for their conductors also. And this select abode we had now chartered for six months, at the rent of half a crown for the whole time, thus diverting all passing traffic to the inns above and below, and relegating the cheery little half-witted Tanguei to the cabin-lodge by the door, where he lived very happily in the dark with his little black pig, among the coffin boards that he had dutifully provided for his father.

But Wolvesden House needed much fitting up to make it habitable. On our first coming, it squatted quite contentedly in a slough of old manure : the slope of the yard was a pigsty, and the house itself lay becalmed like an island in a trackless bog of dung all round, culminating in the high peak of an almost prehistoric midden by the front door, to which we gave' the name of Hill 60. On Hill 60 we planted our flag to dehort other travellers from seeking entrance : but with the rest of the muck we dealt firmly. Channels and drains were cut, the yard itself swept clean, and then shingled with clean pebbles out of the beck bed, with causeways up it, and across, and other causeways outside, leading to the front door. Within doors, Bill had already taken steps : matting on the mud floors, white paper everywhere, and tin stoves from Lanchow, safely encased in loess all over, with their mud-cased chimneys piercing the brushwood of the roof, and perking naked high above its mud surface.

The problem of illumination had next presented itself. The rooms, being meant merely for tired muleteers to pile themselves upon the kangs and sleep, had no other light at all than that which came in through the door. But we, of course, to live there, had need of more. So Bill had removed two or three courses of poles from the outer walls, and covered the long gap thus made with paper. This admitted a soft white glow of daylight into the little cabins, but not enough to read by. Accordingly, spoiled camera plates now came in handy : they were washed clean, and inserted as panes all along the paper window-gaps. With these and the demolition of the kang in the drawing-room to make more space, our quarters were complete. In the bedrooms the kangs remained. Bill slept flat on his, and on mine my camp bed (the room just held it) was superbly enthroned : had I slept convulsively and rolled out, I should have had a far fall to the floor.

This was our installation for the summer : with boards slung on strings for bookshelves, and our goods and chattels unfolded on various tables, we could feel handsomely at home in the hills ; and with feet put up in the evening, one pair on each side of the stove, we could savour the warm delights of domesticity *à deux* after the hardships of the day. And now the local nobility came to call : up from Bridgehead rode the Chinese landlord there, and down from

her *villeggiatura* in Southerly Valley came Grandmamma
Aoo. The landlord of Bridgehead was an exile from Shansi,
for what crime in his native country driven to so remote
a nook of the Empire I never discovered. But down at
Bridgehead, in that warm fertile widening of the Da-Tung-
Hor, China has characteristically achieved a little colony,
amid these inhospitable fastnesses of Tibet. For, let no one
mistake it, the Da-Tung ranges are as purely Tibetan as
the Satanee Alps, though bravely included in Kansu on the
maps.

But here the Gwan (Sovereignty) of China is much tighter.
For these Tibetan chains fill up the void of the great Y
made by the two main Chinese highroads that diverge at
Lanchow—the one running North to Kashgar and Russia,
the other West and then South, to Sining, Koko-Nor, and
Lhasa. Held in the grip of these two roads, with the
complete machinery of Chinese Government active on both,
like two jaws of a pincers which are the Viceroyalty of Kansu
on the right hand and the Viceroyalty of Koko-nor Tibet
on the left, the Tibetan monasteries and villages that fill
the pinch are in no position to be as free and savage as they
would like, after the fashion of the Chagolese, or Siku's
evil neighbours, or the Black Tepo's, fronting immediately
on the last faint fringe of the Empire, with only the lawless
Roof of the World behind them. Thus, though the crumbled
frontier walls of China and Tibet meander sadly over these
Alps at different points, they are a mere symbol : the
whole country is now China, but the whole country remains
Tibet. (And may I here say, in the interests of rhythm,
that I maintain the accepted pronunciation of the sacred
and mysterious name ? Let no one, in my pages, aspire to
the austere correctitude of reading it as " Tibbit.")

Therefore the rare Chinese settlements in these ranges
hold a privileged position, and the Tibetans are glad to use
their enemies as ambassadors to persons of importance. It
was in this capacity that the landlord of Bridgehead now
arrived upon his donkey. He had been, indeed, Bill's first

friend and *point d'appui* in these parts, and came laden with presents for us on his own account—eggs, and hens, and a keg of wine. But it was as the emissary of Tien Tang that he now had special importance. For on the goodwill of the big Abbeys depends, as we had soundly learned, one's whole chance of peace and prosperity in the Tibetan Alps : and at first the monks of Tien Tang had shown a surly and evasive attitude that promised ill. But by this time, it seemed, they had realized the error of their suspicions and the danger of their ways. Official and Viceregal letters had satisfactorily explained our presence, and now, by the Bridgehead landlord the Halls of Heaven (which is Tien Tang Ssŭ) sent up messages of apology, and good intentions, and welcome, making us free of the Alps, and offering us all hospitality.

This was a load off our anxieties : we sent back our cards, and a special scarf of blessing. For of these, in Sining, we had prudently laid in a good stock, much superior in quality to the ragged little web of white that I had received the year before from the Living Buddha of Nalang. Indeed, it is impossible to travel successfully in a Tibetan country without these kataghs, which really take the place of visiting-cards, and, when exchanged, seal one into the friendship of household or Abbey, covering one with its protection, and making one free of its hospitality. Ours, in 1915, were so fascinating that I could never part with one without a pang. They may be of various colours (and all made, as I told you, in the far South of China), but our lot was exclusively of the very palest eau-de-nil, in shimmering soft silk, exquisitely fine and frail, with Buddhas and Bodhisatvas throned in glory, flickering and fading in their fabric as one crumpled them or flung them wide.

So away went the Bridgehead Tanguei with his burden of thanks and compliments : and now came Grandmamma Aoo. Grandmamma Aoo really was the local noblesse. Like Sidonia, she was a lady of castles and lands, owning most of these Alps, with grazing rights and stinting rights

and gaits, and court-leet and court-baron and all the glories
that swelled Maria Bertram's heart to the point of turning
her into Maria Rushworth.   And in personal presentment,
too, she was very like Sidonia in her outcast days—a
charred little withered old witch of a woman, very small and
bent and wrinkled, brilliant-eyed between the thin strings
of ringleted elf-locks, like the strands of a poodle's mane,
that fell on either side her face from beneath her round
cap, so dense with grease and eld that one could hardly
tell if it were felt or leather.   One ancient leathern petticoat
and bodice was the rest of her wear, with silver reliquary,
rings of silver set with turquoise and coral in her ears,
and down her bosom a swinging cascade of silver chains.
On her bare legs, crusted with the mud of ages, she
wore, this being a visit of ceremony, an ample pair of
leathern buskins like enormous Wellingtons.

She brought her husband, too, a comparatively insignificant person : and two grandsons, tall, strapping, splendid
fellows.   All of them were to be our constant visitors, for
Lady Aoo and her family were now in residence up in
Southerly Valley, where the two higher glens converge, in a
large low tent of woven yak-hair.   They were never weary
of our magics—the siphon, the clock, the cameras, the
mincer, and the legendary marvels of the ice-machine.
From the first moment we had a *succés* with Lady Aoo
in particular, which pleasantly resulted in her feeding us
all the summer through with the most delicious milk,
and bladdersful of golden butter from her Alpine steading.
Milk does not, indeed, usually move me to such epithets :
I incline rather as a rule to the Chinese view that it is an
indecent and unclean fluid out of an animal.   But when
you get milk that is the result of a cross between cow and
yak, even the most jaded milk-teetotaller may relax his
strictness.   Milk of the pure yak, indeed, is too heavy and
rich to be borne, but from the almost infinite series of
intermediates between cow and yak you get a milk more
sumptuous than that of any cow, yet not excessive for the

frailty of human stomachs. Such quality do you get, in fact, and such a flow, that I now never see the sad moulting yaks at the Zoo without seeing them also with a mystical eye, as possible forbears of new blends of milk-bearers that will revolutionize farming, and double both quantity and quality of our milk, as soon as some sage soul shall have either caught my own enthusiasm, or independently conceived the obvious notion of intercrossing cow and yak.

The first few days at Wolvesden passed in exploring the nearer reaches of the Dene, and in finishing the fittings of the House. But if further evidence as to altitude were sought, it might be found in the fact that, as late as the first week in May, this high-Alpine valley still lay sere and brown as if it were December. Of all the tuffets and tussocks among the shingle stretches of the beck-bed, only a little golden Draba yet showed colour, and in the cold mossy rocks that overhung the other side of the stream the promises of Primula were still undecipherable. We rambled far and wide, but the one treasure of the moment was within a stone's throw of Wolvesden House itself. I climbed behind, up the flat of the sheltering delta-bank that Southerly beck has accumulated at its debouchure, into Wolfstone Dene. I crossed the green lawn, humpy with emerging hassocks of Iris : and hopped from boulder to boulder among the splashings and clear cataracts of the beck, towards the hot dry spur of rock and cypress-woodland that descends immediately upon it, and juts out into the Dene. This slope is a true sun-trap, fully sheltered and fronting the South : here, if anywhere, the first heralds of spring should be awaking. And here, sure enough, I soon saw gouts of blueness from afar, and all over the bank, among fallen leaves and under grassy tussocks, the first primula of the year was gladdening the sunshine with its fragrant lavender bunches, no longer pinched and weazen with snow as I had seen it down the Pass, but now ample and serene in its expanded happiness.

My first primula of the year : it brings me to a stop.

Oh readers, patient and impatient both, let us now pause to perpend. I do not wish to rouse either party to unseemlinesses of indignation, but my previous experiences on the Eaves of the World have shown me that my attempt to sit gracefully between two stools was even more desperate than I had feared, and less successful than I had hoped. Criticism, in fact, of that immortal work, resolved itself into two definite streams, as irreconcilable as the Rhone and the Saone. "*Such* a delightful book," said one party, "if it hadn't been for all those *beastly* plants," : "*Such* a delightful book," said the other, "if it hadn't been for all those *boring* people and landscapes and things." No *via media*, evidently, had been found : nor do I believe that any exists. Even now, with all my good resolutions, and in the illumination of criticism, I am sure that to some people this book, too, will seem overweighted with plants, and, to others, underweighted.

In no case, however, let either party expect from me, in dealing with either plants or scenes or people, that jejune and dust-coloured dullness of expression that alone, I gather, passes current as sincerity among those who have no emotions to render, or no words to render them with if they had. In sum : criticism here, criticism there, it is all helpful and guiding, but I must remind myself, as I here remind you, that I am writing this book for the relief and release of one person only in the world. I am strenuously re-living, in fact, the dead years, in order to win free for a while from the present ; and, out of my own memories and stored emotions, spinning a rainbow bridge, far-flung over black depths, towards the golden irrecoverable past. As the need is greater now, and the gulfs deeper and darker, and the distance farther, this bridge must be higher and stronger, of firmer texture and closer construction than that which first took me back on to the Eaves of the World : but the material must still be the same—*my* experiences, *my* pleasures, observations, ardours and achievements, with " I," " I," " I," for the inevitably recurring rivet of the whole.

Those, then, who think that this rainbow bridge of mine will carry them also out of storm, back into a forgotten country of calm, are very welcome, indeed, to make the journey, step by step, with me as I build ; but they must always remember that it is with myself, and my own colours, that I build my own rainbow, and that therefore the risk is theirs if they stub their toe against some lump of opinion they dislike, or find themselves puttied up in some purple patch of Primula or Poppy, when they don't in the least know which is which, nor care, nor want to know.

I, meanwhile, must go forward steadily, casting no glance right or left at possible opinions. On the perilous tight-rope of creation, it is vital to concentrate entirely and undeviably on one's own footsteps, and on keeping one's own balance true to itself, unmagnetized away to John on one side or Jane on the other. No real book is ever written for anybody but its writer ; first and foremost : and only afterwards, by the chance of Fate, for the greater or lesser multitude of other people, who reflect his various facets and react to his personality.

Be patient, then, you who don't like plants and do like prattle : and you others, bear up against the prattle for the sake of the plants : I am not writing exclusively for any set of you among the lot, and in my rainbow bridge there are many colours, of which you must accept those you don't like as the price of enjoying those you do. And if you like none of them, you are very welcome to stay at home and not set foot on my bridge at all : and if you come a certain distance, and then find yourself really helpless— well surely there is always an Aunt Lottie to whom you can give the book for Christmas.

So now, unabashed, I assert to you Primula stenocalyx, under the more appealing name of Clusterbeauty. Not that even this will save skippers from here having to skip : for I intend to present to you the Clusterbeauty in her habit as she lives, on all the dry warm banks of loam and loess in these parts, and on the scantier fringes of the woodland.

Her green, ground-hugging rosettes are so exactly like those of any common daisy in a lawn that had I had the naming of the plant, and were not the epithet already occupied, I should certainly have called it Primula bellidifolia. But then up come sturdy little stems of three or four inches, unfurling a head of some five or six large and lovely lavender-blue flowers with a white eye, and the clean dry scent of their group. For, though no one could guess it from the size and amplitude of its blossoms, P. stenocalyx comes into the group of P. farinosa. Indeed, if its character becomes established in cultivation, I should put P. stenocalyx and her other Wolvesden cousin right up at the head of that group.

Unfortunately the test has not yet been as successfully passed as I had hoped. About Wolvesden, and all the country over, from 11,500 down to the hot dry 9,000-ft. levels about Tien Tang, Clusterbeauty abounded so lavishly on all the crumbly banks and braes of loess and gravel and loam as to make me feel quite sure that in cultivation she could not possibly have any fads. But hitherto, in England, I am sorry to say that Clusterbeauty cannot stand corn. She has, in fact, a tendency, like Jeshurun, to wax fat and kick the bucket. Rich soil in summer disposes her to grow so lax and luxuriant as not to be able to withstand our winter wet. Out of very many plants in the open but very few have survived with me : and I already see that starvation and fullest sunshine alone will probably acclimatize Clusterbeauty in the paler conditions of our cooler, moister country.

I mentioned her cousin. For a long time I thought the two main Wolvesden Primulas were forms of one species, but now, with further experience, I grow certain that despite their amazing likeness they are really two quite definite and distinct species, though both the same in rosette, in stem, in shape, size and colour of flower. But the one only begins where the other leaves off. From Wolvesden downwards, limp-leaved, green, entirely powderless, single-crowned,

H

Clusterbeauty monopolizes the ground completely ; and after flowering in a tight fat head, that seems to have no pedicels at all, the seed-bearing footstalks lengthen out surprisingly into a most fantastic spidery effect. This, then, is typical Clusterbeauty, and the genuine, as I believe, P. stenocalyx (P. St. genuina of my articles in the *Gardeners' Chronicle*).

But from Wolvesden upwards to the pass, and on all the Alpine heights, Clusterbeauty never occurs at all, and her place is taken by a twin cousin, with stiffer leaves, and pedicels that never, even in seed, lengthen out in the Procrustean way of P. stenocalyx. And the stems, and calyces, and the underside of the leaves of this are all heavily coated with white powder, thus notably enhancing the loveliness of the lavender blossoms. Otherwise the two plants are identical to the gardener's eye. But the differences are constant and, I am sure, specific. The high-Alpine, which we may call Lavandine, is, of course, even more fascinating than Clusterbeauty : its flowers are perhaps a trifle bluer, its stiffer leaves are conspicuously mid-ribbed and regularly toothed, as the limper dust-green foliage of P. stenocalyx is not. It also grows in clumps, whereas Stenocalyx never does.

But it is only on the high tops and the Pass that you find Lavandine : as you descend the northern slope, and down through the scrub and coppice of the Dene, gradually the leaves seem to get flabbier, and suddenly you are in the undisputed territory of P. stenocalyx again. Lavandine is P. St. dealbata of my articles, but must certainly now be promoted to specific rank. And it so happens that Prof. Balfour has given the name P. leptopoda as an invalid synonym for P. stenocalyx. (P. Biondiana is another vague name in this connexion, too, as is also P. cognata.) But P. leptopoda is described as being powdered, whereas P. stenocalyx as definitely is not. Therefore, out of the confusion bred by their very close general resemblance, I think that P. leptopoda must emerge once more as a sound and definite species from under the shadow of P. stenocalyx.

But in early May Lavandine was still abed, or barely

stirring : and far down in the Dene it was only on the summer banks that even Clusterbeauty was beginning to appear. The only other sign of life was a thing most paradoxical to find up here, in Alpine solitudes so austere. For on the hot bank lay sprawled out the ample rosettes of Incarvillea grandiflora ; and among them, huddling, but soon to rise up on lengthening stems, the glowing rose-red flowers like Dipladenias, or wrong-coloured Allamandas, culled from the stoves of the very rich, and here strewn callously upon the Alpine mountains cold. Indeed, one can hardly believe that these blossoms belong to a real plant actually living here ; so tropical-looking a thing it is, so floppy and flimsy in the overdone magnificence of its enormous flowers, to be really native to such bare spartan places as these, at altitudes so stern.

I browsed to and fro in the Dene. Above Wolvesden House, towards the West rounding the river-cliffs, you come on another shingle-coppice in the flat of the beck, hazy with alder and willow : and on opener places of the Bank, among the Cypress, colonies of Clusterbeauty shone already radiant. But there was nothing else as yet, and on a lap of the hill above, in a fold, a Tibetan dog disliked my presence vividly from a little Alpine steading there. Below Wolvesden, again, round the bend, you look into the farther reaches of the Dene, with the fourth inn about a mile down, and the blue-grey river roaring below on the right, deep in a forest of willows and a chaos of boulders. But there were no flowers here either, not even in a delicious fairy-dell down from the track, where, in a cup of turf as fine and springy as velvet and as green as emerald, a diamond-clear spring welled sluggishly into a wide pool, so tranquil that the brown fur of mosses on the boulders in its depths was never stirred.

And when I adventured up Southerly Valley, I very soon found myself in midwinter again. The rise is smooth and easy and gentle, but rapid and definite. You wander easily up the grassy floor of the glen, and before you have realized the height, you are among patches of snow in the tangles of the cold Cypress wood, with Clusterbeauty only beginning to glimmer bluely here and there, in a world all dank and dark and sopping. Down behind you Wolvesden House and the Dene are sunk out of sight in the depths, and already the vast mountains above them are beginning to unfold. The topmost peaks, indeed, are still out of sight, but the Buttress which impends so awfully over Wolvesden is now dwarfed to a mere basement of the high jut that stands out from Crest Royal, still higher : and above Crest Royal, Pope's Nose and the Dome are coming into view. And all as white and frozen still as the Ortler.

In the opener places of the coppice, and all about, such masses of the Harebell Poppy give signs of life as to show very plainly how high you are. Farther South, on Thunder-crown and Chagola, and the Jo-ni Alps, Meconopsis quintuplinervia is only an outlier, on the fringe of its distribution : and so it is, too, away in the Tsin-ling. But the Da-Tung Alps are evidently its main home, and here it abounds in bewildering profusion everywhere above 11,000 feet, universally prosperous, and notably delighting in dank damp slopes on Northerly faces. But in the early days of May, one could only tell the Harebell Poppy by the gaunt skeletons of its seed-stems ; and there was no other indication of life, or recognizably interesting plant.

And so at last I came to the top of the glen, where it bifurcates on either side of a mountain spur with a huge peak soaring high. The beck comes round from the right, where a new mountain wall comes into sight, far above a long slope of coppice. It was still a glacier, and the coppice perfectly sere. I turned back, and there, up the left-hand glen, I saw a large low gable of black and white blanketing and minor tents, and trodden paddocks with wooden railings, and demon-averting flags on sticks, and a small fluffy puppy tethered on a midden-heap, rending the air with barks. . It was Casa Aoo : Grandmamma herself came forth to wave a friendly hand, and her grandsons ceased their labours, to grin and shout a greeting. So, disappointed of novelty but bewitched by the vast view of the mountains opposite, straight in front of me as I returned, I came down again to Wolvesden, and strolled the river shingles in the sad calm twilight (for the daylight dies very early in the close depth of Wolfstone Dene), and great eagles, perched on boulders of vantage, watched my approach with careful but not timid glance, until they could no longer turn their heads straight back to look at me. Then they would fly off a little way, wheel about, and very soon return.

But it was now clear that even May was much too early for these frore elevations. We decided, after adjusting the household, to move down for a few weeks' exploration of the big Abbeys and the lowlands. The staff, in fact, was a fluctuating quantity, but had to be reduced, owing to the difficulty of getting up sufficient provender for a crowd into so wild a mountain valley. Indeed, had it not really been a highway, of a sort, we could never have solved the problem. As it was, we felt bound to reduce our numbers. This was a nice question, for our personnel included Mahomedan soldiers lent us by Mâ Dâ-ren, and the perfectly useless old opium-soaked " interpreter " lent us by the Chang Gwan to cope with the Tibetans. And how, without damaging the Chang Gwan's " face," were we to return him his interpreter, and at the same time retain, as we wished, the best of Mâ Dâ-ren's soldiers ? Even as far as Mâ Dâ-ren was concerned this seemed a little invidious. However, by dint of cautious and cunning letters the work was successfully accomplished.

The carriage of letters was yet another problem. The Chinese post does not run in the wild Tibetan Alps of the Da-Tung. Accordingly we had to make arrangements for a private post of our own, to bring up our mail from Sining. Fortunately, there happened to be a very respectable elderly gentleman there, who had had the ill luck to marry a shrew. This lady so embittered his existence, and made his home such a hell, that he was being steadily driven into evil courses abroad, drinkshops and gaming-houses. Those interested in arresting his downward progress now, therefore, hit on the happy notion of saving him from his home more wholesomely, by keeping him constantly on the trot, with a five days' trip to Wolvesden, out and back, with our mail. He accepted this plank of rescue with gratitude, and once or twice a week would appear in the distance, advancing down the Dene on a little white donkey, burdened with packages. Anyone could have seen that he was crushed under the load of life : he was a gentle, sad and philosophic old person, white-haired and silent : for the day after his arrival he would sit and rest among the servants, and then on the morrow set off home again with my answers to the letters he had brought.

But I cannot say that his appearances were wholly welcome to me. Letters and newspapers, all packed and quivering with far-off and bygone miseries, did not so much give pleasure, as burst, in a quite unprofitable bomb-explosion, through the cloistered calm into which one had succeeded in secluding one's mountain life. All was peace and work and concentration on it : then would come these shattering mails, and for two or three days one's brain would be kept uselessly bombinating among anguishes one could not help nor hinder nor heal : and by the time it had quieted down again, another mail would be very soon arriving.

Our own staff was more complex than it had been in the previous year, owing to the introduction of the Wicked Wa-wa, whose forceful little personality altered the composition. He was now the dominant figure, snubbing everybody right and left, and allowing no one to wait on me but himself. At the top of the hierarchy, of course, still loomed the Mafu. But a change, like a film of rust, was coming over the Mafu. Even the best of Chinese servants, it is said, eventually reach a stage in which their master has to fight against becoming their slave. Mafu was evidently reaching that point. The old simple alert resourcefulness and personal energy were under a cloud :

he was grown a little grand : his surliness intensified, and there was no longer quite that unremitting zeal with regard to our comforts and interests. So that he counts for less in 1915 than in the year before. But nothing, of course, could ever alter the ingenuous devotion of the good Go-go : and there was still the charm of Gomer, that beautiful radiant creature, brimming over with the joy of life, always interested and amused and eager, no matter how odious the hardships he was enduring.

But others appeared on our staff, supplementary hands necessary to the upkeep of so stately a palace as Wolvesden. We clearly realized the need, on seeing Wa-wa's face, set in a sulk like an unbaked bun, when he was pulled down from his high estate and made to do coolie work with the others, fetching baskets of shingle from the beck to make a floor for the yard, with paths across it. We already had Mâ, of course, the Mahomedan soldier, a trim smart gentle-man of excellent effect : and stray serving-men mysteri-ously appeared, and as mysteriously faded away. But the first permanent novelty was the Sa-wa Wa-wa, a small and stolid-looking Mahomedan child, with broad pale face and wide baggy trousers. At least a child I called him, and as a child I always treated him : even after I had been brought to realize that he was, like Mr. Elton, an old married man, a highly respectable householder of standing, with at least two wives and a family of children. But to see him meekly submitting to being hectored and bullied by the real Wa-wa was to lose all possibility of considering him anything but a child : and as for the Wicked One himself, his bristly little black head seemed visibly to expand with self-importance at having this raw young savage to " form."

We had, by now, a very pretty collection of religions represented on the staff : to complete the set Bill introduced Black Buzzler the Tu-ren. The Child of Earth justly bore his name : he was a dark stocky little man, stained with mud and coal, whom we detained in our service from a string of coal-mules going on their way over the pass from

Ping-fan to Sining. The coal comes down from the North, one enormous glittering block slung on each side a mule. It was by stray purchases from these caravans that we kept the home-fires burning—indeed, had it not been for them, life would not have been possible in that Alpine glen—and it was thus we acquired the Autochthon. Even when washed he was like no one we had yet met. He was not in the least degree Chinese, not in the least degree Mahomedan, not in the least degree Tibetan. He was most of all like a perpetually grinning Chimpanzee out of a chimney, lost in a haze of sooty wool, short and curly as a retriever's, though not so dense. Keep him shaved no matter how carefully, his face always looked as if it were masked with coal-dust : and out of it gleamed two limpid brown eyes, with the devoted doglike look of a retriever. Now the Chinese are egg-smooth, the Mahomedans and Tibetans only less so : and their hair invariably as straight as honesty. Judge then the strangeness of thus coming on a little knot of hairy curly folk secluded up in these mountains from the dawn of time, like a little islet in the hairless ocean of Asia.

Our settlement acquired fame. Indeed, had it not been for the Viceroys of Kansu and the Koko-Nor, I doubt if our occupation of the one livable mule-inn of the valley would have escaped active expressions of unpopularity. As it was, the mule-trains had to pass by in the dusk up towards the little higher inn, or else camp out in the boulder-meadow beyond our door, where their jangling and jinglings and chumpings kept one awake all night. The climax of exclusiveness, however, was reached one evening, when, through the stormy twilight of the gorge, a Living Buddha came riding up in glory—and had to pass on. Many, perhaps, have entertained angels unawares : but to how few has it fallen to turn a Living Buddha from their door ?

But little Tanguei rather relished the change : he now had very light work, helping the servants with odd jobs, instead of catering perpetually for hard and rapacious muleteers, generally Mahomedans : for the rest of the time he could sit happy in his dark little lodge by the doorway, among his coffin-boards, along with the tiny black pig that had previously been the only sharer of his solitude. But I am sorry to say that our advent destroyed the harmony of this union, and distracted the pig from its allegiance. For it now, with paradoxical violence, fell into a quite unprofitable passion for the brown pony. Wherever the brown pony went, the black piglet would pursue him, with ears streaming upon the wind ; and, on his down-sitting or uprising, would always be found entangled in his feet. The pony, however, reciprocated these attentions with a mild friendliness : work, and family affairs, sustained the Tanguei.

For now came up his uncle, pursued by the usual charge of murder, to take refuge beneath our shelter. I began to feel that, what with Uncle, and Wicked Wa-wa, my caravan was rapidly taking on the aspect of a gaol-delivery. Even about Sa-wa and Black Buzzler, there hung dark suspicions that they had somehow stumbled, like Antigone, against the high pedestal of justice. However, when I saw Uncle, all fears for my own reputation were laid to rest. Quite obviously the murder-charge must be a fake. A milder, neater, more petrifyingly respectable person was seldom seen—a pew-opener could not have been more overpowering. So far from bringing suspicion on my household, I felt that Uncle conferred on it an air of solid worth that it had previously lacked. Indeed I looked on Tanguei with a new wonder, as having such a relative, and felt like the Duchess about Mrs. Ponsonby de Tomkyns, that " I had no idea Mrs. Tomkins had such respectable connexions."

The only other inhabitants of Wolvesden are the marmots. At the mouths of their countless holes they sit, large black-and-brown beasts, with an expression of fat and aldermanic importance : or perk erect like begging dogs : or lope across the lawns, with their tails jerking up and down behind, like those wooden cockyolly birds who make antics on the end of a string when pulled. They are all over the country, and wherever you go your advance is shrilly heralded by the whistling of the sentinels. In the evening, when darkness is brimming deeper and deeper in Wolvesden, while overhead the peaks are still flooded with light, they sit like monuments on their mounds. And then the glorious starlit night unfolds, and the enormous silence of the mountains, broken only by the silvery brawl of the beck, and by strange muffled rumblings and bumpings, which for long we thought might be the dim noise of avalanches or remote stone-falls up in the Alps, but realized at last were only boulders churning in the bed of the stream. It was very pleasant, after days of exploration in the wintry combes and glens, to sit in the evening over the stove in our snug little cabin, relaxed in the comfort of a Chinese quilted gown, with the cold Alpine night outside.

Not but that the Chinese gown has its disadvantages. Water having failed to destroy me (in 1914), fire now had its try. Bill was out with Mafu and the Go-go, exploring the white enwintered snowfields of the great Alps above, and I, having done my tasks with the specimens, was standing with my back to the stove, in grateful enjoyment of the warmth. " How very, very nice to be so hot." I felt the heat glowing up my legs. And there seemed a specially pleasant glow of. light, too, beginning to suffuse the room. I basked in beatitude, till a sudden movement showed me the facts of the case. Heat and light were both being emitted by myself : my padded petticoat was in a vivid blaze. To shed the garment promptly seemed a prudent course. Easier said than done. Chinese gowns loop under the arm and down the right side. And now not a knob would part from its loop, no matter how I wrestled and strove and tore, like Herakles helpless in the fatal shirt. Flaming and cooking, a pillar of fire and smoke, I whirled forth into the yard, emitting sounds of protest. Whereupon shrieks arose from all quarters : both the Wa-wa's and Gomer and the Buzzler all converged upon me passionately and put me out with buckets. A fine tale they had to tell the others when Bill at length returned, red-eyed with the bitter Alpine winds up above, but cheered by the promise of huge peaks and lawns and basins and Alps, though all was still perfectly dead and white under unbroken snow.

CHAPTER VII

WOLFSTONE DENE AND THE HALLS OF HEAVEN

On the Eve of the Anne-Queen's death-day, by which the merest schoolboy will easily recognize May 18, our procession formed to ride down Wolfstone Dene to the Halls of Heaven. It was also the anniversary of our intended flight from Satanee the year before : but now how different a scene, how universally peaceful and prosperous. It was a steely pale-sunned day : we got off brisk and early, leaving Tanguei and the pig in charge, under the supervision of poor Go-go, omitted perforce from the procession. Down the reaches of the Dene the caravan proceeded : long grassy bays and projecting buttresses of cliff succeeded each other, with dry copse of Cypress, and the river roaring below us on the right in its forest of willows ; and on the far side the cooler slopes descended from the Alps in a vast voluminous wall of the Red Birch, soon beginning, but not ascending as high as Wolvesden, nor, anywhere in these Northerly ranges, as magnificent as on the flanks of the Bastion and the Felsenhorn by Satanee. None the less it was in overwhelming beauty here, up the filmy forest to the pinnacled points far above, across the river.

Gradually the buttresses grew rarer and less abrupt : the bays longer and blander. We were getting down into the quieter stretches of the Dene, past various Tibetan steadings and the successive mule-inns, each more ramshackle and decrepit than the last. It is a very long way, down the forests and coppice and open stretches of Wolfstone Dene. And still it was too early for flowers, nor did the copse

suggest anything better than wild rose, Berberis and Ribes,
—except for a pretty little tree-Prunus at one point, with
shell-pale flowers profusely pendent all along its flattened
sprays. Everywhere in the brushwood there was promise
of peonies, and Iris ensata promising too, in a Sargasso sea
of glaucous foliage, in every open reach of loess. But brown
winter still reigned, and the heralds of spring were all old
friends—Clusterbeauty flickering in blue multitudes on the
banks and, in the woodland, drifts of a golden Fabaria that
made the effect of Onosma ; and here, too, an older friend
still, from far across the world, in the person of well-beloved
little Maianthemum bifolium, whose delicate modest charm,
it seems, is just beginning to be appreciated by the learned.
The only novelties were things of small moment—an anæmic
creamy Lousewort, and in the lawns the violet and lavender
stars of Adonis cœrulea, among the splayed-out ferny
foliage. But let no one scream out in rapture, at either the
name or colour of the Blue Adonis. She is only called blue
because her blossoms go turquoise-colour in drying : in
themselves they are of a pale silken purple, but not nearly
large enough for the foliage, which spreads out, rank and
coarse, enveloping the rather squinny stars in an over-
whelmingness of greenery.

One big valley comes down on the right from the high
snows, soon after you leave Wolvesden : and another a
very long way down, bringing a dwindled beck in a vast
boulder bed, from the huge white Alps that here come into
sight, up at the valley head. Otherwise Wolfstone Dene
has no tributaries, and no variations of any moment, and
no sight of the snows anywhere, as it coils its way deep
among the enclosing wooded ranges, until you are far away
down, in warmer, drier regions, well below reach, now, of
the Red Birch. And then, right out ahead, over intervening crumpled ranges of lesser hills, open and arid, there
comes into sight, across the distance, the stark white wall
of the Gadjur range.

Often you are in the beck, or crossing it. At one point

there is a brushwood bridge. Hard by is a holy place, a lawn of tussocked Irises and big boulders, nestling under the wall of a rust-coloured precipice that here stands boldly out across your way. Pools of clear silent water well from under it, and over the Holy Spring presides the Buddha, frescoed in dim fading tones of red and green and gold, on the wall of the cliff. Clusterbeauty shines on the ledges, and the Fairy Bell rings her elfin chimes here in little ghostly carillons, and the holiness of the spot, the smile of the Perfect One, have their influences even on the vegetation.

But by degrees you are down the Dene, out of the harsh heights and the cold Alpine air, into the hot dry lands of the lower valley where you sweat, and breathe warm deliciousness. On the sunny side the ruddy cliffs and bluffs are quite like those of the Riviera : you expect to see them clothed in Cistus and rock-rose. And indeed they are dense with the thorny little dunes of the small gorse-like Caragana and in their time hazy with the rose-red airy featherings of Hedysarum multijugum. Now comes a last stretch of woodland, bending to the right : a final curve, and, round the corner of the last fell, the stream and the track run gaily down towards the vale of the Da-Tung, following the bend of the hill to Bridgehead, past the blacksmith's shack, and a few decrepit houses.

The vale of the Da-Tung-Hor is a smiling open basin of fertility, undulating up towards rolling low hills. Being rich and prosperous and sunny, it is once more China, its houses and inhabitants Chinese, and Chinese the hands that have tilled its laps of culture. There is nothing rugged or Alpine anywhere in sight here to suggest the neighbourhood of high inhospitable peaks where demons dwell. The river roars royally down upon the scene here from the left, at a right angle to the debouchure of Wolfstone Dene—a mighty volume of turbid snow-water, emerging violently from a dark defile, and broadening out over vast shingle-flats all a rose-red fog of Hedysarum. And as you gently ride along the iris-flats towards Bridgehead, the fine velvet of the lawns

is gemmed and threaded with the pink little heads of the
Tibetan Androsace, in such abundance that the green is shot
and filmed with a veil of rose : and on the earthy slopes
away to the right, across the Irises, climbing the flanks of the
hill, Clusterbeauty abounds as never yet, in the hot low loess,
a curtain of blueness in the shady corrugations of the bank.

Full in the middle of the scene rises the Great Bridge,
soaring high and far over the breadth of the Da-Tung, in
so brave and magnificent a span that surely this may well
be the finest Tibetan bridge in Northern Asia. It is the
erection, care, and property of the monks at Tien Tang
Ssŭ, and at either end there is a little lodge, with a holy
man inside to take toll. As Mafu, on a former visit, had
made trouble about paying this, and put the monastery
thereby in a fluster, we anticipated to-day the possibility of
an unfriendly reception, and accordingly, for the proper
impressing of the refractory, I now, on Bill's advice, mounted
my steed, and rode forward up to Bridgehead with all the
majesty I could muster. For the Bridge starts its flight
from a knoll of rocks and lawn above the river, and here, on
the height, the Shansi landlord has his ample dwelling of
loess, neat and clean and spacious. No monks were to be
seen, in fact, but out he came to welcome me, and induct me
ceremoniously to rest in a parlour behind the wide yard.

Nor was the monastery in sight either. After the Bridge,
the river swings away in a fierce bend, round under a series
of red precipices, above which rise a series of huge high
downs, bare and grassy, with rare woods in their folds, and
a deep ghyll of woodland at their foot on the near side.
And because of those impassable precipices, and the river
battering along their base, the road to Tien Tang has to
climb out of that ghyll, and round and about over the whole
height of those downs, before at last it can drop arduously
down to the river-level again on their far side, and round
under the fells to where, quite out of sight from Bridgehead, the Halls of Heaven bask under their amphitheatre
of sun-flogged cliffs, fronting the broad Iris plain and a

swing of the river outwards again from the sunny to the cooler side of the vale.

The Tanguci of Chao Tor has wisely chosen his post. He is the trade-centre of all the countryside, the agent and contractor for all the Abbeys hereabouts. Even while I sat there he made some eight or nine pounds out of orders for paper and so forth, from various local monasteries. He was thoroughly a friend of ours, too, and his influence had evidently radiated in favour of us in all directions. For now the caravan proceeded cautiously over the quivering span of the bridge, to be received, and passed with the utmost cordiality by the guardian clerics in their hutches at either end. I myself lay resting on the lawn on the knoll-top, among the Androsaces, and watched the procession defile along the far side of the river, till it was lost to sight in the ghyll. And there, far away above, across the brown-green crown of the fell, a raw streak marked the aspiring track to Tien Tang, so near in distance yet actually so tantalizingly far in travel. The delicious place it was, and the delicious day, and the ecstasy of my heart, almost irrecoverable now, even by the long arm of memory !

At last I rose from the scented velvet of the lawn, to continue after the caravan. A golden Star of Bethlehem shone in rare jewels from the green, and a freak-faced amethystine violet of intense fragrance and clawed leaves, in which I did not then recognize a very old friend that I need by no means have come so far to find, seeing that Viola pinnata is as happy in the European Alps as in the Tibetan lowlands. With bows and smiles to the monks I clomb the arch of the Bridge to its topmost span, which rocks and quavers ominously to the tread. Down on the other side its poles are piled up from a massive buttress of stone in which sand-rats skulk, and little hopping things like jerboas. And then you come to meadows again, with Stellera beginning to push ; and along above the river and its shingle banks uneventfully, till at length you turn away to dive into the darkness of the ghyll.

Tien Tang Ghyll is very lovely, deep between high rugged precipices, full of coolness and moisture and shadow, with Clusterbeauty on the ledges very brilliant, and peonies promising, and the Purple Adonis really beautiful, and, on the higher reaches, a small bush cherry in clouds of delicate clear pink. Up the fantastic stretches of this fairyland I toiled in a perpetual rapture at its perpetually changing and unfolding pictures, each more wild and noble and sombre than the last : and then we turned abruptly up into the wall of woodland on the right, and by harsh violent zigzags mounted fiercely and far through the forest, up and up, till suddenly the forest ended, and out we came, round a bare corner, upon the bare front of the down : and away below us lay the river and its vale unfolded like a map, and the bridge and its hamlet bird's-eyed and minute ; and away beyond it the dark wooded ranges, and the debouchure of Wolfstone Dene, and the long coilings of its course, to where, all along the horizon, built up in a gigantic wall of white magnificence across the world, ranged the whole massive line of the dominating Alps.

We were now at a powerful height already, but the path continued climbing among the folds of the open fell, winding upward in the bays of what might have been a gigantic Sussex Down, with the dwarf Caragana for gorse, in sheets of prickly little hummocks, all showered with golden blossoms. Now and then the hot air was stabbed and set quivering with a hot violent scent of violets, almost unbearably delicious. For a long time I could by no means trace this to its source : but at last realized that it was the breath of a rather feeble spidery-flowered purple Iris, that now and then peered among the coarse brown tussocks of the grass.[1]

In and out we wound, along the down-top, with the backward view more and more magnificent at every bend, but by now too steely in the thunderous warm greyness of the afternoon to be photographed. And then began the

[1] I. Bungei.

I

descent, down and down and down, by a steep and craggy tumbled way, among tumbles of red stone and raw red earth and fantastic rounded strata of red rock like the rankest Pulhamite or concoction of cement. And all the rocks and earth-slides were ablush with the Tibetan Androsace, in cascades of colour almost *too* virulently pink for their setting. At the bottom we were in a glade again, descending back into the river plain. On the steep rocky banks Clusterbeauty blazed in abundance, and the Fairy Bell was more profusely chiming than anywhere else, even in this, its region, evidently, of main abundance. Here, indeed, for the only time in my experience, it had overflowed from the rocks to which, as a rule, it so rigidly adheres, and had come down into mere steep earthy banks of soil among the Primulas.

And, close though I now be to Tien Tang, I needs must loiter here a little over the loveliness of the Fairy Bell. Some people may not find Lloydia alpina sufficiently "striking" for their taste : to me its phantasmal bells have a quite special charm, as they swing out and float and hover, like glassy bubbles, along the stern dark lines of the cliff, the thinly-touched streak of mahogany down the outside of each silvery segment contributing a curious look of elfin transparency to its already elfin grace. Much more sparse and pendulous and ungettable in the Min S'an and Satanee Alps, Lloydia alpina riots in the most massive abundance on all the rock-faces in the Da-Tung range, whether limestone or azoic, and its lovely stems carry three or four flowers, and its triangular pod stands out erect. But nowhere is it in livelier multitudes than on the cool wall of the ghyll that opens out on the Plains of Heaven.

For now, like a level sea, the green ocean of Tien Tang lies before us, flat and vast as a race-course, with here and there the crumbled bones of dead Abbeys lying in long lines of green, and the skeleton of a chorten standing forlorn. Its far horizon is made by a long band of poplars bounding the river, now all budding and making a rolling cirrhus cloud of amber, sulphur, crimson and vividest pale green, against the dark fir-forest that clambers to the very tops of the high craggy fells on the other side. And in mid-May that whole plain is a pale-blue rippling sea of Iris ensata in its loveliest Tibetan form, of freaked creamy fall and china-blue standard, sweet as hyacinths, and filling all the air with a scent as if one were in Holland.

Oh, you dyspeptic people, who despise the pleasures of others, and with peevish pens depreciate rapture into rhapsody, it is already clear that you must not come with *me* to Tibet. For there is loveliness and glory everywhere on those far hills :. I cling with all my zeal to their memories, I will not deny them, and I could not exaggerate them. So stay at home in the suburbs, good people, and cultivate calceolarias : I, and my little band of the elect, will fare forth unashamed across the Plains of Heaven, swishing through that soft blue surf of fragrance, with every nerve tense in the intoxication of delight : and on the gravelly open bank along the track the Tibetan Androsace ripples and falls and cascades in tumbling sheets of colour, as brilliant as Saxifraga appositifolia on the Western face of Penyghent. All notable joys in life should be prefaced by a grace of gratitude : those scented flower-fields inspire a fitting prelude to arrival in the Halls of Heaven. For now, only a few more hundred yards up the plain, under a high hot hill of barrenness and stone, with rare barberries and caraganas drooping under the cliffs, and we are riding round a bend ; and there at once, snuggled into its hot bay beneath an amphitheatre of great red precipices, in which the slanting sundown is cutting folds of deep blue, lies Tien Tang Ssŭ, a serried town of low, flat-roofed white houses, with big churches rising massively from among them, and their golden finials flashing.

Huddled into its bay of warmth the Halls of Heaven fronts the South. No cold winds can ever visit it, no snow lies : winter never comes near it. The cliffs embrace it, and keep off all cold, and concentrate all warmth; in front lies the broad sweep of the Iris plain, and then the poplar belt of the river, and then the fantastic pinnacled blackness of the fir-forest, the only one in these ranges, and the cherished property of the Abbey. Even on first sight, my heart went out ahead of me to Tien Tang—though nothing in the world could have been less like one's notion of a big Tibetan Abbey, the vast cliff-palaces of Lhasa, the squared Egyptian barracks of Labrang, than this dense flat-lined accumulation of whitewashed houses filling the bay and clambering up the steeps towards the foot of the precipice, with a holy pilgrim-path yet higher, circling the entire precinct and set at intervals with invocation-wheels, relic-houses, chortens and stations of devotion.

In the powdered gold of early sunset I rode leisurely into the Halls of Heaven, and in and out among its tortuous streets to where a crowd, gathered in the doorway of a white wall, indicated our quarters. Amid general bowings and smilings I alighted and passed in. I found myself in a long narrow court, with flat-roofed buildings on either side and at the end. On one hand the servants' rooms and kitchen, and across the way Bill's suite of two wood-panelled parlours opening on either side of the entrance room. And at the top you went up by a flight of steps on to the high verandah of the main building. Locked store-rooms took up most of it, but at one side, opening down on to the verandah by more steps, was my own little panelled wooden parlour, with big square window of latticed paper, and shutters to close at night : and at the other end of the verandah you could look through the latticed doorway into the owner's oratory, with altars tended and furnished, and Buddhas and Bodhisatvas smiling from their thrones in the fragrant dimness along the shelves, with flowers in front of them perpetually renewed, and little gleaming brass tartlet-pans of holy water.

Amid a mighty buzz we settled in. For all the rest of

that day, and the morning of the next, passed in entertaining
the conflow of holy people who came crowding to see this
unique peepshow of foreign Lords and foreign devices. It
was a select throng, though, for while the supreme authorities
would not, of course, make themselves so cheap, the monks
and students of the lower grades were not judged worthy
of calling on us.   So that it was only the more (and not
the most or the least) venerable dignitaries who appeared,
a stately handsome type of man in their voluminous swathings
of dull purple, attended often by disciples and acolytes.
Scarves of blessing again came and went between us and the
higher eminences of the place : at length the Prior or Almoner
of Tien Tang made his appearance in person.

The Gwan-ja of Tien Tang is one of the finest men I have
ever seen—or rather, he was, since the office is held only
by the year, and my old friend will long since by now have
sunk back into the lower ranks of the Abbey, with nothing
of his former glory but the envy and animosities that are
always bound to attend on one who has held the public
purse-strings.   For the Gwan-jas of these Abbeys are the
link between monastic meditations and the outer world.
While the Abbots and Living Buddhas lurk in august
seclusion, the Prior has charge of the Abbey's secular
affairs, its rents, its contracts, and the entertainment of
its guests.   In fact, so large are the labours involved that
there are usually two officials, Prior and sub-Prior, to dis-
charge them : and our friend was only the humbler of the
two.   But you could not easily conceive of his having a
superior, so stately a figure he was, well over six feet,
magnificently built, alike in limb and body, and that bold
splendid architecture of face and skull which makes a
fine Tibetan head such a satisfying thing to contemplate.
He was like some statue of a great period come to life,
moving superbly in draped lines of musty scarlet, and surmounted by that massive and marmoreal Roman head,
round and close-cut, and lit by big soft eyes of brown
velvet.

From the first the Gwan-ja was our friend, though confessing that for some time there had been a party in the Abbey hostile to our coming. Meanwhile, wo were going through all our hoops, again and again, to successive " houses " : the siphon squirted, the mincer minced, the cheap little clock we had bought in Lanchow repeated its fallacious chimes to general enthusiasm (you never knew what hour it was going to strike, except that by no possible chance did it ever strike the right one). After reverend eld now came enthusiastic youth : the throng of dignitaries became suffused with younger faces : every make of monk was now surging round us, from the tallest to the tiniest. Evidently the children were not forbidden—such gleeful gay little mobs of monklets, acolytes, novices and students, with keen clean faces and vivid eyes, as lithe and spry as sticklebacks under their purple folds : all hungering to be photographed, yet twinkling about on their bare white legs in such a restless enthusiasm of curiosity that they could hardly be got to stay still for long enough. Finally there arrived the babies of the place, a brace of microscopic pontiffs, about two feet high, in pleated capes of scarlet, as solemn as two Popes beneath enormous crested yellow mitres as tall as themselves.

But now, with twilight gathering, the crowd diminished for the day, and we strolled peacefully down out of Tien Tang and across the Iris plain to where the poplars tower over what proved to be a vast park of soft bare grey sand, soundless as a vale of the dead, with Oxytropids in clusters, flaring violently purple from amid their huddles of feathered silver foliage. Then round, down all the length of the lawn, and up into the glen again, to look at the Primulas and Lloydias. Here we came up with a red-skirted little bare-leg monklet of about eight, telling his beads on his homeward way from lessons in the Abbey. He was as bright as a button and as friendly as a kitten : we lay out upon a fine lawn starred with a tiny pale-blue Gentian, and had fun and laughter with him, hearing about himself, and answering his questions and teasing him a little about the photograph that it was now his chief earthly ambition to get. So, when he had got it, he departed up the glen, padding softly on his bare feet, and devoutly telling his beads as he went : we came back down the other side of the clear beck, and thus home to Tien Tang.

The dusk was green and balmy and bland : we went up on to the flat roof, and had the deck chairs brought up, and lay in luxury. And then, over the profile of the undulating down-tops that crown the precipices round the abbey there appeared first one strange diabolic shape, and then another, and then another. We gazed incredulous through our glasses at these horned blacknesses against the shrill pallor of the sky. There was no doubt of it, though : despite the fact that those hills are only hot and low and arid, not more than 10,000 ft. at their highest, these were the real Big Horn Sheep of the high Alps, coming forth to browse within a stone's throw of the Abbey, secure, for all ·their shyness, in the immemorial protection of the Holy Law.

I need hardly say that the sight of them immediately set Bill's manly heart aglow to violate it : my own heart jibbed, not only because I hold the Holy Law myself, and have no lust for the blood of the confiding and unoffending innocent, but also because I feared that so flagrant a contempt of the Buddha and His Dharma might well give a handle against us to the hostile party in the place. However, now came in the Gwan-ja for a private visit, and was reduced to shivers by our introductory letter from the Magistrate of Ping-fan, threatening the Abbey with mighty mulcts and extortions if its hospitality should fail to give us perfect satisfaction. Then, when we had explained how we had deprecated all these dangers and quieted all the alarms of authority, he grew quite melted with gratitude and, on the question of shooting, declared that, though it was, of course, officially forbidden, he was sure, after the assembled dignitaries had heard the Ping-fan document read, we should

safely be able to shoot anything we pleased, even in the
very gardens and temple-courts of the Abbey itself. So
away he went with it, and now an aged monk with a frail pale
old concentrated face like carved ivory came into the yard,
and craving permission, mounted up on to the verandah,
unlocked the chapel doors, and lit the lamps devoutly before
the Buddhas, murmuring prayer. I contributed a bough
of lilac, and then retired to the roof again, to expand once
more in fatigue and tranquil success, crowning the long
sweltering day of bland and varied delights.

Nullus in orbe sinus Tien Tang prœlucet amoenis :
Nowhere is there such a basking bay of delight, and no
stars in the sky are so big and blazing as those that shine
down on Tien Tang out of the sapphire velvet of summer
nights. The next morning the yard was again a-buzz with
monks, and I found that Bill wanted me to prove my
innocent dilettantism by publicly going out to make a
sketch, on the spot, of the Iris plain. So forth I fared
accordingly, in proper state, with Lay-gor carrying the
paint-box, and Go-go the sketch-book, and Sa-wa Wa-wa
promoted to charge of the brush-case. Immediately the
crowd, as was foreseen, rose up and came also : in a horde
of holy persons I took the field, crowded upon by red and
purple skirts, and an ancient holy odour of rancid butter.
Out we poured along the path round the bend, till, where
the lone poplar dominates the wide blue sea of Iris, beyond a
little beck as clear as a kitten's eyes, I sat down on the turf
and fell to my task. All the crowd sat down around me in
thronging rings : we were joined by the schoolmaster-
monk and all his flock of tiny Lamas, murmuring prayers
methodically in the intervals of pushing for a good place.
In acute discomfort the work of art proceeded with tolerable
success : prayers were very soon forgotten, in the fun of
watching how the brushes went, and conversation was
general, assisted, from me, by bows and smiles and fragments
of Chinese. The expedition handsomely achieved its purpose, and I felt that I had really thoroughly purged all

suspicions of secret and sinister motives in my coming to Tien Tang.

All continued to go well. Bill had an interview with a superior Prior to our Gwan-ja, and learned that a Living Buddha was expected on a visit ; and the stream of monks and little purple people never ceased in our court. Tien Tang is a " town " of many streets and winding ways : and takes time to learn. Between the low blank walls, white or washed with pink, you blindly meander in the cool shadow : sometimes a dark wooden door afar gives you a glimpse into a sunny court, and a verandah of latticed woodwork, with a small son of the Church sitting in a corner chanting his lessons from the broad shallow strips that are Tibetan books. The big churches tower here and there over the flat lines of the town, noble and stately places, standing apart in wide open precincts, and mounted up on flights of stone stairs : or verandahed high in shady courts all a jungle of lilac and peony and Ligustrina. The topmost one is the newest—a bold square white block of a building, aloft, up a steep climb, close under the precipice behind. Inside it is bare and neat and clean, frescoed all round with Buddha-scenes in no contemptible style. Above, under the rocks, clambers the pilgrim-path, and below rises the big rose-red Church of Our Lady of Mercy, with lovely arching roof of turquoise and emerald tiling and gaping blue dolphins for finials, and all the dark woodwork and galleries carved and painted in bold and various colours of crimson and green and white and blue. Round it runs a deep verandah, set at intervals with clanking invocation-wheels, and down below in the well of the courtyard are huge old bushes of tree peony, and a tree of lilac one solid mountainous fountain of lavender blue, and holy Ligustrina, silvery and dapple-barked as a cherry, with heavy bright-green foliage and pyramids of white foamy blossom like a twelve-times-magnified privet.

On holy days the main doors are opened, and the Colossal image of Our Lady smiles out upon the world from her high throne. She is all of gilt, gigantic, crowned and jewelled with fantastic magnificence : and across either end of the building two minor majesties sit looking on her. In the middle, at her feet, the altar is furnished with fresh flowers, and in the doorway sit prelates in swathings of golden silk, telling beads, and chanting, along with devout worshippers come in from the country round in their Sunday bests. Along the verandah, down the wooden stairway, and in the garden, the choirboys frolic and riot, and scramble for cash if you throw them, but it is a holy day, and speech is taboo, so, whatever you say to them, they only put their fingers to their lips, and wriggle and look roguish.

Devout women, too, are on the scene, going the rounds of the verandah, over and over again, turning the clanking invocation cylinders as they come. They, also, are in their Sunday clothes : round felt caps and elf-locks hanging, and silver chains and reliquaries on their breasts, and broad leathern stoles over their purple skirts, adorned with the usual big white plaques of porcelain. A different rule from ours obtains in Tibet : it is the lady who removes her hat in passing a holy person or object. Accordingly these visiting women uncover devoutly each time they pass the open door of Our Lady, or meet with an eminent prelate on the street.

Hard by is the storehouse, filled with many thousands of scarves of blessing, hanging densely in every degree of dinginess, dirt and antiquity, down to the pure eau-de-nil freshness of our own. And down below again, in the centre of the town, is the main church of all. This is a very big building, long and low and massive in outline, standing superbly at the top of a long expanse of pavement, with a gabled smoke-black cookhouse slinking on one side, set out with row over row of noble brass-bound tea-buckets. Long flights of stone stairs lead up to the deep arcade of its triple entrance : inside it is cold and dark and high, filled with the icy scent of old butter invariable in Tibetan churches. The seats, or kneeling-stools, do not run in transverse rows like our pews, but in widespread parallel bars across the length of the building : and at appointed places under the huge dim red pillars are pulpits and lecterns with the altars and the Buddhas aligned along the gloom of the distance.

Services are frequent in every sense ; even in the grey dawn your sleeps are penetrated by the long sad wail of the conch. For when church-time approaches, a monk, wearing his high yellow mitre like a crested cocked hat, mounts up on to the roof, and in the centre of the parapet calls three several times to prayer, at long intervals, in blasts upon his white silver-looking conch, so sustained and drawn-out and unvarying that it seems a miracle how he can hold out with his breath. Some five times a day you hear that mournful hollow-sounding summons, persistent as life itself in its drab undeviating melancholy. Gradually the novices and monks gather at the foot of the steps. They all have their mitres, either towering on their heads, or folded flat beneath their arms. But are not at all oppressed by the solemnity of the occasion or its pontificals.

In fact it is the great game to pluck off somebody's mitre unawares, and cuff him over the head with it, and then throw it down the steps in a general scramble of squeals and giggles and twinkling of frisky bare legs from among their reverend wrappings of purple. So the fun rages, eyed by the Wicked Wa-wa with an expression of sublime and bun-faced scorn, just like a page-boy at the Ritz condescending to despise the antics of guttersnipes in the street. But now the appearance of the monks restores a fair decorum, though still little spurts of laughter erupt. One by one, or in knots and groups, the purple-clad congregation gathers under the steps : across the square, hand in hand, come the two wee mitred toddlers, like a pair of severe Popes through the wrong end of a microscope ; suddenly the three doors are unbolted and thrown wide from within.

Instantly the congregation floods into the glacial dimly-

scented dark, the youngers in a chaos like a beck, the
elders in a staid and orderly stream. Everybody squats
down cross-legged in due order, on his flat cushion. When
the rows are filled and settled the service begins. And first
of all emerges the Gwan-ja to do his part, looking more
superb than ever. For now he has discarded the usual
folded red drapery and cocked-hat mitre : straight from
his broad shoulders falls a pleated cloak of scarlet, in long
austere folds, almost to his knees, and on his head there
aspires a new form of mitre, like a gigantically-crested
Greek helmet, carried out in cardboard covered with
citron-coloured silk. He looks, in fact, exactly like an
actor rehearsing Julius Cæsar at His Majesty's. Majestically
moving to match, he goes his pontifical way, up one row
of kneeling monks and down the next, bearing an enormous
trunk of incense, like a section of the largest church-candle.
Holding it horizontally he inclines it this way and that,
so as to envelop all the worshippers in the swirls of its
sanctifying savour. When he is nearing the end of his
stately progress, there follows a lesser dignitary, who, at a
feverish trot, runs up and down the rows, aspersing them
from side to side with holy water out of a glorious old
brass urn, with wrought spout in the likeness of a spewing
dragon.

And then the service proceeds, with ringing of bells, and
chimes and chanting, litanies, antiphons and psalms :
and a stout ecclesiastic, flat-faced and whiskered like a
butler, is predicating from the pulpit, to an occasional
obbligato of his bell. On he goes and on, sitting cross-
legged and hieratic in his place : but as soon as attention
seems likely to flag, devotion is opportunely sustained—and
in a manner that Christian Churches might very profitably
copy. For now, out of the depths of blackness far away
in the left-hand distance of the dark, there arises a bustle ;
a door is thrown open, and on a shaft of light there pours
in a procession of novices and acolytes from the cookhouse adjacent, each bearing one of those sumptuous

buckets full of tea. A new liveliness perks up in the congregation : everybody produces a wooden bowl : the shaven-
headed Ganymedes go round, administering sustenance
to each from his bucket. Contentment shines, and the
sound of sipping takes the place of sacred song : after
which the bucket-bearers retire again to replenish their
store against another later interval in the service, and the
holy offices are resumed with revivified attention.

There could be no doubt that we were liked in Tien
Tang. Day by day the stream of Lamas and Lama-lings
never ceased, and our stock of marvels never seemed stale.
They loved looking at picture-books and sketches, too.
Murray's Japan, with its reproductions of Buddhas and
temples, aroused the enthusiasm of the old schoolmaster-
monk and his flock of pupils : he wrote me their Tibetan
names, and his own, with my stylo, as a thrilling change
from his own clever pen of wood, cloven like our nibs at
the end. They had a very sharp eye for the flowers, and
looked at the sketches long and carefully, with one eye
telescoped through the hand as their habit is. Gurgles
and snores of satisfaction followed, and an astonishing
aptness of recognition. Not only had they their own names,
in fact, for the wild flowers, but also a smart instinct for
relationships and differences between them. " Nig-munk,
nig-munk," they nodded approvingly at Primula stenocalyx ;
and when they saw Androsace tibetica pictured, they knew
that that also was " Nig-munk," and said so—thus making
my heart clap with delight, after many years of worthy
people who can never be got to see that all Pansies and
Violets are Viola, and all jonquils and daffodils, Narcissus,
to say nothing of such a further flight of perspicacity
as detecting, at a glance, the essential identity of Primula
and Androsace.

The sheep-stalking duly came off : I was able the better
to dissemble my relief that it resulted, as usual, in no
victims, by the fact that poor Bill, besides the disappointment
of a fruitless day, had also had the aggravation of its being

a very wet one. He had, however, sighted big rams abounding on a near ridge, within sight of the Abbey, and was able to report the country up behind it hot and arid and barren and wholly without promise. Hardly had he returned to bed, sleepy from his dawn-start, than judgment descended on him for his nefarious intention. For now behold the Lord Abbot himself come up in high pomp to call. Bill must needs emerge sulphurously from his blanket, to assist me in condignly receiving the pontiff, attended by acolytes, and very stately in bowings and ceremonial courtesies, and exchanging of yet more scarves of blessing. He also brought presents : bladders of butter, and bowls of Silverweed tubers, little nutty things, so delicious (like young asparagus or new potatoes) as to make me feel that one's greed need never flag in England, so long as Potentilla anserina abounds by every wayside, one of our loveliest and most odious of weeds. However, the visit was brief and formal : the big-headed smiling old ecclesiastic (so typically such) had hardly got through with all his bowings and compliments than the summons of prayer-bells sounded afar in the church square : whereupon, with yet more bowings, the Abbot rose up and departed to pontificate, leaving Bill at leisure to go back to bed.

It seems to me now that rains and storm never interrupted the torrid serenity of Tien Tang. But it was not really so : often the sweltering glory of the day accumulated thunders that broke at dusk ; and winds perpetually drove down the ghyll where Lloydia lived, and perpetually ruffled her multitudes. It took half the monastery to accomplish the portrait of the Fairy Bell, gathered in a semicircle under its cliffs, with purple skirts held out to quiet its unceasing sarabands. But not even these holy influences could quell its pervicacity : it danced and fluttered to the lightest flow of air, and when one group of its bells was at last silent, another would immediately set up a chime.

While this task was achieving I myself rounded up the remainder treasures of the ghyll. For here, under a light scrub of briar and barberry, big crimson peonies lurked by now, and in the fine green velvet of the lawns there appeared a pink-faced slender Primula along by the runnels of the beck, and in the marshy laps where it overflowed.[1] Yellow Fabaria was beginning to glow in drifts across the Iris plain now unfolded to its fullest blueness : Stellera was bushing up in domes of blushing white, and among the rosy cascades of the Androsace on the sunny banks and lawns of the small crumbling bluffs there stood up here and there the metallic golden star of Gagea.

The Primula was heartening and pretty and clean as a modern nursery frieze, like a little Cinque Cento flower jewelling the lawn of an Angelico heaven with its pure innocent round faces of pure pink : but an even more precious vision was the rare Iris that peered coyly from under a bush higher up the glen. Iris tigridia is quite a small species, with glaucous leaves in a refined tuffet, and stems of three or four inches. But each of these supports a single flower-de-luce of singularly perfect build and balance, a boldly upstanding exquisite bloom in blended tones of soft blue, with lavender, and fawn and dove-colour and bronze, thunderously haunting the purple of the falls. In the hot bay of Tien Tang it dwelt all round, hanging beneath the scrub and brushwood, over the lip of the little banks and braes and bluffs. But it is an early species, and now only lingered in blossom here and there in secluded corners. The Columbine, on the contrary, was now in full bloom. From its delicate volumes of foliage, marbled exquisitely with white, as if some one had sprayed it from the milk-jug, aspired its many brave and airy stems of fantastic flower.

Aquilegia viridiflora has a monstrous charm that yet is not evil. Alone of its race, so far as I know, it loves only hot rocks and torrid exposures ; and there it flaunts with a curious self-assured beauty of its own, that seems at first to evade notice rather than to miss it, and so ends by

[1] P. Wardii.

capturing the attention completely. Not that the flowers are large, and certainly they are not lovely or alert in colouring : the cup opens of chocolate black, with long curl-horned petals of hyaline green : and gradually the whole bloom passes to a glaucous pale-jade colour with fluff of golden stamens standing out. Not, therefore, at all a showy or " striking " species : yet once you have been caught by its subtle and refined fascination, you will not be able to escape it again. And at first, having heard of its fragrance, I was disappointed to detect none. But, by degrees, with the plant sitting in front of me for its portrait, I found the air dimly haunted with sweetness : I put my nose to the flowers, and still they were quite silent, but there could be no doubt that the Columbine was somehow mysteriously emanating its message—a charm of scent as consciously coquettish and elusive as the charm of its restrained beauty. The monks would give me no name for it that I could catch ; the Iris, on the contrary, was Hsiao Ma-Lien, the Little Horse-Lotus—" horse," I suppose, being used here in the same sense of sham or inferior substitute that we also give the word in " horse-chestnut," " horse-mushroom " and " horse-godmother." (" Horse-sense," too, is mock-modest for that quality which would like to be cleverness, but isn't, so takes refuge in piquing itself on plain bluffness.)

I made another discovery in etymology, too, that set my mind at rest on a matter that had agitated it. Somewhere in these parts, we knew, there lay a large monastery known to Przewalsky, and marked on his maps as " Cheterton." Now by all the signs, even to memories still surviving of the Russians' visit, " Cheterton " ought to have been no other but Tien Tang itself : yet inquire where I would (like Mrs. Norris) I could neither make Cheterton out of Tien Tang, nor hear of any other Abbey in these parts bearing a name at all like it. So " Chesterton," as we called it, was rapidly becoming a mere myth in my mind. But one evening I sat out in the serenity of sundown on a hummock in the Iris plain, engulfed in flowers and fragrance. Around me sat some dull-crimson monks, telling their beads, and making a remark now and again. In front of us the Abbey basked in its bay, above the sea of blueness : devout people, small as emmets, could be seen streaming steadily along the higher reaches of the pilgrim-path behind it, round towards a deep little chine between the cliffs where a Chorten shone white. It caught the eye of a monk : " Chorten Tang," he meditated, " Chorten Tang." As he said it, quickly and easily, I saw at once that this was the original out of which, by an obvious transposition, Przewalsky had made " Cheterton." And sure enough I now discovered that Chorten Tang is indeed the Tibetan name of the Abbey, as Tien Tang is the Chinese alternative—the former meaning the Halls of the Chorten, and the latter, the Halls of Heaven.

The pilgrim-path is in full activity at the end of the day. As the sun begins to sink over the amphitheatre of cliffs, the Iris plain is dotted with venerable figures in sad scarlet sauntering over their beads in the tranquil end of the day : and in the limpid water-runnels that thread the lawn and turn the mills of flour or invocation, the bare-legged schoolboys scutter and splash. And all the time the procession of the devout continues. For a mile or so, in front of the Abbey, the pilgrim-path curves uneventfully among the Irises : seated on hummocks of the green, scattered monks watch the passers with dispassionate eye. There are many ways of doing the round, and many motives. The monks themselves go round methodically, sauntering at ease, and pausing at the stations of devotion, and sitting down in groups here and there to have a chat. And all the time their hands are busy with their rosaries, and in an uninterrupted rumble as they go the Invocation of the Jewel drones from their lips in such a rapid monotone that you cannot detach the syllables of Om Mani Padme Om, so blurred together in the aspirant's zeal to get as many thousand of it as possible done within the hour.

Then there comes along perhaps a woman of the neighbour-

K

hood, discharging a vow or trying to get a benefit. She is in her bests, a-glitter and a-clank with silver chains, and her white plaqued leathern stole depends over her violet skirts, and her round felt hat is on her head. On her back she carries a volume or two of the Scriptures strapped, roughly like two drawers out of a mahogany chest of them —long thick baulks of stiff paper strips, bound between boards of varnished wood. Straining forward from her burden she goes slowly, performs due rites at each station, and often sinks to her knees and then straight forward, flat on her face on the grass, with hands outstretched before her. Rising again in a quick spring she proceeds ; and now comes a little choir-boy who has been naughty, and has to make the pilgrimage of penance, with the good little boys giggling and poking fun at him, in groups alongside.

This is a serious process, for the pilgrimage is accomplished wholly in prostrations. Standing, you fall forward flat, stretched as far as you will reach, with your arms straight out in front of you, as far as they will reach. Then you rise, stand on the extreme point where your finger-tips rested, and fall straight forward again, repeating the process indefinitely till your bourn is attained. It is on record that an offending monk once had to make this penance-pilgrimage all the way from Urga to Lhasa to placate the Sovereign Pontiff. Imagination staggers at the thought of what it must have been to journey by unbroken pros-trations over those appalling Alpine-passes between Litang, Batang, and Tachien-lu. The toil took six months, it is said ; and on his arrival the Dalai Lama refused to see him, and the doors of pardon stayed shut, and home he had to go again, inexorably prostrating himself still, all the way back from Lhasa to Urga. But the bad little boys of Tien Tang have no such rigid rules ; so long as the severe eye of some old monk, squatting on a hummock, is fixed on their performances, all goes faithfully and well, and each pros-tration duly starts from the precise point reached by the last. But now comes a stretch of sward with no one sitting

by, and the other boys have tired of the fun and fallen
away to a new game among themselves ; the penitent looks
furtively round to see that no one is watching, and then,
with feet together, takes a mighty jump forward before his
next prostration—and then another, and then another,
so that a deal of ground is covered with a celerity most
suspicious to anyone who suddenly looks up and sees
him much farther on than he had any right to be, unless
a miracle had sped him forward.

But when the Iris plain is ended, and the path turns
round the far corner of the Abbey and begins to climb into
the cirque of cliffs behind it, the process is no longer so much
impeded by prostrations as by the points of devotion.
The path scrambles up, and then runs level under the
precipices : tucked into corners of rock there are invocation
cylinders to be turned, and, by the track, square whitewashed hutches, man-high ; and at length the path coils
round into the little ghyll at the back.   Here there are
more cylinders, and more holy hutches, and a flagstaff of
prayer standing starkly up out of a base of boulders.   And
here, close under the gloom of the gorge, embowered in
golden cascades of Caragana, the Chorten itself looms
pure and pale, bulging upwards from its four-square pedestal
of straight tiers.   Over the foreground impends an abrupt
jumble of cliff in vast blocks fantastic as a compilation of
sham rockwork, violently scarlet in the slanting sunlight,
and hanging out from its blazing red crevices dense valances
of Polypody in blazing emerald : and, behind, the Chorten
is embraced in the cool deeps of the Chine, between straight-
sided walls of cliff.   On its swelling face it wears an arched
panel containing a Buddha outlined and framed in cobalt :
otherwise it is all of cold white, but for a touch of cream
in the steps on which it rises.   Some holiness rests here,
some relic of sainted Abbot or Living Buddha ; it is the
culminating point of the pilgrimage, and here the monks
sit down again to have another chat.

After which the rest of the circuit is brief and easy :

round behind the Chorten into the combe, and out again
by the flagstaff: and so off the hill-side and forth into the
Iris plain again, on the other flank of the Abbey. The
holy circle is accomplished, and now the sun dies down off
Tien Tang Ssŭ, and the sad blue wail of the conch calls to
vespers, and the little old monk comes up into my chapel
to light the lamp before the Buddha, and on the darkening
down above the topmost lingering flush of the cliffs, the
curly-horned heads of the big sheep emerge in black silhou-
ettes, one by one.

CHAPTER VIII

TIEN TANG TO CHEBSON

Meanwhile the work of exploring the ranges round Tien Tang was diligently proceeding, nor need anyone think that churchgoing monopolized my days. In a cloudless crystal day we started off one morning up on to the summits —Mafu, Gomer, Wicked Wa-wa, and Mâ the Mahomedan. The air was full of joy and spring after the storms ; it was a day of high festival, too ; most of the monks had gone up in procession to the topmost summit of the downs, there to " Nien Jing," with crackers and gunshots going off before an obo-pile on the apex, like a bonfire of long poles built up in a sheaf. And, down below, the Monastery itself was filled with parishioners and devouts from all the country round, and the shrines stood open, and holy musics abounded.

Very serene and heart-free I jogged up the long climb to the grassy saddle on the down-top : but here dismounted. Mafu took the ponies onwards down to Bridgehead, to be shod, while Gomer and Wa-wa, carrying my various paraphernalia, accompanied me up the grassy breast on the right, rosy with Androsace in the lawn towards its culminating crest. In these latitudes and at these altitudes climbing is not the lightfoot affair it is on our own smaller-scaled Alps where, at 6,000 ft. or 7,000 ft., you already have all the flowers you can do with and in no circumstances need ever go higher than nine. But Flora, here, flies a much higher flight ; from 9,000 ft. to 10,000 ft. you toil arduously up braes comparatively barren, with a heart so burdened and bounding that what looks from below like a bank, becomes a voluminous Alp in the ascent, up which you cannot go more than a very few yards at a time before pausing yet again, to pant apoplectically against the unfolding glory of the world.

From that high crest, indeed, when once I had attained it, the view was superb ; but I was even more grateful to the views from the lower reaches, as giving me such sound excuse for my frequent rests. The tops of the down are surfy with a small scant scrub of Potentilla davurica, among which peep the soft blue-purple butterflies of Iris goniocarpa —an old friend from last year, but always welcome. Above Siku, on Thundercrown, the Butterfly Iris so violently differed (according as you found it on the Alp, dwarfer, large flowered, brindled and blurred in blues ; or lower down, among the coarse hot grass on the hot flanks of the spurs, fine-drawn and smaller-flowered with wax-white falls peppered densely with violet velvet round their rims) that I long distinguished it as two definite species, feline and pardaline. The Da-Tung, however, gives you unvaryingly the exact median type of Ir. goniocarpa, not quite so large and blended in the flower, or so stocky in leaf and stem as the feline, not so *élancée*, little-bloomed, thin and vividly varied as the pardaline. But in all its forms the Butterfly Iris is among the loveliest and kindliest of the smaller Irids, and the only thing about it that I deplore is its weakness in the pangs of pregnancy. For hardly has the pod waxed fat, and begun to pale with the promise of ripeness, than her stem grows correspondingly tired, flags by degrees and ultimately flops down completely, among the grasses which by now have grown up into a towering jungle, compared to the neat sprouting lawn from which the Iris had sprung in blossom : so that hunting for seed of Iris goniocarpa is a really desperating business, indeed like questing needles in a world of hay. The pods are practically undiscoverable, in fact, till at last, discharged of their burden, they stand up again stiffly, pale bare skeletons, mocking the eye everywhere with their blatant visibility. For it is by the cruellest of ironies that when you do ultimately see them you no longer want to : for all their seed is shed.

From that high crest all the distant snows lay clear in the
clear air, and on the North, through the topmost fringe of
the coppice that clothed the cooler slope, a lesser pyramid
looked unjustly Alpine and magnificent in a vesture of new
snow. I made towards the coppice : far off, on a green hill-top,
I could see the monks, dark crowds of specks pontificating
round the pale sheaf of the obo, and through the golden
tranquillity of the morning faintly came the blares and
explosions of their music, muted to sweetness like fairy horns
in the distance. Then I passed from the warm grassy side
of the crest into the forest on its farther side. Down and
down I plunged ; it was beautiful and fresh in dawning
green, wonderfully English. Neither in the opener glades,
nor in the woodcutters' clearing, nor in the mellow obscurity
of the woodland did I see any new thing. But the irradiating
loveliness of the day and the scene was such that this made
no matter, and in placid delight I descended the fell, by this
time down in open glades of turf, drifted deep in Irises, till
at length, quite unexpectedly, I came immediately upon a
cosy little folded Tibetan steading, securely concealed in a
lap of the glen, where a number of horses were grazing in its
paddock. Great dogs vociferously disapproved me : I
diverged from my course, and soon found myself dropping
into the depths of the Tien Tang Ghyll. Down its arid
bouldered beck-bed I proceeded, under stony banks ablaze
with the rose of Androsace, and through the gorge, and
round in the open by the bend of the river till I came to the
bridge. Here I paused awhile to make friends with a pigmy
hare who lived among its stones—a pleasant person, like a
wee short-eared rabbit with a dark brown face—then crossed
the bridge, to sit out on the bummock above and take my
nuncheon.

After this, having passed the time of day with Tanguei, I
strolled along the track towards the smithy, hoping to see the
horses shod. But the smithy was too far, so I turned back
at the corner of the bend (high over which the budding
poplars of the impending forest were all a coppery flame),

and returned, above the drifts of storm-dashed Iris, under the immediate shadow of the hill, where Clusterbeauty abounded in colonies of quite bewildering loveliness, in the steep rippled banks and earth-fans. On the knoll I then rested in the sun, and scanned the distant heights of the down, and pondered the waste of labour and time in toiling all that way, when there, much nearer, along the cliffs at the curve of the river ran that short cut which would bring me immediately round again into the plain of Tien Tang. It is true that as I lay and scanned the precipices through my glasses, I could discern no trace of any track at all, but only blank russet-coloured walls of precipice with the river at their feet. However, there the short cut undoubtedly was, and nobody in the neighbourhood ever dreamed of going by any other way, unless they had horses or mules in charge. Where monastic limbs could go, surely mine could follow. So I descended upon Bridgehead Tanguei, and catechized him as to where, precisely, the short cut ran, along those formidable faces. He pretended to show me: I pretended to see. " Little-road, good—not good ? " I inquired. " Good," said Tanguei. " Easy—not easy ? " I precisified. " Easy," replied Tanguei, faithful to China's invariable courtesy in giving the pleasant and obviously desired answer.

So, reassured, I returned across the bridge, with Gomer on my heel: and round to the mouth of the glen. Here amid fierce hot shafts of violet fragrance shot up from clumps of Iris Bungei that peered between the big coarse tussocks I diverged from the track, and addressed myself to the steep fell-slope on my right. Steep, it soon became steeper, and much steeper: slippery and treacherous, it rapidly became much more slippery and treacherous: till suddenly I climbed round a sharp brow, and found myself immediately above the river—high on an open cliff, going furiously hand over hand for fear I should fall off if I stopped to think. It was a hectic climb: Aquilegia viridiflora mopped and mowed at me out of the burnt dark crevices:

with a gasp of relief I at last surmounted a shoulder, and saw a real track, though tiny, coiling on the level, placidly, round a deep chine in the fell.   Glory be, the worst of that fearsome Hsiao Lu was over.   I panted with a self-complacent sense of achievement.   What a mercy: for, if there had been worse before me, and it had become a case of going back, down over that grisly cliff I had just scaled, assuredly I could never have done it.   And otherwise there was no choice: overhead the chine towered up to the down in terrible bluffs, below it descended in yet more terrible ones, starkly to the river.   But now there was no more to do but saunter leisurely round the corner, and up to Tien Tang. I sauntered, I came to the corner, I came round it.

I saw nothing before me any more but a blank bare wall of rock, far and sheer to the bird's-eyed fury of the Da-Tung, darkly roaring below, in its wildest rage, round the bend of the cliff.   The path had wholly vanished, and in front there were only more naked precipices, and more beyond, rosy in the fierceness of the sunlight.   My heart became a petrifaction, and did not by any means thaw when at last I perceived a very small crevice, about four inches wide, slanting obliquely down the bald sheerness of the cliff, with dim slots cut for foothold, long since worn faint as hope and smooth as ice by generations of bare Tibetan soles. For them, or for string sandals, that way would offer small terrors, and evidently it was down there that the Short Cut continued.   But I, cumbrously booted, was in quivering stresses, between the Devil of a backward descent down that first cliff (with an accompanying sense of defeat, and all the high downs to do in the end after all) and the deep sea of that river, roaring so far down, straight beneath the precipice across which, apparently, I was meant to adhere like a fly.

Between the choices I wavered, but Gomer now came along with his radiant air of everything always being such fun, and ran a little way down that cranny like any cat, and smiled up at me reassuringly to say it was all quite easy. Easy, indeed! short cut, indeed! I peevishly reflected that a short cut indeed it was likely to be for me to the Halls of Heaven, supposing I could so far presume on the blamelessness of my past as to count on such a destination. Hoping, therefore, that I was not too sanguine even in my pessimism, I gritted my teeth to the adventure, seeing that no other way lay open. Unluckily Gomer had already things to carry, and could not be further burdened with my boots : and I myself depended on the freedom of both my hands. So down I sat, and deliberately began my downward journey over the face of the cliff, from slab to horrible smooth slab of the cranny, with Gomer backing down below me, arranging my feet with nice precision wherever foothold was dimly indicated. Had I worn nails that day, my death it would assuredly have been ; as it was, I put the very smallest trust in my boots, and went as nervously as any old maid in a marsh, levering myself down inch by inch on my seat—a method of progression that makes up in security what it undeniably lacks in grandeur, seeing that one's posterior curves, in such moments of difficulty, develop a quasi-prehensile and adhesive quality, which no doubt derives from radiating ancestral memories of the tail. No such high anthropological considerations, however, occurred to me then, to distract the caution of my going : bit by bit I slithered and sat, down and down along the crevice, until at length I was safe among a brawl of boulders at the base, hard on the river, with nothing more before me but a scramble over and among them, and then a languid easy saunter up the levels to Tien Tang Ssŭ.

I found Bill very busy amid a crowd of monks, developing photographs and printing plates. For the camera was a very considerable social asset in Tien Tang, where everybody was anxious to have a portrait of himself. One monk, too, possessed a most 'special treasure, which all the others coveted. This was nothing less (here in this remote heart's heart of Asia!) than a picture-postcard of the Potala at Lhasa : and above the vast square bulk of the castle-palace, there hovered aloft, amid woolly little sham clouds, the thin pale face of the Dalai Lama. We were accordingly able to make ourselves generally popular by re-photographing this, and supplying as many replicas as there were eminent ecclesiastics to desire one ; and there were also copies to be made of the Abbey's most cherished picture, a meritorious effort, in hieratic convention, with mitred Saints and Buddhas embedded in a dense multitude of smaller fry, segregated from them by haloes, and circumnavigated by coils of polychromatic cloud.

After this, I myself strolled round with the camera, catching corners of the Abbey and groups of mitred little choir-boys. Then into the dark of the church again, and up on to the roof, to find a long cold vault here, with a big bell. The balcony outside immediately overlooked the yard below : I watched the congregation gather to evensong, all dight in their cocked-hat mitres, and singing psalms rather disorderly distracted by intervals of horseplay. Finally all got in, and I descended to join them. The laity consisted only of me, Mafu, our two Mahomedan soldiers and a local Child of Earth who came in at our heel. The whiskered bland dignitary, who is like a sainted butler, declaimed his litany from the ambo, followed by a gabbly chorus, the acolytes and choir-boys woolgathering in every direction ; but the two little wee, wee people sat motionless as images, with great eyes fixed, an entrancing spectacle of rapt uncomprehending solemnity.

When night was down, Bill and I embarked after dinner on a hair-raising adventure. In the inebriating balmy light of a moon three-fifths to the full, we sauntered artlessly out, as if without any aim in particular, and in a careless-seeming leisure made our way deviously over the scented sea of Iris in the plain. We were, in fact, bent on securing clumps of two special forms, and were anxious to avoid any suspicion or enmity that we might incur from the monks, by openly putting spade into their sacred soil. Personally I believe that by that time we might have carried off the whole plain-ful by cartloads without comment, if we had liked : however, it was huge fun, feeling so surreptitious and conspiratorial. One might have been going secretly, by night, to disentomb some hallowed corpse.   On the bank, just above a particular albino, I remembered two monks were sitting, in fact, drumming and chiming and chaunting in the starry stillness : but we crept past them severally, unobserved.   I discovered my plant pale as a phantom under the moon.   Trepidating, and in a breathless hush, for fear any rash noise should distract those two devout dark blurs on the bank to noticing our sinister attitudes and activities, we successfully got up the clump unnoticed, and made off through the scented surf to the other.   This, too, without suspicion, we achieved, and so triumphantly returned across the grassy plain, toward the sleeping white smear of the monastery, cold and dead in the moonlight, under the cold ghostly pallor of the enveloping cliffs behind.

Disappointed, on the whole, with the floral possibilities of these lower ranges, we now had the fir-forest opposite to explore.   Seeing that, from the river-shingles hardly ten minutes down from Tien Tang, one could almost throw a stone across the river to its farther side, it seemed a night-mare of irony that to get there we should have to go all the way back down the plain, all the way up on to the fells, all the way down to Bridgehead, and then all the way up the far side of the river again—six arduous miles at least, to reach a goal immediately in front of our starting-point, which a bridge would have turned into a traverse of some five hundred yards.   But so it was : no bridge existed here, nor even the pulley-haul basket on a rope which, it was said, the monks occasionally rigged up in later summer.   Nor is the Da-Tung a stream to be forded : as we found in many probings out into its turbid furies.   So off went I and Mâ and Mafu, riding over the downs, while Bill and Wicked Wa-wa went round by that grim Hsiao Lu along the precipice, ultimately to be rejoined by my procession at Bridgehead.   And thence we all came uneventfully backwards again, up the green flats on the other side of the river. It was very tantalizing to see Tien Tang so close over the way, unfolded beneath its cliffs ; so close and yet so unattainable. I could not help laughing, the irony was so acute as to be comic : but Bill fretted at it all day, and made many furious attempts to find a ford, riding òut into the river wherever a broad race of ripples seemed to promise a passage. But it was nowhere any good : sooner or later the violent water roared belly-high, and soon the pony would have been swept off its feet, and engulfed, and carried away even if it tried to swim across, for the Da-Tung-Hor is no river to be lightly treated : even in the end of May, when its full volume has not yet been released by the loosing of the Tibetan snows.

Along and along we drifted, under the sun, till at length we came into the shadow of the forest, round a deep curve of it where woodcutters had already begun their devastations. For the forest of Tien Tang Ssŭ is one of the most important, if not the most important, wood-supplies of Lanchow. The revenues of the Abbey owe much to this almost inexhaustible resource : contractors bid high for its timber, and float it down the Da-Tung-Hor in rafts, and thence down the Hwang-Hor to the capital. As for the Viceroy, he commandeers as he pleases, on nominal prices or none, and woe betide any grumblings. It was, in fact, for some Viceregal work that the felling was now going on, as we rode round amid the heavy boscage that so soon springs up in a clearing, and climbed an ascent, and found ourselves on what now seemed almost a carriage-drive, broad and level and smooth, and white in the hot black shadow of the firs. Now we were in the heart of the woodland : in a vast wall it impended unbroken on the right, and on the left as we went, or in front as we rested, the river rolled beneath, under a deep precipitous fall of cliffs or chalky-looking ghastly soil. Beyond it rolled the rounded cirrhus wave of the poplar-belt, and then the Iris plain, green from here, and level as an unruffled sea : and then the low white stretches of the monastery, huddled beneath its bay of precipices.

Delicious was the day, and delicious the balmy breath of the moth-eaten spruces, and delicious the occasional glades that starkly clove the flanks of the forest. Up some of these we explored : it was like going up a topless stairway, till at last the clearance faded upward into the eternal midnight. But it was all bone dry, dry as no woodland I could have imagined, and far too dry for any flowers, besides being far too deep-sunk in unbroken blackness of dark. So down we came, sending Mafu upward still, to see what might be to be seen over the invisible crest of the ridge : and threaded the greener jungles at the foot of the climb, where the firs are not so dense, and slants of sunlight, filtering through, engender the vivid green of shrubs, and the lesser world of Peonies and Anemonies in their shade. But even these were rare and poor and well-known—the magenta crimson peony of these ranges, that lacks alike the roseate soft tones and the roseate soft sweetness of its cousin on Thunder-crown : and the spidery ugly tangles of Anemone obtusiloba that starts with small five-pointed creamy stars sitting tight in the grass, and ends in lanky spraying fountains, as rank as Geum urbanum (and very like it in effect, but for the colour), with heads of hooky green seeds that catch on to your clothes like burrs.

So in vain search we wrestled among the tangles, and explored the frontage of the fell, till on the lower slopes the forest thinned out, and became a mere occasional outbreak of firs, above green lawns. We got quite clear of the trees at last, to where, round the corner, a stony beck-bed comes down through the fell in a deep chine, with a fantastic high peak of russet-red precipices towering beyond, dark in a vesture of firs up its skirts, and outlined delicately with firs along its crests. Here, among the boulders, deep in a shady hollow of the beck-bed, we rested awhile and drowsed, beneath the murmurous music of poplars, silverily rippling overhead in the dance of the wind. Then slowly we returned along the carriage-drive.

Below, immediately above the river-cliff, was a secondary
lap of grassy glade, open and grilling in the sunshine.   And
here, picnicking alfresco, were two dear old pontiffs at their
lunch, attended by a chaplain, with their palfreys grazing
in   the   background.   " My   Lords,   My   Lords,"   they
rapturously cried up at us with nods and beckings, " Come
down, come down."   So down went Bill and I and the
Wa-wa, and made salutations, and took our seats on the
grass while the chaplain served us all to a lunch of buttered
tea in broad shallow bowls that might have been of boxwood,
and large square sippets hard as marble, out of a bag.   We
lapped and supped and munched as best we might : but,
even when sopped in tea the sippets defeated my dentures
and endangered them : apologies had to be made for my
general defectiveness of construction.   The two old gentlemen, however, were perfectly genial about it, and beamed
upon us through their round horn-rimmed spectacles.   They
were evidently dignitaries of high degree, robed in red and
purple, with important rosaries, and one wore an enormous
red-lacquer hat exactly like a Cardinal's.   The chaplain,
meanwhile,   assisted   by   the   Wa-wa,   inconspicuously
attended, in the background, to the iron tea-porringer
simmering over an improvised tripod of stones and a picnic
fire of sticks.

And so we said Au revoir, till they also should have arrived
at Tien Tang (to which they were on their way) : and ourselves continued homeward ; stopping only to descend the
cliff into the boulder-bed of the river, where, in a placid
emerald back-water, we ate our own lunch, beneath the filmy
shade of the poplars that here make just the same forest as
on the far side, like a phantom park in the underworld.   And
when we got home it was still quite early : and early were
the sheep, too, in emerging from their lairs.   So that, lying
on the roof, we could clearly study their shape and colouring
through our glasses—the straightish out-bent horns of the
rams and their black bell-tuft ; and the mousy tone of all,
with creamy bellies, the colour lining the thighs and the back

of the hind legs, and rounding the blackscutted rump. This will show how close they come down upon that holy spot. Finally, we spotted a ewe, squatting tight beneath a sunny cliff just beyond the Chorten in the chine, so near that we could not refrain from going out to try a preposterous snapshot from the pilgrim-path, watched by monks and pilgrims. And then, to crown all, came down the wonderful night : in the cold intoxicating glare of the almost full moon we roamed along the flat roofs, while the cliffs above looked perfectly Mediterranean, luminous and ghostly, with the ranges of low white houses huddled beneath.

But by now the Irises were gone dashed and dingy in death, like fading daffodils : the Lloydia was blowzy in the rocks, and Androsace tibetica weeping to its end with a blurred eye of blood-crimson : all present work at Tien Tang was accomplished, and it was time to move on, however sad we were to be leaving so delicious a haven of peace. In a morning almost too cloudless to be trusty, the caravan packed up and shouldered its burdens, and rode out of Tien Tang, amid many promises of a quick return : and with us tumultuously in a crowd poured the monks and acolytes, these last in brand new petticoats of deep violet, brief and bunchy as a ballerina's, which, under their equally new upper swathings of bright scarlet, made them look just like old-fashioned fuchsias. At the debouchure of the Lloydia-Glade they fell away, with cries of good-will and farewell : Bill and Mâ went up over the downs to Chao-lo, thence, on their ponies, to make the rough wild trail along the gorges and gullies immediately above the Da-Tung-Hor, but the rest of the caravan had to take a much longer detour, in order to get down to the river again, at its crossing-point. For Chebson Abbey was now our destination ; and Chebson Abbey lies far out on the Western side of the range, whereas Tien Tang snuggles close under the Eastern : so that a long traverse of the chain lay before us, and a transit of the river.

Up the long glade accordingly lay our present course, into the hot dry hill-country behind Tien Tang, but winding perpetually leftwards after the first few miles. Between fantastic red ranges of pulhamite, rounded and eroded, the valley coiled, with scrub of rose and barberry on either side. The little stream was pure as crystal, and made pleasant noises : but ere long the way grew very monotonous and dull.

These open Tibetan vales, in the uneventful foothills of the Alps, are strangely oppressive in their sinister yet unassuming sameness : they are very high, and they seem very high, close up under the immediate lid of the sky : but there is nowhere any sign of it, so that their pretence of being mere lowlands seems an evil sham, and with an evil magic their very dullness, hot and sterile, seems haunted, and the marmots themselves are a magic population, imprisoned by a spell in their present gollywog shape. As I rode slowly along in the ominous silence of the sunshine, I chanted snatches of song to charm away the weight of that watchful stillness : but the only fragment that survives is a Wordsworthian line to the effect that " A marmot's life has few amenities."

All this time, though, the way was gradually rising : and at length we came to a point where a little beck came down another valley on the left, at right angles to our own, now hardly more than an extended saucer sprawling along between the downs. And here, so high we already were, the open slopes were sheeted in a little Rhododendron, occasionally sighted in cooler stretches on the way up, but here for the first time seen in mass, and beginning to clothe itself in colour. This is the universal representative, in the Da-Tung Alps, of that small, grey-leaved, blue-flowered group that has already rejoiced our gardens with Rh. Fastigiatum and Rh. Imbricatum and Rh. F. 119, off Thundercrown. But here the habit is light and graceful, and the foliage minute and almost silvery, so that the shrubling of two feet or so has a special airy charm of its own, even without the comparatively large little flowers, that open in pairs all over the plant, in such profusion that the whole bush goes blue, and the mile-wide stretches of it

L

in the upland moors of the Da-Tung are a sheet of lavender, which fills the farther distances with a film of grey haze.

Up this right-angled turn it was now our time to proceed, at first through coppice of cypress with Primula stenocalyx glittering on the bank, but ascending so rapidly that quite soon we were in the cooler air of an almost Alpine woodland, splashing in mossy pools of the beck in successive laps and hollows of the hill, as we ascended steep over steep. Along one shoulder there was a clearing, and grassy glades with burnt black stumps upstanding, and Iris goniocarpa beginning to glow among the tuffets in more abundance and brilliance than ever I saw it elsewhere in the Da-Tung Alps. And here, among the rest, gleamed two perfect albinos, fairy flowers of an almost flagrant purity, with even the deepest purple frecklings faded into a faintest memory of green. These were most preciously collected, and wadded up in moss : it gives me a special thrill to record that those two plants, after being carried sultrily round all the length of this tour on which we are embarking, with its long sojourn in Chebson, arrived undaunted back at Wolvesden, were planted in the little garden that I made there in the shingle of the yard, and there bore fertile seed (a mouse picked it before I did, but no matter) : that then, in due course, replanted in empty biscuit-tins, they came all the way down across the blazing distances of China to Peking, wintered there in a yard of the Legation, and then, in my own hand and steam-heated sleeping compartment, all across the frozen wastes of Russia and Siberia to Petrograd, up the lagoons of Finland, down the flanks of Sweden, over the fjelds and along the fjords of Norway, and all across the mine-strewn estranging seas to Hull : and are now, one of them at least, thriving as happily at Ingleborough as they ever did (except for the unanticipated attentions of slugs, which bewilder them).

Their immediate neighbour there has an only less romantic history of travel, too : this is that very plant of Androsace mucrenifolia which, four years ago, was making pats of

hawthorn-scented snow, 15,000 ft. up, on the high tops
of Ardgen, and was there photographed in situ, and will
be found immortalized in the first Eaves of the World.
But her Odyssey had not the dramatic touch of being
personally conducted : she travelled home to England comparatively prosaically, all the way from the Tibetan
highlands, by post, in a biscuit-box.   Anyhow, so much for
the ridiculous old legend (even now still lingering) about the
perils of taking up a plant in flower : why that is the very
moment of moments to take it.

After this blissful episode, the path climbed steadily, high
and far, up a coppiced fold between great fells, towards a
distant neck. Gradually the woodland thinned out, and
scant Potentilla-scrub took its place, with coarse tussocky
grass forming its foundation.   All, here, was still drab and
pale : only Primula tangutica, from its cabbagy crowns,
was unfolding, on its lanky stems, its tiers of miserable
squinny chocolate-coloured stars, that make it, as a rule, so
really hideous as to bring shame on the august name it bears.
And I also saw here, one beautiful tuffet of Adonis cœrulea,
concise in the foliage, large and silkily purple in the flower.
By now we were toiling up bare moorland toward the high
neck before us, and on the right hung dark heights, with
scrub of Potentilla and burnt emerald ghylls of grass between
them.   Here from afar I spotted a series of mysterious
blobs, large and rounded and pale up on the flank of the fell,
on a green strip where boscage was beginning to sprout.   I
could not believe them to be anything but baby donkies ;
when I got near it was the Lampshade Poppy, pallid and
preposterous in such a place.

On the pass itself I noticed a track, ascending still higher,
by coils, up the left-hand peak.   But as our own path still
continued, broad and unmistakable, down the other side, I
had no hope of better things, and went straight on, past
bays of brown scrub crowded with the sulphur-pale orbs of
Meconopsis integrifolia.   Still downwards, a broad comfortable road, cypress copse beginning, and beyond, far over

the tumbled distances of wood and moor, a noble range of Alps, ominous in the new brooding gloom of the day.   But hardly had I come on a new aster at the path side, than Gomer came running after with the news that the upward track from the crest had, after all, been the right one.   So back we turned, Go-go, and the stupid-faced pony and I, and laboured up to the pass again : and thence up along the arête still, to the culminating point, which was a bare dark shingle and shale and rock, with nothing of beauty or interest either appearing or promising.

And here we emerged suddenly into sight of our own Wolvesden Alps once more, expanding very magnificent and white before us, high over the black crumples of the lesser hills.   Very steep and very far and difficult was now the descent towards the river, down a precipitous wide gully of moorland, dead and brown and sopping, with tussocky marches, and large loose track of wet stone and shale, empty of hope, with only the little Trollius beginning to appear in buttons of gold.   Lower yet, we came under crags into a ghyll full of a big white rhododendron that was in flower, looking like lodged lumps of snow in a thaw, all over the wet-looking glossy foliage of the tangled bushes. But I grew a little leaden, in the leaden overcast thunderousness of the afternoon, to find no new plants.   It was a tedious descent, too, the donkeys and ponies stumbling cautiously down the steeps among the boulders and pitfalls. Safely, however, we all at length attained once more to the lowest levels, where at once the Iris resumed, in drifted backwashes, filling each bay of the hillside.   There was still a long descent before us, though, to the river, with the marmots now for sole diversion, scuttling about, fat, great, bandy-legged teddy-bears, with their perpetual ridiculous jerking up of their tails at each pause : or sitting up inquiringly at us, with a goggle-eyed plutocratic expression.

But now we did at last got down to the Da-Tung-Hor again, and thence continued easily forward, along the bends of its turbid tide, till, among open meadows, we arrived at the rope ferry, with a mountain slope of birch-copse opposite, and a brightly white-flowered rowan hovering in the coppice beneath. Into the ark we packed, and across the river it was pulley-hauled by the whole staff, sliding along the wire hawser on a ring. Now up and down along the ribs and gullies of the birch-copse we continued our progress up the river. The wood was very luminous and green and lovely, but soon the Da-Tung-Hor came round a wild coil from the right, while our own way ran straight away from it, up an open beck vale with a village, towards high Alps ahead. There seemed a choice of tracks by the stream ; we chose the most convenient—and the inhabitants immediately issued forth and howled at us. We had got on to one of those taboo tracks, that are closed to caravan traffic during the time of springing corn, when demons, if offended, could blast the crop.

Remembering Chago, we hastily retraced our steps, and tried another way—only to find ourselves on a yet more forbidden track, wedged in with walls and prayer-flags. The howls increased in number and volume, dogs bayed and guns went off. However, we continued undaunted, and gradually the unpropitious noises died out in the backward distance, as we jogged quietly through the rural calm of the evening. The glen by degrees grew narrower and deeper : till at length we came into an Iris plain deep down between the fells, with lovely cloudy poplars all ruinously cut and cleared and prone. And above this, high on the flank of the fell, clung Gan Chang Ssŭ, our night's destination, packed on the steep slope. From far above, Mâ called to us : we knew that Bill had duly arrived, and prepared our welcome. By a bridge close by we crossed the beck, and very steeply up into the steep streets of the neat little clean monastery—there to find Bill, indeed, gone out for a stroll, but the people quiet and friendly, and a beautiful new yard-compound allotted to us, in which I was glad to settle for the night, after sustaining a visit from a nice little round French-faced Gwan-ja, who had been to Lhasa, and was accordingly delighted with a present of the post-card photograph.

Gan Chang Ssǔ is not a large religious house, nor a wealthy : it has neither the homely bustle of Tien Tang, nor the stately calm of Chebson. Along the steep hill-side it clings and clambers, looking across at another steep fell-side opposite with the beautiful park of the slaughtered poplars lying deep in the vale between. I visited the main church, square and white and solid, but no rival to those of Tien Tang ; and in a side-room of my own lodgment I came on rood screens and other decorations in coloured butter, stored away for festivals. In all these parts coloured butter is the staple of religious adornment : in the composition they make it is hard and firm and enduring, susceptible of infinite twisting and carving and moulding. At Gan Chang there were merely conventional flowers, roses and peonies, sculptured in pink and red and yellow butter amid green butter-foliage and mounted on frames, but one of the most celebrated festivals in all Buddhist Northern Asia is the Butter Fair at Gumbum Abbey, whither, in the opening of the year, uncounted multitudes flock to see a show of tableaux and holy scenes, episodes in the lives of saints and Buddhas, all carried out, with the most marvellous artistry, in sculptures of coloured butter, modelled and tinted to the life. These are new every year, each exhibition trying to rival the last, but in the ordinary run of things, the lesser monasteries keep their butter ornaments stored in some loft from year to year, as here at Gan Chang, to be produced in due season for decorating the church at Harvest Festivals and such-like.

But I cannot tell you more of Gan Chang Ssǔ, for at grey of the next morning we were up and out of it, with a tremendous day before us, of crossing the Alps and descending upon their Western slope. High as we already were, we had yet to go much higher, up and up the windings of the valley, with the willowy little blue Rhododendron now abounding in beauty on all the banks ; and another one also appearing, a size larger, like Rh. (azalea) amœnum, with much bigger flowers of a similar lavender blue, but dying magenta. By

this time, too, the prevalent Daphne of those ranges was in.
bloom, and proved in general to be, or to fade, of a rich
ivory white. And still we climbed : up on open moorland
now, with a pass ahead of us, by many coils, at the end ; and
behind, in the cloudless morning, a noble backward view
over the whole Gadjur range in the far distance.

When we topped the crest we saw ahead of us the
track continuing, level and broad and white, round a vast
open flank of mountain, that fell away below in a smooth
moorland sweep, towards a tumble of valleys and hills
mapped out below, filling the leftward distance to where,
high up the sky, the Wolvesden Alps themselves now reappeared in all their candid splendour, though too switchbacked
in outline for anything approaching the wild ferocious beauty
of the Satanee Alps and the Min S'an. The road ran flatly
along, half-way up the mountain : on the right, above us, the
moorland ere long died into savage screes of naked russet
stone, descending from savage naked peaks and pinnacles
far overhead, that sometimes also wept themselves away in
wild couloirs cutting deep grooves down the flank of the fell
and widening away to the valley below. And so we went—
another breast, another wide level sweep of bay : another
breast, another bay : it was like a marvellous gigantic
Bindelweg, but with even more sense of exaltation, of vast
openness and freedom, suspended half-way up in space with
the world mapped out beneath, and those massive snowy
pyramids deployed in procession across the sky above it,
and in the middle of the leftward distance, above the tumble
of hills and hollows intervening, a pale high saddle, from
which, on the feet of thought, I saw clearly that one stepped
straight down upon Casa Aoo, and, farther still, on
Wolvesden in its Dene. And on all the banks around us the
powdered blue Primula glittered in the brown moorland
edges in unbelievable abundance, and in the deep-scored
" rovine " that we again and again had to circumnavigate,
in the couloirs streaming starkly from the imminent red
shingles and savageries up above.

Few Alps have given me so memorable an " easy " as this.
But at last our skirting of the Red-Peaked Range was
accomplished, and we reached the culminating neck of all,
a scrambly little pass of gleaming shale-shingle, on which,
in one solitary lavender-coloured dome of loveliness, there
squatted close and tight the rounded stemless head of an
Erysimum scented like a clove.   And from this, round the
corner of the range, we descended upon a much duller world,
clearly leading down into the lowlands by a long, long drop
of soggy dead-brown moorland vale, with eruptions of marsh
in which a little Draba thing was beginning to promise
sheets and hassocks of shrill yellow.   And over the lower
fells the willowy blue Rhododendron was in such drifts of
colour that all the hill seemed veiled in a haze of cold grey.
The track was steep and wet and bad and dull, with only
dull high rotundities of fell enfolding it, and no more Alps :
but at last, at the bottom, we came out into the flat wide
shingled bed of a river, which had torn its way from the
heart of the peaks up behind.   Into this our own little
half-born beck converged, and down the shingled levels we
proceeded, sometimes under eruptions of impending cliff,
and all the time more obviously advancing out of the
mountains towards the upland plains on the Western slope.
On the edge of these the river drew near to a " klause " of
cliffs, so that the path deserted it, and climbed out along a
rolling fell of grass and Daphne and Potentilla scrubbage on
the right.   Here, to surmount the rib that terminated in
those cliffs, we had to cross a small moorland saddle where
among the tussocks the golden Gagea reappeared rarely,
in such magnified form as almost to suggest a starry golden
tulip.   And on the far side, human life at last reappeared.

For now we were looking out over a vast champaign of
cultures and dead river deltas, the Westward fall of the
Da-Tung chain, such as we had already seen at Officialton.
And away below us to the left, about a bummock on the
moorland, there was a lively crowd gathered, and the little
red mud wall of a crumbling fortalice beyond.   Guns were

going off in disorder, and flags waving and gongs and crackers contributing their quota, round a dark central figure performing pious evolutions.   At first I thought it was a Living Buddha pontificating, but soon it appeared that it was only some Chinese ceremony being discharged by an official : disillusioned, I continued my way, and the Beano, meanwhile, also moved on, but not before the din of it in the distance had so terrified a brace of enormous shaggy yaks as white as milk and tethered together like cuff links, who had previously been advancing quietly over the brae, that now they tossed up their heads and wildly bolted down upon me like a discordant pair of earthquakes, barging tempestuously this way and that, and plunging in all directions with their terrific horns.   So we judged it best to dismount and get up off the track, while the twin cataclysms surged by, and their pavid attendants trotted after in the background, with useless shoutings that carried no conviction even to themselves.

After this we were out of the mountain country, down in an endless vista of rolling cultivated lands, all the breakwater spurs and vast river deltas from the Alps being alike diligently cultivated to the last inch.   Over spurs and across deltas we alternately toiled and jogged, with our faces set steadily away from the mountains that lay behind us, up to the right, with only lovely clouds to diversify the dullness of the way.   This is so very huge a country, so leisurely and ample in its naked lines, that the distances seem almost as great as they really are.   I paused upon a stretch of river sward to dismount, and to unhook the bag at my pony's neck, and sit down among the pale little starry gentians to take a snack upon the brink of a pellucid brook, there brabbling.   But not even this Arcadian diversion succeeded : for the honey, with characteristic malignity, had come out of the pot and flooded everything in a morass of stickiness, and the sardine-tin would not open, and altogether I felt too empty and empeeved for any thought of food, mounted my steed once more, and joggled forward again across the sunlit world, raising myself above earthly rubs as I rode, by the reflection that no matter with what mishaps I might meet in the way of robbery, murder, massacre, martyrdom, or even the misery of an effusive honeypot, by no possible malignity of fate, at all events, could I here meet with Aunt Albinia.[1]

In a high chaunt I proclaimed this uplifting consolation to the four winds : I proceeded with lightened heart, and the sun once more resumed its brilliance. For, dull and long though they may sometimes seem in the going, how infinitely golden, really, and in retrospect, are those days of effortless uneventful abstraction, drifting across the enormous immemorial smile of China, in perfect openness of light and air, in perfect openness of freedom from all earthly cares, duties, ties and domesticities, with nothing to think about at all but when one will reach one's destination, and what one will eat when one gets there.   You might fancy, indeed, that such days of untrammelled mental leisure would lead one to a course of high and holy thinking, solid reflections (like Mary Bennet's) and wise resolutions : instead of which (I personally find) the vacancy of one's mind, sunk in a hebetude of happiness, dwells, exclusively, with what the incomparable Elizabeth justly calls " a shameful persistence, on the succulent and the gross."

In such an elevating train of thought, accordingly, I now devoured the distances.   Isolated, far ahead of us, above the undulating hills of tillage, a huge high hog's back of purple down dominated the view : towards this we made, across yet another delta of two or three miles width, parcelled out to the last inch, in a patchwork of culture.   Here there was a factory of yak-dung fuel, with cakes of it baking in rows on boards outside, and a new Iris suddenly flared blue on a red loam-bank that was not loess, and in places the bare earth was exploding oddly in humps of glossy greenness and

[1] Not an absolutely certain consolation either : does not the proverb say, " Although mankind numbers a million millions, and although the desert of Shan-Tz' be boundless, yet there did Li-Hing encounter his mother-in-law " ?

big chocolate-purple bells of blossom. And on the rise we
passed, without notice, a little crumbled wall of loess, grass-
grown, negligible, melted almost back into the downs again,
but running, if you look to right and left, indefinitely up and
down the distance, over the downlands Westward, and Eastward imperturbably up across the Alps. And this poor
relic, that a crippled child could now almost take at a stride,
is no mean symbol.   For it is neither more nor less than a
boundary wall of China and Tibet.   Since the days of its
building the tide of Empire has ebbed and flowed, and far
beyond her actual limits China pervades. But this
mouldered rampart still remains to show a line where once
she cried halt for a while.

And even now you are definitely in Tibet on its far side.
For on crossing the rise you see below you yet another of
those vast deltas, expanding fanwise from the mountains
about six miles up to the right ; but this one is not cultivated,
like those in China : it is a moorland plain of rough virgin
pasture, grazed over by herds of yaks that look like emmets
on its vast brownish expanse, and dotted here and there with
the yurts of the nomad tribes that keep them, and shift
their pasture from place to place.   Below the green downs
across the delta (one of which showed a dark fringe of fir-
forest from its farther slope) the untilled pasture plain vastly
continued : and the great hog's-back fell was now close at
hand, closing in the distance below the plain.   How much
farther we still had to go, I neither knew nor recked : what
was my amazement, then, when Mafu indicated the forest
fringe with his finger and said, " That wood under, Chebson
Ssŭ."   We still had the delta-flat indeed to traverse, but it
seemed a trifle, and I marvelled at the rapidity with which
our destination had burst upon us.   However, no trifle was
the delta-flat after all ; it was at least two miles across.
And it was some time, therefore, after my first rapture of
relief, ere we were breasting the green rise on its far side,
had topped it, and found ourselves immediately riding down
on Chebson Abbey.

CHAPTER IX

CHEBSON ABBEY

Chebson Abbey lies closely hidden in the last green hollow of the downs, and you come upon it abruptly, lying unsuspected at your feet, with a shock of surprise at finding such a hive of humanity lurking in the face of this enormous featureless land. The downs descend in a long spur from the Alps, some five miles back in the West: and at their end they widen into a cup or pincer-shaped hollow from which a little open vale sinks down to the pasture plain beyond. And in that cup lies Chebson Abbey, facing due South, secure and snug in that hollow of rolling hills as open and green as Sussex Downs. Behind it, a steep breast black with a copse of cypress fronts the sun, and on the corrugations of the fell that forms the leftward rim of the cup, there are rather mangy strips of fir, above the Potentilla scrub: otherwise the scene is wholly bare and treeless, until you come to the big hog's back across the plain below, whose dry flanks and chines are similarly scattered with parched-looking firs. So much for the mighty forests in which the pages of Przewalsky had made us expect to find Chebson Abbey richly enveloped.

It is a noble place, though, huge and serene—a very select and exclusive foundation, with only some seventy monks, all of the " best " people, living each in state alone in a wide-yarded low white house. Here and there rise big churches, and full in the middle the main church of all, a splendid great block of soft crimson, roofed most gorgeously in gold with golden dragons spouting off the rainwater ; golden dragons are the finials on the roof, and

golden stags and wheels and pillar-boxes adorn its parapet.
This resplendent structure stands isolated in a vast
quadrangle of lawn, which is walled all round its four sides
with a spacious frescoed cloister, whose inner railing is set
with hundreds after hundreds of invocation cylinders that
you set clanking one by one as you make the circuit. Up
behind the blank red outer wall of the cloister stands a
small sumptuous church all by itself : and up above this
again, close under the steep of cypresses, are the guest-
cloisters.

These match with the scale of the whole Abbey. Even
the lower one, where guests of lower distinction are accommo-
dated, is wide and solid—a big square, lying on a slope,
with a big raised causeway of cobbles descending down the
centre, with living-rooms all round, and even lesser lateral
yards on either side. At the top of the causeway you pass
into the upper guest-cloister, and find yourself in an even
nobler square, a cobbled empty yard of spacious silence
with an arcaded cloister all round, and the living-rooms
cool under its shade, and above, by stairways from the
four corners, upper galleries of rooms, which, at the two
frontal ends of the square, project out in square roof-loggias
that command an untrammelled view over the whole Abbey
and its downs, and the plain below, and the hills beyond.
These belong each to a small suite of rooms that faces
upon it, cut off by doors and steps from the first-floor
gallery of apartments behind. They consist of a little
central hall, and two panelled rooms opening out on either
side—delicious sequestered suites of tranquillity, open to
all the air and sunshine. These are reserved for Living
Buddhas on a visit ; but even our own quarters down below
left nothing to be desired in the way of comfort, constructed
on the same triple scheme (which obtains all round the
quad.), roomy and cool and dark, panelled all over in wood,
with kang and table and cupboard. And up behind the
upper guest-cloister again, you pass into ramifying stone-
walled yards and court of yet another church, with yet

another up behind it under the hill—trim gawcy buildings, both of them, high and square and white, with bold hard-browed Egyptian windows, and, close under their caves, that band of beautiful decoration they make here, of brush-wood packed together, and then all cut off evenly in a flat surface. This makes the effect of a deep belt of brown velvet, on which great monogrammed bucklers of gilt and other gilded ornaments flash sumptuously.

A huge collegiate calm and solemnity broods unbroken over Chebson ; its atmosphere compares to the bustling popular pieties of Tien Tang as a wealthy old Oxford college's to the stir of an urban parish. When, on my entering the cloister, the Prior came forth to greet me, and induct me to my apartments, he also continued the comparison, for, though everything that was friendly and courteous, he had the assured calm, the gentlemanly sufficiency and ease of any Master or Bursar—not curious or effusive or aloof, but taking himself and us for granted, with a proper unconscious sense of his own competence. He looked the part, too, to perfection, a portly old body, of immense dignity, voluminous in his crimsons, with a huge powerful head, and like a Tibetan Coquelin in his mobility of feature. He had a little the presence and port of a magnified Mr. Asquith, but with elephantine ears like the handles of an urn, and dense luscious jowl and lips, and dense black eyebrows almost too artificial looking to be true, that waggishly went up and down, and worked as hard as George Alexander's.

In an easy flow of compliments and mutual admiration our talk proceeded, and he told us details as to the age and population of the Abbey. It is not an old place, in fact dating back only about a century : but handsomely endowed and handsomely built, though run up in a hurry, with a regrettable scamping of solid work. It does not even, for all its wealth, and the sumptuous furniture of its sumptuous buildings, appear to possess a Living Buddha of its own, though at the moment of our visit it had the borrowed glory of one on loan, a Manifestation from far parts, and of such importance that he had with him a bodyguard of soldiers from Peking, a trim, well-set-up lot of fellows in their tight grey uniform, strangely modern to see, in the somnolent vacancies of this sedate place. He was, indeed, so big and holy a person that we were most unlikely to forgather with him : and had his abode apart, in a neat square Church-house, walled away in an orchard-paddock up at the top of the hamlet. Where the Abbot lived or whether we should see him, did not transpire : meanwhile our friend in charge was the Prior or Bursar, no mere temporary appointment, as he of Tien Tang, but as permanent an established dignitary as Mr. Bidder himself.

But these passages were put a stop to by anxiety about the lateness of the mules. Evidently they must have missed their way. I myself had laid them open to doing so, by riding ahead with Mafu. And missed the way they had : and only at long last were discerned from the col above the Abbey, a scattered string of mites, proceeding far away down across the bottom of the plain. Mafu rode down the Abbey-vale between the horns of the down, to intercept them, and we returned to our quarters. And there, as I walked up and down the quad., I became conscious of a waft of unconsciousness shooting most oddly up through my heels. At first I diagnosed mere emptiness, and then a set of earthquakes, but ere long joined on these symptoms to the strained staggers I had had in my eyes during the last part of the journey, and realized that the brilliant light in this high altitude must have given me a touch of the sun.

Poor Bill, too, was under a cloud, with an ill-tempered tooth, which had already begun grumbling and growling at Tien Tang, but by this time had risen to a real roaring rage that defied palliatives. Sterner steps were tried. Bill lassoed the offender with a piece of string, of which Mafu held the other end and pulled. But from this grisly tug-of-war only howls and agonies resulted : the tooth would not budge. So it became plain that he must ride away over the hills to Sining, and have it removed. The next day passed in preparations. The sky was steely and stuffy, with a pale blurred sun : it was not till dusk that I went out, and up on to a green bummock of the down above, from which I had a full view of the Abbey, mapped out at my feet : and, turning my back on it, a panorama of the Alps, now some seven or eight miles distant, still pale and sere as if it were winter. Then down I came into the town again : for so Chebson Abbey really is, with wide ways and open spaces. No one ever seems to be about : few noises break the comfortable grey calm, and rarely do the resident prelates pervade the sleepy streets and alleys of whitewashed walls. It was almost a shock, on going up into the outer court of the big church, to find the Buddha's bodyguard sitting about, and playing, and mending their uniforms. Then through one of the three gateways (the main one, in the middle, is kept shut) I passed into the arcade of the cloister, and in front of me, beyond the railing and its line of cylinders, lay the smooth expanse of lawn, and the rose-red mass of the square gold-lidded edifice itself, looking, but for its colour and gilding, astonishingly like some big English country house, with wide-spaced windows, and drive running up to an especially ample portico. Yet how much more beautiful by virtue of that colouring, the husky rich rose, with windows heavily outlined in square belts of white, and above, under the gilded eaves, the deep-brown velvet band of brushwood, set with plaques and clasps and hinges of gilded metal, and the gilded curve of the roof, over all, with its flashing dragons on the angles, and golden stags and wheel and pillar-boxes crowning the frontal parapet.

Across the silent emptiness of the precinct I advanced to the verandah, and tried one of the big painted doors in its depths. It yielded : a wave of solid butter-scented black cold came out to meet me, in an exhalation of icy wind. Into the enormous gorgeous gloom of the interior

I cautiously peered, but, in the distance of the dark, shouts of warning reverberated at me from a lamp-lighting monk on one of the altars : so, fearing to be tactless, I retired.

When I got back I found Mafu in one of his wild gorilla furies, and the court re-echoed with his shattering shouts. It appeared that we now had a fellow-guest, some quite small official up from Mao Be Hsien : and this plebeian person had actually had the audacity to come and peer, uninvited, into our apartments. However, Mafu soon " showed 'im 'is error, plain " : away he slunk into his own, and the evening concluded in a long visit from the Prior, who brought two keen-faced English-looking friends to see us. They were all most affable, but cast such marked glances at the Chartreuse bottle, and made so many leading remarks about " foreign wine," that I became torn with the desire to offer them some, as they so obviously desired. Bill, however, restrained me : it would be taken as a shocking insult if we tried to tempt them from their vow of abstinence. I could not, myself, feel that they were quite so morbidly sensitive as all that about their vows : but Bill must always know best. So I continued stony to their hints, and at last those holy ones went sadly away, with many backward glances of longing, and grievous waggings of the head ; murmurs about " Wai-gwe Jiu, Wai-gwe Jiu " dolorously re-echoed as they drifted out.

But, in my grief at their disappointment, I reckoned without the universal ingenuity of the priestly mind, which never fails to find a sanctified road to the desired end. For now, in a little, they all came drifting in again, much more alertly, and with a radiant look. This, however, must have belied their real feelings : for they had all, it seemed, in the last five minutes, developed painful stomachic affections, for which, after the Apostolic prescription, a little wine was indicated by the Faculty. And they had heard that the foreign variety was specially efficacious : might they try some, in the interests of medical science ? Mrs. Crupp and her spasms find strange echoes all the world

M

over : we poured them forth each a dose, and down it
went, with such instant good results that the exhibition of
another was declared desirable. The Prior, in particular,
justified his bonhomous aspect, by absorbing this new
medicine with flagrant gusto, though also with gurglings
and gaspings of depreciation, and pantomimic pouting and
pulling of faces and wild agitations of the eyebrows and
resounding slaps of protest upon the purple bow-window of
his belly.

Bill got up early, and I rose late, to a leaden-lidded day,
stifling as a Turkish bath. Hardly had I got to work on
a sketch of the big church, than the Prior came heaving
round to take me down on a visit to it. And a huge sombre
hall of darkness and magnificence it certainly is, filling the
whole ground-floor of the building, then contracting, to
rise high in a central clerestory, which thus leaves room
for the quadrangle of galleries on the upper floor, and
also lets shafts of daylight down into the gloom of the
great hall below. The enormous altars stand aligned
between the distanced columns all up its farther side,
fronting the three doors. They are chapels in themselves,
or giants' pews : up in the depth of each a colossal Buddha
Saint or Bodhisattva sits enthroned, securely boxed off
from the rest of the church by wooden panellings and
stairways, but out before him, along the broad frontal
barrier which is really the altar, arises such a congregation
of lesser holy figures, together with sets of altar vessels,
and flowers, and flat convolutions of coloured butterwork,
that when near at hand you can hardly discern the closeted
golden colossi behind, dimly glooming above, from the
seclusion of their huge magnificent shrines. Dimly, too,
the slants of light from the clerestory filter down into the
solemnity of the church, and fade into the further darknesses
among the flat-faced columns that stand like trees in an
ancient forest. From capital to base these are densely
hung and flounced and valanced with streamers and lappets
and pennons of old embroidered brocades, and on each

high altar, in front of the gilded Buddhas their altar vessels
are of cloisonné or wrought metal-work, or Kang-Hsi
blue-and-white : and scattered pavilions and pulpits of
woodwork look like pillar-boxes in the vast expanse : and
high overhead the daylight in the clerestory strikes straight
on brilliant rolls of fresco hung all round, and then dies
downwards to lose itself in the cavernous fragrant darkness
among the columns in a vague haze of sumptuousness and
colour, filled with a sense of long-established splendour,
august and sacred and serene.

I won permission to throw wide another of the big doors,
to get more light, and try a photograph. This did not turn
out well, but photographs of Tibetan church-interiors are
by no means things you come by every day, and anyhow
the vague amorphous blur that the camera produced
gives, after all, no such bad impression of the blurred and
vague impressiveness of Chebson. Then, when this was
achieved, in a remote corner of darkness we came to a
stairway, and climbed to the upper roof. Here we found
ourselves in a flat quadrangle, with the clerestory rising
in the middle to its golden roof high overhead. Into this
we were not able to get, but peered along, through its
latticed and wire-meshed windows, down into the well of
the church below : then turned our attention to the galleries
of libraries, shrines and relic stores that wall in the quadrangle
all round. And then again up by another stair on to the
roof of these, which is the flat rampart frontage of the
building, with the golden-roofed clerestory still rising high
in the middle. But here you are very close to the glittering
splendour of it, and the dragons come mouthing down upon
you at its corners : in all this gorgeousness there is one
homely touch of modern times. For the effective gutters
and waterspouts are of plain European lead piping.

So, on this level white causeway we roamed awhile and
examined the strange colossal gilded pillar-boxes that stand
at its corners, and along the front, with the golden wheel
and the golden stags (or whatever these hieratic beasts may

be, that squat in a pair, on either side of the wheel along the high parapet of Tibetan churches). And then retired down to earth again, to go and see other shrines, which, however, proved a bathos—new, and garish, and dull. So now I turned my attention to flowers, and fared forth with Gomer on to the downs. At Chebson the loess has reached its end, and only seems to lie in hollows of the main formation, which is a hardish reddish loam. But the flora does not alter very much, and over the green undulations of the grass Stellera dances everywhere, and the hill-sides have a chintzy quattrocento prettiness of flower-bespangled lawn. Among the rest, however, there is the new Iris. And this is a lovely thing, forming in the course of time huge old hassocks of coarse mahogany-coloured fibre, like old bass-matting, the desiccated wreckage of years, from which sprout grassy fountains of foliage, and large flowers of limpid blue, with a white throat and a golden flame down the fall, suggesting absolutely in colour, and approximately in shape, a bright but thinly-built form of I. sibirica, though only springing from the earth on a stem of four or five inches. At least so it looks : but that stem is a delusion ; the bloom of I. tenuifolia, in fact, not only has no stem at all, but actually begins underground. All that you see is its throat and its style : the ovary lurks half an inch below the soil, embedded tightly in the hassock. If you quarry with a penknife, you can enucleate the pods not only of last year, but of many bygone seasons, still lingering perfectly sound and good in the mass of the plant.

How this astonishingly inconvenient system can result in the abundance with which Iris tenuifolia is seen all over these grassy downs wherever there is no loess, I have no idea. It looks as if the plant laid itself out never to be distributed : yet distributed it is, very widely, from the remote hills of Quetta, away to these fells of farthest North-Eastern Tibet. Not only, though, does its seed take no apparent steps to get itself scattered, but it also, good and fat though it seems, has no alacrity in germinating. In

due course I collected large quantities : but not a single
seedling have I raised myself, nor have I heard of anyone
else doing so. Alas, then, for Iris tenuifolia, still uncom-
municatively blooming in little spurts of cornflower-sapphire
on the green downs of Chebson, without chick or child in
England to prove my tale of its beauty. However, for
a consolation, I do not believe that either child or chick
would have done so. For despite that massive cheerfulness
and immortality it shows round Chebson, I. tenuifolia proves
to have no generous nature. There exist in cultivation two
small plants, from its Quetta kingdom : and these sulk
obstinately and wholly refuse to make headway, never
grow, never thrive, never increase, never flower.

Below the ·Abbey the right-hand horn of the enclosing
down is bare and voluminous and green as Wiltshire, with
white Chortens perched in its flanks, but never the trace
of a tree. On the left side, however, up each successive
groove of the high hill-side, the grass gives way to a dwarfish
moorland scrub of Potentilla, and then to a more or less
wretched streak of spruce-wood, which at the top coalesces
into a small forest close and dense and pitch-dark inside,
with an undergrowth of the stark and spiny drum-shaped
gooseberry throughout. I hoped from afar for flowers,
and mounted the slope. Immediately I drew near the
Potentilla heath it became alive, all over the hill-side, with
big hares loping and leaping in all directions, with rather
long black tails, heavily outlined with white, sticking out
straight behind them as they ran. And in the dumpy
Potentillas themselves the azure-blue Corydalis peered
forth, in glints of turquoise. The elusiveness of love is
nothing compared to that of Corydalis. I made the most
solemn vows and vigils to get seed of this lovely C. curviflora,
and of the almost unbelievably beautiful C. melanochlora :
but never once could I catch the propitious moment as it
flew. Come too early, and the pods are hard and green :
turn away your head to sneeze, and, when you next look,
the pod has burst open like a popgun, and shot out all its

little glossy black bullets far and wide. You have to wait upon a Corydal as a gourmet waits upon the ripening of his pheasant : with the further disadvantage that, whereas the pheasant, when it has fallen off its tail, lies inert on the floor, the corydal-seed, in the twinkle of an eye, is over the hills and far away.

On the cooler side of the fold there was now the woodland, scurvily beginning, and in its lower reaches cruelly cut. Moss and promise filled it, and a fat Primula unfolding like a cabbage. But all was still so wintry and unrevealed that I could well believe the aneroid was right in putting Chebson at almost the same height as Wolvesden. And the Primula was clearly only going to be P. tangutica, an entirely contemptible plant, rank and robustious in growth, mean and squinny in flower, muddy and morbid in the dull chocolates and greens of its colouring, even when you get the very best forms, where the livid greenish-yellow of the starved-looking star stands out in good contrast to the mahogany-crimson of the tube. Nor did I find hope of anything better, though by degrees I thoroughly ransacked each groove of the hill-side, and the moorlands and forest-fringes along its crest, from which, on the one hand, you look down upon the Abbey with four big white Chortens sitting in a row at its lower end as a sort of entrance-gate, and other Chortens lodged here and there on the verdure of the enveloping hill-sides : and on the other, out over the delta-plain, sweeping round below like a great sea, into which Chebson fell stands out and sinks, like an enormous cloven promontory with a chine in the middle. But Chebson is too far from the Alps, in fact, for a rich or an Alpine flora.

The brooding calm broke in storms, and the weather turned clear and cold, with new snow on all the peaks. I took an early opportunity of going up into their immediate roots. Attended by Mafu and Wa-wa, I rode over the saddle above the Abbey, and down into the delta-plain, and up its enormous vista, towards the distant disgorgement between the hills, that never seemed to come any nearer. Miles wide and miles long, the delta is flat as a frozen sea, one unbroken sheet of moorland pasture.   Here and there, on its vast face, we passed various encampments of nomads, and their dark round yurts (yurt is the mongol tent, a drum-shaped affair), with herds of cattle at pasture.   This they take by stints and stretches : different families have different " gaits " : when one is finished with, the tents are struck and the clan and all their kine come farther down the plain to another.   Higher up, we now entered at last into the hills, and found ourselves in a deep narrow glen, squeezed closely in between bare grassy bulwarks of mountain, so topless and enormous that they seemed positively to bulge over above us on either hand, holding the ghyll in a breathless grip.   Right away ahead, between more moorland masses, loomed a distance of jagged white peaks ; the glen bottom was a flat stretch of tussocky marsh, threaded by clear runnels and pools from the main beck : and on its far side, a deep steep ghyll towered up in the face of the right-hand fell.   Everything here, in the beginning of June, at some 12,000 ft., was still as dead and sere and pallid as you would find them at the same date upon Moncenisio at 7,000.   But though the rise from Chebson had been so smooth and gradual as really to be imperceptible a very genuine rise it had been.   We could judge of it better now, looking back over the delta, to where the spur of Chebson dwindled down into the distance, like a ship hull-down over the rim of the sea.   And we could judge of it as well by other evidence nearer at hand.

For now that we were in the gorge the vegetation was at once perfectly Alpine, and all the three poppies, unknown round Chebson, immediately reappeared.   There in the bushy bog-hummocks flared the lemony orbs of the Lamp-shade, the Harebell was pushing buds of green from the brown pats of sodden silky mess, and in the shingles were showing the thorny grey leaves and black-dead seed-spires of the Celestial.   At least, I hoped that this time the prevalent thorny Poppy of these parts might mark a change, and that here we might at last be coming on Meconopsis racemosa. I had a reason for my hope. The original specimen of all on which the description of Meconopsis racemosa as a species was built, is one of Przewalsky's collecting, and is said to bear " Chebson " on its label. Now, round Chebson itself clearly there was no Poppy of the Celestial group : therefore it seemed reasonable to suppose, on finding one of the group in the Alps behind, that this must be the missing M. racemosa—which I will hence-forth be familiar with as the sapphire Poppy, seeing that, while M. Prattii has blossoms of clear light blue with creamy-drab anthers, M. racemosa tends to a deeper tone, with orange anthers gorgeously contrasting. It is in fact, if our present knowledge about the original description of type-specimens be adequate, a mere variety of M. horridula, which has a special habit of often sending up its flowers, not in a spire, but each on what looks like a single stem of its own, all these "stems" springing at once from the base. The true spire is as it were squashed down and telescoped under ground, so that its feet stalks have to come up in a fountain, each apparently independent of the rest, even as the common Primrose seems to carry its flowers separately, while all the time the common stem which holds them all together is hidden safely below stairs. When the stem lengthens and becomes apparent, the primrose becomes a Polyanthus : so, in the same way, when Meconopsis horridula (which is the real species) sends up a spike, it becomes the racemose variety ; and, M. horridula racemosa, when it gives way to its odd habit of obliterating the spike and flowering altogether from the base, passes back towards M. horridula in a manner quite unknown to M. Prattii, which in some forms has very long strict footstalks, and, in some, quite short ones, making a mace-like effect instead of an airy spire, but never, by any chance that I have seen in many myriads of specimens, suppresses the main stem altogether, though in the Ardjeri Alps it does, very rarely, send up such a number of basal scapes as almost or wholly to obliterate the central one.

Let us not, however, anticipate. For dead winter still ruled in these depths, and vegetation was so little advanced as to give no hint of the glories it would probably unfold by late July. Across the beck I splashed and plunged, and up into the riven mountain-side above its far bank. Here another tiny rill came dancing and bubbling darkly down to join it, between the pale brown turfy hassocks that overhung it, in which the Globeflower was already just beginning to unfold, in little stemless clusters of huge golden buttercups, huddling close as yet into the pallid deadness of the turf, on which they flared like dropped splashes of sunshine. Of other life there was none, though, as I climbed the steep of the ghyll's cold Northern face, I found it all a soggy wall of deep ancient moss masses, ice-cold and indeed half ice, in which the roots and branches of the Little Rhododendron straggled and sprawled. And here the whole mountain-side was curtained with cushions of the harebell Poppy, coagulated so abundantly in every moss-fall as to show me not only that here, in the Da-Tung, we have the very central point of the plant, but also that, above all other Meconopsids, it thirsts for moisture and abundantly repays it.

I clambered high upon the fell-side, to where the ghyll died out into the vastness of the open moor above : but clearly there was no use in exploring any farther as yet. So round the bay of the hill I made my way, and down under hot little cliffs that impended over the sunny Southward slope. But even here there were only old friends— Lloydia still in being the Lavender Primula, and Androsace tibetica only just beginning to open her eyes. So back I came into the marish flat below, and thence, after a snack, homeward down the delta again, pursued by sleet-storms out of the violated angry mountains, sent after us on the wings of a wind as cold and keen as winter.

And on the way we met with a wee woolly white yak-let, no bigger than a lamb, who took so violent a fancy to us, that nothing could prevent him from adding himself to our company. We could not beat him away or throw stones at him, he was such an innocent little engaging beast, with his bulging black eyes full of a naïve enthusiasm, and the glossy blackness of his cold nose, and the curly white of his coat, and the endearing knock-kneed awkwardness of his amblings and plungings. Yet desist from us he would not, despite our persuasions : if we stopped, nothing would induce him to go home : if we put our ponies to a canter to get away from him, he cantered and galloped also, among our cantering hoofs, and death bade fair to be his portion. And already, from the yurts now diminishing to pinheads up the distance, faint howls began to come floating, and the baying of dogs : though it is as well to be hung for a sheep as a lamb, it is no part of prudence to reverse the process. If we *were* to die the death for cattle-lifting on a Tibetan moorland, it seemed absurd to do it for so minute an object. So I detailed Wa-wa to sit down firmly, with the yak-let in his arms, and there hold him until the ponies should be well away beyond reach of his wambling little legs. And away we rode : when I looked back Wa-wa was making a perfect Academy picture, kneeling down strenuously embracing the reluctant yak-let in both arms. It only wanted " Tronger zan 'oo " or " Tuggy-Tug " or " Pitty Ickle " or some similar touch of domestic pathos, by way of a title, to qualify immediately for a Christmas Number. But all the time the baby yak was refusing to play up, straining wildly to be after us and sending despairing bleats down the distance, derelict like Dido.

However, his self-immolated phantom did not come gloomily to meet me, when under the deepening grey lid of the afternoon, increasingly cold and bleak, I rode down the vacant streets of Chebson, and up into the outer stable-yard of the cloister, where, on the roof of the inner gateway, a big black hound, perpetually chained, so fearfully bayed and bounded and clanked and strained against his bonds at every entrance into the yard, that I was always glad to be safe under that perilous portal, and inside the vast tranquillity of the cloister.

Mafu now rode out again, down the lower plain towards the defile between the two great hogs' backs, on the chance of meeting Bill returning, while I myself sat out in the noble façade of the upper cloister that faces down upon the lower, to watch in awe-stricken delight the magnificent storms that were brewing up across the South. Such splendours, terrible in gloom and violence, always make one think of God or gods : a lingering relic in us of the Cave-period, when all these huge and inexplicable terrors of Nature had to be given an explanation in some personal source that could be propitiated. To this day, sunny skies and smooth prosperous scenes arouse no specifically " religious " feeling in any normal mind (I exclude, of course, the Saint, who is very far above the normal : and also the professionally devout, almost as far below it) ; amid typhoons and tempests and the titanic terrors of Nature alone it is, by the released furies of fire, earth, air and water, that the God-notion re-awakens in us out of the irrecoverable past. The inner-most mind of man, in fact, takes joy for granted, but fear is its god. Worship is no appreciation of the pleasant, but deprecation of its reverse.

Upon these exalted meditations there now advanced two stately figures that immediately dispelled them—a notable husband and wife, Prince and Princess of their tribe, swinging up the causeway of the lower cloister from their devotions in the big church. They were six foot tall at least, the pair of them, and with that sumptuous Red Indian handsomeness, hard and high, which so plainly gives away the provenance of the Red Indians themselves : on their heads were huge turbaned coils of woolstrands, and they moved majestically in long coats of scarlet lined with sheepskin, upon the breast of which hung square silver reliquaries of special size. And then " When these had gone by with their splendours " what rested to me then, and remained, was the return, before dark, of Mafu, without Bill, indeed, but bearing a big bale of flowers.

Most of these, indeed, were comparatively uninteresting pink peonies and barberries : but out of the bundle at last unfolded a bunch of something so beautiful that it made me jump. An Isopyrum—but what an Isopyrum ! All the previous season I had been moving under limestone cliffs, hung with wide grey maidenhair cushions of I. grandiflorum, besprent with big golden-hearted wood anemones of white or palest skim-milk blue. And all that season, beautiful as I. grandiflorum certainly ·was, I kept wondering over the shouts of ecstasy that it had aroused in previous collectors. It seemed a lovely thing enough, but not really anything to lie awake at night about. And now there turned up unbeknownst, in Mafu's anthropoid fist, an Isopyrum that simply sent grandiflorum supperless to bed—with foliage larger and more voluminous, like a much handsomer sea-blue maidenhair, from out of which came dancing great silken blossoms of sheeny lavender purple, like some glorified anemone nemorosa Allenii, with a fluff of golden stamens at their heart, and five orange-coloured nectaries set round. If that other pretty thing, anæmic and pale, was indeed I. grandiflorum, what then was this full-blooded noble beauty of twice the size ? And how could any other Isopyrum be called " grandiflorum " with this one in existence ?

Throughout the season I doubted if I might not have misplaced the names, especially as I remembered how Mr. Elwes had told me of a lovely purple Isopyrum yet farther North in the Altai : indeed, it was not till the first *Eaves of the World* was passing its final proofs for publication that at last, in 1917, I learned that the Da-Tung Isopyrum was not, as I had modestly called it, I. grandiflorum, but a brand-new species, in whose beauty my own mortal name was to be immortalized. For indeed, I. Farreri leaves I. grandiflorum away out of sight—an introduction so important, so vigorous, hearty and superb, that in itself it would have been well worth the whole year's expedition. At the time, though, I knew nothing of all this : even so, nothing would serve me but to ride off immediately through the night, or at crash of the next dawn, to see where Mafu had first seen this marvel, hanging from a cliff in the defile between the hogs' backs. But Mafu restrained me, and on the morrow the beauty of the flowers themselves decoyed me into sitting down to paint them : and then Bill returned, successfully relieved of the tooth, and laden with a present of blue-ribboned sailor-hats for the servants : and the Prior took poorly and lay groaning upon the Kang[1] in his dark venerable quarters across the yard from ours, inviting us urgently to massage him. So that, amid these distractions, I never got down to the first home of the Isopyrum, but lived, instead, in lawful hope of seeing it often up in the Alps.

[1] You remember : the hollow bed-platform of every Chinese and Sino-Tibetan house, which is kept stoked up, like a stove.

CHAPTER X

HOME AGAIN

In the meantime the Prior's symptoms yielded perceptibly to Chartreuse : though even under this treatment I must confess that they recurred, and clamoured for repetitions of the cure. So that we took an early opportunity of telling the holy man he was well again ; and, to be certain that he should stay so, made preparations for a speedy removal of ourselves and our bottle back to Wolvesden. And, after all, the old man was not there to see us off. It turned out that he had had to go down to another Prior, who lay in such extremity of sickness that it had not been thought worth while to worry Bill for medical advice. And now, the sick man lay dying, the Living Buddha had gone down to him in state, to give him the last consolations of the Church, in presence of the abbot and the other high ecclesiastics of the place. So that with our Prior we had no word of Au revoir, and even with his deputy there were difficulties. We had settled up all our dues for fodder and provender—these being all they let a visitor pay for, lodging, in these holy places, being free—when out came the sub-prior again from his room, staggering beneath a burden of perforated pence on strings. We were not only to go away as grateful guests, it seemed, but the European practice was to be reversed, and we were to go away heavily tipped into the bargain. Proper pride, as well as improper, startled a little at the notion : also one felt that the indignity—so to call it—might be fraught with danger, supposing the tale spread and ulti- mately came within reach of the scandal that breeds like maggots in the mission stations. Taking bribes and robbing the country would be mild terms. However, there was nothing for it, unless we were to affront the Abbey and hurt the feelings of our hosts. So the long strings of copper-sausages—amounting to perhaps half a crown in total value—were slung across one of the mules, and, with deep bows of gratitude, we rode out of the yard, attended by our train wearing their new blue-lined and blue-ribboned sailor-hats from Sining, all rather small in the head and rather short in the brim. We felt as if we were taking out the school or the choir on treat to the Crystal Palace.

Out across the delta we rode, and then past the yak-dung factory, away South-Eastwards, over swards of finest lawn all jewelled in the clear sunlight with constellations of the little skim-milk gentian, like some small Cerastium close into the turf. It was an astonishing thing, too, to notice now, in every cultivated place, the eruption of Scopolia tangutica. This already challenged our notice on the last stage into Chebson, but by this time it was much more evident everywhere. For its cabbagy noses first break the soil asunder in great clods, just as Eremurus thrusts up the solid earth in a fractured star like a stone sent through plate-glass ; and then up its lucent masses come huddling, almost as you watch, like some uncanny green gnome popping up from the cellars of the world. From this, however, it in time develops a stature, ample and even coarse, of two or three feet, with coarse ample foliage of vivid green, and large urn-shaped capsules : but in spring it squats close to the soil, unfurling immediately among the huddled volume of its leaves the enormous bells of its blossom, luridly brown and green. This sinister plant is, like the nettle, a persistent follower of man ; rarely will you see it far from a farmyard or a paddock ; and it even ascends as high into the Alps as Wolvesden House, and the slopes of Southerly Valley up behind, on the way to Grandmamma Aoo.

Then, through the mouldering boundary wall of China and Tibet, we rode down into the next plain, which, being Chinese, was cultivated to the last inch ; and South till we

were within some five miles of Officialton. And now we
kept away to the left South-Easterly, over more ridges and
intervening flats, all barefaced and open as a German lie,
till a penultimate rise brought us up once more close under
the Alps, whose course we had so long been following. And
very magnificent now loomed their complicated procession
upon the left, swept from time to time by violent sleet-
storms, while all the rest of the world was in brilliant sun.

From the col the backward view was very Cumbrian
and wide—far and far over the unfolded undulations, to
where, out against the Western sky, the long hog's back of
Chebson Down rolled in diaphanous purple. From this
point we had a very steep drop, over a curious bare slope
wildly corrugated into rents and hollows and ridges, down
into yet another river-vale, but narrower than its predecessors (being nearer to its beginnings), hand-flat as they,
and heavily cultivated too, but also rich with avenues and
woodlands of the white-stemmed poplar.

Indeed, all along this country they are trying both to
bind the barren slopes and shade the torrid ways by sticking
in bare poles of the poplar, straight sticks like walking-sticks,
with a blob of clay on the top. No further care is taken,
either in planting or in tending : but if fortune favours,
these dead staves bud and burst like Tannhauser's, and in a
few seasons the face of this bare land may be as beneficially
changed as that of Hsin Jang, the New Province of
Turkestan, up in the North, once as forlorn a wilderness of
sand and death as that which now mummifies the glories of
Turfan and Khotan—until a Chinese Viceroy took the
problem in hand, and by prudent and persistent planting
has, in half a century, so wholly changed the climate and
condition of things that the former desert now blossoms as
the rose and produces crops and fruits incredible before,
including the finest raisins in the world.

But now we had really come to the last breakwater-spur
of the foothills, and on its other side rode gently down into
Weston-of-the-Pass, which we had left on one side of us

when first we rode up into the Alps. Weston is a poor little place, straggling along the flank of the spur with the moorland green of the delta below ; and moorland slopes of green come sloping down into this on the left, from the gleaming crags and gaunt precipices of the Alps, whose chines and ghylls now tower up overhead. The houses in Weston are neat and clean and square as a rule, carved and moulded out of the clean loess : and on their walls round plaques of yak-dung are plastered in rows to dry for fuel, and on their roofs, and on ledges cut in the little bluffs of loess cliff from which they are built out (and into which their cellars and stables and store-rooms are hollowed), little gardens of flowers glow daily with Iceland Poppy and China Aster. It is a haunt of the Turen, too, and in its lanes you may often come upon some of those fantastically splendid ladies, in their panoply of plaqued stoles and silver chains and enormous heart-shaped blue head-dresses, valanced with red fringe. But if you turn the camera upon them, they flee at once, with loud squawks of mingled laughter and terror.

The house to which we ourselves went was, however, the smallest and poorest of all, but belonged to an especially friendly host whom Bill had discovered on a previous visit. The House of Many Babies consists only of a small muddy yard with a flagstaff on the middle. There is a stable on one side and miserable ramshackle sheds down the other, and, at the top, a block of three rooms, with a door from the central one upon the raised verandah. Yet here, in the peace and happiness of perfect hugger-mugger the proprietor pigs it with a huge wife, various slatternly stray females, twelve children, three daughters-in-law (including an enormous hodge of a woman who is wife to his boy of thirteen), a prehistoric-looking grandfather of ninety-eight, like a piece of grimy old ivory, and a wee Hampdenshire Wonder runt, with nothing of a body, and tiniest pipe-stem limbs, but a head as noble and large and wise as a Buddha's, with Buddha's calm solemn eyes of endurance and understanding. Add to this population a whole other one of pigs, hens,

N

yapping dogs, donkies, a cat, and a pet lamb, and you may well wonder at the elasticity of the House of Many Babies in being able also to put up our whole party, of nine people, six horses and two asses. Shake down, however, we all at last did : but it was a tight fit. Bill went behind, and laired in the hayloft carved in the cliff ; and even the cat had to go to bed on top of the pigs, moulding for herself a hollow in the heaving fatness of their black backs, as they lay piled upon each other in their loess kennel.

But the House of Many Babies was a pleasant place. A general friendliness pervaded it, and you could see that it held a happy family. The babies peeped and played, and nobody scolded ; the large daughter-in-law looked dourly, but that was only because she was so very large that her face had settled heavily into the massive immobility of a dough cake. But all the other ladies were cheery, and, in particular, one whom I had looked on as a cretin (because she had a goître, and a chinless profile like a teapot, and a slavey's haycock of hair that sagged and flopped to each footstep as she bustled about), proved, on the contrary, the most alert and helpful and intelligent of them all. As for the venerable head of the whole clan, Lao Dada was now so old as to be past hearing, past sight, past understanding, past almost everything. A dim blurred consciousness of existence alone remained, and a physical satisfaction in the sunshine.

Of course, in any civilized country he would long since have been put away in the workhouse by any family of such a condition as this, so poor and populous : or harried out of life by shrewish tongues, for the sake of the bite and sup his continuance subtracted from the household resources. But these benighted barbarians have other views about the sanctity of years : and Lao Dada was being shepherded through his last feeble days with every observance and comfort that the crowded struggling family could muster. Among the vats and pans he had his Kang, in the cupboard-like store-room off the central entrance-room in the verandah

(my own bed just fitted into the opposite one, clean panelled
all round with new-looking wood, and papered with texts
and pictures of saints and Buddhas).   Here he slept, and on
a wet day or a cold one, drowsed through it in the dimness
of the tiny room : a vivacious little granddaughter of six or
seven lay there with him also, to see to his needs in the night,
and fetch him his bowlful of sop in the morning.   Then, if
the morning were sunny and fine, he would slowly rise up,
and come hirpling forth upon the verandah, supported by a
staff in one trembling old white claw, and by the small girl
on the other.   With his patient ghostly face, lined and
lifeless as a carving, and his dead pale blue eyes, and his last
white hairs gathered up into a little topknot on the crown
of his ivory skull, Lao Dada might have served for a picture
of the very spirit of old age, or of some ancient sage out
of the past incarnation of China's unnumbered æons of
wisdom.   Bit by bit, he would grope forward to where the
sun struck into the verandah, and there squat down against
a pillar-post : and so, almost without motion, sit all day
till sundown, in a fading haze of consciousness, broken only
from time to time by gentle little pale croonings to the
granddaughter, or to the other multicoloured babies now
tumbling round him at play, along with the hens and the cat
and the vociferating piglings.

But the sinking fires were not yet quite dead.   Unconscious, to all seeming, of general life, Lao Dada began
perceptibly to take notice of our arrival.   A mysterious
thrill seemed to vibrate through his abandonment : he sat
up with more of an air, turned his head this way and that,
and with his dim sunken eyes apprehended faintly the siphon
and the clock.   As for the rest of the family, it was very
merry with us : we photographed all of it, *privatim et
seriatim*, and gladdened the hearts of the little girls with
presents of scarlet cloth which, we insisted, were to be for
them, and for them alone, instead of being diverted to the
use of the already sufficiently spoiled little boys, as we know
they certainly would be, unless we definitely forbade.   And

so we retired at last to a happy night in that happy tumbling place, and rose in a radiant morning to be off on the last stage of our return to Wolvesden.

Bill had ridden out earlier still, for a copious variety of reasons, among which I was supposed not to see the only real one, which was that he wanted to go ahead and get everything comfortably arranged for me at home before I arrived there. Down into the delta I rode, and up its turfy moorland. Here I was immediately cheered by the aspect of a new little Trolius that shone here and there among the tussocks in starry sparks. For, indeed, I had expected no new flowers, and my spirits were further overlaid with gloom, to think of the correspondence now awaiting me at Wolvesden. It was long since we had had letters, and I trembled to think of the accumulations mounting up for me there all the time. Poor innocent unoffending me, what an avalanche of pent-up disasters, anguishes, and anxieties should I not have to undergo. It is, in fact, no easy thing to launch a successful letter across many miles of the world, to an addressless correspondent (at the far end of most uncertain unrealized posts), of whom you only know that he is somewhere up in the Alps of the Tibetan Border. Chit-chat dies at prospect of such a journey ; even the war, I found, instead of stimulating people to a fevered output of comment and reflexion, crushed even the most intelligent into an inarticulate dullness by the mere weight and enormousness of its horror. Of this I now quiveringly dreaded the infection that would surely envelop me at Wolvesden in its accumulated miasma : and anyhow, the gift of transmundane letter-writing is not one possessed by many except Sara Priceless—and the particular Fair One I happen to be addressing at the moment.

Meanwhile in its rare sparks the Globeflower glittered in the marish bouldered hollows among the hummocks of Potentilla—a smaller frailer thing altogether than T. pumilus, and of a paler gold. And then, in the mouth of the defile, the ivory Daphne bushes were all aglow, and in the levels

Stellera sprouted in shell-pink domes of fragrance. Whereas before, all this had been black-and-white, arctic, alpine, it was now all brown-and-green, torrid and lowland. The gorge, I could now see, is a deep cleavage between huge fantastically uptilted beds of fired conglomerate, dark and barren : the hotter moorland slopes, as we mounted its curves, were covered with a wiry little delicate bushling of silver grey, like straight sprays of some very refined hoar-frosted Rosemary, all springing together, unbranching, from the neck of the plant. What this might be I could not tell : but I had already come upon it in the shingles of Wolvesden, graceful and springy as the spirit of youth : and found that it exhaled the very scent of Lemon Verbena and Eucalyptus citriodora. Above the steep slopes there rose, on the right, high-close volumes of moorland, and on the left, cliffs over sombre cliffs towards the big peaks above. Down in the middle, among mossy boulders, the beck brabbled through golden sheets of Draba : Potentilla and Ivory Daphne sat humpily about on the unfolded lawns, and ahead, there towered out enormous cliffs and fantastic pinnacles of what looked like Dolomite.

At this my heart lightened : the appearance on the scene of limestone is always a sign of hope to the gardener, and my soul had too long sickened at the unvarying igneousness of these mountains, and the unvarying pyramidal outline of their summits that offered no prospect of anything more lively higher up. Cheerfully I ambled up the windings of the vale : true, it was not all so awfully magnificent as last time, but then it was by no means also so awfully uncomfortable. The Go-go led me carefully on a string, for when my mind is on mountains roaming far slopes after flowers, the rest of me is otherwise too much at the mercy of sudden movements, stumblings and stops on the part of that incalculable engine, the horse. Like the White Knight, I drift, and like the White Knight I have a liability to tumble out of my dreamland over the pony's head if it puts its foot into a marmot's hole.

Thus, in safe tutelage, I reached the slopes at the base of the limestone cliffs, rounded their base, and came into sight of a dark little ghyll, deep in their heart, unfolding upon a wide sweep of lawn, with big yaks feeding. And the precipices from here were fully displayed in their enormous mass, corrugated wildly, crumpled, tumbled, hideous : but rosily flushed with promise. I alighted, and made my gradual way upward over the lawn, across the beck, and up the steep rippled slope of white silt, filled with the lemon-scented silveriness, and rose red with the Androsace in between. On the pale walls overhead the Incarvillea flared in splashes of crimson, like any Peony, and at length, up above me, the faint haze of vegetation on the rock defined itself into here and there a spot of yellow, and a misty purple unseen before. And after a moment of scorn for the accustomary dinginess of Oxytropids, I realized that I had come upon a new Iris. Iris Potaninii is a queer little species. I have only seen it at this one point, squatting in tight wads of bluntish grey-green leaves on the ledges of this sunny limestone precipice, and it bears (from the same tuft, very often) flowers of clear sulphur yellow and flowers of a dull husky purple, sitting close upon the cushion. It is a true flag-Iris with golden beard, and fall tucked sharply back beneath the blossom : and wonderfully suggests I. chamæiris as you see it rambling along the ledges of S. Raphael. The purple form, indeed, is rather dim and ugly, but the clear yellow one (which is a little larger) is really attractive, when you see it in a good clump. But I am not going to pretend that Iris Potaninii is anything to write home about in red letters.

I now climbed down the bank again, this time keeping close under the cliff, till I came into the ghyll, where a small yak-byre of stone walls keeps the entrance. Into the cool obscurity of the chine I turned, up the course of the beck, where it darkly gurgled among the grimy crusts of lingering snow-pats. And in the cold shade a new pinkiness at once illumined the sombre ledges of moss and moisture. Instinctively the flower-trained eye detects a fresh note of colour,

be it near or far. There is no possibility of mistake and I
gasped for a minute in the delight of a Primula that was not
P. stenocalyx—a Primula that in another instant I recognized as P. urticæfolia. P. urticæfolia I had known of as a
peculiarity of these parts, but the Paxian description had
been so brief and pallid, and the specific name, with its
suggestion of leaves like a nettle, conjured up such a picture
of coarse rankness, that I had felt no wish to come on P.
urticæfolia at all. But here she was, beyond a doubt, and
atrociously wronged alike in description and specific name.
" Nettle leaved," indeed ! why, her foliage is so wee that
you hardly see it for the lovely great rose-pink flowers that
sit close upon it all over the tuft. And when you do see
them, they are the most dainty delicate little objects, gashed
so deep into five or seven strips that they give a fringed curly
effect of brightest green filigree, no more like the large dank
dullness of a nettle than the finest moss is comparable to a
cabbage.

The plant's real parallels are two. Far away from here,
along the high summits of Tsang Chan above Tali Lake, lives
Primula bella, in cushions of loveliness ; and much further
away yet, along the moorland ridges above the Glocknerhaus,
and all over the Southern Dolomites and Austrian Alps,
P. minima runs riot in a carpet of colour. And at first, so
vividly do the flowers and leaves of P. urticæfolia resemble
those of P. bella that one looks at once for the fuzz of white
hair in the throat that is the distinguishing mark of all the
bella group : until one realizes that memory, not imagination, can best give the match, since here is simply P. minima
come over into Asia, and got a little solider in the star and a
little more purely pink in the face. True, this is a soft and
tender plant in texture, it has a tiny stem that sometimes
bears two or three flowers on long thready footstalks of an
inch or so, and it does not run or ramp, but sits quiet in small
concise tuffets. Yet its whole effect, lying in blushing
blotches along the moss-wads of all the cool and shady alpine
cliffs of this region, wherever limestone breaks out, is just

that of a less ragged and aniline minima, as minima lies in vinous drifts along the ghyll-ledges of the Glocknerhaus. Imagine a hybrid of minima and bella, in fact, and you will have no such bad notion of the Pretty Primula—as I propose in future, more justly, to speak of P. urticæfolia.

There are no joys in life, I suppose, more restfully rapturous than the discovery of a new lovely flower. I have expatiated on this often, and will not do so here again· Embalmed in bliss, I climbed about on the ledges of the Primula, savouring the charm of it at leisure. And then pressed forward through the dark narrows of the chine, to where, beyond, it widened into a sort of cauldron, with cliffs of topless vastness impending everywhere, and two narrow gullies of precipitous grass descending into it from above, one of them bringing down the beck, and the other merely leading up over the top of the right-hand cliff, towards the moorlands overhead. All the herbage of the hills was still quite dead and pallid as in March, and no sign of life seemed to stir yet in the black-brown tracts of deep sodden moss that covered the dark slopes on either side. But the rock-face that fronted me did take the morning sun, and here, accordingly, plastered tightly into all the crevices of its overhung concavity, my Isopyrum was already unfolding its huge purple silk Anemones over the sea-blue filigree of its foliage. This was the first time of my seeing it at home : and of it I will only say that then, as ever afterwards, wherever I saw it, its beauty was so overwhelming as always to hold me spellbound in front of it, almost ill with the delight of its loveliness. Of saxatile plants, haunters of sheer cliff faces, I have known many famous beauties, and no new friend can make me disloyal to Daphne petræa in rose-pink sheets along the blank roseate frontage of the Tombea, or to the King of the Alps in silvered pin-cushions of turquoise on the black walls of Colbricon. But Isopyrum Farreri has a glory equal to theirs, and superior, if only in being different, in combining exquisite grace of foliage and habit with a sumptuousness of colour no less than theirs, to say no more.

And luckily my Isopyrum has no fads about rock in the garden, but thrives in open soil like any Anemone.

Was not this enough ? In front of the Isopyrum I said my Nunc Dimittis, and cast the wearied eye of repletion round the rest of the ghyll. What mattered those golden buttons of Globeflower here and there, and the heads of red-purple stars that Primula Woodwardii was unfolding above the pale tussocks on its eight-inch stems ? I had had my fill, and could feel no further frenzy for any such familiar fry. And in that instant, on the far bank, deep in the shadow of the cliff, where the springy floor was still black and sodden, I saw upon the darkness something new—a delicate white stem and wide ghostly bells hanging. In the calm of complete rapture, I solemnly stepped across the beck, and up to the spot where my latest treasure flickered on the gloom, amid the blue flickerings of the Lavandine Primula above it and below, and occasional furious flares of red-violet from the Imperial Primula. But here was something quite unknown, I could see at a glance, to science—a Primula in the group of P. Nivalis, with a typical nivalis neck-stock, fat and deep and tunicated as a leek's, and a big cabbage of leaves, richly green and glossy, and pure white beneath with powder. And the flowers ! On a stout white stem of six inches they unfold above the leaves, half-hanging in a bunch of half-a-dozen or so. And they are of a loveliness singular and phantasmal in their family, very large and ample and round-faced, of a faint blue lavender so subtle as to be almost a French grey, gradually suffused with a white radiation from the misty bull's-eye of intense black-purple at their throat, which continues down the tube inside and out. And their sad and startling loveliness is echoed by the keen sad sweetness of their scent. There is altogether, despite its stalwart growth and size, something ghostly and tragic about this wistful splendour, so Quakerish in its combinations of colour.

Long I knelt before that isolated specimen, adoring its perfections : then rose and swept a glance of re-awakened

keenness round the walls and floor of the ghyll, high and low.
And there, far up on impregnable ledges of the dark cliff
opposite, I now saw the pale heads of My Primula nodding,
larger and richer than in the lone stray specimen seeded down
at my feet, like phantoms in the gloom, in the cavities and
crannies, and up the inner rim of the knife edge in which the
precipice curved round over the chine.   And, as I saw it
then, so I always saw My Primula henceforward—always in
the gullies in the coldest shadiest aspects, usually on the
limestone, and always (typically) wedged fast in crevices of
the sheer cliff, so small that it seemed a miracle how the
plant could find room for its stout leek-like trunk, or nourishment for the very few thick fat roots like stiff spaghetti, that
emerge from its butt.

The geological confusion of this range is quite grotesque.
The beck-beds are all of rounded granite boulders, whose
source I never found, the base is of conglomerate as hard as
hate, black shales far overhead on the peaks suggest the coal
that the district yields, red shales suggest iron, grey shales
more granite, the main mass is purely igneous and azoic :
and then, at a wild tilt, up comes the limestone, violently
bursting aloft in gigantic reefs and spars and slanted towers
of Dolomite, on the slopes that lead up to the Pass, and the
long arête that climbs to the summit of Kerauno.   And it
is here, among the dark combes and on the cold sides of
those towers, that Primula Farreriana first shows her face ;
while here, too, and only on the limestone, with a far more
rigid preference, the Pretty Primula glows.   But Mine put
all other thoughts from my head : in " singing, dancing,
exclaiming spirits " like Emma, I scrambled out of the ghyll,
up over its buttress of cliff, on to the open moorland, and
there while Go-go and the pony, minute specks in the glen
below, advanced slowly *pari passu*, to keep level with my
adventures, I explored beck-runnel after beck-runnel in the
successive folds of the fell.

In the banks the Lavandine Primula was an almost
enraging loveliness of blue profusion, and beside the bubbling

swirls Globeflowers glowed. But otherwise there was
nothing yet alive, except that occasionally above the drab
pale deadness of the turf hassocks, sombrely flared the
intense violets of the Imperial Primula. But P. Woodwardii
of the Da-Tung differs now and then so oddly from what
seems to be the identical P. Woodwardii of the Min Sán that
Professor Balfour even dallies with the idea that they are
specifically distinct. Completely the same in every respect,
to the gardener's eye, P. Woodwardii here differs from the
completely hairless, downless and powderless P. Woodwardii
of the Min Sán, in sometimes wearing powder on its stems,
and often (if not always) having its leaves clothed in a
microscopic fur of glands that makes them dull and finely
velvety, instead of perfectly smooth and shiny. The flowers,
too, are here, as a rule, of a fiercer, hotter red-violet than
the deep imperial purples that are invariable in the Min
Sán plant. But invariable in both forms is the eye of ashen
black that forms the centre of each flower; which makes
it one of the standing miracles and problems of plant-life,
why P. Woodwardii should infallibly develop, in cultivation,
a clear eye of white round that central blackness of the
tube's throat—a development which exquisitely increases
and illuminates the loveliness of the flower, but which is
entirely unknown in the wild state—at least so far as I myself
can speak, from the hundreds upon thousands of specimens
I have seen on field or fell of the Da-Tung or the Min Sán.

And now back again to the path, over the braes and gullies,
to meet its ascending coils. Immediately overhead climbs
the pass in coils and zigzags and long ascents. Fierce and
long and high it is, but to-day all coming green and alive,
with no speck of snow remaining : a stiff toil, but without
the dark whiteness of mystery and storm that had made it
so marvellous on my first traverse. The last twenty yards
up to the actual crest are a scramble and scree of red earth
and stones. And here the whole scene was blue with the
incredible multitudes of the Lavandine Primula, glimmering
from a groundwork of the little yellow Oxygraphis, in equal

multitudes over the bare soil. But I do not much like this last. It is quite a small thing, of two or three inches, with many-rayed stars of blossom, like washed-out buttercups in colour, but tainted with the metallic greenish shrillness of Adonis. They huddle in abundance close over the tuft of fat dark-green foliage, and in the middle of each pointed narrow petal the yellow suddenly dies out into a sodden transparency which gives each round saucer of blossom the look of having a wide dusky-coloured eye. Otherwise on the crest of the pass life was still very young : the Imperial Primula and the Harebell Poppy were only just beginning to stir, and in the rocks of the arête the tight wads of Androsace mucronifolia were still like a dead rust of lichen.

Down on the far side I plunged, with the led pony stumbling cautiously behind. In no season or circumstances could one ride down the Eastern face of Wolvesden Pass, so very sheerly does the scree-like track descend what looks from above like an unnegotiable series of cliffs, between which the path has to tack to and fro in short violent zigzags, to make its way down among them at all. In the upper rocks there was no new thing : and when I came into the Rhododendron zone, and found big cool moist bluffs cushioned and pedestalled on depths of moss, the only novelty still was that same promising cushion of Porphyrion-looking saxifrage that I had seen the year before, in the topmost limestone cliffs of the Ardjeri Alps. But now it turned out to be only a most measling Kabschia, with tiny moth-eaten ragged flowers of unclean white, sitting close in the delusive prettiness of those tight tuffets of wee silver-margined rosettes. So that really there was nothing to distract me from the view in front, as downwards I plunged and scrambled by short cuts and divergations into gullies and under cliffs very superb and high ; the Omos-Thanatos mass towered ahead over the valley beneath me, filling the scene : and I could now see how this gigantic barrier deflects the Dene, which has to cut deeply round Northward to the left, beneath the cruel needle of Omos, far on high, the last outlier of the massif.

Without ill-event we reached the foot of the pass, where valleys and beck beds converge. Here I resumed the pony and went forward. And this was my first sight of the Dene by daylight. At its very head there comes down into it from the left the blind vale that is born up above between the converging screes of Kerauno and the dolomite tumbles opposite. Behind, the ridge of the pass leading up to the peak of Kerauno : in front, a huge wall of Dolomitic limestone, enclose Dolomite Valley. Never were such wild precipices, stark and perfectly naked, towering up and up, in bulges and smooth faces, and the most frantically contorted crumplings and corrugations of the strata : blankly terrible, and apparently childless, by rights, of streams, yet with deep crazy ghylls at intervals, tearing down from the cliff foot, through the high rampart of the fell in front into the floor of the valley itself.

From the junction of the two streams that meet at the Dene head, the path leaves Dolomite Valley on the left, and continues mildly along above the beck beneath the tame cypressus coppice that here clothes the lower flanks of the Dolomite range in its South-Easterly extension. And all the time the big mountains up ahead of you bulk larger and larger, like things in a nightmare, graceless but magnificently enormous heights, nameless for ever (for Chinese and Tibetans are at one, in giving no identifying names to the various peaks, fathers of thunder and terror that Chinese and Tibetans are at one in hating and dreading and only generically recognizing as far as they must), unless it be for the names by which I myself came in time to know them [1]— Omos the Ferocious, last and least of the line ; Achthos the Burdensome, Axeinos the Inhospitable, and Thanatos the King of the range, the very accumulated bones of Death

---

[1] Since I do not care to follow the fashion so prevalent among explorers, of naming new peaks after personal acquaintance: by which Kerauno, for instance, would certainly appear as " Mount Etherington-Hunnybun," after my dear old friend, " Mrs. Etherington-Hunnybun, of The Hunnybunneries, Hockley in the Hole."

himself. And behind us now, aspiring high, but not so high, the two horns of the Pass-ridge, profiled aloft in the blue— Kelaino the Dark and dull, and pale Kerauno, the home of Lightning, standing out over the lowlands, the advance-guard of the mountains.

Now there is a fording of the stream to its other side, where the most trying stretch of the Upper Dene 'begins. This is a long expanse, a series of bays, of very soggy marshy emerald turf, jewelled indeed with the bright pink prettiness of Primula Wardii, but jewelled also a great deal more densely with round granite boulders of every degree of size and unsteadiness, often piled into a solid wilderness of stone. It was this stretch that had been so cruel when traversed by night, and delusively masked by snow : even by day, how-ever, it is always a trial, and always the bit I dreaded in going up to the pass or down again. It lasts for about a mile, and every step is a torment, with the ponies scrambling and floundering and stumbling, their hoofs scrabbling and slither-ing off a smooth rock, or plunging helplessly with an unbalanced one. But at last relief is reached : an open grassy vale descends from the right along the base of the Omos-Thanatos range, from where, away up there, the Pass-ridge and the arête of Kelaino die dully and indeter-minately into other downs, away round the vale head, against the knees of the Thanatos-mass. This vale brings down a beck, in a wide tract of stones that ends the slough stretch, and on the other side yet another beck converges among shingles, from the back side of the contorted range that walls in Dolomite Valley.

So after this, though the going is still very rough and stony, it is at least firm and easy, over a long flat stretch of grey and white shingle, half overgrown by now with alder and slight willow, but also with open expanses where flowers of the Alps have seeded down, sky-blue poppies and purple Delphiniums flaring on the pallid greyness of the pebbles. But the comparatively level descent that has brought us so gradually down from the foot of the pass is soon to deepen to something more abrupt and violent. For now we are under the immediate shadow of Omos, developing overhead in slope over tremendous slope of coppice and then Rhododendron, to where you have to crane up your neck to see the fierce tooth itself looming into the air, so far aloft that you despair of ever reaching it : and the Dene accordingly has to sink down into the narrows of the gorge. Here again you ford the beck, and on the far side come upon the topmost of the mule-inns, so small and derelict a place that you would never guess it a possible place for human shelter. And from this, in deepening brushwood you descend the left bank of the beck, by now, with its various confluents, a creditable torrent : and in among the pebbles of the way sit clumped leaden-looking humps of violet leaves, illumined all over with bright golden violets that shine like sunlight in the sylvan dimness. And in the rockwalls on the left the Fairy Bell begins to swing, and round a bend of bluffs that comes next, my Isopyrum also appears in glory.

Below, on the right, the stream is roaring away down, close between cliffs and forested bluffs and boulders, in a succession of shattering ice-grey cascades hidden under the quivering green. You are deep in the throat of the Dene now, descending along the bankside through copse of briar and Ribes and Barberry, all of them spiny, and all of them ugly. In the difficult deviosities of the descent, there are crossings and re-crossings of the torrent, giddy skirtings of cliffs, and vertiginous scramblings down beneath them. More and more you feel imprisoned and shut in, sinking ever deeper in the grip of the gorge, with Omos towering more and more terribly high immediately overhead. Indeed, when the Dene has fairly swallowed you, the mountain itself passes out of sight above, leaving you to be throttled by its lowest slopes—only to reappear again lower down, where a momentary widening of the glen reveals it again, culminating the crushing mass of the woodland wall that shuts out daylight across the river. At one point, from under a cliff with such a waving purple cushion of Isopyrum as makes it

impossible to think of anything else, the horse has to make
its own sweet way accordingly, floundering breast high
through the clear foaming green of the torrent and its deep
swirls, across to a long line of limestone precipices : and on
the lower side of this projection, in the cool and the shadow,
the Pretty Primula reappears on the ledges with Isopyrum.
But almost at once we have to re-cross the stream and downwards again, on the sunnier bank, and then along the
rim, and then beneath the base, round bay after bay
of the convulsively coiling stream, under cliffs that are
igneous again, and either too low or too uninteresting for
anything but the Fairy Bell, which here swings out in
multitudes.

The gorges are nearly threaded now, and you are so deep
between the hills that there is no longer any more hope than
from Wolvesden of seeing the high tops themselves, or even
Omos, their youngest born. Here there is a bridge to cross
by, a springy span of poles and mud and brushwood ; and
then a breast of woodland and copse, sparse and dull as all
the rest, with only peonies here and there for promise : next
comes a long bay of emerald turf beside the stream, and
then you rise again, scrambling round a coppiced spur that
sweeps straight down in a taut arête-line from the mountains
up above : and dip among the Rhododendrons on the other
side, with little pale orchids peering among the mossy under-
cut at the path-side like ghosts of green-white flies, and the
Harebell Poppy beginning to flutter purple banners : and
so along with difficulty, but no variety, past the second
mule inn across the stream at the top of the widening vale
(a better place than the upper one, but not a Ritz) to where a
last bend brings you out into the open upper reach of the
Dene, released from the gorges. And there at the end, just
before the Dene sinks deep again into its second set of gorges,
is my own dear little house once more, just discernible as a
new-mudded flat roofline, huddled under the green tongue
of bank that sweeps out behind it from Southerly Valley :
with the white flag flickering on Hill 60 in front of it, and

the ponies grazing, and Wa-wa doing Sister Anne on Hill 60 to see if we are ever coming.

And so, a last smooth stretch through small low copse of Daphne and the purple Rhododendron, and then long open lawns, and a drop to the river, and a final fording of it, and there we are triumphantly riding over the bouldered Iris flats again to our own front door, there to be welcomed by Bill and the whole rejoicing staff, and a bale of correspondence which, like this whole memorable day itself, falsified all my dumps of the morning by containing neither dullness, empeevements nor ill news : besides bales of information about that sinister but supreme genius, who solved all the hitherto unsolved problems of murder by his brilliant new device of drowning a succession of Brides in Baths. And up behind the house the lawn level from Southerly Valley was now all a sea of golden Globeflowers like gigantic buttercups in an English field : and from the little bluff of rocks above, the Androsace floundered in cascades of round-eyed pinkness. So no wonder, with all these glories and triumphs put together, if this apical day left us both quite birdwitted with pleasure and excitement and relief, unable to settle coherently to anything, in the well-rounded completeness of our satisfaction with everything.

CHAPTER XI

SUMMER WORK

The Dene was indeed awake by now : every day the lawns round Wolvesden House, or the beck-shingles down in front of them, revealed some new flower. The little blue Rhododendron was a-bloom on the islets amid the stone tracts, and day by day the blobby whiteness of the big glossy one visibly climbed the mountain-wall of jungle opposite, like an ascending thaw. And in the swirls of the torrent, where it lashes round under the bends of the cliff, beneath a canopy of the pink-flowered Caragana's thorny arms of voluminous emerald foliage, the ice-crusts were daily diminishing to their end, so that when ice-cream was in request, Gomer now had to ride right across the torrent to the darkest lairs beneath the rocks, looking splendid as a young Centaur, as he fought the grey horse, caracoling and reneging through the deep brawls of the water.

Work, therefore, went busily, varied by photography, reading, writing, and the joys of society. For Grandmamma Aoo and her brood were constant visitors, dropping in daily with birch-bark buckets of milk, and bladders full of matured but excellent butter, of which the only doubt was whether the hairs it contained were those of yaks or of Grandmamma. She even brought her own grandmamma, the " aieule " of all the Aoo's, a twinkling little old crone, as old as the world but infinitely more cheerful. And there were casual visitors, too, dropping in on their way up or down the Pass. These were of all sorts and degrees, from small local officials and jolly coal-carriers, to a quite dotty Lama, who came capering in one morning with bell and bowl, and, having been charm-

ingly ragged by Gomer, was in course of being put out by
the two unfriendly Mahomedan soldiers, when he was rescued
by Bill, brought in and made much of, and sent at last on
his way rejoicing. The menagerie, too, kept us lively. The
six surviving hons had now entirely recovered, and proudly
pervaded the place : when a new lot arrived from over the
hills the old lot would at first have nothing to do with these
parvenus, and haughtily went out walking with the pig
instead. However, in the course of time they coalesced,
and fell to picking the Primulas in the yard, leaving the pig
to pursue, undistracted, his hopeless passion for the little
brown pony.

Wild life was also round us in abundance. I say nothing
of the fat-bodied brown moths that used to come flapping
in at night, and whizz round the little room in almost invisible
humming gyrations that destroyed all possibility of sitting
at peace : nor of how I revolted against having them seized
and cast into the stove. Birds were a pleasanter feature of
the yard : there was one in particular that rejoiced me—a
thing like a very large missel-thrush that has fallen breast
forward into a dish of raspberry ice, so that all his front was
of bland soft pink, with crimson splashes among the decent
mouse-coloured smoothness of his head and shoulders.
Then there was a pair of big brown-and-chestnut flycatchers,
who, to my delight, had a nest of babies in the roof-beam of
the stable, just above where I used to sit out in the shadow to
paint my flowers. The morning being favourable, and the
flower alluring, forth I would sally into the little shingled
yard. "One bowl water, two plates," was the cry : forth
came the Wa-wa running with the required paraphernalia,
to set out chair and table beneath the eaves of the arcade,
just out of the direct sunlight, close beside the little garden
patch we had made, with sand and soil from the river-bed,
on the hard floor of the yard, to grow specimens of special
plants on and ripen their seed, and gauge, too, from this, when
they should be ripening overhead on the mountains. So
there, when I had got the table at last as level as it would go

and propped up with pebbles from wobbling, I sat at work :
and above, in the eaves, Mr. and Mrs. Flycatcher whizzed
and whirred and chittered, coming and going perpetually,
with a constant supply of flies and moths for the babies.

Until, on a sad day, the babies having grown older, the
servants thought it would amuse me to have them more
securely under observation, so removed them from the nest,
all four of them, and hung them up in the same place in a
box, with a mesh of string across its open frontage. All
seemed quite happy and prosperous ; the servants were
pleased and I was pleased, and even the imprisoned family
and its parents seemed pleased. And Mr. and Mrs. Flycatcher showed no remission of zeal in feeding their children :
constantly hovering, in a twittering poise of wings, in front
of the cage, administering dainties to clamorous little open
beaks. But one morning a tragedy appeared. Three of
the fledgelings still perked and gaped, but at the bottom of
the cage the fourth lay stark, completely bald in the head,
but otherwise without sign of hurt. The death I deplored,
the baldness I pondered. What could be the cause of this
mortal mange ? More days went by, though, and a few
mornings later I became aware that yet another of the
captives was looking rather lethargic, and on closer inspection
was found to be developing the fatal baldness. Appalled, I
set myself to watch, and the yet more appalling truth was
gradually revealed. Under cover of bringing nourishment,
the parent birds were pecking their babies to death, one by
one, to save them from the horrors of captivity.

In a passion of remorse I seized my scissors, and cut away
the string-mesh, and shook the prisoners out of their box.
Tailless, fat and unfledged, they floundered to the earth ;
and I then had new remorses that their tardy release had
only landed them helpless within reach of the rats. However, they hopped about, and soon perked up, and preened
themselves, and finally disappeared ; to be discovered a few
days later, sitting on logs and tree trunks, and so diligently
absorbing the victims that their parents now brought them

with redoubled zeal that they swelled visibly, and sprouted feathers as vigorously as the Press sprouts rumours. My reward was complete when, about a week later I met one of my late guests sitting on a beam, the picture of prosperity : he cheeped at me cheerfully in recognition, and then flew away, as strong on the wing as any scandal.

Not that rats were the worst of our neighbours by way of *feræ naturæ.* All round the house those fearsome marmots sat up and squeaked and scuttled, hardly now condescending to avoid as one passed by. And there was always something sinister about their cod-fish expression of pursy self-importance. But I wondered all the while about the name of the Valley. There were the Rocks all right, unmistakable and abundant : but where were the Wolves ? The whole place seemed peaceful as a parsonage without the parson. But one wet day, as I sat over a book in the gloaming of my little room, I heard a mighty scatteration, and on coming out into the yard, saw that all the local flocks of sheep and goats had come pouring down over the bluff above in a unanimous cataract of confusion, out of the cypress coppice higher up. Evidently there had been an alarm. I could discern no cause for it, however, and no result, until I noticed one poor little goat, who seemed to ail : and on studying him through the glasses, found that his paunch was bitten out, and hanging. A wolf, big and grey and bushy-tailed, had leapt down upon that placid flock as it browsed among the bushes : and the valley was justified of its name. Excitement raged among the staff : in uncomplaining meekness the little goat stood and then lay, impeded by his paunch from movement, and disarranged for feeding. And the rest continued chumping unperturbed, having by now forgotten all about wolves and the misfortune of their fellow. But I could not bear it, and sent forth the Sa-wa Wa-wa. With all the unholy glee of his age and creed and kind, he shinned up the impending bluff, and knelt upon the little goat and slit its weazand.

Southerly Valley was now a floor of golden Globeflowers, with rare great ragged violet asters here and there, and the

pink-faced blandness of Primulas beside the beck.   We made
(but without a barouche landau) exploring parties up its
various divergencies towards the high tops above.   The
lower reaches are all of green soft sward and flowers, blobbed
with occasional bushes of the ivory daphne.   And so it very
gradually mounts, so gently that you hardly know it, but
that Wolvesden and the Dene are suddenly seen to have
sunk down out of sight, and the Buttress over them to have
dwindled to a mere detail in the unfolded rampart of Crest
Royal, far overhead.   On either side are arid cliffs containing
nothing of merit, that sink starkly out of the cypress coppice,
and then degringolate down towards the valley in long
slides of barren scree, fringed with copse of briar and barberry round the curve of their base, where they die out in a
grassy moundage with the big pale aconite towering among
the tumbles in sumptuous and sickly-coloured evilness.
Then, as the valley climbs and narrows, the beck has to be
crossed and re-crossed : and on its right flank, among the
boscage, which now begins to be of Rhododendron, the Harebell Poppy takes charge, and all the slope flickers with its
lavender butterflies, coyly peering.   The lawns in the groove
grow clouded with coppice as one climbs, and backward the
view is now stupefyingly enormous, up to the gigantic heights
of Crest Royal, with the big peaks still only peering over,
and Wolvesden quite lost to view beneath your feet.   Copse
and lawn now alternate : there are climbs and dips in the
beck bed.   Down from the right a tributary glen converges
through woodland almost at a right angle, round the
flank of the projecting needle from the range behind, so high
that you can no longer see its top.   But higher yet is the
wall of slope and scree and cliff that is now revealed above
the tributary valley, bare and open and vast, until it dies
into the fur of the forest beneath.   But our own way lies
straight ahead, up into an evident gorge, beyond a wide lawn
and a confusion of coppice.   And here, among her green
paddocks, sits Grandmamma Aoo, with her flocks and her
herds and her kindred.

So here we paused, to pass the time of day.   Forth from under the low sagging roof of the dark yak-hair tent came the Matriarch, and beamed upon us, and warned us of supernatural wonders up above.   But we proceeded undeterred, up into what soon became a narrow steep gorge of shade and moisture, with limestone cliffs on which the pinkness of the Pretty Primula shone abundant, amid the blue heads of the Lavandine along the ledges, very lovely, with huge masses of Isopyrum, promising profusely but not yet out.   Above the shingled damp of the chine the valley becomes a dull and rather ugly trough of shallowing moorland, humpy with Potentilla scrub and with ragged cypress coppice still persisting here and there on the little bluffs to the right.   At this point Grandmamma Aoo has a summer steading of two or three lean-to shacks built of poles plastered over with yak-dung, and now all grass-grown and green with age, where she herself or some of her descendants come up in August to pasture the kine on the upper alps.   Now it was all forlorn and desolate and dank : at this height the moorland was still dead and pale.

And here there darkened upon us a weight of cloud, which soon developed into violent thunder and a passion of whipping sleet that ere long quieted into a soft and passionless fall of big-flaked snow.   Under a bluff we cowered for shelter (we were high above the last of the Aoo chalets by now) and the boys characteristically achieved a fire with torn trunks of the cypress.   Up against the face of the rock the smoke went surging in stormy yellow coils, and down upon it, dark against the universal pallor overhead, the snowflakes sank in steady multitudes.   The fire kept life and warmth in us amid the arctic winter in which we were now enshrouded : but the world was clean blotted out in iron darkness.   And then the storm began to pass.   Insensibly the world reappeared : the foreground, the voor groove of the moor, its succession of little bluffs, answering each other on either side, and then, far away below, the sullen green fur of the forests, sinking in long slides towards its lower reaches, from the long wild

lines of pinnacle and precipice profiled pale, in the ghost-
liness of mountains seen through storm in a print of
Hiroshige. Down and down they sank, one behind another,
from their taut sweep into the invisibility of cloud on either
hand.

And the deepest depth below, where Wolvesden lay, down
out of sight and thought, was all a blank of black-violet
gloom in a solid wall, like the curtain separating stalls from
stage. But then, as we looked, a ghostly cleavage dawned
about half-way up in a blurred bar of pallor that widened and
lightened, while the darkness in the depths deepened to
midnight by comparison. And up above, so far up above
that one would never have thought of raising one's eyes so
high, the peaks of the big Alps themselves now gradually
slid into visibility, dim and faint as phantoms, and hardly
more than vapours themselves on the vaporous dark in
which they insensibly dawned behind dense veils of driving
rain. And now, in front of that grim phantasmagoria of
gloom, the sun came suddenly slanting across the foreground,
and the dun moorland flashed into pale fire, and the wet
bluffs shone ruddy and blue, and the gnomish little firs that
crowned them took on a flaring vividness of sun-illumined
wet against the gigantic darkness behind.

But these were the last trees, stunted almost to extinction
by their audacity in venturing so high. As soon as the
clearance was complete we emerged from our shelter and
continued up the long gully of the moorland, bare and open,
shallower and duller all the time towards the shallow col
that we could now see up ahead of us at its end. We continued very slowly, though the going was gentle and easy :
but the altitude forbids speed. Vegetation was hardly yet
at its birth : the Globeflower was only just appearing, and
otherwise there was only a profusion of the clove-scented
purple Erysimum I had first seen on the Gan-Chang pass :
and, in the dead grassy slopes, the Lampshade Poppy,
luminous in the low scant scrub, prettier than I have ever
seen it elsewhere, from the added refinement it acquires here,

by having only one or two flowers, instead of its usual plethoric profusion and its usual crude gollopshiousness of stature. Here our way was diversified, too, by what looked in the distance up ahead of us like a big pale stoat dodging among the bummocks that densely dot the moorland. And the scale of the whole scene, the size of the hillocks may be gauged from the fact that through the glasses we soon discovered our stoat to be a large silvery fox with a beautiful bushy brush. He avoided us, however, and faded unobtrusively away among the hollows. A last pull over the dells and rises of the moor, and we had attained the slack dip of the col.

On the far side it falls steep (occasionally in bluffs and cliffs) and to the very crest it is covered on its further side with thin low scrub of Potentilla and Caragana, in the topmost fringes of which the Imperial Primula stolidly loomed. On the right the moorland slope shoots higher still, in a stark sweep towards the summit overhead ; and on the left the line of the col sweeps upward too, more gradually, to lose itself in an enormous complication of alps and lawns and plateaux. And in front the view is superb, straight away out, over a lower world of tumbled valleys and hills and sharp folds of innumerable ridges and alps, to where, across the distance, tower the bald and savage corrugations, red and grey, of the wild chain of peaks along whose slopes we had climbed, on our way from Gan Chang to Chebson. And there, indeed, were the level windings of that road clearly visible, coiling like a Dolomitenstrasse in a thread of white round the flanks of the range. And it was a day of glory too, by now, to enhance the day : with the intervening depths of rich greens and blues and purples, and the far peaks very cold and clear, and overhead a wild racing sky of clouds and blue, with rolling cloud-banks about, and pale swirls of snow drifting from peak to peak in the distance.

So now we addressed ourselves to the slope on the right. It was a long heavy climb : pull over pull that seemed endless, before we reached the summit. But it was a delight-

ful pull, too, up over close moorland turf, still dead as Queen
Anne, but comfortable to the climber, with here and there a
fragrant little purple dome of Erysimum squatting tight to
its drabness. And the view widened awfully in all directions;
straight across, high over the forgotten darkness of the Dene,
rose the wall of Crest Royal, with which now we were on
such equal terms that we could see how it is only the pedestal
or outlying spur of the gigantic Alps up above, from here
expanded in all their overpowering magnificence : while
away to the right we had full command of the huge laps and
dips and shallow lake-like hollows of moorland, with which
the high tops are diversified under the summits—each one
of them looking as if it must inevitably be the home of six
new Primulas at the least.

From the crest you gaze over down into another vale, like
that by which we had come up, except that this one is much
more profound and abrupt, and deeply filled with woodland ;
under a much more wild and gigantic wall of a very much
higher mountain on the other side, tethered, from where we
stood, to the main ridge, by a wall of precipices, falling sheer,
in smooth naked bulges and faces, on either side. We did
not pursue our way forward along these, but kept to the
right now, along the arête of the spur, skirting its peaks,
and stopping often to rest on the close brown deadness,
springy and dark, and sodden, of the alpine turf, and there
scan out the dips and dishes of the uplands opposite,
mapping out expeditions, and forecasting hopes. As I lay,
my fingers strayed on a pale little thin shoot of green
straggling limp and feeble on the soggy floor of moss, from
which the snow had so lately gone that everything was still
squashed flat : " Hullo, Bill," I said, " here'll be a gentian
one of these days," and thought no more. Little did I know
of what it was I spoke so lightly : nor of the ironical contrast
between our high hopes of those dishes, and our levity with
this contemned little bird in the hand.

And now, from among enormous pinnacles and what
looked Dolomite yet was barren, we began descending to the

new glen. It was like a trackless descent of Wolvesden Pass : very far, and very steep : we zigzagged downwards through cliffs and towers outstanding like teeth from the grassy wall of the mountain-side. Overhead the sky was now coming low on us in a baldachin of darkness, heavy and solid as the murderous bed-canopy in Joseph Conrad's tale. Hardly had we reached the narrow groove of the ghyll below, when a blind white tourmente of snow swept screaming down into the glen from the ridge above. So that we were very glad to shelter here, in one of the two shallow lean-to shacks of dung-plastered poles that we happened upon, one on either side of the gorge, another alpine steading of the Aoo's, evidently. So we lingered, and lit a fire : and the world went white. Low and empty by now, too, with the long descent, we ate a snack : both my eardrums were throbbing in sharp pain, with our deep sudden drop from the heights overhead. And still the snow continued falling, steadily, passionately, yet persistently : and dusk was darkening through the storm.

We decided to run no risk of being penned up by nightfall in this unknown glen : so adventured forth into a virginal world of snow beneath the enormous blue brollies brought with us that day by the boys. These did at least shelter heads and shoulders : one's legs, anyhow, bare in their shorts, must have been whipped in a minute to ice by the frozen thorny jungles of Caragana and other snow-laden scrub, through which we now had to battle for a mile or so down the sinking groove of the valley, laboriously making steam ahead in that thigh-deep sea of dense ice-bound shrubbery. It was an unspeakably odious progress : my soul and my knee-joints wilted within me, and the umbrella grew heavy as lead. But it would have been far worse had there been wind, or a cold rain : as it was the white wet world was calm, and if you whizzed the umbrella from time to time, when it grew too weighty, its solid roof of snow would fly off in a Catherine wheel of clots and clods.

And at length, down a series of banks and coppiced drops,

we came into the main beck ghyll where all the streams of this valley-head converge, in a precipitous chine, so deep under an ancient jungle of alder and willow that beneath their interlacing and almost impenetrable shade huge old snowpats were still lying, grimy but undefeated. As we made our difficult way down the cliffs and ledges into that lovely over-arched ravine, I just had time to notice that its walls were hung with what promised to be a quite special splendour of Isopyrum, just beginning. I could only frozenly peer up at it, however, as we hurried on downwards, over a less difficult valley-stretch now, in deeper coppice, and with traces of a track. The glen was curling round the base of the high peak which ends the spur we had explored and crossed : and ere long, beneath a tall jungle, we were down once more at the top of Southerly Valley where the two branches of its Y diverge. And now all the ardours and endurances of the long day were over. There were the shanties again, and Grandmamma Aoo yodelling salutations from her midden : to the left of us, down and down, ran the delicious smooth descent of Southerly Valley, deep into the Dene. No more impenetrable scrub or difficult jungle : and no more whiteness, for the snow left off here, and none was falling anywhere by this time, and all was pale and clear and still, with the valley glistering in the wet, and pale new winter shadowy against the iron sky, on all the huge heights and masses overhead.

Selection, say the wise, is the secret of art : do not expect me to lug you out on all the expeditions involved in the exploration of such a range as the Da-Tung Alps. But, if I spare your mental legs, on your eyes I will have no mercy : no flower of any loveliness shall elude you, though the precise steps of their attainment be left a blur, from which only the more salient ascensions emerge. One of them was an expedition up to the pass, to explore the ridge away up towards Kerauno. Bill and Mâ went away ahead of me, and ere long I followed with Mafu, in a cross temper that had visibly been growing upon him these many days past. It is a tremendous long hard stretch up to the base of the pass, certainly, and then a tremendous long pull up it. Just by the topmost mule-inn I came upon Bill, engaged in photographing Isopyrum—or attempting to. But it was no use. All the blossoms hopped and danced in a saraband to every breath of air : and when, after an agelong wait, they seemed to have all subsided, one of them was always certain to start bowing and fluttering again at the last moment. So we desisted, and all proceeded onward, and up the pass. As we roamed round the giant flanks beneath the igneous arête, towards the tilted Dolomite towers beyond that make the ramparts of Kerauno, the glorious day began to grey over, and looking up, I saw a thing unknown to all my previous experiences. For there, vivid on the sullen lead-coloured zenith, flamed a perfect solar rainbow, a wide belt of prismatic splendours standing away round the sun like Saturn's rings, but much further away, with a fainter reverberation yet further still.

In the thunderous calm it seemed an omen of doom, a crucial symptom of the Last Day, now brooding down upon us in breathless livid silence. However, we maintained our course, easily and level, beneath the arête and along its convenient teeth and gendarmes, till we came to the combes and chines of moisture and cool shades that shoot up into the blind hearts of the Dolomite towers. At their feet these sink away in white scree-slopes bedizened with the Welcome Primula and Celestial Poppies, threaded by the white-starred promise of a glossy Cerastium, and by the sprawling fluffy heads of a whitish Lagotis that here replaces the blue fuzz of L. Ramalana on Thundercrown. But in the jaws of the chines themselves the shady scree is moist and fine and silty. And here there is much more wealth of beauty. For here the Lavandine Primulas' blue heads are everywhere, and the Pretty One deserts her accustomed ledges, and comes down on to the open slope, and twinkles in a tissue of rose-pink stars all over the gritty damps : while up above, in the closest crevices far up in the darkest folds of the precipices,

My Own Primula flaunts in full splendour of lavender-grey heads and glistering cabbages of white-powdered emerald foliage, often seeding down on to the cool silt of the chine-floors, where the shade is heaviest, and is so always to be seen, hugging the most umbrageous side of the most umbra geous gullies and couloirs, down under all the Dolomitic towers at this high elevation.

Go-go ran up among the cliffs like a monkey, and from unseen chinks and rill grooves in the upper precipices cast down upon me glossy bales and chunks of the stately beauty to be taken home and matured in the yard garden of Wolves-den : while I myself adored it in the shade of the ghylls, and looked reverently up to where I could see it sometimes peering over from its lodging in the crevices.

Mafu, meanwhile, was gone ahead up higher to scout for new treasures on the slopes of Kerauno. In course of time Bill and I foregathered again from our respective precipices, and began making towards the upper ones, already finding Androsace mucronifolia in sheets as yet flowerless, over the finer scree and silt-ripples of the slope, while the Pretty Primula here ventured out, undaunted and triumphant, on to the open alp. From this point I went up hand over hand, in the fold of a cliff, seeing that a rill-gully would give access to its summit, if I surmounted a lower bulge, and then traversed above a bold bare bluff. Suddenly there was a scuffle and a scuttering ; Mrs. Snowhen rose indignant from her brood, and went shambling away, with such an extra-ordinarily convincing pretence of being wounded and winged and helpless, that I stood spellbound to see her running unbelievably on her big pink feet across the blank frontage of the precipice : and meanwhile the babies improved the occasion by squatting so close that not my utmost efforts could subsequently discover them, scanning that small slope of bumpy barrenness yard by yard as I did : it was only afterward from above that Bill was able to discover them through his glasses, perking and prying for their mother again, with little cheepings.

Not for me the pathway of Mrs. Snowhen along the face of precipices. By my appointed gully I grappled my way to the cliff-top, and there found myself in a corrugation of sere alpine moorlands, reminding me of happy days on Colbricon, when the spring is barely born, and only Primula glutinosa flares violet on the pale alpine turf. Here were a succession of tip-tilted limestone ribs with gullies between, where late snow still lay : all the alp was still dun-coloured, and dead, and sodden flat with the recent departure of the rest. No flowers, therefore, either showing or discernible : but yellowed masses emerging from the darkness round the fringe of melting snowdrifts. And, on the open fell, we came upon a new Erysimum, sweet as the other, but downy, and of a rosier pinkness, and standing up on sturdy stems of three or four inches, so that its blushing tight heads were grievously like those of some new Primula from afar. In a bay of the moorland it was prettily peppered : we mounted steadily and far, over bulges and bluffs and bosses, to where, high on the flank of the upper slopes, we were heartened to see Mafu at work. But when we got there, it was only to find the worthy man gone fast asleep. This was a dereliction of duty that called for plain speaking : we administered it, and then, as life was clearly non-existent up here, began all descending again, by different directions, on our ways back to the col, and the horses, and lunch. Deep into a gully beneath a Dolomite cliff I myself diverged, and there found such beautiful abundance of my Primula as drove me almost distracted, like Lydia Bennet. So that the ultimate disaster befel me unperceived, and when, at last, after very long weariful toilings round the fell, I came back to the crest of the pass, it was to discover that my faithful trowel had somewhere eluded my vigilance, and now lay lost, like a Slaughtered Saint's Bones, somewhere on these enormous Alpine mountains cold.

This was a crushing blow. I have a cult for my collecting trowels, and set my pride in never losing them. I had brought four to China ; two had been lost, indeed (for

shame !), in the first week at Siku, but these calamities had
braced me to such a constancy of caution that both the
remaining trowels had hitherto survived all the vicissitudes
of travel.   And now it was by my own remissness that the
culminating crime had been committed.   In itself this was
a culmination : if treasures ARE to be broken or lost or
spoiled, let this, at all events, happen through some one else,
as then one can at least save something out of the wreckage
by showing oneself magnanimous, and mitigating the
matter : whereas if oneself is alone responsible, the irretrievable disaster is complicated by an irretrievable loss of
self-respect.   Even damns are too dim to illuminate the
darkness of one's wrath when oneself is the object.   So that
it was in a mood of penitential depression that at length I
found myself nearing the col.

Suddenly there was a crash overhead, a succession of
dull thuds—and a huge square black boulder like a grave-
stone came crashing and bounding down upon me from the
arête overhead, in a series of widening kangaroo leaps that
gashed and tore the hard flank of the fell as if it had been
cheese.   As I stood and pondered the matter, another
followed and another : clearly the promise of that solar
rainbow was being fulfilled, and my last day was upon me,
at the hands of the high angry Gods of these hills.   But
really—people who lose trowels, what else can they either
deserve or expect ?   In a philosophic pessimism I proceeded
across the danger stretch and the unctuous rich black gashes
in the flesh of the fell.   No more evil, however, overtook me
till I came to the col.   For now I found that Mafu's jealous
domineeringness had refused to let the Wa-wa put the tea-
ping into my saddle-bag at starting.   And so there were I,
and the arête, and all of us, as irremediably dry as any
epitome of Herbert Spencer.   Without my bottle of tea,
how were the crusts and the sausage to go down ?   Crossly I
chumped and choked : they wouldn't and didn't.   Even
more than for the trowel I wailed for my tea-ping : while
Bill gave Mafu another rough side of his tongue for such a

further instance of neglect, and Mafu went more and more blank with rage at such a stripping of his " face " before Go-go and Mâ.

However, this concatenation of calamities inspired me with such a salutary vigour of rage, that, after assimilating the unmoistened sausage, I plucked up heart to go back all along those fells again, on a vague roving quest for the trowel. It might be lying anywhere indeed on those mountain-sides : but the sausage gradually suffused me with inspiration as to one particular spot in the last of my Primula gullies where it might very possibly be. However, when, at long last, I got there, no sign of it could be seen, though all around the silt was untidy with the ruddy scatteration it had made of the rich fat earth. But, though I kicked and sifted the debris up and down, I could find no trowel, and was returning disconsolate and downcast, when there, sprawling loose at my feet upon the open moorland, far from any plants on which it could have been employed, the steely gleam of its blade caught my eye. It must have inexplicably fallen from my pocket : which blunted the acutest edge of my self-reproach. All the same, I beat myself with it severely, to inculcate caution : and then returned, in a high radiance of relief, round to the col again, to where Bill was now photographing a large group of my Primula, looking very made-up, and bedded-out, and artificial—as, indeed, it always does, though (thanks to its habit of always growing in colonies of nicely-disposed single crowns or clumps, instead of in a confusion of masses and tufts all close together) quite as much when wild in a stretch of scree, as when carefully arranged to have its portrait taken.

After which the day's toils and achievements were over. We sent the horses down the pass, while Bill and I descended the sheer steep of the mossy mountain-side, over slopes all glorious with Globeflower and Imperial Primula, and promising an equal glory of the Harebell Poppy later on. It was a far drop to the beck-shingles of the Dolomite Valley : I was glad to get down on to these, as the lower folds and

P

slopes of the descent were dense with small scrub of Potentilla and Caragana, that whipped my bare knees unmercifully
till they were red and raw.

At the foot of the pass we rejoined our mounts and
uneventfully proceeded homeward, where Bill, perpending
the day, in connection with other recent happenings, grew
more and more perturbed over the deterioration of Mafu,
who was now sulking impenetrably, dour and hideous as a
bear, and actually refusing, on two occasions, to rise from
his seat on the kang when Bill went into the kitchen. This
was really too much : strong steps were urgently indicated.
I took them, on Bill's appeal : " Robed in the awful splendour of my place, apparelled in the Godhead that I am,"
the Lord High Keeper of the King's Peace, Law-and-order
incarnate, rose up in person and stalked across the yard into
the smoky dark of the kitchen, where the staff sat *accroupi*
in various corners of the kang, and there, in level tones,
standing stiff as a graven image, addressed Mafu in a few
well-chosen sentences, and then avoided, with majestic
rapidity, before any reply was possible. But this august
intervention had all its intended effect : by such a rebuke
from the supreme head, administered *coram populo*, Mafu's
face was wholly skinned from him, and he went thence-
forward lowly as a lamb, with no more sulkings or neglects.

Days passed now, in minor expeditions, and achieving of
photographs. The Isopyrum, up in the ghyll of the right-
hand gorge above Casa Aoo, was in beauty almost unbelievable, and after cat-and-mouse waitings through several
hours, at last gave us flashes of quiet for photography, with
all its lovely dodder-headed blossoms unanimously still for
the flicker of an eyelid. And then we judged it time to
adventure up on to the main Alps above, where summer must
surely be ripening, as every day the blobbed whiteness of
the Rhododendron climbed higher on the forest wall overhead. In much jollity we set forth, very early of a filmy
grey morning, with all the staff in high spirits, recent rows
having quite cleared the air, and Mafu's repentance being

abundantly evident, not in words indeed, but in extra pro-
venances, and general docility.

Him we did not take, however, but our happy band
consisted of the two soldiers, the two Wa-wa's, Lay-gor,
Go-go and Gomer. Up the long bays of Wolfstone Dene
the procession wound, till it came to the rib that descends
from the Omos massif at the turn of the vale, by the second
inn. Here we dismounted, and home went the horses.
First of all we had a steep high hummock to mount, where
the Butterfly Iris flickered blue in the barer places, but not
in the barest of all, at the top, where the barren climb was
like some steep of the Esterel. But then we struck the
arête of the spur itself, and after that our toil was only
diversified delight. For this arête is like a taut cord, strung
between the depths of the Dene and the vast heights above.
At a swinging swoop it mounts, over teeth, and bluffs, and
serrations and gendarmes. Some of them you climb;
others you circumvent, and across the face of others you
boldly clamber : all the way there is a faint hunters' track
to guide you, and though the climb is unrelenting and
tremendous, yet it is so interesting at every yard, so full of
incident, that the toil of it is unfelt, and the heights you are
so quickly gaining pass unnoticed, unless on some upstanding
bluff you lie down to pant, among the voluminous thorny
branches of the pink Caragana, and see the Dene itself
dwindled to a mere groove beneath the flowing skirts of the
coppice below, and Wolvesden House a mere brown point
in its green lawns. We proceeded easily and delightfully
upward, over the craggy steeps and the easies in between :
till at last, before we dared hope it, we were actually at the
top of the rib, close under the snow-streaked enormous
Buttress that impends so impregnable over Wolvesden, and
on a level with the big snow gully on its right, that can barely
be discerned from below. But this is like a petty glacier,
filling the dip from which a beck descends under cliffs out of
a dish of lawn which is the highland Alp. As soon as you
have arduously toiled up, through thin copse of Rhododen-

dron, along the flank of the Buttress, you find yourself in the upper level, with the height of Crest Royal now fully revealed ahead of you, far above the puny brow of the Buttress, out on the left, with a huge insignificant spur sweeping round from it to the right, from the yet higher masses that loom over its beginning, to fold the upland vale deep in its embrace.

Go-go and Gomer went straight ahead for Crest Royal, up the cliffs of the Buttress by various directions. The rest of us having breasted the Rhododendron slope, attained the highland level and crossed its becks, through marshes filled with a curious little Allium, with few large flower-bells of pale yellow. Here we all had to have food, being so faint with mountain sickness. The dish itself was large and lovely and lush and greening ; abundant with the lovable pubent pink Erysimum, and with the Harebell Poppy already beginning to reveal its inimitable charm. But we climbed now up to the right, to the ridge of the enclosing spur ; and thence along its grassy arête, by successive steep pulls drawing nearer and nearer to the final toil up to the main massif, still bafflingly far overhead. At last we attained the foot of the bulk that dominates the vale-head, and began mounting finally, with many a stress of heart pang and burdened breathing, and many a consequent pause to ponder the incalculable huge splendour of the scene. For now we were so high that the high Alps above Casa Aoo were sunk to crumpled hills below one's vision : over which the eye ranged untrammelled across the world, to the red violence of the naked peaks above the Gan-Chang pass, and beyond even these again, to where, in the far North, huge pyramids of everlasting snow impend over Old Da-Tung. And in front of us now towered on a level with us, across a gigantic chine of scree, sinking down through coppice into the remote darkness of Wolfstone Dene, the whole bulk of Omos, seen broadside on, cruel and vast (with its dank Northerly precipices curtained in cushions of green wetness and big masses that were found through the glasses to be my

Primula)—standing out tremendous in its unsupported
isolated magnificence above the depths below : and behind,
in the distance, the ridge of the pass, and the gable of
Kerauno away up it to the right.

In the cold intervening gulf snow lay, and snow was still
cold in dying drifts on the open shoulder as we laboured up
its increasing bareness, exploring the dank mossy precipices
on either side as we mounted, but without result. These
diversify the way, though : till the last pull lugs one's leaden
legs up the nakedness of the open scree towards the bald
summit. It was all I could do to breathe now : the feat
became almost impossible to me, on perceiving at my knee a
new Primula. Alone it gleamed, one solitary spark of rosy
flame, on the dark desolation. No more could anywhere be
found, nor any other sign of life at all. But this apparition
forearmed me against the toils of the remaining fifty feet,
with hope of what we might see on emerging from the cold
sunless Northern fall of the ridge, over on to its warm
Southerly aspect. " Despair of nothing that you would
attain, Unwearied diligence your point will gain." Our
diligence was far, indeed, from being unwearied, but at length
it did attain its point, if such a name can be applied to the
round smooth dome, on the summit of which we ultimately
arrived, with other bare pyramids before us, and Crest Royal
sinking away to the left, emitting the unconsidered Buttress
from its flank : and in front, enfiladed, the line of Achthos
and Axeinos above a vast intervening sweep of Alpine lawn
down beneath our feet. It was a marvellous golden view,
straight into the heart of the Alps, with those dishes of lawn
higher and higher in their recesses, and a little ice-lake at the
top, and the jewel-green Märjelen See of the Clear Lake
refulgent among green embankments on their lower level.

For a while we wandered awe-stricken, up and down the
smooth shaly lifelessness of the summits—the Dome, the
Pyramid, and Pope's Nose with its stark canine tooth sticking up at the side. We got to the Western fall of the chain
above where the arête, at the corner, tethers Omos, like a

young puppy, to the main mass from which we now dominate him; and looked down and down, over unimaginable desolatenesses of scree and cliff, to the green fells beneath, and the greener valley at their feet, gently sinking towards the Dene; then returned to the livelier ridge of Crest Royal, where awakening Alpine turf sinks sharp towards the universal green of the great basin. And in the topmost ripples, under the rim of each tussock, the rosy little Primula was alert and smiling in the sunshine of that favoured Crest, the first corner of the high Alps to be kissed to life.

It was a most enrapturing sight, so wee, so brilliant, so endearing; but I had no hope of it as a new species, though it made up the last of the five Primulas I knew we had a right to find in the Da-Tung. P. Farreriana, and P. Wardii from the Tien Tang rills, were bonuses of the high Gods : we had already accounted for P. stenocalyx, P. tangutica, P. gemmifera and P. urticæfolia.

About P. gemmifera, indeed, a doubt still hung. All over the range abounded the lovely pink-faced Welcome Primula of 1914, to which Edinburgh had given the just name of P. acclamata; but Pax and Knuth also recorded, rather aridly, a P. gemmifera from these ranges, as being an annual, as having large pale purple flowers, and as producing bulbils. All this sounded very attractive : and might be held an admirable description of P. gemmifera, except for the trifling details that that perverse plant is not an annual, does not have pale purple flowers, and has never emitted a bulbil in her life. For when, in the course of my homeward journey, I ransacked the sheets of the Petrograd Herbarium to corroborate my Primulas, what was my horror on finding that P. gemmifera was nothing more nor less than my own beloved acclamata, softly pink, perennial and devoid of bulbils. But who could have recognized the truth under such an ill-fitting cloak of erroneous description? And, at the very same time, Edinburgh was also making the same discovery : so P. acclamata dies out of the gardener's vocabulary for ever, and the Welcome Primula must appear to him henceforth in catalogues as P. gemmifera, though certainly gemless, and as certainly a gem.

That same visit elucidated also the riddle of the Little Queen of Crest Royal. For the fifth Primula recorded by Pax and Knuth, under the very vague locality "Kansu," is P. pumilio—a very small, tufted, weak little fairy of the highest Alps, forming cushions of tiny flowers in many-blossomed heads. Now "Kansu" as a locality for any Alpine plant does not mean Kansu at all; it means Tibet— the big mountain chains up the border, which are not really Chinese at all, often not even by claim. So that it was plain that P. pumilio must belong (especially as it is a plant of Przewalsky's collecting) to the Alps of the Da-Tung. We had long been anxious for it, long been wondering why we did not find it, and the Little Queen on Crest Royal at first satisfied our anxieties, and made us sigh with relief in having duly worked off all the Przewalsky species, besides adding two of our own. Until I looked closer. It was very odd: there was no cushion, there were no heads of blossom, the blossoms themselves not numerous and wee: on the con-trary, they were big for the tiny plant, they were carried on footstalks of an inch or two from a scape so close to the ground that it looked as if each gay little round-faced gold-eyed brightness were springing solitary on a thread fine stem of its own, and, finally, the plant did not grow in cushions, but in quite small tufts of two or three crowns at the most. Nor did any other detail square with P. pumilio: on the contrary, this plant came nearer to P. Wardii, squashed into minuteness (and still nearer, had I known it, to a minified P. tibetica). So that my heart soon bounded up again in the prospect of another novelty. And a novelty it indeed proved, though one already known in dried specimens from far and wide up the borders of Tibet, but as yet unnamed. For when my own specimens arrived at Edinburgh under the provisional name of P. Reginella (not only in tribute to its own regal but tiny charm, but also to give an *arrière-pensée* of its inventor's Christian name), they came just in time to enable Prof. Balfour to determine the species from them, and crystallize it accordingly under the name of P. Reginella.

This was all very fine, though, but where, all this time, was the real P. Pumilio ? We had got our novelty, but the last of the Przewalskian species eluded our quest obstinately and drove me to despair, as high top after high top failed to reveal it. It was not till I reached the Petrograd Herbarium that the mystery was solved. Primula Pumilio hails only from the heights of Djakhar, an eighteen thousand foot mountain away south of the Da-Tung, down in the Bad Lands below Kweite, in the heart of the wildest Tibetan tribes. More than that; another and an older friend is mixed with it. Przewalsky's sheets of P. Pumilio consist of four square patches of the tiny specimens bedded out on the page. The first is pure P. Pumilio, but the second contains an admixture of P. Reginella, the third contains more, and the last is pure P. Reginella, or very nearly. And this shows what surprises yet remain for workers in Herbaria, where such a confusion can be made between two species immediately and obviously distinct, that a trained botanist will diagnose one, and yet entirely ignore the other on the same sheet.

These dissertations, however, date from " the lonesome latter years." Come we back now to Crest Royal and its twinkling Queen. For here, in such a scene, and in such company, my heart danced as high, I think, as on any day in all my Chinese travels—though it also danced louder and more painfully. We sat in an ecstasy to nunch : then gathered the Little Queen for her photograph, collecting her in tuffets to be taken down and ripened in the yard. After which Bill would be off down into the basin, and across its successive folds of green to the far-off emerald of the Clear Lake : and I meanwhile explored the bluffs and slopes and shingles of Crest Royal up and down, and then lay long and rested, and grew chilly and crushed and paralysed by the enormous magnificence of the mountains ahead. Crest

Royal runs down, and down, in a long dying spur, banking
up the alpine levels from Wolfstone Dene, far below on the
other side. And the alpine basin itself, having collected all
its becks, fanwise from all its fells, at last centralizes into a
funnel that sinks abruptly and indefinitely beneath the
dying spurs of the ridge, towards the distant dark of a river-
gorge that cuts at right angles into the Dene, round the final
bluff of declining Crest Royal. It is all on a scale of bigness,
though, that words cannot convey : and on the far side of the
vague depths rises a new line of alps, only less high than
these, culminating indeed in the almost equal bulk of
Hypsêlos, and then swinging round at the valley head to
connect with the back-quarters of the Thanatos Massif, in a
cirque of gaunt and naked precipices, with a bare wilderness
of uncharted masses behind.

But now, tiny specks on a far horizon, Go-go and Gomer
hove into sight on the profile of the Buttress, and by degrees
drew near, with bales of vegetation in their arms. However,
it all proved to be my Primula, with neither novelty nor
variety. So we played about still, among the pink-headed
Erysimums that densely dotted the slope, and found a white
one. And then Bill was seen returning ; when he reached
us he told a fine tale of how lovely the Clear Lake was, and
what a place for encampment lay hard by it ; but he, too,
brought no news of any novelty. And now, instead of
returning over Crest Royal, the way we had come, he decided
to take Go-go and Lay-gor, and go off down the dip of the
alp into the dark of the valley beneath, and so round, and
into the Dene and up to Wolvesden : to spy out tracks and
directions, and judge the possibility of bringing the tents
up to the Clear Lake on mules. The rest of us, therefore,
dropped over the ridge, and sheer down the screes of its
northern face, slithering and skating in slides of shingle and
shale. It was a long way down into the dish of the alp ;
and it was not till we were at the snow gully that my heart
began to feel relieved ; and we were half-way down into
Wolfstone Dene before it was entirely easy. One of the

soldiers, indeed, had been completely prostrate with mountain sickness all day, and was a pale, tottering wreck by the
time we got him home.

Long delays, however, and many other explorations intervened before we were able to get up on to that alp.   In the
meantime we managed to be rid of our two soldiers on polite
pleas that would not get them into trouble with Mâ-Dâ-ren ;
who, of course, would have flatly refused to believe the truth
of the matter, which was that we were unable to feed them.
Then Bill went down to Tien Tang, in search of an extra tent,
while the rest of us achieved various researches in the ranges
round about ; and, though he found that pious establishment
very empty, most of its inhabitants being busy tree-felling
for the Viceroy of Kansu, or gone away to the local Derby
and horse-fair now raging, he was yet quite successful in
his quest.   And in others, too, for he brought back an almost
fantastically beautiful Atragenoid Clematis, with double-
looking cruciform flowers of a silky china blue, paling to
waxen whiteness at their heart, which he had found trailing
over little low bushes near the top of the wood in Tien Tang
Ghyll.   And there was yet another treasure.   On the Cliff
of the Holy Well, beneath the smile of the Buddha, the
influences of holiness had been so strong that the golden
Globe flower had gone, in two specimens, of a perfectly pure
white, rich and solid as cream or fresh ivory.   Painted and
photographed and delicately nurtured in the garden, Trollius
pumilus Perfectissimi survived all these ordeals, and survived
its subsequent long journey home to England, and now
diffidently trembles back to life on the same bank of the
rock-garden that enshrines the Albino of the Butterfly Iris.

However, at last our pocket Dartmoor, Murdering
Uncle and Wicked Wa-wa and the rest, including even Dien
Tanguei, went off down the Dene and up the lateral valley,
to accomplish the necessary path-making through the coppice-
jungles below the alp ; and on a day, summoned down by
Bill, I embarked for the high adventure.   In gay spirits
I was off, though this was to be no permanent encampment

but a mere preliminary flight of exploration. Down and down the Dene we rode, disheartened by the floral emptiness of the lovely lush-looking coppice-glades through which we passed (so different now from what they were when first we saw them) : and then to the right, up mile after mile of the most abominable bouldered river-bed, until I was heartily sick of its bare stoniness. But at last on my right hand I saw a little green knoll, with the beginnings of a path leading up into the green gloom of a narrow glen down which a grey torrent came roaring. This was the way up to the alp, and here Bill awaited me, almost despairing by now of my arrival. So I alighted, and up the steep gorge we proceeded through the woodland and coppice, where a very fine raw new path was now making, to where, in a most arcadian nook of green shade beneath a big rock, with the beck brawling below, I found the tent established and the staff encamped. We all rested, and the men knocked off work and had tea ; and this was the purposed end of our day. But Bill started the notion that it might be better to push on immediately to the alpine steading up above, and spend the night there instead of here, so as to start high next morning. And this so heartily chimed with all my own wishes, that I pushed the plan forward enthusiastically, till it was definitely decided. So back we sent Dien Tanguei, in charge of two of the horses, and ourselves reloading the other with necessaries for the night struck camp and began moving upwards, with Go-go, Wa-wa and Uncle in attendance, and Mafu left behind to look after the tent.

Soon we arrived at the steep ascent to the upper alp. I had heard terrifying tales of its length and steepness, with the result that I took it quite lightly, and found it not a tithe of the three main stretches up the Tombea. The boys had made good going, too, with a neat zigzagging ascent ; so that one stodged and panted unimpeded upwards through the woodland, rank with Aconite in the open glades, and its shady places occupied by a frail spidery

Saxifrage flopping flaccidly about with hairy-edged heart-shaped foliage like a Parnassia's. There was nothing else to notice, though, as the valley sank down behind us. And so the woodland tailed off, and round a shoulder we came out on the open vastness of the fell, and saw the path winding ahead of us in a level leisure round further bays, belly-deep in a universal surf of Potentilla and sweet Lilac Honeysuckle, over which, fat and fluffy, stood pompously up the thick seed-stems of the Lampshade Poppy, and in and out appeared also the lurid stars of the Tangutic Primula.

In the clear and solemn calm we strolled along, and round the next shoulder. There, on its brow, was the Ma-Chang —a deserted horse-steading, of which only the four-square walls of the shelter still stood. It has never meant, of course, to be roofed, except by a temporary tenting ; now it was made beautifully cosy for us with the Koko-Nor Viceroy's tent unfurled, and inside the forlorn bits of boarding had been fitted up for beds. The Ma-Chang is most beautifully situated, on the forehead of the alp, amid dense scrub of Lonicera Syringantha and Potentilla : from its open heights it overlooks the far depths at its feet, and then, above, there are the vast peaks peering, and wild crags, with dead pines profiled on the sky, impending immediately over the top of the mountain wall to which the Ma-Chang clings. On the right the funnel of the glen dwindles up to where its streams cut down through the rim of the alp that engirdles it so vastly ; opposite, across the abysm, a slope of Rhododendron-jungle banks up and up to where the realm of bare rock begins ; and across the yet further depth of darkness on the left aspires the naked hugeness of Hypsêlos, and the complicated amphitheatre of cliffs that closes the valley head.

In the low loose scrub of the white Rhododendron the wild sheep have their tracks everywhere in the mossy ripples of the voluminous slopes opposite. But on the side of the Ma-Chang the fell is open, with patches of dense lush pasture, thick as hay, and violently green, except for sky-blue drifts of a rather rank Omphalodes. We descended the yak-dunged richness, to where the beck furiously roars, but, though the scene was opulent everywhere with flowers, there were no new ones. So we returned up to the Ma-Chang, perched above on its height; and there lay revelling in the gigantic splendour of the view, while far up overhead among the skeleton pines the silhouetted antlers of an inquisitive elk appeared, far-branched and wide themselves as the wreck of a dead tree. It was a real alpine situation, a real alpine view; for the first time in my Chinese travels a well-known scene, cousin to any one might see up the Val Savine, or beside the Lac Clair, but incomparably larger and grander. With a feeling of being at home once more, I sprawled at ease on my springy cushions of Potentilla and Honeysuckle, contemplating the vast loveliness of the world with that curious proprietary feeling that such loveliness gives—as if one somehow owned it, or were responsible for it, and had a right to be proud of it. And yet, I suppose, a glory so great that it floods and overwhelms one, and absorbs one wholly into its possession, does also, by that very fact pass into one's own possession, too, becomes an inseparable part of one for evermore. The mere fact of perceiving and assimilating such things means that one is storing their glory up to render again for others, even as the giant tree ferns who assimilated the glow of the Coal Age, now render it out again in flame. So that I, indeed, become the medium, the middleman, the mere conduit, to pour forth upon all you who read, a trickle or so, no matter how diluted and defiled and wasted, of the torrential beauty that held me breathless and stupid up on that Tibetan Ma-Chang that you will otherwise never see.

And so, by degrees, the air darkened solemnly like deep water, and a deeper stillness than ever seemed to fill the world. The golden radiance faded upwards, as dusk came swiftly climbing the opposite slopes; at length the last red glow died off the crags of Hypsêlos, and the Alps all stood cold and grey and dead in the cold dead clearness of the alpine night. And a roaring fire was built beside the Ma-Chang, clattering and streaming and swirling up into the quiet air, to keep off wolves and bears and Powers of Darkness. On the morrow the high Gods beamed on us auspiciously in a cloudless dawn, with the Alps sombre and lifeless still against the pale sky. We were off about four, leaving the tent and its plenishings to be disestablished and carried back to Wolvesden ; up and up, along the right-hand slope we continued from the Ma-Chang, round the countless bays and folds that descend from Crest Royal. From the Ma-Chang it had looked a mere nothing, a quiet stroll, just a hop, skip and jump, up to the alpine levels at the glen head. But it proved a very far cry, and a very long mighty toil ; the vegetation was luxuriant, crowded with seedspires of the Lampshade Poppy (but always and only where low scrub filled some dip of the slope) and the gross spikes of hideous Primula tangutica. And so, in due course, we did leave below us the sudden downward sink of the streams from the alp-level, and continued yet higher, for some distance, before crossing leftwards over a dip of runnels and marshes, to clamber up on to the alpine lawns themselves.

And now, immediately, the beauty of the Harebell Poppy began to break upon us. It was everywhere, flickering and dancing in millions upon millions of pale purple butterflies, as far as eye could see, over all the enormous slopes and braes of the grass. The sun was now coming up, and its earliest rays slanted upon the upland in shafts of gold-dust ; in the young fresh light the whole alp was a glistering jewel-work with dew in a powdered haze of diamond, with the innumerable soft blue laughter of the Poppies rippling universally above a floor of pale purple Alpine Asters, interspersed with here and there the complacent pinkness of the Welcome Primula. In the far-off memory of that scene I have to rein myself in, for fear a flux of words should ensue : but do not be embittered, all you who incline to

be jealous, scornful, or incredulous of lovelinesses you
have never shared (and possibly never could) if I tell you
coldly that even I, in those moments, was stricken dumb
and helpless by the sight of a glory surpassing, as I do
truly think, all that I have ever seen elsewhere. Stupid
with a blank delight, I wandered spellbound over those
unharvested lawns, agonizing with the effort to contain
without breaking the infinite flood of glory they were so
mercilessly pouring into so frail and finite a vessel. One
did not dare speak. It was indeed a pain almost like
the water-torture of Madame de Brinvilliers. And at my
side walked Bill, silent as I. What was he thinking then ?
How was this sight striking home to him ? But who can
ever know what even these dearest and nearest are doing
and enduring in the secret inmost rooms of the soul ? We
continued together, voiceless and smitten.

And then at last he turned to me, and in the awe-stricken
whisper of one overwhelmed by a divine presence, he said :
" Doesn't it make your very soul ache ? " It was the right,
the absolute and final word. It did. It twisted one's very
being, in the agony to absorb that sight wholly, to get
outside it, possess it, delay its passing, tear it away from
its native hills and keep it with one for ever—flesh of one's
flesh, and brain of one's brain. But beauty is so big and
enduring, and we so small and evanescent, that for us the
almost physical pain of trying to pack the incommensurable
inside the infinitesimal is, indeed, as if one should try
to decant the Yellow River into a thimble. Let us hope
that even a drop remains inside the poor little vessel round
which so titanic an overflow goes inevitably lost, roaring and
seething in a spate that would baffle any holding capacity.

Meconopsis quintuplinervia ! Will anybody wonder that
even I, hating as I do the Wardour Street popular names
with which Ruskin tried to " affubler " such known beauties
as Saxifrage and Campanula, should now yield to the
same weakness, and try to give my beloved Tibetan Poppy
an English name to which she has no right at all ? But I

hope it is only proleptically that I forge the name of Harebell Poppy. I hope that the plant's beauty and its charm
and its permanence will so ensure its popularity in gardens
as to make a popular name inevitable. And, that being
so, there will be "Harebell Poppy" ready made. For
indeed, to cherish or even to purchase, a plant called
Meconopsis quintuplinervia is as impossible as to love a
woman called Georgiana : mitigating substitutes inevitably
have to be invented. So, as the "Harebell Poppy," may
my Tibetan treasure long enrich our gardens, luxuriant and
enduring in rich moist ground, and inimitably lovely in the
well-bred grace of its habit, as well as in the serene and
tranquil loveliness of its lavender bells. Some there are,
indeed, who misprise these, and find them insufficiently
"showy." Alas, the prevailing fault of Meconopsis is not
modesty ; but it is in modesty that M. quintuplinervia,
alone of her kind, excels. Not for her the blatant crude
enormousness of M. integrifolia, the sinister and snaky
splendour of M. punicea, the hard clear glory of M. simplici-
folia : her fluttering butterflies aim at a more quiet charm,
that only the dull-eyed and deboshed in taste could dream of
calling dull.

So much for the gentle blue-purple of the Harebell as
she normally lives, and so deliriously abounds over that
highland lawn in the high heart of the Alps ; but what
of her varieties ? M. quintuplinervia, indeed, is a stable
species in her variable race, and not one in a million flowers
shows any difference. But in the very many millions that
possess the upper fells of the Da-Tung, varieties at last do
arise. Further on towards the Clear Lake there is a broad
triangular stretch of the moor, between two becks, on which
the Poppy shifts to rosy and amethystine tones ; and,
very rarely, you come on forms in which the delicate loveliness
of the bells is of real azure blue, as it were muted and veiled
with a hinted reminiscence of their normal lavender so as
to have an opalescent effect of shot silk. And then, more
rarely still, there are albinoes and albinoids, almost unimagin-

ably beautiful, like living drops of purity or incarnate snow-flakes—exactly what the Snowdrop ought to be, and isn't. These, though, sickened at Siberia, and perished of Petro-grad : I can only bring myself to tell of their tantalizing vanished wonders, so that you may all see the point of raising seed of the Harebell Poppy and going on raising seed of her (hearty perennial though she be) on chance of one day blooming a drop of mortal rainbow or a whiteness pure as milk. And if, amid the cataclysms of anguish that clamour round us everywhere nowadays,[1] you declare that all this babble about beauty and flowers is a vain imper-tinence, then I must tell you that you err, and that your perspectives are false. Mortal dooms and dynasties are brief things, but beauty is indestructible and eternal, if its tabernacle be only in a petal that is shed to-morrow. Wars and agonies are shadows only cast across the path of man : each successive one seems the end of all things, but man perpetually emerges and goes forward, lured always and cheered and inspired by the immortal beauty-thought that finds form in all the hopes and enjoyments of his life. *Inter arma silent flores* is no truth ; on the contrary, amid the crash of doom our sanity and survival more than ever depend on the strength with which we can listen to the still small voice that towers above the cannons, and cling to the little quiet things of life, the things that come and go yet are always there, the inextinguishable lamps of God amid the disaster that man has made of his life.

This is no idle fantasy : little happinesses may look little, and find no place in the plans of diplomats and prophets ; but they outlast the worst catastrophes and survive the plans and the diplomats and the prophets and all. Dead bones in their grave lie Mary and Elizabeth, Queens ; and dead dust of death is all they did ; but the flowers they grew in their gardens still continue giving comfort and delight perpetually, down through the continuing generations, to whom the people of the past

[1] This was written in June, 1918.

Q

are mere phantasmal fictions in books, diaphanous, desiccated as dried flowers themselves. All the wars of the world, all the Cæsars, have not the staying power of a Lily in a cottage border : man creates the storms in his teacup, and dies of them, but there remains a something standing outside, a something impregnable, as far beyond reach of man's destructiveness as is man's own self. The immortality of marbles and of miseries is a vain, small thing compared to the immortality of a flower that blooms and is dead by dusk.

Therefore think no scorn to linger for a little while on these far fells among the poppies. Slowly we mounted over down after down, and over the vast dishes of marsh and lawn into which the uplands drain. From Crest Royal the basin had looked an undulating expanse : as soon as you are in it, you find a complication of hills and ranges overwhelming you on all sides. And everywhere the Poppy flickered and danced, in multitude and beauty unbelievable, above galaxies of fat-faced dwarf pale Asters, with Primula gemmifera sturdy and pink, and Trollius already beginning to fade rusty and blood-coloured, dark blots in the jewelled tissue of those incomparable lawns. And in the flatter, damper stretches the vivid emerald of the finer turf was sheeted in a uniform flare of sunlight by a yellow Geum or Sieversia (G. Purdomii), growing densely in drifts of half a mile across, lovely in its feathered foliage, but concealing this now from view beneath a profusion of flowers, rayed out in crowds on weakly declining stems in such abundance that though not gargantuan individually, they turned that whole dish to a Field of the Cloth of Gold.

Gently, dissolved in a constant kaleidoscope of ecstasies, we sauntered here and there across the firm springy green, and came at length to the further rise of moorland where the pale Poppies live. It was still a high far tramp, up rise after rise, before we came under a big fell-barrier diversified by the protrusion of a red precipice, as it were a frontal bone that had worn through the epidermis of the alp. This barrier upholds the Clear Lake ; and as soon as we had climbed to the higher level, by the gully at its top end down which a beck drains, we found those virgin waters glittering at our feet like liquid beryl, lapping against the white gritty marge. The Clear Lake proves to be a bean-shaped sheet of water, flawless and serene, about three-quarters of a mile long, set like a jewel in the brown-green lawns, close beneath streaming red screes of desolation, that along the far shore descend upon it from an arc of naked pinnacles and precipices, culminating overhead in a noble pyramid, so gashed with rust coloured outcrops from the grey that it could have no other name than Croda Rossa.

It is curious to see how the Clear Lake is banked up there, and held, almost artificially, by the long rampart of moor that it seems to have pushed forward, while at its top end the steep enormousness of the rise towards the feet of Axeinos is a wild chaos of black boulders as big as houses, loosely compiled, that yet, in the unseizable scale of the scene, seem a mere peppering of pebbles like hundreds and thousands. Indeed, the valley-head, narrowing upwards to its dreary source between the lifeless precipices of Thanatos and the lifeless screes of Axeinos, does suggest glacier-action in a very remote past, if ever a glacier so small as this can have been possible. The embankment of the Clear Lake has all the look of being a terminal moraine thrust out over the alp as the advance bar of a glacier : higher up there is a similar but smaller bar, banking up a similar but smaller water, while higher yet amid the dank desolation of scree and boulder at the feet of Thanatos, there is a last faint hollow, and a final puddle, slinking shamefast among the blocks, and so feeble that it can hardly make up its mind whether to be slough or marsh or pond.

To the attack of the second upland we now advanced, across a flat delta of grit and scree that brings down the streams of the boulder-hill into the top end of the Lake.

This wonderful bare stretch promised flowers in such variety and abundance that I thought of it forthwith as the Jardin. But now we were come to the far side, and were mounting very slowly in pangs of overburdened respiration up the steep wall of fell beyond. At the foot of it, in the marshes that close the Jardin, the Little Queen flamed rosy along tussocks as yet hardly beginning to awake; but now we were at such a height, and so immediately in the shadow of the great peaks, that there was no life yet, and the rippled side of the fell was alternately pale with drab deadness or dark with snow-pressed moss. And over the rim we came upon the Lac Savine, a very shallow, very vivid little sheet of water, spread-eagled among the moorland dunes between the tightening grip of the Alps. Here the marshes were already emerald, but there was no touch of flower-life yet, except the Little Queen, bejewelling the lines of cleavage along the boulders across the pool. Round that side we clambered, and then began mounting again, up a new high breast to the actual valley-head, which coils to the right, round the bulk of Axeinos, to the arête that links Axeinos to Thanatos.

All this is the very abomination of desolation. From the Lac Savine upwards, you are in the very jaws of those terrific dead mountains, biting on you tighter and tighter like a rat-trap at every step. Below, in the chaos, lies the Puddle, and after that the upper course of the climb is nothing but a wild and lifeless wilderness of stone, dominated awfully by the Northern precipices of Thanatos, more wholly dead and cold, in a cold dead greyness, than any other mountain I have ever met. This chill glen, between its enclosing walls, is a grisly place : its mountains might be refrigerated skeletons in the moon ; they have a lunar ghastliness of complete extinction, a glaring staring life lessness that seems to have an almost phosphorescent pallor. Thanatos was still crusted, indeed, with crests and ledges and gullies of snow : but not even when sun and summer sweep these away, can those fearful cold faces, that ugly undignified chaos of crags and cliffs, ever be warmed and kindled to the faintest cheerfulness.

Barren Axeinos is not quite so irremediably grim, fronting the sunlight as it does, across the glen-head, opposite Thanatos. Indeed we were now above the glen, and mounting, more slowly and agonizedly than ever, the skirts of Axeinos himself, slanting across them steeply upwards towards the precipices of the arête overhead. Here we were in the sunshine again contemplating the mortal cold of Thanatos across the depths; and here the Harebell Poppy, accordingly, was beginning to ring her chimes. And here, as hand over hand, yard by yard, I grappled my way upwards, I came on one as white and clean and clear as the soul of St. John, a thing so beautiful as to give yet a new turn to the wheel of the day's delights. One tuft of a pure Albino we already had in the garden, though: so from this one, in reverent appreciation, I withheld the trowel, and left her swinging out her perfect snowy bells unperturbed. And there I like to think of her still thriving through the years, and, still unperturbed, shaking out her snowy bells across all the din of the world, in a delicate and remote derision.

High overhead still hung the cliffs and naked earthpans and screes of the obvious col connecting Axeinos and Thanatos by its shallow dip. The way was very long and steep, and the scale of the scene so huge that one never seemed really to be any higher, not even after the most heart-breaking bursts of upward effort. And there were no new flowers; all down the slope, even into the mossy turf below, ran carpets of Androsace mucronifolia, and among the stones of the bare scree shone the humped white and azure heads of Corydalis melanochlora, sitting close on the fat sea-blue ferniness of their foliage. But there was nothing new. And soon there was nothing more at all in the lifeless crags and slopes ascending to the neck itself. Up the crags and along their ledges, and up in the jaws of the narrow gullies between them, we made our way, beneath bare cliffs descending on us from the peak of Axeinos, now immediately above. And so, at length, attained the despaired-of crest, and looked over—out above the moorlands tumbling indistinguishably " like mastiff pups at play " across the deeps below—to where, along the distance, in a dark high barrier, towered the wall of Wolvesden Pass, with Kelaino at its nearer end and Kerauno remote at the other.

And in the sunlight of the col the Little Queen was very pink and gay and charming along the mossy cracks ; but otherwise, after such toils, we were dulled by the complete (though characteristic) dull lifelessness of these high primary rocks. However, below at our feet lay the third of the big highland dishes to which we had so aspired from afar, on the pass, in sure hope that those three pale laps that lie between the respective knees of Omos and Achthos, Achthos and Axeinos, Axeinos and Thanatos, would certainly yield a sumptuous harvest.

So now we started forth again, questing along the enormous Western face of Axeinos himself, which is a bewildering world of steep little slopes of lawn and scree, interspersed among a grey chaos of crags and spars and boulders, upheld by successive tiers of naked cliff, away and away downwards to the alpine lawns below. It was heart-breakingly huge and dreadful : by degrees we worked downward, scrambling and dropping in the empty gully of one of the many evanescent torrent-falls that have scored this front of Axeinos all along in a succession of vertical wrinkles. Or so they look from the pass ; but when you are in them, they turn to wild chines of gloom, lifeless, except for my own brave Primula, sprouting opulently in the tightest crannies of the darkest dankest faces of the cliff. Indeed, it is remarkable with what rigidity the plant selects only such nooks and niches as are rarely if ever visited by sunlight. And in that titanic Baalbek of naked ruin, its fat splendour, its sumptuous lavender-grey bunches, have a more than ever unbelievable and artificial look, as if somebody had gone by just ahead of one, and poked pale purple Polyanthuses into all the sunless crevices for a joke.

So gradually we got down beneath the bastion precipices at the base of the summit mass, and the torrent-course, now languidly alive with a little water, lodged in pools and dribbling down the gulches, brought us round at the foot of a huge cliff, on whose face shone here and there a spark of purple that for an agonizing instant we thought might prove a new Poppy. But through the glasses it turned out to be no more than dull mauve variations of Meconopsis Prattii. So, disillusioned, we turned away and descended into the dish of our last hopes. And the dish held nothing—nothing but a wide shallow wetness of very coarse tussocks, drab and pale as parchment still, illuminated only at intervals by such re-hashed cabbage as the Trollius, the Erysimum, and Primula Woodwardii. And even these were so rare as to leave that disheartening saucer virtually empty. Stale and leaden we dropped at last over its lower rim, and began descending the vast and bulging slopes of the lower fells that descend in merciless enormousness, towards the depths of the valley, mapped out clear and green far beneath our feet, with the horses, like fleas in a fold of baize, awaiting us, much too remote, away down its course.

Never were there such slopes as these of the Da-Tung Alps. In our own, the upper fells descend upon lower ones, and so to the valleys; even in the ranges of Jo-ni and Satanee, the alps decline by folds and ridges and long convolutions. But here, from the base of the peaks, they soar away down in an unbroken sweep to the glens below, and there is no describing their weariful hugeness except by saying that they do indeed seem to bulge. From beneath they swell up over your head, and you cannot see their top : from the top they swell away below you, and you cannot see their bottom. Blanked by disappointment as I was, my knees felt very old and tired, and I could go but slowly down the stair-steep interminableness of the descent.

Even the soil here seemed coarse and common, and the mountain-side had mange. All decent alps—even in the Da-Tung—are densely clothed in turf, but the Western slopes under Axeinos and Thanatos have only a scant scab of grass, through which the crude plebeian soil everywhere appears, nourishing even the Celestial Poppy grudgingly.

For Meconopsis Prattii alters its habit in the Da-Tung Alps. In the Min S'an and the Satanee ranges it had always and only been a plant of the precipices and topmost shingles—whether you get the short pedicelled form, like a stocky mace of azure, or the long-pedicelled one, strict and *élancé*, it is always either in the cliff or in the scree, never out on the open grass of the alps. But in the Da-Tung the plant strikes a compromise in every way. It is neither quite a mace, here, nor quite a spire—tending more to the latter development, perhaps, but laxer in spike, and looser altogether in habit than any prevalent form of 1914. And not only does it haunt the cliffs and high shingles everywhere, but also, in the Da-Tung chain, it ventures down into the grass of the alps, and wherever this is not too dense and coarse to be suitable, universally bejewels the high slopes with its floppy array of blossoms, rather larger, to my fancy, and of a rather brighter blue, than most that I remembered in the Min S'an. But still the same species.

Here skip, Aunt Agnes : I am having an aside with such experts as are ambitious to perpend upon Poppies. In particular the Horrid Group of Meconopsis is especially entangled, confused, and difficult to decipher. All its members have bristles, all are monocarpous, and all have flowers in varying tones of blue and azure. The Indian species may here be left out of account, but the Tibetan ranges up the Border give us M. Prattii, M. racemosa, M. rudis, M. horridula—and the disappointing M. eximia —all differentiable, but not always easy to differentiate. Yet, after much experience in the field during 1914 and

1915, with many hundreds and thousands of specimens, I remain convinced that the Horridulous Blue Poppy of the Min S'an and the Da-Tung is always the same species, M. Prattii, with the unvarying ash-grey anthers.[1] But in almost every other respect—shape of leaf, shape of pod, length of style, the species appears to me to fluctuate despairingly, and I grow more and more struck by the temerity with which Herbarium botanists build up a species on half a dozen dried specimens on a sheet, whereas in many a detail the species would give them the lie, if they could see it by the thousand blossoming on the hill-side. In point of fact, a specific difference is merely the least common denominator in a vast generalization of individuals, all of whom vary this way and that to their own sweet will, but all of whom possess the one or two quite unvarying details that by their universality and invariability constitute a species.

And, to arrive at these bedrock differences, it is really imperative to see the plant not only living, and wild, but abundant. It is only on a vast number of living individuals that you can satisfactorily establish a general formula for a "species," since only a vast number can yield you its one common factor, by giving full perception of the plant's range of variation, so that you can arrive at the one point (or more) in which it never varies at all. Thus, Meconopsis Prattii (my beloved Celestial Poppy) may, in my experience of it, have flowers of every shade from pure white through all tones of azure, mauve and lilac, to clean pink; it may have quite narrow foliage, or foliage so broad as to seem, in the second-year seedlings, almost round; the leaves may be quite entire or faintly waved at their edge; and the footstalks can be either quite short or strict and long; it may have the widest diversities in the shape of its pods and in the length of its styles. But it never varies in the smallest degree from the ashen-

[1] I ought to say that Professor Balfour sometimes hovers on the verge of wanting to separate them.

cream colour of its anthers. And thus, out of an incalculable multitude of diverse individuals on the mountains, I generalize a definite species—Meconopsis Prattii,
with ashen-cream-coloured anthers ; and, if I came on a
specimen with golden or orange ones, should attribute it
at once to M. racemosa ; or if other indications pointed,
realize a new species.

But I never have, and in M. Prattii I never, assuredly,
shall. At the same time, in gardens I often have to clutch
my faith in those anthers like a sheet-anchor in stormy
seas : when I am shown two or three Horridulous Blue
Poppies, apparently all as diverse as chalk from cheese,
yet all grey-anthered, and all bearing the name of M.
Prattii, and every one of them children or grandchildren
from my own collected seed. And then I appreciate the
enormous advantage of having known a species in the field,
living, and in bulk, instead of only in a herbarium, dead,
and in a few specimens : for, while my own eyes, and my
host's tongue, are both loudly saying, "Those two poppies
can't *possibly*, both of them, be M. Prattii," my brain is
busily remembering the high lawns and shingles of the
Da-Tung, the topmost screes and precipices of the Min
S'an, with their many myriads of Celestial Poppies, individually so diverse as to embrace, in their vast definition, not
only both the variations before me (on each of which,
separately, you might base a new species quite plausibly),
but many others yet wider and extremer, connected by a
thousand gradations, yet all gathered into the one fold
by their unvarying monopoly of ashen-cream-coloured
("gilvous" is the learned word) anthers. (For when other
poppies have gilvous anthers, they have other definite
specific marks that differentiate them from M. Prattii.)
So variable and yet so constant is the species. Cultivation
may also encourage diversity, as may, too, the difference
between living on the high limestones of the Min S'an,
and on the azoic summits of the Da-Tung. But it is all
M. Prattii—until you come on, or breed, a specimen identical

with the rest, except in having differently coloured anthers.

Cease to skip, Aunt Agnes : I resume my descent of that endless, endless bank, never seeming to get any nearer to the microscopic stream-bed beneath. The horses were still painfully far away, too, infinitesimal down the valley ; Bill cut across the fell to fetch them, while I continued stolidly stamping my way down the earthy wall of the mountain, now dappled and quite gay with the azures of the Poppy, and the comfortable pink of the Welcome Primula. And overhead Axeinos and Thanatos had now shot up so sheer and far and high that it seemed incredible that we could ever have scaled such altitudes ; and almost equally incredible that we could have come down from them. No wavings could attract or awake Dien Tanguei, asleep at his post by the ponies ; Wa-wa and I got down at last into the valley, and tramped along its trough, traversing two deserted Ma-Changs with crumbling precincts of stone-walling and dungy tracts of pasture round them, sodden and pale, but beginning to spring into rich green. It was like a suggestion of the Granges Savines in its savage abandonment, and rich harvest of nettles and cow-pats to tell of human activities. But lower down, the reaches of the glen were come to life ; and now appeared Tanguei, galloping up on the brown pony, which I then mounted, and so jogged on to join the rest. On a grassy lawn I found Bill pleasantly resting ; hopped off, and hoped to rest there also. But now, for the first and only time of my experience anywhere in the Tibetan border-alps, we were so pestered with horse-flies as to be driven headlong forward in flight like Io. And the poor horses were so tired with three tremendous stony days that they could hardly put one foot before the other, and drearily stumbled at the boulders in their path. By marshy green flats aglow with Primula Wardii we slowly descended to the junction where this valley flows into Wolfstone Dene over that wide tract of shingle about half a mile above the first inn and the beginning of the gorges ; and thence, more slowly still, down them and back to Wolvesden, serene in the achievement of so big an expedition accomplished, and so large a tract of the Alps explored, but both of us quite flattened out with the leaden lack of result.

And I hate getting in from the mountains while light still lingers over the depths of the valley : the rest of the day is such a lagging bathos, in which one can settle to nothing. Nor, now that I had got home, did I feel so very tired. For these huge Tibetan days, in fact, neither in hours nor in labour, equal those of the Torsoleto and the Tombéa, for example ; and though one climbs at double the height, and with heart-fettered slowness (I had felt the altitudes less that day, and worst at the Clear Lake), all this is compensated by having everything carried for you, as Chinese etiquette commands. So I pottered emptily enough over the golden lawns of Globeflower, where Pylzow's Geranium was now sprawling through the grass, with its thread-fine stems and large lovely flowers of clear pink— the same species, it now proves, from the Petrograd Herbarium, as the pink Geranium I had got in the Ardjeri Alps the year before, leaving the high alpine treasure (Fzoi) to stand, after all, as a separate new species; both of them, in different ways though, precious adornments of the garden, the one scrambling and spreading and brilliant, the other concise, high-alpine, and delicately lovely.

None the less it was sadly that I digested our disappointment over this granitic range, of which the Russians had left such misleadingly rosy accounts. A sense of failure pressed me down like a lid ; there was no longer any good denying it. The summer was fleeting by, and the ranges had been duly visited, without revealing any novelty or variety of flora : nothing to rival the rich lovelinesses that await one at every turn of the track above Li-kiang, or Sung-pan, or Tali-fu—nothing even to compare with the high flanks of Thundercrown, and the uncharted alpine wildernesses of the Stone Mountains. I had always had a fear that we were too far North ; and that fear had been intensified when first I saw the pyramids of the Da-Tung chain and realized that they were non-calcareous. And by this time I had to face the facts of the case, and the poor dull harvest that was all I bade fair to gather for appetent friends at home. The mischance of the latitude, the altitude, the geology, all seemed to be my own fault ; and now there only remained the dolomite precipices opposite Kerauno and the Pass. Limestone alone (as usual) had yielded us the few chief treasures of the year : its main outcrop might surely yield us more ? So I went in, and Bill and I spent the evening philosophizing over our failure ; hoping even yet to retrieve it by wild diversions, we agreed to recognize that here we had drawn blank. But here, meanwhile, I was to remain for the seed-harvest, to go round the district and collect all that was worth having (for not even in extremity could I bring myself to violate my own standards and promises by fattening out my seed-list with worthlessnesses of ugly bramble and briar), while Bill, with Mafu, sped off to the Koko-nor and the Kweete-Salar Alps to see if he could not save the situation even yet, with some new Poppy or Primula. But first we would explore the Dolomite Valley, go up into camp for a time beside the Clear Lake, and also do the highest of the high peaks above Casa Aoo.

CHAPTER XII

THE HASTENED END

When the day came there was packing and preparation in the lovely morning, and off we all set, up Southerly valley, and up its right-hand confluent below the Casa. In the ghyll my Isopyrum hung in waving masses of loveliness, but we could not linger in this most perfect of Nature's rock-gardens, and pushed on high and higher, till we came to the upmost steading in the gully. My little green chrysalis of a tent was then pitched on the brow of the fell, while across the beck the rest encamped in the yak-dung lean-to's, sadly disturbing Mrs. Bird,[1] who had hitherto had it all to herself for her nursery. We then ambrosially lunched off bread and milk and apricots, and spent the rest of the day exploring the vast slopes above that look so trifling. But we found nothing new, except the true Lloydia tibetica (which is a dull and ugly gawk), and a very pretty little yellow Cremanthodium like a golden Dahlia, with pendent head on a four-inch stem, which haunted dank shady ledges of the wetter cliffs and shingles up above, in the gully of the torrent, where Isopyrum was also bewilderingly magnificent, and the Poppies, Harebell and Celestial. So at dusk we came down again into the dark of the ghyll, filled by now with blue swirls of smoke from the camp-fire—and in due course, feeling rather " einsam " and depressed, I retired to my splendid isolation across the beck.

I woke very early, and felt yet more depressed. No sign of life appeared in the lean-to down below ; I lay empty and wretched in the cold shadow, awaiting developments.

[1] Not Mrs. James Bird, who was *née* Partridge.

And then, when the sun did come round over the hills, he came over so very high an edge as made it evident he must be well up on his journey. Clearly I must call the men, or they would snore on till Doomsday. And now there was much bustling for breakfast, and the four little bobtailed baby birds in their nest woke up and cheeped, while their mother, on a log outside, reassured me by chirruping cheerfully back at them. And the sun, in two minutes, flooded out the cold blue darkness of the glen with light and warmth. Off we set, up the alp at the back, so steep as to seem positively heaving over at us, and as high as Heaven. It was, however, quite as monotonous : at first of grass, and then of bare earthpans sliding down in long fat breasts from the cliffs above ; and all of it occupied with nothing but our old friends, except for a violet Delphinium still in bud, that evidently meant to be D. Pylzowi.

Finally, working along upwards to the right, we attained at last to the col, on which a fresh snow cornice still lay ; the cliffs on its far side were still dark in winter, with soggy curtains of moss and straggling Rhododendrons. We lay here awhile, contemplating the vast noble view over the Gan-Chang pass ; then strolled along the moist, fine silt of the arête to attack the final climb up slithery shingle-slides that mounted with fierce steepness up and up, in a desolate barrenness as naked as truth, towards the culminating mass overhead, which seemed to wear a ridge or coif of grass, such as surely, at so great a height, *must* yield a treasure or two. Up we moiled, panting ; all I found on the way was a strange Lousewort among the stones, with dark claret-crimson flowers, and the whole plant enveloped in a crystalline fluff of wool that glistered thickly like spun glass. But nothing else. And when we achievèd that high grassy crown there was nothing else there also ; and nothing more on the highest rocky peak above, in which the mass culminates ; and nothing more on the secondary peak below that dominates the Dene. Slowly we ascended to it, along that arête of coarse turf, and vindinctively named that nasty mountain

Mother Hubbard. Here we rested : the scene was very
grand and lovely, fronting on to Crest Royal and the Alps,
but I was sick at heart with so many days of failure and so
monotonous a flora, with no distinction between alpine and
high-alpine zones, and the very valleys not low enough for
even their typical treasures. And poor Bill, I could see,
was as sick as I was, if not worse : each of us was " bright "
for the other's benefit, and a more dreadful thing could
hardly be. So, in the end, we dropped down the interminable fall of coarse scree beneath us, until it tailed off
into equally endless slopes of coarse barren grass. And at
length, through a peppering of dead or sickly firs, we reached
the coppice, and came straight upon the Isopyrum gully,
and so home ; the staff, meanwhile, collecting the camp,
according to instructions. All that night I lay feverish
and wakeful, haunted by visions of the various lovely new
Primulas that might so easily have been there, upon those
ridges : only that they weren't !

Weather now imprisoned us, though as yet I saw no signs
of the six weeks' unceasing rain which had been held out
to me as so charming a feature of the season here. All that
happened was constant broodings and violent storms : the
afternoon would often bring a furious deluge, and end at
dusk in lovely pictures of broken clouds above the sundown,
flooding the valley with brassy light, while all the darkened
hills and their folds were filled with fleecy white rolls of the
unravelled storm. In the twilight the Dene is a mysterious
place, and its darkness seems something private, peculiar to
itself. One evening I strolled down beside the beck, lonely
in the silence. And suddenly I seemed to hear a pistol-shot,
followed by a vast dim chorus of wailing voices that came
flooding up the valley on a cold violent blast. But this
was after the expedition up to Dolomite Valley, by which
time " fiddle-strings was weakness to expredge my nerves,"
—and I might easily have heard anything, except comfort
or reason. More especially as Bill had just told me that
Gomer was now to be clawed away from us by his old

grannies away in Na-Lang, imperiously summoning him home to take a wife, so that they might thus have a general servant to support their declining days.

Altogether, gloom brooded. Indeed, the Rainbow Bridge has long since reached its bourn; we have long been roaming at ease on the far golden shore, and found it barren; now, upon a bridge of sighs we must embark upon a return journey across the abysm of tears towards the desolated shell-holes and slag-heaps of the present days. Yet do not be misled if I seem to grizzle and peeve as I return. For there is laughter in every sigh and complaint, and a twinkle of not unkindly derision that any such should be emitted. In fact, for the fun of the thing, I exaggerate my attitude, to make you the better share that fun. My glooms, then, are all part of it; and, indeed, what perfect fun the whole adventure is, in retrospect, with even its disappointment, and flatnesses blended by distance into the rainbow radiance of the irrecoverably remote. And laughter is the salt of life, assimilating its bitter savours and its sweet ones alike into one digestible meal; and the mere exaggeration of a dark mood provokes its dissipation into a burst of mockery. But those who stand outside, though sharing the laughter, are sometimes apt to overlook the exaggeration that bred it, and to take the grumblings as much more serious and heartfelt than they are. And therefore I must warn you that much of what is to follow will be " only Coleridge's fun."

Meanwhile, a detachment of the boys were gone down the valley and up towards the Ma-Chang, to prepare for our expedition to camp beside the Clear Lake; and we ourselves, on a fine morning very early, made off up the Dene with the tents for a sojourn in Dolomite Valley, our last hope. From the pass, long since, we had marked an abandoned Ma-Chang lying in one of the gullies that cut down from the cliffs; and this was our objective. But when we attained the open alpine bosom of Dolomite Valley, we considerably overshot our mark. For the walls of precipices tower indeed

R

enormous in their incredible, untidy crumples ; but enormous
lies in front of them their foothill of fell, through which the
ghylls come cutting a deep and narrow way, giving successive visions of a widening bay behind, and a big blank front
of precipice. But these V-shaped revelations are like each
other as pea to pea ; and it was only after several false tries
that we penetrated up into the right gulch, and there, at
the foot of the rocks, above where two rills converge from
the huge faces overhead, we found the Ma-Chang lurking
among nettles and big white boulders, a ruinous little square
of crumbled walls.

But it was a delectable spot none the less, and, from the
cliffs of the little chine below, my Isopyrum flaunted in
delicate sheaves ; while up above the eye soon got lost in
bulge over smooth bulge of topless white precipices, in a
bewildering compilation of cliff and grottoes and grooves,
and narrow gullies down which, occasionally, there came a
dark smear of wetness, or a swaying string of illuminated
diamond sparks from far up above. So here we unfolded ;
and in a little while began exploring the combes and scarps
near by. But their slopes and crannies and overhung caves
produced only our old friends ; away and away upwards
over the face of the impending enormousness, so overpowering as hardly to be believable, there flickered occasional
specks of mauve and blue ; but even these, through the
glasses, were seen on the lower reaches to be merely the
Celestial Poppy, and so were no doubt still the same on the
higher. Towards the topmost ridges, therefore, we must
now remove our hopes.

In due course we separated, Bill attempting a way straight
up the wall, clambering amid the smooth shelves and
slabs and cañons, in hope that by successive traverses and
scrambles he might at last be led to the top ; while I, up
the smooth waterworn little ghyll immediately behind, where
a trickle from the cliff slumbered or gurgled among the
boulders, made upward towards the same goal, over the
opener frontage of enormous earth-pans varied with bluffs

of precipice, that faded higher up into scree, and higher yet into grass. It was a curious scene, like none I have known elsewhere—completely bald and naked mountain-side of unctuous ruddy soil, stiff like shaly clay, and on a giant scale, swelling away below to remote cliffs and depths, and swelling away above to remote cliffs and heights. And all quite empty, except for abundance of the welcome Primula, which particularly loves these bare places. Gradually I attained the first sprinklings of grass, and then the steep ripplings of unbroken lawn. But all the way I saw nothing of interest anywhere, except a big mountain sheep up ahead of me, seeming darker-bellied and shaggier than those of Tien-Tang; and, from the ridge itself, a glorious storm going down in a dense darkness over Wolvesden, with an almost continuous drone of thunder hoarsely rattling.

Very cold blew the wind along the topmost arête. And very cold was my mood, as I roamed its sharp dells of turf and examined its dorsal fins of rock, only to find nothing new whatever; far along I roamed, and up and down, and nowhere came on any better luck, though rocks and turf alike were all, of course, moderately gay with the usual flowers. Only a minute high-alpine violet, with a freaked little peevish face, rewarded my search. And at last it was evident that there was no more to be hoped for on the lawns and wild screes that engirdle Dolomite Valley; all I could now do, as I dispiritedly slithered down the stairways of the shingle, was to buoy myself up on the notion that Bill would now be returning from the cliffs with at least four glorious new Primulas and half as many new Poppies. But I cannot say the buoy was very solid: I felt rather as if I were clinging for security in stormy seas to the unsafe iridescence of a soap-bubble. And when at length I fore-gathered once more with Bill at the Ma-Chang, it was to find that he, on his part, had been consoling himself with similar hopes about me. He, too, had found nothing.

All was over. The visions of romance were as effectively dispelled as Emma's. In a frozen gloom we faced failure;

in extremity reversed all former schemes, and took Napo-
leonic new decisions.   There should be no high-alpine camp-
ing yet, and Bill should go off immediately on his tour to
the Koko-nor, while I collected the harvest of the Da-Tung ;
and then, when he returned, we were to bolt off immediately, down across the whole depth of China, to where the
Da-Ba-S'an ranges intervene between Kansu, Shensi and
Szechwam.   The Da-Ba-S'an ranges, we knew, did not run
very high—only to some 8,000 ft. or so, which is as nothing,
of course, in Northern China ; but so far South we hoped
that they might at least yield woods, and the tail-end of
flowering-shrub seed—if only we could finish off here in a
month, and then make a clean run of it Southward, on our
way to the Yang-tze-jang—and so down by water to the
coast.   It was a desperate long journey, and on a desperate
hope ; but anything, we felt, would be better than returning,
tamely thin-pocketed and in failure, across that Northern
face of China which we had traversed with such warm hopes
in 1914.   But it was altogether a bad business ; not even
the Jiu-ping could irradiate the gloom, or discover any real
point of hope in it anywhere.   Sunk in lethargy and silence
we sat through the evening, endured the broken feverish
sleeps of nerve-exhaustion, and on the morrow hectically
broke up the camp and hurried home to Wolvesden, too
disgusted to linger, and in a fever to polish off work in these
parts, and shake their barren dust from our feet for ever.
It is an ironical commentary on human joys and miseries,
despairs and complacencies, that (though we did not know
it) perhaps the three most important alpines of my whole
expedition belong to this second season that now seemed so
dull and disastrous—new species all, and new species of a
rank so towering that my Gentian alone, so far as the happiness of future gardens and generations is concerned, would
of itself have been easily worth all the trouble, anxiety and
expense of the entire two years' tour.

But this still lay hidden in the future ; and as yet I had
no presumptuous thought of hoping that the Isopyrum and

the big Primula could be mine. In a flopping mood we
returned to Wolvesden, and flung ourselves furiously into
preparations for finishing up with the season. Home, on
our summons, came the staff, in an abrupt break-up of the
camp on the alp, and all our jolly preparations—yet another
sad reminder of the sudden abysm of failure and new
unknown plans into which we had been plunged by the
lamentable omission of these alps to cater properly for
plants. Even the limestones of them lazy and monotonous !
And now my dear Bill whirled away from me across the
pass, carrying with him Mafu and Black Buzzler the Turen,
on his wild flight of exploration to the Koko-nor ; leaving
me with only the Wa-was and the Go-go. Not even this
charge of responsibility could cheer me at the thought of
being alone, and sole manager, for a month or so, mighty
tribute though it was to my increased mastery of Chinese,
humans and language. More especially as he took with
him Gomer also, *en route* for the grannies at Na-Lang.
" I could have better spared a better man "—if I could
have found one, which I greatly doubt. I liked all my
servants—the ridiculous and wicked Wa-wa, the simian
dourness of Mafu, good simple Go-go ; but it gave me a
quite special and personal pang to be parting for ever from
Gomer's *jeunesse-dorée* gaiety and enthusiastic interest in
life. I had him into my room before he went, then ; and
endeavoured personally to explain what I thought of him,
and how sorry I was to lose him. I think he, too, was sorry
to be going : he did not want either the wife or the grannies,
he wanted to stay with us, and ultimately see Peking. But
those old grannies, all the empire over, are the supreme
power in China, incarnating in themselves in each household, however humble, the immemorial matriarchy of its
religious system that finds its supreme incarnation in the
figures of the sacrosanct Empresses-Dowager, who dominate
the Chinese Empire all down its history, from behind the
veil of their " deep seclusion in the palace."

But no such meditations could distract me from my

depression in being bereft, at one blow, of Bill and Gomer. I attempted minor expeditions to divert me and to fill the days while the seed continued ripening. In particular I was determined to conquer Kelaino and Kerauno. My first assault was baffled by the weather : as I rode up the Dene such terrifying cauldrons of dense black darkness seethed round the summits that for once even I, who believe in bluffing the weather, turned back betimes—though feeling rather diminished by doing so. I need not have been anxious about my prescience : the day soon settled to a soaker that would have sunk the Ark itself.

Ere long a good day came, and Go-go and the Sa-wa Wa-wa and I set forth. Without event we reached the foot of the pass, and toiled up it. By this time its shingles were growing purple with the crowded big butterflies of Delphinium Pylzowi, and Corydalis scaberula was very handsome in the rubble at the pathside near the top, with luscious ferny foliage and stalwart spires of claret-crimson helmets darkening richly to black at their tips. The sky, which had grown doubtful, cleared ; but still the big blue umbrella seemed a desirable adjunct. I sent Go-go along the left-hand ridge to explore Kelaino, while Sawa and the umbrella and I set out towards Kerauno, looming lonely and pale and very high to the right. Up the huge fells and folds of the grassy crest we proceeded, occasionally balked by scarps and bluffs of dolomite that forced us to cast back and try elsewhere. The weather now threatened awfully again : the main massif behind was veiled in a blank of violet storm, and black dark brooded over the darkness of Kelaino, and other murky glooms lay out over far Gadjur and the northerly ranges behind ; while ahead of me, up the giant's causeway of the grassy arête, Kerauno soared into the greying air, pallid as an old rain-sodden bone. I was prepared for the worst, as ragged rain-clouds seemed converging on the peak from all round ; but all passed off in a spit, and sun was bright on the turfy knife-edge of the crest when I attained it. Up, and up, and up, hand over hand, in sharp tussocked steps the crest ascends, narrowing to the final sword-blade of the actual summit, where the lawn dies into desolate depths of naked grey shingle on both sides.

Kerauno stands out, huge and solitary, like a headland commanding wide lands and seas ; beneath the low canopy of cloud the westward view was incomparable, far and far, over all the Sining region, undistinguishable ripplings and expanses away into the undiscoverable remoteness of the distance, with here and there the glint of a river like a twist of silver wire dropped among the flatnesses and faint folds of some unfolded pall of soft blues and purples and dove-colour. Otherwise there was nothing more tangibly to reward me in the way of plants ; I find that my diary rather acidly records, " only the usual Nobbutnowtia invariabilis, and a poor show even of that." However, the loveliness of that vast scene was such that I could not but be in good heart all the same ; fie upon the vulgar greed that will not be content with a high-alpine lawn anyhow ; and clamours for " novelties " and richer things than the clustered snowy Lychnis, the orbed butter-coloured fluffs of Garlic, the pink domes of Erysimum, that here and there diversify the brown-green moorland along the high-aspiring neck of Kerauno.

But the peak itself is absolutely and resolutely barren— a mere wilderness of scree and shingle, squatted over by flat dull wads of what appeared to be Sibthorbia europæa, but yielding no other life whatever, not even the usual children of these exalted nudities. Down into Dolomite Valley I slid and slithered over the scree and slides, taking half the mountain with me it seemed, as I plunged and skidded and tobogganned, quicker and quicker downwards on my feet, in a scuttling scattering roar of shale and shingle. Then, through the Potentilla and Rhododendron scrub of the lower slopes, and along the valley bottom, more modestly proceeded along the beck-bed, to where the horses were coming down the pass to meet me at its foot, and carry us home, in a mood of satisfaction at having achieved the two peaks—though Go-go had discovered nothing more on Kelaino than I on Kerauno. But my evening meditations were diversified by the stove. I sat quiet, and felt how pleasant and warm it was ; when lo ! sparks fell, and the thatch round its chimney was seen to be in a red glow. There ensued violent whizzings-about by all the staff ; water was applied, and the smoulder got out, and fresh mud securely plastered round the chimney where it passed up through the roof. These alarums and excursions inspired me with the thought that now the time might be ripe to go down again to Tien-Tang in search of seeds. I issued orders accordingly, feeling as amazed as Fanny Price at Portsmouth, that here should I be, all alone in the heart of Asia, in sole responsibility for my flock, and issuing orders to it in a version of the Chinese tongue, which, however incorrect, was not inadequate.

The train was dispatched ahead, with many polite messages to the Gwan-ja : so that when I arrived I might find my quarters prepared, and my things set out. After allowing an hour's start, Go-go and Wa-wa and I set out. The Dene was dense and umbrageous in summer dullness ; but the long winding course of it was pleasant, though the only novelties it yielded were a rather poor Philadelphus and a rank Hydrangea ; and its only event a little aged woman going by us, with a wee white kitten enfolded in her grubby bosom. But about two miles above the debouchure of the Dene, as I rode through the silvery haze of willows like a Corot picture, which here fills its shingled bed, I could not refrain from crossing the torrent to the opposite bank, where the open steeps of the hill-side were now luxuriant as a hayfield, with sheaves of pale China-blue Adenophoras swinging out their branching chimes, amid the violent sealing-wax scarlet balls of the Slender-leaved Lily, all tangled up together in a lovely riot, with many another large lush beauty.

When I got within sight of Bridgehead the sky had

darkened, and winds blew furiously and rain splattered. But duty called me to dismount, and go and seek for seed of P. Stenocalyx on the banks, wading through the wet sea of the now knee-high Iris. And the seed was ripe, and so was the Stellera's, which greatly enheartened me. Very far away ahead, streaking along the high brow of the downs, I now saw the caravan : so followed slowly on, in what seemed by this time like a soft and settled soaker, very wet but by no means odious. Up in the ghyll I could not see the Blue Clematis in seed and could not be bothered to go poking for pods of the Violet Iris at its mouth. So we reached the top, and I walked down, amused by fat big tailless " mice " that scuttled like lightning over the rock-slabs. Riding into Tien Tang was like coming home again to old friends : how different from the strangeness and muffled uncertainties of my first visit ! An enthusiastic welcome awaited me in that happy place, from the Gwan-ja and the rest : and also my old quarters made ready again with all my possessions unfolded, and the Wa-wa presiding over them immediately with his most characteristic air of serene and stolid patronage. In a warm complacency I settled down into that warm environment of company and welcome ; and, after abortive but cordial interchanges with the Gwan-ja, went early to bed, an enormous moon meanwhile, just past her prime, coming palely up in a milky cloud-wrack, looking almost painfully like some production at His Majesty's.

No words can express the pleasure that I had in this sojourn at Tien Tang ; so exalted as I was by its soft balmy warmth that I could hardly bear myself for the sheer delight of it. The very air was like cream to my excoriated nerves and lungs ; and the blue breathless nights incredible with their blaze of stars, and moonshine that drove one delirious with its white cold magic. I need not tell of how the days passed in collecting all the seeds required, and drying them in trays of cardboard paper on the verandah, to the admiration of the monks : where the desiccating

pods of the graceful Caragana would amaze them by exploding in the sunshine with a sharp report, and smartly hitting
one of those holy men in the eye with a pellet of seed, to
the huge hilarity of the rest. There were new beauties
about the place, too. The poplar-park down by the river
was now at its very loveliest, with its stately boles support-
ing a uniform canopy of green shade, beneath which one
roamed the soundless bare sand in a breathless rapture of
calm through the submarine twilight. And all the cloister
yards and gardens were ablaze with Iceland Poppies, in the
richest shades that I have ever seen, and on the flat mud
roofs fields of young green corn had sprouted thick, illuminated by the flaring scarlet blobs of the Slender-leaved
Lily.

Happiness flooded into me again, like wine into a cup;
life went in a sort of leisurely roar of bliss, in work or in
rest, and the only spicules on that perfect rose of delight
were the countless moths that would come to commit suicide
in my candle as I sat out on my loggia in the starlight after
a long day of toil and sweat, and the barking dogs that
used to tatter the moonlit stillness and break my slumbers.
But even these had their compensation, in luring me indig-
nantly out on to the verandah, where the annihilating glory
of the starlight held me immediately spellbound, drowned
in a drunkenness of delight that obliterated thought of dogs
or sleep or me.

Let no one think it frivolous or frigid of me, that even
now, after all this length of intervening days, I thus hotly
speak of Tien Tang, and fly for refuge to its remote radiance.
Nor does a thing like this, once seen and felt, pass out of
one's grip. It is good for one to have seen the sun : coal
burns in the dark. Not so long since, I stood on the levelled
land out beyond Ypres ; all the world was a flat indis-
criminate muddle of raw mud, without a blade of grass or
living green thing anywhere as far as eye could stretch in
every direction, along the livid leaden lines of the distance,
with trees and houses now unguessable, mere blackened

splinters and spars of matchwood here and there; and the waste was pitted universally with shell-holes like bleared eyes, full of foul water; and the clammy mud oozed horrible colours; and the whole air was sick with a stale vile smell; and all the earth with horrors hidden or revealed—abandoned wreckage of equipment, and rusted weapons broken and thrown away; and tattered tanks like stranded dead whales on a mud-flat, and bloated carcasses of beasts immobile and mountainous, whitened with limc; and grcy broken trunks and clods like sodden sandbags, that had long lost the horror of even suggesting humanity, except where the clogged slime just displayed the spiked bulb of a helmet that was not empty, or the soles of two boots peered out of a bank; their juxtaposition showed you the whole lie of their owner's body, slack and at rest inside; or where, down in the filmy clear depths of a pool, the eye followed the strange line of a seeming tree-stump, pale and gnarled, until it startled to discern the tranquillity of an upturned mouldering chin at its end, or discovered a clenched mummified hand, brown as smoked old ivory.

The pleasant garden of European civilization! And even this, as nothing to such a garden in the actual making. But quite enough to bear. And then, when the crushing misery of it, its immortal smell of despair and defilement, were growing upon me too heavy for the limits of endurance, there suddenly rose up clear above all this, obliterating and triumphant, the reverberating cliffs of Tien Tang, rugged and high and radiant in the rose and gold of sunshine, with the long tranquil lines of white houses at their base, and their overpowering fragrance of pleasantness and warmth and peace.

Foreign travel, O reader, has its very real advantages, and all the pleasant scenes you have collected are so many medicine-bottles stored on your shelves against the maladies of life. For ugliness is something local, detachable, evanescent, while beauty is something preponderant, impregnable and eternal. It is a very small slice of earth after all that man has made into Hell : and only for a very short time. And the conches are all the while still waiting to worship in the scented sundown of Tien Tang.

I could have wished they didn't. How true it is that the wakeful night only subsides into slumber with the breakfast bell : hardly had I become able to close my eyes from the barking dogs as day began to dawn than devotion on the church-top would begin to penetrate my drowse with its melancholy note. Church services punctuated the hours more faithfully than my poor little clock, whom altitudes and rough treatment and jogglings on mule-back had so completely perturbed that no wonder if it jumped about, and marked any hour it chose, except the right one. Nor were these its only trials. Returning one morning from a seed-hunt, at what was palpably lunch-time, I was horrified to see that lying gimcrack say it was half-past four. But lunch-time it indeed was ; and Lay-gor immediately proved this by producing dishes. So that I realized it was his wicked Wa-wa who had been playing with the clock, putting it through its chimes, so as to amuse the little novices, and show off his own importance before them. But the jingle had not worked, and he had gone on turning the hands from hour to hour, in vain hope of making it do so ; and had then found himself unable to turn them back again ; and so had called in his father to cover his crime. So I sent for him, and expounded my reading of the case, and how dreadful it was ; and flared my eyes at him for a warning. Little good I got by it. With bun-faced blandness, and a sanctimonious air of innocence that would have put Job himself in a fury to take that bad child face down across his knee, the Wa-wa denied everything, and with such a candid assurance as left me feeling completely in the wrong by my unworthy suspicions. However, I maintained a stern upperlip, and continued to hope (without the smallest reason) that that nefarious infant was properly impressed.

But earthly heavens have two gates : of entrance, and of exit again. The time grew ripe for me to quit Tien Tang

with my harvest, and hie me away across the Alps to Chebson. Sad at heart to be quitting the beloved Capua of Tien
Tang—probably for ever—I nevertheless gave Spartan
orders for departure. And only then discovered that, the
Da-Tung River being now in summer spate, the rope-ferry
was in disuse, and the only remaining means of traversing
it was the bridge. So back we should have to go up to
Wolvesden, and over the pass, and down to Weston—two
nights and three days on the long trail, instead of making
for Gan Chang, and duly arriving on the second afternoon
at Chebson. However, there was no help for it : I gave
my last instructions, and on a day rode out again from Tien
Tang over the downs. In the Da-Tung shingles the little
fragrant rose, so lovely with its fine bluish foliage, and its
pink bloomy shoots, and its profusion of rich red flowers,
consoled me by being now only less lovely with its heavy
burden of scarlet hips, from which the calyx falls away
immediately, so that they look like crowded vermilion fruits
of some magnified Cotoneaster in their thick clusters all
down the bending sprays. Also at the mouth of the ghyll,
Anemone vitifolia was splendid, in one wide colony, waving
now in a boscage of big fat flowers of soft pink—the only
occurrence of this plant that I know, save one, throughout
the length and breadth of the Da-Tung Alps—whereas, in
the regions of Siku and Jo-ni, far to the South of these, in
1914, it had been a commonplace of all the warm open stony
places and field edges, up the whole of the Tibetan border
lowlands.

The next day I spent at Wolvesden, accomplishing minor
jobs ; it was as blazing hot up here as it had been down
at Tien Tang ; in nothing but shorts and a pyjama jacket
I roamed up Soùtherly Valley, and was ecstatically blissful.
A little dull Ephedra that had hitherto only made mats of
dusty grey wire among the shingles had now sheeted itself
solid with bloomy rose-scarlet drupes ; and there were
many other seeds near at hand to collect. On the morrow
we removed over the Pass, to the House of Many Babies,

en route for Chebson.   And anything like the Western face
of the Pass I have seldom seen.   All the uppermost zigzags
and open scree banks were dense with rounded low clouds
of the Violet Delphinium, among which stalwartly stood up
the azure spires of the Celestial Poppy.   It was a stupefying
sight, and one of these combinations that Nature alone can
effect with complete success.   But none of the seeds in the
limestone ghyll were ripe, and I could only discover one fat
pod of Iris potaninii, and by the time I emerged towards
the Western foothills the day had grown leadenly grey.
Tired and dehilarated by the lurid dark, I drifted at length
into the yard of Many Babies, and sadly anticipated a soak-
ing day to follow.

But by a miracle the morrow turned out so gorgeous that
I even got another tiny touch of sun.   We were off early,
along a new track, indicated to us by a new Do-fu (donkey-
man), who had lately accrued, mysteriously, to the staff.   I
raised remarks, but he was so confident and reassuring that
I let the matter slide.   Blandly and in acute good humour
at prospect of a short easy stage I drifted over the broad
plains of corn and flax and violent yellow mustard, and
over the ruddy intervening spurs between them.   But
gradually the journey, which I had flattered myself would
be so brief, began to be long ; and, to my horror, I realized
that the officious Do-fu's new track that he was so sure of
meant to lead us South of the two big down-masses that rise
in splendid isolation below Chebson.   This added many
miles to our journey, and I longed for command of language
adequately to comminate that Do-fu, as the distances trailed
out behind us and lengthened away ahead.   With rage I
saw the real downs of our destination away up on the right,
and grew to appreciate the enormousness of having to strike
back at them, all the way up the stream-course that intervenes between the two fells.   They themselves, too, and
their gorge, were depressing.   The gorge, indeed, was really
more of an open vale, extremely long and hot, and entirely
void of interest ; while the fells, though steep and high, were

evidently both dry and dull. As the distance increases behind one, so increases on one the weariness of a prolonged day's stage ; and I quailed to contemplate the stodge of toiling all the way up those elephantine bulks, with the almost certainty of finding nothing there but Nobbutnowtia. But so I always incline to feel towards the end of the day, when my climbing ambitions strangely dwindle.

And so, after what seemed almost the period of a patriarch, we had done with the windings of that uninteresting stream-bed, and emerged upon a level sea of grassy plain, down into the head of which ran a cloven green promontory. And in that fold of the promontory nestled the four white Chortens all of a row, and the crowded low white lines, and the golden roof of Chebson Abbey. The close of that tedious journey was by far its brightest part ; for not only had I now our goal in sight, but the plain itself was very lovely, lush with tall beautiful plants of the damp moorland turf, among which the most striking was a stately Senecio [1] with handsome sea-blue foliage, and very big bright-golden flowers set rarely and at reasonable intervals near the top of its three-foot stem. Also, having alighted to examine this and to walk across the moor and collect its treasures, I was struck by the likeliness of the place for the little starry Trollius, of which I had failed to find any seed in the plain above Weston, where alone I had seen it in flower. And on prying round, I found the seed-heads abundant here, and fully ripe, lurking among the elongated sword-tufts of Iris ensata. And so at last we rode slowly up the final mile into the downs about dusk, under a sky now dark and brewing as ever over all the Alps ; and found the rest of the train comfortably settled in, having come the right way ; and the Prior a-beam with smiles, and his own quarters across the courtyard allotted me this time for mine.

The lapse of time was evident in Chebson. All along one side the red outer wall of the church precinct was now

[1] In cultivation it has bloomed a dowdy weed, says E. A. Bowles.

propped up on poles to prevent it falling down altogether. Other repairs and alterations were proceeding in the other churches, but a denser calm than ever seemed to brood over the place. I saw nobody but the Prior all the time I was there, and the chief signs of religious activity were two small novices, who sat about and practised on the conch with the most devastating effect. Even when, by request, they were induced to remove their pious ardours to a remoter cloister, the brief and broken monotony of their blasts was maddening. I judged it would be very long before they attained the *sostenuto* strength of lung exhibited at Tien Tang; but anyhow, the patient persistence of their efforts deserved success.

On another occasion, when the spacious calm of the cloister had ceased to reverberate with the news of Violet Asquith's engagement, I was wandering up and down the arcades, when my ears were assaulted on all sides with a droning thundering blare that seemed to come from everywhere at once, like a tiger's purr, sinking and soaring and re-echoing hollowly all round the cloister in the most baffling manner. For a moment or two I stood smitten, casting my eyes around for some monstrous demon of the air; then addressed myself to discovering whence these grisly boomings could proceed. For quite a while I vainly peep-bo'ed with the invisible band, but at last, warned by yells of especial ferocity, lifted my eyes on high (for I was now in the deep well of cloister behind the guest-yard) and saw that the concert was raging overhead, on the roof-loggia of the church. It was a chaos of queer muffled wailings, as if on muted violins played high up on the lowest string, accompanied by duets on two enormous trumpets, at least fifteen feet long, projecting out over the parapet on which they were propped. In a vast mimallonean buzz the noise continued till seven in the evening, assisted below by the big bell in the cloister: often the trumpets took fresh breath, and boomed and droned and blared with very splendid effect; but would often collapse and cough and break

wind in the most lamentable manner instead, like the sharp
ripping of trousers.

But of other holy activities I saw no sign. Nor went out
to look for them, indeed : nor could expect to see them
otherwise. For here I wish to enter a word of caution.
There is one very silly section of the world, which talks of
all other religions and religious bodies than their own, as
" heathenism " and " idolaters " ; but there is also another
section which rushes to the diametrically opposed extreme,
in a silliness which is hardly less extreme than the other
—though very much more respectable, in that it is an
exaggeration of sympathy and interest and curiosity,
developed all together into a gross credulity. For these
good people, who would be cold as pebblestones about any
ordinary European monk, grow moist-eyed immediately
on mention of a Tibetan one, and seem to think the mere
word Lama is not only equivalent to a saint, but pregnant
with all the arts of magic. They look upon me with wonder
when they hear I have frequented Tibetan monasteries,
and seem to think that I must there have been submerged
in a sea of Mahatmas and miracles and all manner of other
such unholinesses as are most strictly forbidden to any
follower of the Buddha, no matter how remote. Even
round my own head I find a reflected aura of mystery ; such
are the sights and secrets I am considered to have absorbed
during my sojournings in the Sacred and Mysterious land,
that on a day, when I tried to play up to this reputation,
and told somebody at a party that I saw in her a mongoose
being evoked, the poor lady immediately turned pale and
faintly shrieked, and sank in a swoon upon the .tea-cups,
declaring that she felt herself becoming one indeed ; while
all the other feathered hats twittered together, in terror-
stricken envy of her mystic experience.

The plain truth alone shall be my portion. Perhaps I
have not been long enough or deep enough in Tibet to
develop that rank and riotous imagination with which it
sometimes seems to inspire the people who say they have

s

seen it.   But, anyhow, plain truth is always a great deal more
interesting than the most flaring fantasies of fiction.   And
the plain truth of the matter here is that a Tibetan monastery
is very much the same as any other monastery all the world
over.   The percentage of good and evil in any accumulated
body of religious students and devotees is a very stable
quantity; and of saints and sinners no doubt Chebson and
Hilmi and Hiei-Zan contain precisely the same proportion as
Monte Cassino, Stonyhurst and the Grande Chartreuse.
And, beyond a doubt also, the main mass of monks, in all
these establishments, are neither the one nor the other, but a
body of men exactly like other men, except for their robes
and restrictions, not very good, not very bad, but rather
bored and obliterated in their profession, and sodden in lust
of body and lethargy of mind, thanks to the unnatural conditions of a life for which not one of them in ten has any
aptitude whatever.

As for the powers, who is there that shall prescribe limits
to will-force, and to will-feebleness ?   No doubt there are
various people in all countries whose faith is great enough
to move mountains, as no doubt there are very many more
whose folly is great enough to see the mountains move.   The

And, in any case, it must be remembered yet again, that
in such a community it is not the real saints and students who
have time to waste on a casual visitor, or who naturally
occur to his casual glance.   It is not from loafers in the
church-court that you can gauge the high flights of the
secluded saints you never see.   And from the fact that you
never do see them, one section of opinion is much too apt to
jump at the conclusion that they do not exist, as the other
is to exaggerate, credulously, alike their multitude and their
powers.   Therefore, of saints abounding I can tell no sentimental tale : Buddhas and Bodhisattvas do not grow on
every bush; the men in Tibetan monasteries that I myself
have seen were simply men very like all other average
ecclesiastics in any creed or country, and the others I take
on trust.

Buddha, however, teaches a profound disgust and distrust for material miracles. No matter how enormous they may be, they can never be any argument (as an evil and adulterous generation always takes them) in favour of a spiritual truth ; which would be their only *raison d'être* ; therefore, the follower of the Buddha, however vivid an academic interest he may take in marvels and the marvellous powers of man, will always leave them aside in his course, and refuse to be preoccupied with them, or to try to prove things by them. Of what mysterious and supra-normal feats the Living Buddhas in Tibetan monasteries are capable, I cannot rightly speak ; everything is possible, but nothing is proven. But Mahatmas and Maskelyne-Cookeries are mere inventions of a scheming folly that has nothing whatever in common with Buddhism but the name ; which it has not the smallest right to bear. In none of its true branches has Buddhism ever gone a-whoring after such nonsenses ; whatever powers the Arahat or the Bodhisat may possess, these are the simple collateral results of his development, not ends in themselves to be made a gaping-stock and argument for the silly. Therefore, once and for all, the general atmosphere of a big Buddhist Abbey is neither more impressive and holy, nor less so, than that of any other religious foundation. No special awe hangs heavy upon it ; miracles do not occur at every corner of its streets, nor its casual monks exude conjuring-trick rabbits with each wave of the hand.

There was much work, meanwhile, proceeding among the seeds. The two high downs below the Abbey, indeed, yielded nothing at all, as I had rather dreaded ; but the green folds round about the Abbey itself, beside their harvest of seeds, were now also at their prettiest with flowers. There was nothing of special interest, of course, but all the big grassy downs were thickly enamelled with blossoms, and Stellera particularly abundant. With penknives we delved into the hard tussocks of Iris tenuifolia, to pry out its astonishing fat pear-shaped pods, fleshy and rose-coloured at the top, like prickly-pear-fruits embedded in a fossilized clot of bass-matting. Then we crossed over on to the side where the folds of coppice are, to quest for the blue Corydal in the Potentilla tuffets up the slope. But not a trace of seed was to be seen, nor, indeed, any trace of the plant remaining at all. So, by degrees we came up on to the crest, where, among the russet-coloured hollows and rises of the moorland, my Aster rose glorious here and there, with solitary ragged flowers of rich violet over the low scrub. And there was also a big fringy Pink, of ravishing fragrance, that was none other than our old and valued friend Dianthus squarrosus. So here, with full packets and pockets, we long lay out upon a crest, languid in the wide loveliness of the scene, with the green plain at our feet, sweeping round the base of the promontory like an unrippled sea ; and then those two lonely and gigantic purple downs beyond, abruptly blocking the view.

Even the Abbey yielded seed and flowers. For the stone-walling and the flagstones of the yards and cloisters were now a-flaunt with Iceland poppies, and in the guest-cloister itself, at the foot of the stone lions, Trollius Chinensis was blooming luxuriantly in fine bushes, throwing up far and wide its gaping patens of rich orange. And there was an older friend still. For along all the lines of the walls in the deep quiet of the yards behind my cloister there fluttered gaily a charming little tri-colour Pansy, of violet and butter-yellow, with its two upper petals of richest purple-velvet, but outlined with a thin line of cream all round, that gave the flowers a most perky and intelligent expression. And Viola Chebsonensis must have come a very far journey, to be Viola Chebsonensis at all. For there exists no tri-colour Viola anywhere in the Eastern borders of Tibet, or the inlands of China. So that this little pansy must have been of foreign descent, a cousin, though indefinitely removed, of Mr. Dobbie's giants. Some lover of such delights, English beyond a doubt, assuredly gave pansy-seed to some big monastery near the coast, such as Wu-Tai-S'an ; and in course of time some Abbot or Living Buddha on pilgrimage must have conveyed a pinch of its descendants' seed to Chebson. And here it is, now flourishing and cheery as any wild plant established on the spot since the beginning of time. It was with a never-failing thrill of emotion that I always used to contemplate those multitudinous little old friendly faces, flickering along the eaves and gutters of the courtyard walls in Chebson ; trying to figure out the long romance of their arrival here, and the kindly thought of the kindly people who passed it on from hand to hand up-country, in no desire but to give pleasure. How vivid a contrast, O readers, to the results of that merely utilitarian and profit-seeking thought which introduced the rabbit to Australia !

Now only remained my expedition up into the Alps at the head of the delta-plain. Untaught by experience, I had nursed a hope that perhaps, by starting very early, I might achieve one of the big heights that same day, and so shorten my visit. However, the pace of the caravan was so slow, and the length of the moorland level so immense, that it was at least midday when we got into the throat of the gorge, and it now took another hour or more to put up the tent. The first place I picked for it, up under the shelter of a little cliff, proved too small, and we had to move it down nearer the floor of the glen, close to the track. It was rather a public spot, for the delta-plain below was now quite populous with yurts and camps of cattle, with jolly people passing down the path all the time, pulling carts of cut shrubbery for bedding. But peace and security seemed to rule, and everybody passed us a happy time of day as they went. Across the flat of the glen where the beck brabbles greyly through the sombre-coloured waste of hummocks, two Lamas and their attendant were encamped, each in a little white tent of his own, like a bathing-box. But they held austerely aloof, and took no notice of us, except for a beautiful but wall-eyed peasant lad who was visiting them ; and presently came splashing through the beck and the dotted pools to give us a greeting, and watch our proceedings with the tent.

But by the time everything was fixed, I looked up and saw the Alps swelling upon me overhead so dishearteningly enormous that clearly, in what was now left of the day, there was no possibility of achieving a serious ascent. So I distributed the staff, and sent off the officious Do-fu back to Chebson for *Northanger Abbey*, which that polypragmatic person had managed to omit. After which I waded the beck hard by where the monks were shuttered up in mysterious seclusion; and set myself to climbing in the deep ghyll-fold of the fell that I had already visited, while it was still sere and bare in early summer. But nothing was yet ripe; which confirmed my conviction that this place stands even higher than Weston. After me came Lay-gor and Go-go: the latter I sent ahead of me, to prospect, while Lay-gor and I roamed around the bay, above and below. But we saw no sign of anything new; only a very lovely albinoid of the Harebell Poppy, with bells of pure white, deepening to a violet base. The afternoon was grilling and glorious: I lay on tussocks, and conned the vast green fells opposite, heaving away up and up and up, to their culminating peaks; with smallness and cold fear in my heart, to crane up and see how big they were. So at last I rambled slowly downward again, still seeing no pod of the Butterfly Iris, whose blossoms had so beautifully abounded here in June, beside the beck. It was soon dark down below, and there was yet a long dull time of waiting before the Do-fu reappeared with the vital volume. And when he did reappear, it was with *Emma* in his hand, not *Northanger Abbey*! People who will always do everything do everything invariably wrong. And I had so longed for that letter of Isabella's, so "faithfully promised"! However, no alternative in *Jane* can be unwelcome: I got into bed and became very happy at the "worthy Coles'"; got out of it to dine, and then, getting back, was happier still.

I rose very early after a poor night to find the day had

dawned ominous, filmed over with cloud-threats. But early
as was I, the monks on the scrub-flat opposite were earlier
still. For now those blank white bathing-tents had come to
life and given up their secret; the pontiffs had emerged in
high yellow mitres, armed with trumpets and green drums.
And now on these they boomed and droned and palely
tooted, perlustrating the place in a solemn measure, this
way and that, forth and back. I wish I could have known
what it was all about, that curious lonely liturgy, up in the
heart of the Alps. But Go-go was ignorant, and the unutterable scorn on the face of the Wa-wa was enough, of itself, to
congeal curiosity on my lips.

So now I set forward, and rode about half a mile farther
up, to where, by a gate of cliffs, a left-hand glen converges,
revealing gaunt red screes and crags and naked peaks away
at its far end. Towards these, then, I sent the Go-go forward, with his collecting-tin, while I myself, and both the
Wa-was, bearing both the big blue umbrellas, set ourselves
to breasting the rib on the left, which is like a steep toe to the
great green fell overhead. The climb was so enormous as
to be quite stupefying: in a mechanical endurance we
mounted and mounted; all I saw of novelty was a queer
Lathræa once or twice. And still we toiled on upwards, ten
yards at a time, while the day grew rapidly more baleful.
It was a long age before we had surmounted even the first
bulge of the fell. Here we came into sight of yet more, and
higher, billowing away overhead in vast swells of lifeless,
browning moorland. But here our way was also unexpectedly diversified, and the incalculable loneliness of the
scene unwontedly exhilarated. For, scattered across the
face of the slope, like beaters, came along a carolling gay
crew of Tibetan maids and matrons in blue and scarlet, very
vivid on that dun-coloured scene, with copious chains of
bead and silver and coral swinging from their bosoms or
their many-plaited heads, as they stooped along the moor at
their task of collecting the round yellow garlic heads. We
hailed them and shouted; but they were coy and startled

as wild deer, and floundered away over the fell in a flight as we pursued them, like a flock of Oreads surprised by hunters on their mountains. But high squeals and laughter floated back at us through the cold threatening dark of the air.

So onwards we ascended still, leaving these lesser thoughts below ; up and up a long series of steep grassy rises, towards a red and green crest above, and a peak now becoming visible far overhead ; no new flowers anywhere in the coarse russet-coloured lawns of the moorland ; the clustered paper-white Silene was pretty, but, *proh pudor*, the prettiest, brightest and most abundant show of all was provided by nothing more nor less than the common Dandelion ! And this is an insult which has never yet been inflicted on me by any European height, be it no higher than the mere Moncenisio. But here, at some 13,000 ft. or 14,000 ft., I felt it the outrage almost incredible—the night work of some enemy. It takes a granitic alp of the Da-Tung to achieve so grotesque a violation of Alpine proprieties.

Jaundiced in my views, and peevish, I accordingly proceeded up to the stony slides and arêtes, close beneath the black overwhelming darkness of the sky, that now began to spit. In all the shingles there was rich glory of the Delphinium, the Celestial Poppy and Corydalis melanochlora : but nothing was ripe in seed, and there was nothing new at all, except for the little dwarf yellow stars of a Cremanthodium. Sick with so stale a set of beauties, I wandered to the right, along the rib-saddle which ties this flying buttress of the mountains to the main mass, where the naked red peak impends. The saddle would have made a very lovely Alpine scene, had its views on flower-production been less restricted —a long rippled series of lawns and dips and shallow blunted outcrops almost worn down into the turf, which, at this altitude, was springy and dark and sodden. While, on the far side, the scree-slopes sank indefinitely downward, jewelled as they went, with azure maces of poppy, the golden stars of Cremanthodium, and the excruciating loveliness of the

Corydalis, in humped blobs of snow-flecked turquoise, squatting on its sumptuous blue foliage over the raw red face of the scree. Under a sky so imminent and black the air takes on a cold ghastly pallor in which flowers seem actually to flame ; on the charnel-house gloom of that voor alp, the blues and purples and yellows of the blossoms were like multitudinous flecks of electric fire, luminous as ghost-lights. But otherwise neither the view nor its presentment was rewarding ; the mountains being all dull huge green downs, or else dead pandemoniums of craggy pyramid and scree : while the distances of plain out in the West were only a boring ocean of monotony in the greyness.

And so I came to the foot of the Red Peak overhead, now beginning to swim in ominous vapour, while behind it, on the world of black or russet crags that formed its universal background, the heavy-lidded night of storm was momentarily sinking lower. Through the glasses I diligently explored the cliffs and ledges above me. But the peak was a crumbling pyramid of wholly lifeless ruin, blank and naked. And in its lower reaches there were only the same things as I had seen everywhere else. Meanwhile the darkness was settling down upon me, in a sort of universal droning boom, as if the consummation of all things was approaching, through a dark crescendo of silence. So, completely disillusioned, I set off sliding downwards, in the couloir of fine shale where the ridge flies out at an angle from the Red Peak. It sinks ere long into a widening gully of rough coarse chaos, shingle and bald shale, wreckage of the Red Peak that has now flown up overhead into the pale Coan swirls of cloud. Among the stones a small purple Aconite was pretty, and, on the shady side, I came on one large mass of Androsace mucronifolia ; and the violet of the Delphinium was everywhere glorious. As the spitting of the rain ceased, I sat on a boulder to take a midday snack, and a funny little bush-tailed weaselly creature, as long and thin as some heraldic beast on a royal shield, emerged from its lair in the scree, and bounded about on the stones near by. Both the Wa-was were, of course, immediately agog to kill it : but I repressed their degrading ardours.

And now, as I plunged downwards in the corrie again, the long-delayed rain began descending in force. For a while we sheltered under a brow of cliff, hoping that the deluge would lighten ; however, it clearly had no such intention, and grew steadily worse. So desperately we plunged on downwards, beneath the big blue umbrellas, the Wa-was bobbing away below me. In time the corrie became a torrent-ghyll ; far and far we dived towards the depths of the glen, where gradually scrub and sedge resumed sway ; we kept as closely as possible to the rill-groove itself, which offered the one clear channel down the dip, otherwise filled with sopped Potentilla tangles that birched my bare legs under my shorts to raspberry ice. And so descended at long last into the lower valley, whence it was still more than a mile back to the tent. Here immediately I retired to bed, blander and in better humour than could have been hoped after so weariful and disappointing a day—that had not even been very pleasurable as a walk, owing to the general lack of beauty in weather or air or scene. But, with each successive death of hope, the passing pang comes easier. Even when the Go-go returned from his expedition, he also brought me, in his crowded tin, nothing newer than clumped masses of Corydalis melanochlora.

And of all my failures, this lies heaviest on my memory and my longing, even heavier than Primula hylophila and Primula Violagrandis. For Corydalis melanochlora is so specially lovely a plant, and bade so fair to prosper in our moraines as well as in its own shingles. Its name, indeed, is very silly (I only discovered it from Przewalsky's dried specimens in the Petrograd Herbarium : Professor Balfour had meanwhile called it C. Purdomii), yet has so liquid a loveliness of its own that I retain it, though in no way does " black-pale " or " black-green " give any hint of those amazing snow-white helmets, huddled together on the glaucous foliage, crested and lipped with a blazing violent light azure, with just a point of black at their vizor. And so hearty and abundant a plant, too, raging over all the highest open screes and shingles, from Thundercrown (at least) equally luxuriant up to the Da-Tung Alps in the far north—and farther yet, no doubt, whether on lime or shale or granite. Nevertheless with all my work and waitings and watching, I was never able anywhere to catch its seed on the hop. It had always either hopped already when I came to it, or was too remote from the moment of doing so. For no plant did I try harder, but in all the thousands of specimens we attempted, the tale was still the same. So I then sedulously collected its bunched tubers, and gardened them up at Wolvesden in boxes. But though they throve and appeared to ripen their seed, it all turned out no good, and though I sent home such germs as I was thus able to achieve, none of them proved fertile, and nothing more has anybody heard or seen of Corydalis melanochlora in the living plant. For, unkindest cut of all; though I copiously sent home those tubers, and though they travelled well, not even these went any further, but died off after arrival, despite the plump healthiness in which they appeared to arrive. So that C. melanochlora still awaits introduction, on her gaunt screes—and is well worth the pilgrimage, all for herself.

No more expeditions yielded any more results. A chilly mizzle universally prevailed. In a dull hopeless morning I caused the camp to be disestablished, and rode away down to Chebson, so weary and mountain-sick with all this steady failure that I could have found it in my heart to forswear alps altogether, and henceforth cultivate no more difficult eminence than Brighton Esplanade. The monks across the beck had shifted their tents up the scrub-flat, and then down the scrub-flat, and now were busy as usual at their mysterious pontifications, lugubrious in the drizzling greyness. And the day darkened to deluges as I rode. But then it cleared to brightness again, and by the time we had left the mountains behind, had developed into balmy pleasantness. Chebson received me with its large august benignity, and I sustained various visits through the rest of the day from his Eminence the Prior, who now developed an alarming assortment of stomachic symptoms, on each of which in turn he came to me for advice—the reason of this abrupt failure in health being the arrival of the Post Lao-han, bearing, among other things, a bottle of Hennessey to replenish my depleted store.

He also brought a letter from Bill reporting chiefly barrenness and monotony from the Koko-Nor and the Kweite-Salar ranges, except for a pretty form of Iceland Poppy, and a big white-flowered bush Potentilla, "with the leaves of a Sorbus," which abounded in the sterile river shingles. But in such a state of nerves was I by this time, as to be timorous over even this lovely acquisition; and then by "one of those sudden bursts of mind that do sometimes occur" I flashed into memory of P. Salessowi, of which Bill's description gave an accurate picture. And P. Salessowi had already been in the garden at Ingleborough for more than ten years, and had there once produced one flower, and ugly at that! "What a life!" peevishly exclaims the diary at this point. The ironies of fate and time! For now, with what a tearing hunger of heart could I say ἠλίβατος ὑπὸ κευθμῶσι γενοίμην of Tien Tang or Chebson, never staying at all to be pernickety about their productions in the plant line. But Bill's Potentilla did indeed prove to be none other than P. Salessowi; so that all I learned from that soon-extinguished hope is that if anyone possesses this handsome shrub, and wants to see it beautiful in blossom, an arid treatment of gravel and stones is indicated, rather than the soporific fatness of garden soil.

But now good-bye to Chebson. Long affectionate handholdings with the Prior; many a promise of return—and forth I rode in the tail of the cavalcade, over the brow of the down. And the hills closed round on Chebson Abbey, and hid it from my sight. Sadly I traversed the Deltas, insisting this time on keeping the proper way; and the day was a pathetic fallacy to match that of my extinguished hopes—

a level day, of ugly arid atmosphere, ha'ary and colourless; with much of the sky now overcast with clouds, like me. The journey, though, was greatly shortened by keeping to the straight course, and the House of Many Babies received me warmly. Here I lay a little while collapsed with illness for hope deferred and defunct maketh more than the heart sick; and the Go-go ailed also. The return was yet further procrastinated by black storms, alike in the staff and on the Alps. Feebly I tried to comprehend and cope with the former, and abjectly went to bed from the other, while appalling thunders raged for hours all around, and the Alps overhead were lost in bellowing midnight, and the green world below went white with hail. The temperature, too, had by this time turned arctically cold through all this high region; and, even in warm sunny Chebson, lying far out from the Alps as it does, had been so chilly as to make me remember, with embittered regret, the gorgeous heat that had reigned, even on the higher flanks of Thundercrown, a month later than this.

In intervals of the converging storms I looked up anxiously to the gleaming combes and chines of smooth precipice overhead above the green folds of the impending Alps. In flaccid feebleness I sent off the convalescent Go-go to prospect, while the rest collected seed of Stellera and Daphne in the plain. But, as he returned empty-handed without having attained the highest heights, I was more than ever haunted by the feeling that we ought to go and camp up there definitely. But really, in the wintry cold, I could not manage to lug myself into entertaining the notion of undergoing so much, for the inevitable reward of nothing at all. Finally the situation was taken out of my hands, and I was vastly relieved when Lay-gor and Go-go came to ask me if we might get off early on the morrow, so as to be over the pass, and home in Wolvesden, before the worst of the weather had happened. My heart glowed proleptically at this decision: in Wolvesden, at least, one would be able to have a fire again, and once more feel that one had feet. So for

half that idle afternoon I drowsed, and for the rest I slept :
in the evening I got up to dine in the little central room
behind the verandah. But the cold was piercing and blew
in by every crevice ; and the yak-dung cakes on the fire-pan
were powerless to dispel it. I felt strangely empty and
bloodless, and powerless against circumstances : delighted
when dusk at last descended, and the day was done.

Marvellous revival next morning in me as well as the
weather ; for the latter was in a glorious mood, after all,
and so was I.   And there was a nip in the air like iced wine,
and the Alps were grizzled with new sleet. Scruples and
duties faded from my mind like cloud-wracks from a peak
at sunrise. Looking neither to right nor left, I set off with
the caravan, crammed all my pockets with seed of Stellera
in the plain, and then, with various diversions after other
seeds by the way, addressed myself to the Pass. And from
afar, as I rode up towards the glen-head, its upper half
seemed lost in an odd dull cloud, like slate-coloured smoke
lying immovable and solid over the final zigzags. Only
when I got nearer did I realize that this was Delphinium
Pylzowi, now in its fullest zenith of glory, in myriads of tight
domed masses all over the open path-side scree, each of them
perhaps nine inches high and a foot wide ; and every one
of them almost hidden from sight by its abundant flights of
big violet butterflies, aggregating into a sheer sheet of
richest purple all up the slope, interspersed with myriads of
bristling azure poppy-spires, as if an army of small pokers
had been dipped in Heaven and then stuck upright into the
fell-side, with Heaven still adhering to their poke in gouts
and clots and splashes. It was a sight to make one shout.
But being alone, I had to do most of my shouting internally,
which always hurts more. If only D. Pylzowi will condescend to grow as stout and dense and stocky at home, and
to give that abundance of blossom, and of as rich a size and
brilliancy, as on its own Alps ! So far I only know of it as
rather lank and spindly in growth, rather dull and squinny
of flower. But perhaps, when it has settled down to new

surroundings, it may revert to its true domestic style—
though I must confess that my Alpine Delphiniums have both
seemed hitherto rather ominously inconstant to their original form under the seductive influences of garden culture.
Even D. tanguticum, from its perfectly dwarf and enormous-
flowered form on the scree-tops of Thundercrown and Ardjeri,
too often maintains in the garden a fatal new propensity
to length of weakly shank, and pallid diminished blossom.

Now followed hot and glorious days of seed-collecting, all
about Wolvesden and the neighbouring hills. The grilling
little yard was full of big paper trays with stacks of seed set
out to cook in the sun. These had to be weighted with
stones at their corners against the wind ; but even so, or in
the toil of getting them all indoors again at sundown (which
sometimes left a corner of some tray unguarded while its
neighbour was removed), there would come a sudden draught,
and the trays would lift and flap and flounder and threaten
to blow away, until with shrieks I had summoned all the
rest of the staff, who with answering shrieks would come
pelting out of the kitchen to weight them down again, or
carry them in—everybody, meanwhile, vehemently cursing
everybody else for neglect.

No event, and no high adventure, marked these days of
awaiting Bill's return. They were long. He had written
again, by this time, and was as sickened and disappointed
as I, with unvarying disappointment and sameness in the
Kweite-Salar Alps, and round the Koko-Nor. Evidently he
was as keen as I to finish up quickly with these ranges, and
get away. He sent a hamper of plants ahead of him now,
but they all looked very much the same as those of the
Da-Tung, except for a fat dwarf Gentian, bilious and pallid,
which I soon learned to believe only a variant of blue G.
triflora, universal on the high Alps overhead.[1] For now was

---

[1] Aster F. 75, from the marshes of the Koko-Nor, was also in
this batch, and Mariae, form of Androsace tibetica, thin leaved
and so late in bloom as now to be at its full, whereas the type was
already shedding its seed.

the hey-day of Gentians, alike on the heights and in the depths. Only tiny Gentians rule the spring in North China ; the prime of the big ones begins in August. By now they shone all about Wolvesden—a big straggling coarse affair with flopping stems and creamy flowers, which is probably G. straminea, and a handsome stalwart thing growing into a dense bush, with such myriads of flowers that though they never open properly, the rich sapphire blue of their outsides, and their thick-set multitudes, produce a most sumptuous effect of colour—which I hope will be no duller or poorer at home, seeing that this Gentian affects just those common open sunny places in common ordinary open soil, as are affected in the Alps by weed-easy G. cruciata. While down in the hot lands by Tien Tang, the open banks and path-sides are abundant in yet another floppet, with upstaring violet flowers along the ground-hugging sprays that radiate from its crown. And this is the *real* G. Przewalskyi, leaving the very much handsomer sapphire velvet beauty of 1914 (F. 303) to take its true rank at last as a new species, under the name of G. Purdomii, a hardy treasure if ever there was one, delighting the torrid lowland banks and road-sides round Jo-ni, as heartily as does G. Przewalskyi those of the more Northerly regions. But all these, and all their beauties, are but as an opening chorus of supers for the autumnal Gentians of the high Alps, from whom is now soon to step forth and take the stage, the Primadonna assoluta of this season, if not of both my own seasons, and most of everybody else's.

For now, one afternoon, I sat resting, after an expedition for seeds up Southerly Valley, from which I had sent the Wa-was ahead of me home with the harvest, since their indefatigable good manners in keeping close on my heels had worn even closer on my nerves. And as I sat, there arose simultaneous rushings in the yard, and cries of " Por-loy ! " Out I ran, as eagerly as the rest. And there, indeed, was my dear Bill, afar off yet, but riding smartly down the last green bay above the beck, cloaked in a Jaeger blanket, and

waving a yak-tail fly-whisk.   Ecstasies of reunion followed ;
we sat and prowled and prattled till far into the night, and he
gave me such an account of the sad enormous dull monotony
of the Koko-Nor as quite let me off all wish to see it.   And
we decided to make off immediately up into the Alps,
on a final inspection ; and then to pack up and be gone
for the sunny South, and the remote hopes of the Da-Ba
S'an.

   But the next few days, after all, were rather niddering.
The staff took ill with a sort of influenza.   And then I also
followed suit.   And the weather, angry at having given no
smallest sign of that six weeks' rainy season that had been
held out as my summer prospect, developed sullen rages
that evidently preluded the Alpine winter.   Long I lay
abed, low and poorly, listening to the incessant rain : only
quinine could lug me so far out of coma as to be capable of
even Pride and Prejudice—a drug of itself which I had
always hitherto believed could cope with the highest temperature and the deepest lethargy.   And when I resumed
consciousness, it was to find a white world, with densely-
falling thawing snow.   At thought of what this must portend
up on the Alps above, the energy of desperateness hauled
me into convalescence, and I insisted with myself that I
must be perfectly fit again by the time the staff had prepared
the way up to camp, as they were now forthwith dispatched
to do.   Meanwhile the weather obeyed my commands to
clear ; and so did I.   In glorious days I sat about ecstatically, though kitten-weak.   And in the night, unable to
sleep, I cast all my padded coats about me, and sallied out
into the huge moon-flooded silence of the Dene, where the
beck mysteriously roared and blattered up into the velvety
supernatural calm.   It was an intoxicating hour, almost
unbearable in the glare of its black-and-white glory and its
breathless tranquillity.   On successive boulders beside the
beck I sat and basked in the ghastly blaze ; it was warm and
still as a night in Kandy.

   My own method, when I more severely ail, is to rage

T

through Burroughs & Wellcome's black box, and take two
pilules out of every pill-tube ; if one does not cure, the next
may.   Anyhow, some effect is bound to be produced, even
if the method be a trifle drastic and empirical.   Unfortunately, on this occasion I took too comprehensive a variety
of medicines to combat my ills ; though the effect, indeed,
was produced, it was almost excessive ; with the result that
when, on the morrow, we did at last set off for the Alps, in a
fine but filmy morning with a hard cold wind, I suddenly
" came over " abjectly weak and weary, and felt myself a
fool for going.   But there is no medicine for megrims half so
good as mountains ; I was ere long completely preoccupied.
Down the depths of the Dene we rode, and up the shingled
miles of the confluent river, meeting, in the alder-coppice of
the boulder-bed, with the abandoned antlers of an elk, left
there till its lucky murderer should have time to come and
reclaim them.   Then up the mountain-side we still rode, and
up to the Ma-chang, and up and up and up into the Alp, and
over its bays and folds, till we actually attained on horse-
back to the mountain of black blocks above the Clear
Lake.

It is a curious place, so loose a compilation of sombre
vast rocks that the turf between is springy with unfilled holes
beneath, and there are deep caverns and hollows everywhere
among the boulders, and water trickling and lurking, as if
the whole hill were a sponge.   As it indeed is, a slack-woven
texture, full of pores and passages, lightly accumulated, and
never settled down into solidity.   Here we encamped ;
Bill in one tent, and I in another, and the staff in the
big white one, lent us by the Viceroy of the Koko-
Nor.

Close below lies the Clear Lake, down a steep climb among
the dips and dells of the boulder-mountain.   But at its head
there intervenes the Jardin of which I spoke, a smooth delta
of becks and rills converging to the Lake.   And, as I now
patrolled it gently, while the tents were being established,
I realized with a certain sardonic amusement that all my

other expeditions in the Da-Tung Alps had been wasted.
For here, in this stretch of a quarter of a mile across and a
hundred yards deep, occurred every high Alpine flower that
I had found in the whole course of the season's arduous and
unrewarding expeditions—with the solitary exception of
Primula urticifolia, immovably calcicole. It was a bewilderingly enrapturing place, with its paradoxical population,
seeded down from the heights or translated by the becks.
All the Poppies were there, all the Primulas, and many
another adminicle of delight. And they all looked like guests
and aliens, gathered together in one space by Nature's special
invitation. I benignly revelled among the seeds, now ripe
for the gathering, even to the prevalent Alpine Saxifrage of
these ranges—a feathery spire of white stars, rising from a
rosette of very handsome glossy primuloid foliage : and each
star with a pompous fat eye of black-purple, from the conspicuous swollen carpels. I suspect this of being S. egregia ;
anyhow it abounds all over the high lawns of the Da-Tung,
and descends to the foot of the Pass. But why pause on one
pleasure, when there were so many more ? I was soon as
fat as Humpty Dumpty, with swollen seed-packets bulging
me out in every direction. Indeed, that Jardin at the head
of the Clear Lake is perhaps the most entrancing collecting-
ground I have ever struck ; it was not with the altitude alone
that my heart went boppoty-bop as I perused its gentle
swards and shingle-flats.

That over-tried organ suffered greatly indeed, and did
the oddest things. Wakeful through the nights I lay, with
its rumblings and bumblings and stoppages ; it seemed to
me to make such a noise that often I wondered if it was not
avalanches in the silence of the lonely Alpine dark ; but
heart-anguishes, hunger and weakness were all obliterated
by the deifying glory of that place. Even in the doorway of
my tent I was so happy that I could hardly breathe. All
around me that tumble of mountainous dark conglomerate
boulders, big as houses, with Isopyrum flopping purple in
their crevices ; and down between them deep mossy caverns,

or elastic turfy dells beneath which you could hear surreptitious waters gurgling ; and the Jardin mapped out below ; and then the paralysing clean emerald of the Clear Lake, set in a bevel of sloped green lawns beneath the raw red stone slopes from Croda Rossa, high overhead on the right. And all around us nothing but the untarnished empty glory of the Alpine lawns, incomparably gigantic beneath the naked piled wilderness of the peaks. Not for the first time did the exalted loneliness of high places take hold of me, and seize me out of myself, " and charm away all wrinkles That cares and frets and worries of our days Had written in the forehead of my soul." But never, I think, have I known quite so scarifying a spring-cleaning as I endured at the hands of that high basin of the Alps, so vast and pure, without touch or taint of man since the beginning of time, and on to the unutterable end. No wonder if the Holy Ones haunt the great heights and draw from them their holiness.

How powerful are the wings of man's fancy : how feeble the efforts of man's legs. Small marvel the Hebrew Lord takes no delight in them. Despite the blank white bliss of my inner mood, it was a toilful puffing person who agonized up and down the swells of those virgin lawns. They were now all fired to russet by early frosts : their brief life was over, and their winter at hand. But meanwhile they had burst into a final flare of glory with Gentians and Saxifrages. The Saxifrages were golden creatures of the Hirculus persuasion, varying in size, but superb at their best (F. 200) with blue foliage and big blossoms of gorgeous clear glitter. The Gentian had not the massed meek loveliness of G. hexaphylla, but all the same it sheeted the whole moorland in a film of milky blue ; being G. triflora, bold and upstanding, with three or four fat big trumpets gathered together at the top of a five-inch stem, rather like a magnified and glorified G. Pneumonanthe, but of a softer, paler, watery colour. I even found a pure albino, ugly and disappointing as albino Gentians almost always are. What ails the mortal mind so to crave for variations that are bound inevitably to disappoint, in so far as they are, *ipso facto*, variations from a beauty such as that of a blue Gentian, on which no improvement is conceivable ?

CHAPTER XIII

FAREWELL TO WOLVESDEN

The rambling days went by in expeditions hither and thither up among the breasts of Axeinos and Thanatos, and over the enormous alps, in search of seed : to end always in an ecstasy of happiness, as we sat at rest in the tent door, absorbing the panorama of the fells, browning to autumn, while away over the Clear Lake, beyond its mountain barrier, the distances opened out infinitely far, over the crumpled lower ranges away below, in ripple over world-wide ripple of softest and most entrancing blue, with the gaunt naked-ness of the Gadjur range for crest of its culminating wave. Often Gadjur bred level banks of violet darkness in the afternoons, and Thanatos, not to be outdone, ere long filmed over the glory of the day in dullness, and out of dullness ere long brewed dark, which became violent, became a torrent of rain, became deluges of snow that fell in soft cascades all night. I would wake from fitful slumbers to what sounded like alarming stone-falls from Croda Rossa or Axeinos, possibly threatening the camp ; but on looking out it was only Bill and the servants clearing the solid masses of snow off the tents. And so would dawn, in time, a new day of stark diamond-clear radiance, almost unbearably brilliant on a new world of whiteness, which, however, rapidly began to resume its normal colours under the hot lances of sun-light.

Off one would start, this way or that ; and on return would find the camp in a mighty fluster of consternation, black-and-violet layers of storm having by now accumu-lated over the whole northerly region, soon to materialize over us also, in furious squalls, thunder and lashing hail, together with the penetrating grisly cold that floods all these high alps the moment that the sun has ceased to smile.   But seed-gathering went very well ; in one fold of the Alps a Celestial Poppy gave us pods of so special a size, shape, wartiness and thorniness, containing seed so brown and fat and big and square that I almost dared diagnose a different species—a wild hope which the whole habit, up to date, of F. 735 in cultivation goes far to encourage, though of its flowers not even Bill (who had passed down that dell in summer) had any clear recollection, to differentiate it from M. Prattii.   The only new treasure of any moment lived in the very highest scree-slopes of all, where every other form of life had faded out in the universal deadness and ruin of Axeinos and Thanatos.   This was an Aconite that sat dumpily in voluminous masses of very handsome foliage scalloped and glossy, close over which emerged stocky masses of very large blossoms in a close buzzle of helmets, in texture like Japanese silk-crêpe, and of the oddest, most subtle and lovely colour, like oyster-coloured chiffon over a blue slip, so that its effect was that of a delicate French grey or smoke. This strange and sinister beauty had a tap-root that seemed anxious to get down again to the bottom of everything ; however, with much delving, I worried up a few of the smaller plants, in a faint hope against hope that I might get them home alive ; but Alas ! it was not to be.

It is a wonderful walk round the Clear Lake.   First of all down our cataclysm of loose-piled monoliths, porous with deep mossy chasms, and waters flowing far down under them ; and so across the Jardin to the far shore, where the red scree shoots straight from the ruinous peak of Croda Rossa into the green water itself.   Here you must scuttle, for fresh stone-falls come constantly cannonading down the couloirs and cliffs overhead, like sugar-blocks clattering down from a scoop.   Then comes a curious rounded swell of boulders, settled and old and moss-grown, standing out into the lake.   Being cool and dank and shady, this is matted with large loose masses of rather sad-looking and flowerless Androsace mucronifolia. And after this you resume the scree-slope, loose and raw and red, sinking in steep taut lines to the Lake.

Here, as I went, precautiously, quick and light, I was gradually engulphed in a great pervading roar that seemed to come from everywhere, and yet evidently came from nowhere. I pried about anxiously, but could discern no visible cause : there was nothing round me at all but the dry red scree, and down below, the Lake, and up overhead, the lower cliffs of Croda Rossa. And yet here was this voluminous muted roaring, like some continuing stone-fall not so very far away. It took me several minutes to place its source ; this, like Hamlet's father's ghost, was in the cellarage. Down under the scree, in fact, beneath my feet, a subterranean torrent was making that hoarse uncanny sound ; and yet, up above, there was no sign of any water at all on the dead precipices and gullies of Croda Rossa, while the Lake lay perfectly smooth and tranquil below, with no trace of receiving any such volume of water, even beneath its surface. Evidently the torrent is a secret birth in Croda Rossa, and sinks sheer down towards some tardy emergence in the valley below the alp.

Round the far bay the circuit of scree grows milder, and so you come to the end of the Clear Lake, where the real stream brims over the lip of its moorland barrier in a delicious stretch of clear bubbling pools and whirls, rippling darkly round among the dark boulders that lie sunken and becalmed over the face of the fell and its shallow dip. And the near marge is green alpine lawn again, all along, velvety and elastic, with the green water lapping lazily against a hem of white silt, in which springs a new tall Aconite of no particular attraction. Ahead of you, over the dwarfed chaos of boulders from which the indiscernible minuteness of the camp dominates the flat of the Jardin beneath, now towers the lumpish massiveness of Axeinos ; while, with any luck, as you serenely wander close. along the shore you may get the entire pyramid of Croda Rossa mirrored in the unflawed emerald of the lake.

But now the harvest was all gathered, and with our burden of bulging packets it was time to break up the camp and get down again to Wolvesden to prepare our final departure. August 30 dawned in golden brilliancy with a foretang of winter already crystalline in the air, and in the hollow blue folds of the alp and over the browned and sparkling open faces. Beyond the dip, the whole of the distance was filled with a fleecy milk sea of white cloud, out of which, one behind the other, in clear soft blue, the remote ranges rose like islands. With Go-go and wicked Wa-wa I set out betimes, to return to Wolvesden over Crest Royal after Primula reginella, while Bill and the rest were to scour the descending alps and get down by the Ma-Chang, to secure the pendulous Cherry, and so forth, on their way.

And hardly had I started when, in the fine turf that crowned the top of a sloping boulder, there stared at me a new Gentian, a Gentian that instantly obliterates all others of its race, and sinks even G. Verna and G. Gentianella into a common depth of dullness. When the first awe was over, I gave tongue for Bill, and together, in reverend silence, we contemplated that marvel of luminous loveliness. Not the faintest hope possessed me that this glaring miracle could be a new species. Had not Przewalsky crossed this range ? How then could he possibly have missed a splendour so assaulting as this ? I forgot the chances of the season, and the complete and abject insignificance of Gentiana Farreri when not in flower. For Gentiana Farreri it indeed is, first seen as a Gentian-promise on the crown of Mother Hubbard, and even now, in its overwhelming beauty, attributed by my pessimistic modesty to G. Przewalskyi.

The collector's dream is to have some illustrious plant to bear his name immortal through the gardens of future generations, long after he himself shall have become dust of their paths. Mere beauty will not do it ; for the plant may fail and fade in cultivation, and his name be no more known, except to the learned, as attached to a dead dry sliver on the sheets of a herbarium. To become vividly immortal in the Valhalla of gardeners, one must own a species as vigorous as it is glorious, a thing capable of becoming, and remaining, a household word among English enthusiasts, such a constant friend, for example, as Gentiana Gentianella or Primula auricula. And how few of our new Chinese importations will probably do this! Already Professor Balfour had refused me several of my Primulas, as being, despite their loveliness, of a temper so tricky as evidently not to be long for this world in English gardens, and therefore not fitted permanently to bear aloft my name in them. Only reluctantly, in fact, had he consented to give me P. Farreriana on my urgent plea that a Primula of my own I must certainly have, and that a lovelier one there could not be, and that no more were likely to be got in my season anyhow, so this one I must certainly have, permanency or no permanency.

But Gentiana Farreri is of a very different kidney, and bids fair to be as solid a permanency as G. Gentianella itself. It is perfectly hardy, and—what is very remarkable in any Gentian but miraculously so in a Gentian so miraculously beautiful—it is perfectly vigorous and easy to deal with in any reasonable conditions of culture in a cool place not parched or water-logged. Here, indeed, it forms masses many times the size of any clump you will see on its own alps; and already special pilgrimages go to Edinburgh in August and September, to see those jungles of my Gentian, a yard through, with some three hundred gigantic trumpets opening at once. Shall I add that, in addition to growing so freely, and flowering so lavishly in so late and dull a moment of the year, this preposterously good-tempered exception to the rule of its race keeps its glory open, rain or shine, can be struck from cuttings as copiously as a Viola, and layered along its shoots as complacently as any carnation.

And its beauty! Nothing could I foretell of its temper

and future history that day, as I stood rapt in contemplation before the actual plant, the last and greatest event of my second season, and well worth the whole two years' expedition anyhow, merely to have seen it. A fine frail tuft like grass radiating some half a dozen fine flapping stems—that is G. Farreri, quite inconspicuous and obscure in all the high lawns of the Da-Tung, even down into the Dene as low as Wolvesden House. Until it flowers; and every day in early September brings a fresh crashing explosion of colour in the fold of the lawns. For each of those weakly stems concludes in one enormous upturned trumpet, more gorgeous than anything attained by G. Gentianella, but in the same general style and form. But the outline is different, with a more subtle swell to the chalice, and that is freaked outside in heavy lines of black-purple that divide long vandykes of dim periwinkle blue with panels of Nankeen buff between ; inside the tube and throat are white, but the mouth and the wide bold flanges are of so luminous and intense a light azure that one blossom of it will blaze out at you among the grass on the other side of the valley. In no other plant, except perhaps, Ipomœa Learii, or Nemophila, do I know such a shattering acuteness of colour : it is like a clear sky soon after sunrise, shrill and translucent, as if it had a light inside. It literally burns in the alpine turf like an electric jewel, an incandescent turquoise.

Do you wonder if I stood spell-bound ? Do you wonder if my heart also sank to my boots in despair ? For how was I to get this glory home ? A plant that only blooms in the beginning of September—when will it seed ? The only possible chance that I could see lay in transporting living clumps ; for we clearly could not go on waiting in Wolvesden for the seed to ripen. Nor was there anyone we could trust to collect it after we had gone. And yet to miss this would be to miss the apex of my whole expedition, a thing that ranked already with my Isopyrum—and even above it for the uniqueness of its colour. So I did transport the living clumps ; with what awe and attendance you may judge.

And the Trans-Siberian journey killed them all. My disappointment cut so deep that I put it behind me, and resolutely banished the memory of that Gentian from my heart. Months passed, and the War submerged me in work, and London engulphed me, and the garden ceased to exist, except as a remote memory. But in August of that year (1916) a little package reached me from the Botanic Garden at Edinburgh. Would I give the history of the enclosed Gentian ? I tore open the box, and there, large and lovely and luminous as ever, was the lost Da-Tung Gentian, which I had dismissed all hope of ever seeing again.

Do you ask how the miracle was wrought ? I hope you do, for I intend to tell you. Can you remember how in 1914, over the high lawns of Thundercrown and the Ardjeri Alps, I collected the elusive seed of Gentiana hexaphylla— on Thundercrown, with my own hands, and vicariously, by the servants, on the fells of Ardjeri ? And do you also remember that some of the packets brought down by the servants seemed to show a different form, to be larger and thicker and darker in the pod than any of G. hexaphylla's ? So different, indeed, did they seem to me that I ultimately sent them, as a precautionary measure, under different numbers, as F315^A, and F473. And these germs it was that in due course revealed the despaired-of G. Farreri to the amazed eyes of Edinburgh. On so frail a thread, and across so complete an intervening gulf of gloom, was accomplished the introduction to our gardens of so pre-eminent a plant. In any Comtist calendar, that reckons only the really important things for human happiness (rather than the mere deaths of Sovereigns, and passing of Bills that make no difference, and conclusions of peaces made of pie crust), large and red will be the letters that mark the August day which first revealed my Gentiana to cultivation.

After this vision of beauty you will easily figure to yourself how easily I sailed across the undulations of the Alps, and towered lightly to the ridge of Crest Royal, illuminated and drawn on, as I climbed, by occasional flares of the Gentian, just beginning in the turf of the hill-side. On Crest Royal there was the Little Queen to be got, and the sweet pink Erysimum ; for long I agonized vainly for the latter, and at last saw the clustered spectacles of its seed heads at my very feet, and away down the sunny slope. Broken-backed by the minuteness of my search for the Primula, I straightened out to descend the scree on the other side, in which a flannel-leaved Saussurea was the only sign of life, with elongated domes of straw-coloured fluff and wool in a dense web like crystallized wadding. In the big dish below the Harebell Poppy was now in the pleasantest state of seed, all the pods fat and just dehiscent, not yet dried out, nor dashed by storms. I spent a very happy hour or two snapping off their jolly plumpnesses till I was bulged as a barrel in all my pockets. And so, over the rim of the dish at last, and down the enormous descent of the rib-ridge into Wolvesden again. And at the very bottom, in a lawn of the Dene, what should once more blaze upon my sight but my own Gentian ? And so ended the crucial and final expedition of my second year. Poor Bill was tired and depressed with the monotony of our matter, but I, who had feared crossluck up there, alike with the weather and the seeds, now concluded the book of Wolvesden in a climax of radiance, so to have been spared by the former, and so triumphantly to have conquered the latter.

Bill now went off to Sining again, to fetch back more mules for our departure. Meanwhile, there were some final chores of seed-collecting to be done, as well as the boxing up of the plants we meant to take down country. More tasks filled the intervening days to Bill's return ; I even crossed the Pass to try for seed of the lovely Chickweed (Cerastium melanandrum), which rambles with its dark and glossy shoots in the earth-slopes of the Western face, and snows them under with immense flowers of purest white, flushed often to the softest and loveliest shell-pink. Of this, though, I failed, and had to take plants ; on my heels Lay-gor had better luck, following with a pillow-case in which to cram pell-mell the terrible thorny spires of Meconopsis Prattii. All the other seeds being also satisfactorily collected, I returned to camp at the Ma Chang in Dolomite Valley, in high delight to find there such abundance of Isopyrum pods, big and baggy, precisely ripe for the picking, just browning at the tops of the opening carpels, but without yet having scattered their precious germs, as it has a maddening habit of doing as soon as the pods are really mature, each flow of air rattling them out right and left. On the cliffs, too, there were three very lovely soft rose-coloured specimens of the Celestial Poppy; but all of them impregnable.

Not that it would have been any use if they had been accessible, they were not ripe in seed, and transplanting would have been useless. On the morrow I set out to return, all along the frontage of the cliffs and into their ghylls, prospecting and collecting. At the foot of the last, the pony was led up to meet me, saddled only with a jadz', on which the bedding was strapped. Elegantly I stepped off upon it, straight from the rock. Whereupon the jadz' tilted delicately away on the far side, and in an instant fell off down the slope with me on top of it, impotent as a sack. Consternation raged; I felt it a great comfort to have English to swear in, as nobody understood, and therefore nobody's feelings were hurt, while my own were duly relieved. I was now assiduously picked up and hyked on again, but for a long time the jadz' continued very uncertain in its equilibrium, and I had several more near shaves, as I rode and dismounted down the Dene, where my Gentian was by now beginning to reveal the fullness of its inevitable glory in the lawns of the lower reaches.

In my activities I was not left wholly lonely. Grandmamma Aoo called frequently in with milk and butter; also her splendid young descendants. And one day two gorgeous Tibetan ladies in blue and scarlet went flapping down the boulders of the beck just as I was collecting seed of Bill's Dracocephalum from what had once been blue-sheeted drifts of it in the mud-flats alongside the clear rills and pools that lurk in the wide reaches of the alder jungle across the torrent. Behind them there followed a lone stray dog, whom in vain they tried to detach from their tracks by throwing stones at it.

But once a decision has been taken, I am always immediately afire to carry it out forthwith; and now I was growing desperate to pack up and be done with Wolvesden for ever, and off on the southward trail. I even wondered if I could haul up sufficient zeal to accomplish the one remaining seed-hunt—up Southerly Valley to the col, and down again by the converging glen. But of course I did: incomplete unclean finishes are an abhorrence to me, and I could not rest till I had got my season thoroughly achieved. Accompanied by both Wa-wa's, Go-go, an accidental idiot, and a new intelligent coolie originally called Wongar (but, for a certain resemblance, known as " Bongie " instead), I rode up, past the Aoo's, on the idiot's bright little red pony. And very comfortably I rode, on my folded blanket, and actually continued riding all the way, up the gorge, up the glen, right away up to the col itself. It was quite fair going anyhow, and I felt disinclined for gratuitous exertion. As I intended this to be τὴν πανυστάτην ὁδῶν ἁπάσων in the parts, I meant to accomplish as much of it as I could, ἐξ ἀκινήτου ποδός. On the col I alighted, and the pony went back to wait at Casa Aoo, while the rest of us dredged the heights for seeds. All the turf was gay with golden Saxifrages, and sturdily stood up the milky blue clustered trumpets of Gentiana triflora; every now and then out crashed the azure note of G. Farreri from the mild general beauty of the chorus; and each time made me jump anew with the rapture of its piercing clearness. Across the ridge I descended to the steading where we had slept, and thereabouts made a sumptuous harvest of the Isopyrum. Furies of rain now supervened, and we sheltered in the opportune lean-to's. When we went on downwards the pleasure of that last pleasant day was done. For now the sky was black, the wind piercing, and the soaked scrub drenched me

to the thighs in no time : below, in the Ghyll, this was
succeeded by soaked coppice of just such a nice height as
to flap ice-water in our faces or pour down deluges on our
heads. Altogether it was odious ; when I at last reached
the pony I could not think of riding, but raced ahead for
warmth towards the Dene, although the idiot in charge had
had the surprising sense to put a waterproof over the bedding.
With Wa-wa on my heels I tore down to Wolvesden, shifted,
had tea, sorted my harvest, and then folded my hands in
supreme achievement, feeling now so heartily satisfied with
my closing stodge among these Alps, that it was evident the
odiousness of the day's shower had been merely the final
spite of these grudging old granite mountains at our having
so triumphed over them all along the line. And now arrived
Lady Aoo with a present of clotted cream, and in a little
while more cries were heard, and quite unexpectedly Bill
himself came riding in with news of the required mules
following behind in charge of fat, comfortable Sining Tanguei ;
and laden, too, with a rich cargo of furs, coats and robes of
lynx and sand-fox and squirrel, looted from Peking long
since, and now sold off at a bargain by the robber, established
in security at Sining.

When the caravan at last came jingling up there was
accordingly a great unpacking, and the Dene that night
saw strange pavanes and perambulations, as we strutted
stately in first one sumptuous vestment and then another,
sweeping in the exuviæ of squirrels, or opulent in depths of
lynx, or merely picturesque in parquetries of sand-fox. For
the Chinese excel in picture-puzzling with their furs : it is
not enough for them merely to make up a robe of skins, but
they cut and slide and slice them till the reverse of the coat
is like nothing so much as a mad mosaic of stitchery. But
the outer result is often parcelled and panelled fantastically
in contrasting squares, or peacock-eyed with a different fur ;
particularly lovely are the coats all creamy and primrose
with the breasts of Tibetan sand-fox, appliqués with round
dabs of pale blue and soft chestnut from squirrels.

But now the preparations for departure went furiously forward, further exasperated by the fact that autumn had clearly arrived in the Alps, made manifest in universal cloud and mizzle, and continuing Arctic cold. Gradually everything was packed, even to the plants in their boxes, and our happy little house dismantled. It was a miserable delight. I grudged each wasted minute before we got away, yet looked comfortably forward to the regret of years. Out may come the stoves and chimneys, back may go the K'angs and the black dark of unbroken walls, but Wolvesden House, I feel, though abandoned again for evermore to mules and muleteers, remains perpetually my property. Dear little house, how dull you sometimes were ; how desirable you always are !—sitting up there, far away, lost and lone in your deep groove of the great Tibetan Alps. Those who may wish (in days I hope still distant) to commune with my ghost must take a long journey ; to where it will be found cheeping and chittering wanly round the mud-plastered walls of Wolvesden, rather than on the Schneeberg or the Tombia or even Moncenisio.

And now, in the break-up of the home, came out the full extent of Grandmamma Aoo's ambitions. All the summer through that noble little old lady had so plethorically fed us on the best of butter and cream and milk that by this time we bulged. And all the time she had firmly refused to entertain a single penny of payment. But now, at the end, the inmost desire of her heart was coyly unfolded. Might she, *might* she, did we think, be allowed to possess one of our empty bottles—and, at that, not a dull opaque black bottle, such as is favoured by whisky, but a crystal bottle, such as once was the shrine of Chartreuse or Crème-de-Menthe ? Behold the fatal error of those who travel teetotal in the Tibetan highlands, where glass in every form is precious and rare as jewels. And how lucky that we ourselves had been more provident, and not heretical to the plumpy deity of pink eyne : for now Grandmamma Aoo could be amply repaid with about half a dozen specimens of her heart's

U

desire. With these, as much too precious to be trusted to other hands, she went home staggering up the glen herself; then returned with all her descendants and collaterals, to gather up any other flotsam that might be giving away. A proud lady was she, these days, twinkling delightedly from amid her elf locks; and a proud lady she undoubtedly continues, probably the best hated hostess on the Border— triumphant in a more general jealousy than if she went pranking it in three tiaras at the Opera. Let no one, I repeat, who proposes to travel in Tibet, abhor the bottle: it is a very present help in time of trouble when moderately full, but especially, when empty, the pilgrim's most precious coin of barter.

Cold and clear as a diamond dawned September 13 into Wolvesden, flooding the deeps of the glen with gold and striking sparkles from all the frosted lawns. Like Attila on Cormons watching the burning of Aquilia, I stood on the breast of lawn behind, to watch the dismantling of the home. All around me were Aoo's, bearing burdens, and seeking more. Every rag and scrap had been torn out of the rooms and enthusiastically garnered; gone were the stoves, their chimneys, the windows of plate-glass, and everything down to the minutest scrap of metal—all compiled on the broad backs of the gleeful Aoo's. For why, meanwhile, does little Tanguei sit sad and sullen on Hill 60, deserted even by his pig (engaged in a final despairing philander with the brown pony), and taking no part at all in the packings or apportionings? Bad little Tanguei, a goodly proportion of our relics had been carefully set aside for his due perquisite indeed; but at the last moment it was discovered that he had anticipated matters. Concealed among his father's coffin-boards were sundry of our possessions brought to light. Justice accordingly proclaimed that he had forfeited his share in our rejecta, and that the entire stock must now be transferred, instead, to the Aoo's. These, then, were in the broadest grins of glee. But Tanguei sat silent and aloof, in a disconsolate sulk, like the little boy with a smarting tail in the *Ingoldsby Legends*. I am afraid there was bad blood brewed that day between him and the Aoo's.

Breakings-up are dreadful ; I will not dwell on my farewells to that golden place, where my Gentian was now in the full of its splendour beside the stone-shoots up the lawns across the beck, so unsufferably beautiful that even now my memory staggers in the thought of it, as I saw it that last morning, and said good-bye to it (as I feared, for ever) in the nippy sparkle of that virginal air, filled with strange haunting autumnal fragrances, chill and delicious and sad. But now all was ready, and Lady Aoo presented us with a poor fluffy sheep that one of her descendants had been out all the previous day on the hills procuring. Away rode Bill down the Dene ahead of us toward Tien Tang : away moved the caravan. In a fury of joy to be going, in a fury of regret to be gone, I hastened to mount the grey pony at last, and for the last time turned my back hastily on Wolvesden.

Uneventfully, in a stupor of distracted feelings I shepherded the caravan down the Dene, and over the hills to Tien Tang. Seed-gatherings delayed me here and there, so that when I at length arrived in that delicious bourne, it was to find the staff already installed. But no longer in our old quarters : this time we were the guests of the Chancellor, or Prior, in his own wide-house with L-shaped yard. He himself was not yet at home ; but soon arrived from across the river by the pulley-haul basket contraption that the monks had recently rigged up (since a mighty business of tree-felling was now going forward in the forest opposite, on order of the Viceroy) to save the waste of that long trail down to Chiao-Tor. A kindly and charming host he proved ; all the civilities passed, and in procession across the yard we bore him presents of Missionary jam in a tin, Pulu (Tibetan) serge, cakes, kataghs, and an enamelled wash-basin. These were accepted with vehement protests and deprecations ; then, immediately on our return to our own verandah, requited with butter, sugar, grated cheese, and a dishful of those little tubers of Potentilla anserina, which make such good eating on the Border (they taste nuttily, of Asparagus and new potatoes) as to make me now feel that whatever may be the future rigours of rationing in England, our greed need never suffer, nor its belly be constricted, so long as Silverweed abounds along every highway-side all over the country. And after dinner both the Priors came across to call, and hankered round admiringly among our possessions.

In chat and pleasantness closed the evening, and on the morrow, very early, we rode on for the last time out of Tien Tang. Rode in the wrong direction, up the steep slant of the track round the big bluff below the Abbey, that impends upon the Da-Tung-Hor. For a little while the Sa-wa Wa-wa trotted alongside, after the farewell good wishes of the monks had faded, but soon even he dropped away, and the curve of the cliff shut out Tien Tang and everything of Wolvesden was left behind now and safely sealed into the past. My heart, like Fanny's (though in no other respect, I hope), can never resist the sad influences of the word " last " ; exactly three years ago to-day as I write I rode for the last time out of Tien Tang ; and through blurred eyes of memory I still see each step of the way as blurred as I did then— looking back and looking back, till that golden bay of sunshine was hidden finally from sight.

CHAPTER XIV

BACK TO LANCHOW

Between Tien Tang and Ping-Fan the journey is one of five days, up and down, over the big ranges of arid open downs that intervene between the Gadjur range and the Da-Tung Alps. In due course it crosses the last fading extension of Gadjur, and then, by long vales, sinks to the Ping-Fan River and Ping-Fan. Here you have regained the Great North Road, which carries you thence across country, from the Ping-Fan River to the Hwang-Hor, and back to Lanchow.

But I could take little joy in the journey. My face was set in the reverse direction from my heart: the Da-Tung Alps soon died out in the backward distance, and there were no more anywhere at all, and the soul within me was like lead. Even when various little passes of 9,000 ft. or 10,000 ft. might have offered farewell sights of Thanatos and his colleagues along the skyline, there never was any skyline, but the remotenesses of Heaven and earth were blended in one monotony of dun-coloured haze. Occasionally the track ascends by wooded windings in the fell. These were softly lovely, and led to lush and pretty upper lawns, filled with all manner of autumnating herbage. And there followed happy windings up a deep forested chine down between the big fell masses that one sees from the high tops of Tien Tang. At the top of this was a marshy upland plain where the stream meandered level with its fount, amid drifts of yellowing Iris, and tussocks fringed with what looked like a Swertia but proved to be a pretty little Delphinium of palest water-blue. In ranges so dull, this was evidently to be my last flower of

293

the year. But now Bill was lost, and after long waitings we
went on again up over the hills by hidden coilings to a pass
amid hideous knubbly peaks of conglomerate, faced with
here and there a mangy scab of vegetation. On the other
side we descended into a broad river bed, with the ragged
splendour of Gadjur now quite close at hand up at its head
incredibly gaunt and stark and cruel. But away from it,
down the river vale, we had to proceed, still between the
fantastic red Pulhamite freaks of conglomerate that fill all
this intervening region, wherever peaks emerge ; and
through a smiling homely scene of fields and harvest, and
golden stretches of stubble, and cornstocks arrayed for
carrying. And finally, in a village of fine houses so square
and solid that I felt they must be Tibetan (though the blue-
clad bending Ruths among the corn were all Chinese, and a
Chinese temple posed alone in the ridge of the hill above), I
found the despaired-of Bill already awaiting us in the wide
yard of an inn.

Tao-erh, despite its solid houses and its abundance of
prayer flags, was a Chinese village after all, of agents and
traders in wool with the Tibetans. Hence its combined
atmosphere. The morrow gave us a very long stage : there
is no recording its windings unless with a special map, and I
am sure my publisher, like him of the Wrong Box, would be
averse to the expense. Miles of serene vales, miles of
downs, phantasmagorias of red pinnacles : the glorious day
was like that of a fine shoot at home, with a colourless ha'ar
over the distance, and an autumnal delicious nip that perhaps
intensified my feeling that the wooded Northerly slopes
and the rosy conglomerate peaks of the valley recalled the
foothills of the Alps. Over a pass commanding a vast fell
panorama, as it might have been Ribblehead on a huge
scale, with Potentilla scrub for heather, we dipped into a
new vale, and up a converging valley, and across it to a ridge
which we mounted in a bold zigzag. All about were big
untouched masses of wood. I might have known their
reason, for, as we mounted the zigzag, what I had fancied

was a walled granary fortress ahead of our track in the
valley below, now unfolded beneath us as a very comfortable
large monastery—with two big churches squarely sitting
within its wide half-occupied square.   It was a strange
outpost of Tibet in a country now so wholly Chinese
again.

More valleys now, more passes, and then in and out along
the wide open faces of the fells towards a valley-head, and
the highest pass of all, a height of some 10,000 ft. or more.
No flowers of any moment, however, could be expected at so
contemptible an elevation and in a region so un-Alpine.   But
as we mounted towards the actual col, I perceived the moorland turf to be veiled in a film of blue.   A little nearer and it
was as if the azure zenith itself had descended solid all along
the tops (but no lower), for here, quite suddenly, was my own
Gentian again so vehemently abounding, and in such a
unanimity of glory that hardly could you set your foot down
anywhere on the moor without crushing at least half a dozen
of its imperious trumpets.   I raged about, in a stupor of
rapture, searching, of course, for Albinos, but retaining
sense enough to be glad I found none.   And the other side of
the pass was a complete bathos—raw plebeian loess and
commonplace Asters, beautiful indeed in their pessimistic
purples, but dull on the retina after the luminous glare of
the Gentian.

And after all this, " *such* a much."   For the journey tailed
on and on, and each successive hope of our bourne proved
delusive, and on we had to go again.   The day began
declining ; the flat wide champaign of golden stubble was
filled in the centre by a long sloping three-sided hill, with a
three-sided little red fortalice on its apex, and all its broad
triangular face a blaze of gold in the slants of sundown.
Away behind it loomed up a huge rounded headland of
precipices, mistily pink on the powder-blue of the darkling
sky.   Surely beneath this watch-tower of China and Tibet,
that village crouching at its feet must be the Thirty Brilliances, our destination ?   No such thing.   Another twenty

li. A climb, a drop, sunset; another col, and then another drop towards a village in sight away at the foot of the vale which this time really could not help being Thirty Brilliances (or Thirty Names; I do not know the character for Ming in San-shir-Ming). But still it was no such thing. Away down the richly cultured valley we had to go on winding, and all the hills had now died away into low dull ranges of hummocks that are hardly less tedious and sterile in their summer life than in their winter death. It was dark, and everybody tired and heart-sick with hope deferred : a kindly soul by the wayside cheered us with " Dao-la " (you've arrived). But where ? It was still long before we wound again leftward round a buttress of the hills and came at once into a village which surely, *surely* must be Thirty Brilliances —or Thirty Names, and all bad ones. But on and on we steadily went, right through it : I despaired. Till abruptly at the very extremity of the place, just as hope had completely forsaken me, we did actually find ourselves turning into a vast-yarded inn with two small dungeon-sculleries at either end of its wings, to serve for Bill and me.

It was not San-shir-Ming at all, but Man-che-Tang. We rode out of it betimes, in a grilling morning, up through rich lovely open lands of waving corn, white to the harvest, up to a small col, and over this still upward, towards a mighty down-mass running South-East and no doubt the final fading tail-tip of the Gadjur range. Here it was all open turf with outcrops of rock : Iris tenuifolia abounded in grassy swathes, as it does all along these high downs where the soil is not loess. I was soon exhilarated again to be winding in the sunshine along the voluminous naked flanks of that green fell, in that sparkle of the air crisp with the decadent autumnal deliciousness of dying Artemisias. Down we descended far into a very deep ghyll, glorious in rich woodland on its other side with the mountain ash magnificent in cascades of blood-drops. And then abruptly up to the left, up and up, towards a pass so imminent and high that I never dared hope we should have to cross it. But we did : thus traversing the big down. On the crest, however, though we were at a greater height than anything we had achieved since leaving Wolvesden, there was no sign of my Gentian, or of any other interesting Alpine—either because this crest was of loess or because the scene was now too far removed from the Alpine region.

On the far side we descended placidly down long, long vales of browning moorland, till gradually we came into an enormously lengthy, dull and hideous shallow valley, with bursts of red rock, and fantastic toad-stones and boulders squatting on the right-hand skyline. And ahead at its remotest leftward coil reappeared at last the crumply and ochre-coloured downs of all the Lanchow region. Clearly we were making here our farewells to the fading hills, and coming back to the river levels of Kansu, with Ping-Fan and the Great North Road somewhere round the corner at the end of our stage. It was still a long stretch. By this time I was completely tired. The weariness and labour of the trail increase upon one steadily in China, and after nearly two years of it, on and off, three days of trekking at the end are more arduous and exhaustive than three weeks at the start. No doubt it makes a difference, too, that the start *is* the start, with all the joys and glories of the journey still ahead ; while the end *is* the end darkening hourly to the depths of Finis, with all the joys and glories receding hourly further into the irrecoverable past. Nor were the prudences of the cat befriending cook without their influence on my mood. For, though she had so far modified as to dispatch a few of the stores on which I had counted to carry us through the culminating fatigues and exhaustion of the close, yet these were so very few as merely to make a mock of our necessities, having to be so agonizingly economized that all the time one's rumbling wolf was neither sustained nor satisfied. But all the same, to show that the heart-loading length of these stages was not subjective only, but very real, I need only say that poor fat Sining Tanguei, who had brought us the new mules to Wolvesden, was now painfully hobbling, with my stick as well as his own to help him forward, while, actually, the wicked Wa-wa grew so tired that he had to lag and rest behind, and ultimately had to be sent back for and fetched with a mule when we got down to Ping-Fan.

For get down at last we did, out of the hills into the broad river-flats below ; and, turning a corner to the right, now saw before us, some three miles ahead across the plain, the noble irregular many-angled walls of Ping-Fan (Easy-Food ?) picturesquely engulphed in volumes of verdure ; while on the near side of the river, along the downs overhead, the most fairy-like temples perched along astoundingly fantastic pinnacles of loess. On we went, after a vain wait for the Wa-wa ; the Ping-Fan-Hor has a hugely wide shingle flat for its bed, but now was flowing in only two channels, swift and dark and vicious. Successfully we made the ford, and had no difficulty in finding our inn, in the street of inns along outside the Western wall, facing to the river, and now a grilling suntrap in the Westering glare. Bill now went back to guide in Lay-gor and the lagging little tired asses, and send for the Wa-wa. We decided, seeing how completely done up was all the staff, thenceforth to take a cart for ourselves down the remaining stages to Lanchow, thus freeing the ponies and the bed-bearing mule for the various servants in turn, while the Wa-wa could come with us.

Easier said than managed ; not a Peking cart, it appeared, was in the place, important stage on the Great North Road though it be. Easier managed than said, after all ; for, characteristically, after all the negations and impotencies of last night, there in the morning a cart duly was. My spirits cast aside their dolefulness and danced ; the hot soft balmy air made me feel as if I had just got down to Bozen from the Stelvio, and even the being in a Chinese town again after so much mountain solitude set my heart aglow with the delight of humankind. And now the cart came up—betimes, too ; I bundled in, and set thankfully off, ahead of the caravan, padded upon my bags and bedding in such an ecstasy of comfort as only those who have been on trek for a

whole season can understand one's finding in so ingenious
an engine of torment as a Peking cart on a Chinese Imperial
high-road—which, for surface and quality, is comparable
only to a fading cart-track across a Yorkshire fell. But
the Great North Road is deep and velvety, and soft with
looseness along this stretch ; blissfully I rolled out of Ping-
Fan with the Wa-wa perched in front of me on the cart-sill,
immovably superior, as usual, to all he surveyed, needing
nothing but a livery to turn him into the most typical little
Tiger who ever carried compromising correspondence in a
Victorian comedy. I felt, indeed, that I myself could by
no means live up to the crushing superiority of my little
squire now once more mine only : the monks of Tien Tang
had been so shocked in their sense of dignity to find Bill and
I had but the one between us, that we had felt ourselves
forced to engage the Sa-wa Wa-wa, if only to equalize matters
and save appearances. But now that the need for this was
over, the wicked Wa-wa reverted to his original post, as my
own particular proprietor.

It was very pleasant, rolling at ease out of Ping-Fan, past
the many fine walls and towers of the Manchu city, and
through a noble new pagoda'ed gate-house. Down the
empoplared lanes we lumbered in the radiant morning,
Rivieran in the sweet tang of the sweet breeze that came
dancing up to meet us, and was shovelled into the depths of
the cart by the big square awning built right out in front at
an upward slant, over the mule. The country was the same
as that between Lanchow and Sining, but now all heavily
plumed with lovely green in the wide valley of this river,
which is evidently fast shrinking. For its actual bed is
to-day a grass-grown permanent plain, with only room for
runnels here and there ; thus showing how all this sad
ancient land is rapidly drying up, and must, ere long, unless
the former forests are gradually renewed, go the same way
as Lob-Nor and Turfan and Khetan the Old. Even the
Koko-Nor is dying from its former rims. But in the midst
of these melancholy musings Bill overtook me at a canter,

in towering spirits, and packed off the Wa-wa ahead on the brown pony, while he himself clambered into the cart. We achieved the rest of the way very happily in chat, refreshing our throats with gulps from one of the huge but insipid pink-fleshed melons that are always meeting one in stacked cart-loads up the North Road, and are so seductively lovely in their great piled quarters on Chinese fruit stalls, in the contrast of green rind and rose-pink flesh with bright black seeds embedded. Our eyes we perpetually refreshed with the verdure all round us, and with the distant right-hand view, which down its length was a long fantastic *chevaux de frise* of pinnacles and spires and towers, each crowned with a fairy-like temple as delicate and poised as if it were a bird alighted from Heaven ; and all softly blue and dove-colour and far away.

Our stage was the quiet little mouldering town of Red-borough (Hung Chung). And on the morrow we plunged into the abomination of death once more, turning away Eastward from the Ping-Fan-Hor, to cut across the angle that it makes with the Hwang-Hor. This is all a wholly desert land ; we spent the long day coiling and winding in and out and up and down among hideous lifeless hummocks of red and ochre and grey, and then down an endless and horrible shallow valley of dry bones, between slag-dump hills of desolation ; and then upwards and Eastwards through more ranges to match, till our way was temporarily cheered by a temple lodged on an efflorescence of crag ; and by reviving cultivation in the flats, and by a new appearance of that solid erosion-resisting red-rock, which had emerged from the hill-side above Nien-Bi-Hsien in what looked like pillared frontages of an imperial tomb. Here it stood up occasionally, stark and lone, in gigantic blocks like Egyptian temples gone a little blurred, with a crumbling cap of earth a-top. The road sank soundless in depths of sand : the going was slow and very bad. It was late when we reached our stage at Black-Dyke-Water (Hai-dja-Shui).

And here we rummaged out our belongings to try and

make some sort of decent reappearance in Lanchow on the morrow. Off went Bill, very early, and in a kind of flutter I proceeded after him, tremulously agog, after all these months, to be re-entering what the accomplished Amanda McKittrick Ross would call " the heightened haunts of high-born socialism." (She means, I think, Society : not its exact opposite.) The way was very long and dull, but the day so fine and lovely that I drowsed along through the balmy air in a soft beatitude, though nothing was to be seen anywhere but those lifeless hills of red and grey, with one more burst of the ruddy castellations. Then we entered a narrow gorge, and wound and wound and wound, till the hills faded at last, and suddenly we came out upon the vast valley of the Hwang-Hor again, and then more suddenly still, round a last Easterly turning, and there was the whole distance opened out ahead of us, and the wide sinister face of the river, and miles of green orchard beyond, away and away, to where, up the enfolding hills, appeared far off and tiny and pale, the guard towers of the capital.

The last stretch of the stage was much the worst, for the road now left its deep sandy velvet, and became bone-hard, and very stony, so that we agonizingly boppled along in the full anguish of a Peking cart, till my head felt like rolling from my shoulders. Nor did the distance ever seem to come nearer. However, the laws of nature prevail even over the fancies of fatigue. Bill and Bongie had cantered ahead, and now Bongie came riding back to meet me, and houses appeared, and increased, and there was the city developing, and now we were in the suburb, and ahead of me a steep rise towards a gate house, and on its parapet, bobbing up and down for welcome, the white parasol of Mrs. Post Office, with Bill and Mr. Post Office in attendance. I lumbered out of the cart, to go courteously up to greet them. And the simultaneous cry that hailed me back into the crowd of my kind was " Oh, how you *have* grown stout ! "

Dissembling my wrath against Grandmamma Aoo for leading me to this reproach, I exchanged heartinesses, and off we all set into the city. But no large beautiful house for me this time : the inn was quite good enough for the short time which was all I intended to spend in Lanchow. The next morning I woke from a bad night to another glorious day, and with the sun's ascent my spirits towered and I had all the glow of waking to a lovely London day in June—such was now my emotion to be in a big city again, and in soft air, hot and sweet and full of urban scents. And urban invitations now flowed in : Mâ pestered us for the inevitable banquet ; Mr. Lo and Mr. Li came calling in their smoothest silks and brightest smiles and bade us to dinner : and the Viceroy sent asking for an early conference. But these joys were darkened for us by the sensation of the hour. For there arrived a piteous letter.from the Sining Missionary, asking us to do all we could for the poor old Chang Gwan of the Koko-Nor, and relating the tragic tale of his crash. The superficial story was all we were told, but Chinese official life has so many undercurrents and dark silent pools that the apparent reasons are rarely the real ones, and never the only ones ; especially in such times as these were, gravid with change, overshadowed by Yuan Shih Kai's now evident and determined ascent towards the Dragon Throne.

So that the true tale of the Chang Gwan's fall remains yet, perhaps, to be told. The official tale related how some wretched young trading agent was up at Sining on a wool-deal and came to some arrangement with the Chang Gwan, in contravention of which it was rumoured that a certain rival wool-office was opened. It was never proved that this had really been opened at all ; certainly never proved that it had been opened at the order or even with the knowledge of the Viceroy. The agent, however, young and rash, and ignorant of all the ropes, leapt at the worst conclusion without further inquiry, and precipitately wired a complaint to the central Government. All this story, however, if true, can only have given the Government a handle for a long pre-determined stroke. For by return of cable, they asked no explanations, made no preface of remonstrance, did not

even in due form accept the resignation of the Viceroy.
They ordered his instant arrest and dispatch to Peking.
The order was carried out with calculated brutality, and as a
crowning insult entrusted to Mâ Dâ-ren the Mahomedan.
Without warning or decency, the Military Governor marched
into the Viceregal Palace, and arrested the Viceroy in full
Yamen. With the shame and the shock the poor old man
went stone-blind. And thus vanishes from history the last
Manchu Viceroy of Koko-Nor Tibet. In a greater actor and
on an imperial stage, the tragedy of Great Lord Fang of
Siku was here re-enacted. But when I remembered the
Chang Gwan, that genial kindly little old gentleman, and
all he had done for us, and the friendliness he had shown, I
confess that I should have liked a few plain words with that
wool agent.

The next day I had my interview with the Viceroy of
Kansu. In three carts went Mr. Li and Bill and I. Bill
mocked at my tardy strivings after tidiness; and difficult
buttonings into a suit that had once been decent. After
libertine months of décolletage, I myself felt strange and
imprisoned in tie and collar. When we reached the upper
courts of the Palace, behold the Viceroy himself, heaving
forth enthusiastically to greet us, more massive and monu-
mental than ever, in a wadded gown of pale blue silk over
many others. He convoyed us directly to an inner room,
and there showed us many pictures and an ebullient
cordiality. This was by far the most interesting interview
I ever had with a Chinese official. For some reason all
guardedness was laid aside, and the Viceroy unfolded openly
in questions and answers and comments. He seemed to
want particularly to discuss the downfall of the Chang Gwan,
and pointedly asked us what we knew, and how we knew it.
In answer, of course, we did what we could to enforce the
Chang Gwan's case and urge consideration for him. But
for all his smilings and acquiescences told us, the Kansu
Viceroy might have been his enemy, personal or official.
However, everything we said was very well received, before

we passed at length up characteristic avenues of aimless amiable talk, towards the real object of the interview.

The Viceroy of Kansu was one of the many cousins whom Yuan Shih Kai had been diligently planting out in the big Viceroyalties for some years past, to prepare public opinion for his own ascent of the Imperial Throne. And now events were moving rapidly; the President, at the Temple of Heaven, had recently performed certain pontifications that appertain only to the Emperors of China, high priests and mediators between Heaven and Earth. Though the rites were modified, this was meant as a *ballon d'essai*, and made his purpose unmistakably plain; and the calm atmosphere of China was thrilling throughout with a sense of the imminent change. And the Viceroy, no doubt on instructions, was anxious to find out what we thought of this new move, and how Europe would accept the establishment of a new Imperial dynasty. Fortunately what was desired on one side harmonized with what was thought on the other, smiles broadened and nods became more frequent and vigorous as we expatiated with courteous enthusiasm on the prospects of a China once more secure in her immemorial system of democratic autocracy. Public opinion, indeed so far as we could see, (in the North) hailed the president's decision with satisfaction usually, with acquiescence at the worst, and nowhere with hostility. The oldest and wisest of the world's Empires asks only for peace : that sovereign or that system which brings her peace must inevitably be the one that will appeal to China ; yet writing now more than two years since the collapse and death of the Emperor Yuan, there seems no more reason than before to hope at last that out of the very extremity of chaos and misery and aimless antagonistic egoism in which that collapse plunged her, the unhappy lacerated Empire has effectively learned the value of solidarity, or is turning in sheer weariness towards harmony and concessions and quiet again.

These, however, are posthumous reflections on what then appeared like a rosy prospect. No doubt the Viceroy of

Kansu looked for his share of profit in being a cousin of the throne. He had certainly borne the burden and heat of being a cousin of the President. Yuan Shih Kai had thorough notions of playing his part, and no one knew better than he how profoundly Chinese opinion appreciates fine sentiments, especially when backed by an ostentation of fine actions. And a would-be Emperor, especially, must go very cautiously forward on his almost blasphemous climb, panoplied in an unvarying nobility of phrase and attitude. Accordingly he had put forth (after that Imperial tradition and model so touchingly followed, on occasions, by the Grand Dowager) the most beautiful and self-denying edicts, ordering that on his birthday, and other such festal occasions, no valuable presents were to be sent him by the provincial Governors, lest their populations be overburdened in their poverty. This was all very fine and impressive, but the Kansu Viceroy considered himself, as a cousin, behind the scenes. Realizing that the heart of man, not excepting Emperors in posse, is always, whatever his tongue may say, capacious of presents and so elastic that its capacity even increases with their number and importance, he filled a whole train of carts with precious pictures, bronzes, furs, silks and cash, and dispatched the caravan towards Peking, heralded by a telegram of cousinly congratulation on the President's birthday. He reckoned without the Roman virtue of his relative. Indeed, what use are relatives to an aspiring President, unless to be snubbed *coram populo* for a good example ? Yuan Shih Kai made full use accordingly of his rights, and all China was edified to learn that the Viceroy of Kansu had had his procession of presents stopped on the way by special telegram from Peking, and sent back in disgrace to Lanchow, under cover of a stately rebuke, for an action so calculated to corrupt the pure *candeur* of the President, and at variance with his express directions. Results ; a great loss of face for the Viceroy, but an enormous accretion of credit for the President. Meanwhile we do not ask what private letters softened the blow, nor what treasures of particular price were packed off later to Peking, in a less obtrusive manner.

No wonder the Viceroy now beamed over our gracious assent to the President's Imperial programme. The toils of the business were over, the sweets were now to begin. And so he took leave, promising us a special garden-party in a few days' time. That night we relaxed in a lesser Beano, at Mr. Li's, at which the fun waxed fast and furious, there being no Mrs. Post Office present to supervise the revels. I think a happy Chinese party would surpass even Mrs. Musgrove's notion of a little quiet cheerfulness; nor could Cordelia have ever excelled at the morra-game. The two players simultaneously throw forward their hands, with a varying number of fingers extended; in the same instant each yells his estimate of the combined number. If neither is right neither wins the coup : if one is right, the other takes a nip from the wine-cup, or a no-heeler if his mood prompts. The Chinese are agile as a *prima donna* in altering their guess-number in the middle of their yell. And when you get four or five couples at a party, all bellowing like bulls of Bashan, in a shattering pandemonium of duets, the effect is something to be remembered; more especially as the Chinese pad out the numbers with allusions and associations from the Classics. Thus, while the uncultured foreigner, hurling forth his fist towards his opponent, yells " Six " for his guess of the total fingers extended, his lettered rival, in even more stentorian tones, is shrieking about the Seven Humours or the Eight Fairies.

In quieter intervals, too, Mr. Lo and Mr. Li did not forget the chance of bargaining about their bronzes. Mr. Li, the more dexterous and practised of the two, had not Mr. Lo's warmth of heart and engaging ingenuousness. Mr. Li stuck sweetly to his price, yielded nothing, and gave no luck-penny ; but there was no resisting Mr. Lo's incomparable innocence and round little earnest candid face, as he would press upon one some acquisition of his, with the endearing assurance " Good things I kip, bad things I sell you." But

now, the bargain clinched, Mr. Lo relaxed into generosity,
and pressed upon me as a present a crystal " dlak'n "
(dragon) which proved to be a little couchant unicorn ; then
becoming a little embroiled in speech, had a long passage
with Mr. Post Office about some " pixtures " that he wished
to purchase of him ; and so was at last removed, still
clamouring proffers for the " pixtures."

Packings, payments and dispatchings were now going on.
It was a question of getting the specimens, the furs, bronzes,
china, scrolls, and all our heavier possessions carted down
country to the railhead. The packing-cases proved dis-
concertingly numerous and vast ; it took two large wains
and a Peking cart to hold them. Ma-y, meanwhile, held the
contract—80 taels (£12) for a thousand catties, only to the
railhead. And the weight of our chattels amounted to
two and a half thousand. The price, looking back, seems
little enough. At the time, under the load of big disburse-
ments on every side, I felt this the final straw that crushed
me. The caravan was to break up, too. Ma-y, in charge of
the chattels, and supported by a special escort from the
Viceroy, would see the goods down-country, and up the rail
to Peking, there to await our arrival. And Bill intended
to fly round by Ardjeri and Jo-ni, to gather up a few omitted
or scantily-harvested seeds of the previous season, notably
of the beautiful Drokwa-Land Senecio (F. 400 [1]) that I have
never seen. Thence he was to fetch a wide bend through
Kiai Chew and down Kansu, and meet me again somewhere
on the Szechuan Border or in Shensi. I, meanwhile, now
travelling almost as light as Bill, discharged of everything
but bed and bedding and comb and cook-pots, and attended
only by Go-go, Bongie, Lay-gor and the wicked Wa-wa,
would forge straight ahead Southward through the Province,
and await Bill for a night or so, in such pleasant places as
should seem probable, until finally we rejoined each other.
The original caravan was quite dissolved, and the ponies (all

---

[1] Abundance was got, but it never seems to have germinated
anywhere.

except Bill's vivid little brown one) traded away in Lanchow for " pixtures." Bill was going to ride, and I myself proceed luxuriously across the face of China in a mule-litter, secure reliquary for my wearied bones.

Everything went well; and the day of the garden-party approached. But now, with shattering suddenness, a fatal blow befell. All these days the Wa-wa had been visibly swelling at the thought of going down-country with me, and seeing trains and steamers and Peking, and the world the flesh and the devil generally. And, under his charge, I did not quail before the loneliness of my long solitary journey. But one fine morning Lay-gor returned from some errand at Wa-gung-Hsien, on the Tao-jo trail, and I was aware of a commotion in the kitchen. Down I hurried, to find him in floods of tears, and his Wa-wa alongside, his bun-like face congested with rage, and his eyes glinting a few painful squeezed-out diamonds that were meant to express pious grief, but really expressed only anger in the capital degree. For down was gone the castle in Spain, and ended, in an instant, all prospects of Peking; Lay-gor brought back news of a Grannie moribund at Nâ-Lang, and imperiously summoning back all her descendants to her death-bed. There was nothing for it; father and son must instantly say good-bye to us and be off. Never did a face so speak fury as that Wa-wa's, as he knelt before me, trying to conjure up an expression of filial dutifulness, but obviously rent with the bitterest disappointment. My own was hardly less; such a bad little boy perhaps, such a good little servant for sure.

And our mutual emotions were further complicated, my condolences hollowed, and his assumption of dutiful woe made more difficult, by our common knowledge that Grannie, of course, was perfectly well all the time, and going about her business, never better in her life. But she had issued her fiat: immemorial custom forbade question and commanded instant obedience even to the empty formality of a pretended death-bed. It was Gomer's case over again—the undisputed autocracy of the Dowager in Chinese life, from Tz'Hsi " in

the deep seclusion of the Palace," to the publicity of
Appu in the corner of the Kang. And Appu is not going to
have the younglings of her house straying long, or straying
afar, to get corrupted with foreign countries, women, drinks,
diseases. To avort the latter she goes any lengths, and if
her descendant tries to be deaf to her call, Appu takes
officially to her death-bed and summons all the clan to attend
it. Woe betide the truant if he stays away. Truly, despite
the nonsense often talked about the status of women in
China, it is certain that in reality no other country gives
woman anything like such a dominating position as she
holds in Chinese life—if only she can live through the neglect
of her girlhood, the drudgery and subjection of her married
life, and emerge at last into the sacred majesty of Dowager-
hood, with full revenge in her hands to take for all the
previous servitude of her days, and daughters-in-law of her
own to bully in turn, and sons and sons' sons to dragoon.
No impotent Dower-House, no parish relief or grudged corner
or workhouse for a Chinese Grannie : she succeeds auto-
matically to the mastery of house and hearth and home,
representing, as she now does, the accumulated sacro-sanctity
of the ancestors, the apex of the family, guardian of its
traditions from the past and its continuing branches of the
future.

But all this sociology could not save the situation. We
were to lose our Wa-wa, and at once. Bundles were hastily
made, and the little asses got ready ; almost before I could
realize the blow and all it meant, father and son were on
their knees again before me saying good-bye. And in a few
more minutes Lay-gor and his Wa-wa and the four little
wise donkeys were nothing but a memory, specks of blue and
grey vanishing down the Southward road, merged in the
incalculable millions of China. And what has now become
of that precocious infant. I hardly dare to wonder. Disappointed of foreign travel, yet already fleshed with a taste
of it, he must have burst upon Jo-ni as a furious portent,
heady with some knowledge of the world, yet droughty for

more. A perilous combination. Without doubt he is by
now high in the dissolute entourage of Yang Tu-Ssu ;
unless, indeed, he has ousted his sovereign, and is now himself
the reigning Prince of Jo-ni ; or, as is indeed much more
likely, I fear, has long since had his head bashed in by what
Michael Finsbury called an injured husband, or his throat
slit by some rival or stay-at-home, provoked beyond bearing
by his serene and ineffable presumption and monstrous
man-of-the-worldishness. In any case, I tremble for that
Grannie who cut him off from his prospects ; though her
first death-bed was merely official, I feel confident she soon
found a genuine one.

At 4 o'clock of a radiant afternoon arrived our summons
to the party. Rather to my disappointment I had learned
that it was to be a big and formal affair, including even the
Missionary element. Well up then, on our hind legs, and in
our tightest clothes, off we duly set in carts, and in a remote
garden-house of the Palace were joined by a knot of fellow-
guests, who had not been admitted till our own arrival.
Then hove in our host, and a long period of courtesies and
chat ensued. Weary at last of nothing-saying over cups of
tea, I asked if we might not see the garden. The move was
well taken, and forth we all streamed, impeded by a great
deal of ceremonious modesty at each doorway. When we
came to the *œil de bœuf* gateway into the actual garden,
there might have been a longer pause than ever. But Bill
had developed a real friendship of chuckles with the Viceroy,
and now, in particular, wanted to fix arrangements about
the escort of our goods down country. So without delay or
deprecations of any kind, he seized the Potentate's black
satin arm, linked it close in his, and they wallowed through
the wall together in whispered gurgles and laughter, followed
by an almost audible gasp from the other guests at such an
unbuttoned display of informality.

The viceregal garden is really almost a park in size, and
its then tenant was on the way to making it very delightful.
Its first part, near the building, was a huge extent (canopied

by noble old trees) of mounts and monticules and rockworks,
with pools and gazeboes and terraces and towers and
summer-houses, and little Chelsea-Show-ish stretches and
corners of walling and flights of steps, with gay pots of
flowers along the parapets. In the dappled green of the
overshadowing trees it all sparkled with a discreet brilliance.
Here and there, in cages and enclosures, were pheasants
and rabbits and storks. An ape had once illustrated the
collection, but had by now been gathered to his fathers.
And the Ma-ji, shorn of their *raison d'être*, drooped sullenly.
Ma-ji (Horse-chickens) are a species of mountain pheasant,
whose plumage, in old Imperial days, was very highly prized
and priced, as a ceremonial adornment of the highest officials.
This plumage, though, is nothing exciting, but nevertheless
Ma-ji always captivate my fancy, for they are exactly—but
exactly—like *very* stout old ladies from the suburbs, come
up to town by tube to the theatre, tightly bound in grey
alpaca dust-cloaks, with a wisp of white choker just showing
under their chin on either side, and fierce little red eyes
a-sparkle in an expression of restless and vindictive propriety.

The remoter part of the park is flat and more given over to
flowers, planted in by rectangular stretches, with irrigation
runnels between. The gaiety of these was gone : I saw
drifts of what had been a Lily, and alongside a plumy feather-
ing filminess of green, to which the Viceroy delightedly drew
my attention as a particular beauty. Very lovely indeed it
was, but do the Chinese take the wrong end of the stick in
this matter, or do we ? For " Dragon's whiskers " is an
article of beauty in China, but of diet in Europe. We eat it
in its younger stages with Sauce Mousseline, or melted butter
or vinaigrette. It is, in fact, no more nor less than Asparagus
officinalis. But China does not eat it at all in any stage, any
more than she eats the tomato or the quince. These are all
grown for their beauty or their fragrance, and for nothing
else. At least, up-country, where Lanchow alone rises to
the rare æsthetic luxury of a few tomatoes, which are piled

high on a dish to adorn the drawing-room in summer, even as quinces, big and pale golden, similarly piled in winter, see the long months out in their beauty, and flood the place with fragrance to boot.

When we had thoroughly pervaded the Palace grounds the crowd began moving back towards dinner, but diverged to a beautiful walled pool, with water-plants abounding, and a summer pavilion on the far side. And now it appeared that Mr. Kwai, one of our fellow-guests, had grounds adjoining, which he wished to show me. So we passed through a gate into his enclosure, and found a quite charming formal garden, trim and neat and gay, with parterres and palisades, and a vine-arbour in the middle, as it might have been in some Albergo-garden in Verona. But I thought I could discern that the Viceroy was not wholly pleased at this rival attraction : the long-delayed dinner was now announced, and he shovelled us all indoors with firmness and promptitude.

The meal was good and very " foreign " ; the merriment went high and disposedly, the Viceroy alleging a sick stomach. But his real pleasure came later, in having us apart, to show us his pictures. Now he could really unfold and expatiate with chuckles over the beauty of each, and the complimentary scrolls of calligraphy that he was doing with his own viceregal hand for Bill and me, as a special sign of friendship. His collection was a big and fine one : he clearly delighted in it, and delighted in showing. " Hoo-hoo ! " he said with gurgling deep joy, lovingly indicating some delicate touch of colour or following some suave line with a downward sweep of his sumptuous long-nailed thumb, girt with a great napkin-ring of jade. We admired to his heart's content, and then were escorted out, down lateral courtyards, silent and empty, with big earthenware vats containing little trees in them, formally aligned, or smaller jars brilliant with annuals—singly planted as specimens— among which we were shown with pointed pride the Pansies and Cornflowers and Petunias that we ourselves had procured him from England.

In one of the courtyards, decent and withdrawn, sat the Vicereine of Kansu, sewing shoes in the quiet sunshine, while around her the viceregal marmaille tumbled and played in their brilliant little scarlet breeches and trousers. The proud father chuckled delightfully, and tweaked the nearest pigtail with approval. And after a moment's contemplation of the scene we moved on. Indeed, these are a very pleasant kindly people, so paradoxically combining the extreme of simple homeliness and domestic affection with the most exacting and elaborate code of ceremonial etiquette in the world. And this they can do because they are so completely sure of themselves, serene in the unassertive self-confidence that only the consciousness of four thousand years of civilization can convey.

Without any serious word said this time, we parted from His Excellency, and bumped home in our carts. But hardly had we arrived than Mr. Li appeared with a solemn and secret message. Would we deploy our influence in the highest quarters at Peking to protect His Excellency against any scandals or hostile manœuvres that might be engineered against him by his enemies in that vast and sinister mechanism of wheels within wheels? This was a large contract; I carry trowels in my pocket, not Viceroyalties. However, the chance word in season to the powerful is always among the possibilities of our wonderful mortal kaleidoscope; I was able conscientiously to assure Mr. Li that should the President-Emperor insist on coming to tea with me in Peking, I would not fail to impress him to the best of my ability with the prowess and loyalty of the Kansu Viceroy, all libels to the contrary notwithstanding.

And now, as if to bind me to my promise, the complimentary scrolls arrived from the Palace, with all His Excellency's compliments and a large head and shoulders photograph of him, in military uniform, with the pupils of the eyes pecked in with a pin to give the required glare of official ferocity. A brace of scrolls for me, and a brace for Bill, a column of big black characters on each from the Viceroy's own hand, with the Viceregal signature and seal attached. My legends announced that I had crossed ten thousand oceans to come to China and that the tale of my virtues was endless as a circle—an ambiguous compliment, since a circle has no beginning either, as doubtless my detractors will discern. Anyhow, this was glory, and great " face " : the servants and the fellow-guests of the inn pressed round in awe. Mr. Lo, however, was illuminatingly candid on the matter. It appeared that the Great Man's calligraphy, in the eyes of those who knew, was, as a matter of fact " plen'y bad." But why tell him so ? Accordingly all the Province flattered his harmless delusion of penmanship, and when in doubt as to obtaining an office or deprecating displeasure, the surest method was to beg for a specimen from the Viceregal brush.

But now the time is come. One farewell stroll, out of the South Gate, and afar round by Wu chuen, over the enormous waste of dimpling graves with the crumpled Egyptian hills of the distance very lovely and golden in the late shafts of the sun, over the illuminated walls and towers of the city, and the flat green ocean of tree-tops from which they rise. And then—the Shandz' is at the door of the inn, a thing like a big drain-pipe of matting on a frame of laths, with a pole protruding in front and behind. In its depths my scanty baggage is packed, a lumpy bed, if it were not for the depth of quilts and coats and cushions accumulated on top. Good-bye Mr. and Mrs. Post Office, Good-bye Mafu, Good-bye Mr. Li and Mr. Lo, Good-bye Lanchow. But just as I am about to crawl into the recesses of the Shandz', arrives a breathless message from His Excellency. Would we go up and take his photograph ? Yes, indeed, at whatever cost of trouble and delay. Had he not crowned all his friendliness by giving our chattels a flaming passport down-country and two of his smartest guards for its escort, not only in his own province, but right through to the railhead ? So up we hurried to the Palace, and there, in the garden, the Keeper of the King's Peace and the Keeper of the President's were duly immortalized side by side. But I do not reproduce the

result ; it is not a portrait on which I dwell with complacency. You may imagine a reformed burglar in black satin,
cheek by jowl with an elderly and dissipated-looking Caruso.
And now, after renewed and tender farewells to Mr. Lo and
Mr. Li, back we returned to the inn. Into the matted ark
of the Shandz, I crawled and there was so securely packed
and wadded up in my bedding as to be like a chrysalis
in its cocoon ;—Houp ; it was hoisted up in front and its
frontal pole lodged on the leader mule, and then—Houp—
equalized again by being hoisted up on the mule behind.
Lying out my length, swaying high above the earth, I felt as
tyrannous and splendid as Cleopatra borne aloft in procession. And now the moment was come ; Bill thrust in
his hand for a farewell grip, and off I went swinging out of
Lanchow for the last time, low in my spirits that it *was* the
last time, low in the prospect of affronting the infinite distances of China with only Go-go and Bongie for my sole
support, and low beneath all, in thought of such a long
parting from my dear Bill, and our uncertainty as to when
and where we should join forces again.

CHAPTER XV
THE DOWNWARD TRAIL

But the day was very glorious, and I grew serene in spirits as equably I balleted along through the hours, across the glaring downs and ravines of bare loess with glimpses of what may still have been the Hwang-Hor away to my left, in a cañon of rock with fragments of an apparently ancient wall alongside. After trudging it and trekking it for months, there is no restfulness in life like that of a mule-litter. Relaxed in absolute ease, ensconced in comfort, one lies wedged into the softness of the bedding, with every muscle gone loose, every curve and protuberance fitted and moulded by the bedding. The movement is undulating and bland, the hours slide by in a stupor of incredible comfort, so acute as almost to be plausibly mistaken for happiness. It was out of a roseate havoc of dreams that at last I alighted at Han Tao, down in a broad river-plain, joyous in greenness and poplars, and under a sky now gone brazen and sulphurous and violet with brewing masses of storm. There was a little delay in finding an inn, and then followed the worst of the day—the fuss and confusion of the first stage out, with nothing to be found in its place, and everybody ineffectually doing everybody else's work—except the donkeymen, who did not even do their own. And poor Go-go, of course, had no more command than a kitten. Sad and cross for my Wa-wa I coped with the chaos ; all the packages had to be uncorded, and the litter itself completely gutted—as indeed, it always had to be each night, to get at the bed and the wash-pot, and then repacked each morning.

Mid-Kansu is a land of glaring loess, with clean-cut spotless loess villages here and there. Always so neat and new, because when your house begins to show signs of wear, you do not restore it, but take a pail and a trowel and some chopped straw, and go out and make a mud-pie wherever you please to build a new one. As the paste of the walls rises higher and higher, you corset it flat between braced boards on either side ; and so it hardens, and you take away the boards, and there is a faultless square block of yellow mud walls, with only the roof needing to be added. I spare you the detail of my uneventful days, broken only by the noon interval, when they would unyoke the mules to go in and rest and feed in some village, dumping down the litter with me inside in the middle of the public street for all the world to crowd round and gaze at, unless the inn had some dark little private room where I could go in and sit on the Kang and take lunch in such comfort as the flies would leave me in the intervals of whacking at them with my yak-tail whisk. My last touch of my former world occurred to me on the second day out. As I neared the midday stage I looked ahead. And wondered why a khaki-clad gorilla should be at large on the face of China. Could it be ? Impossible—but it *was*—Mafu, in charge of the chattels and their escort, grinning all over his face as he saw me approaching. For Mafu, what with the civilizing influences of Lanchow, and a public beating he had incurred at Koko-Nor, followed by public kowtows of apology, was now apparently as good as gold again, and the sight of him, though our ways were now to diverge finally, was refreshing as a tonic in that large lone land.

Kan Tsoo Tien is a typical mule-village of this great highroad, with a long row of clean open shops containing everything a muleman could need, and clean wide inn-yards running back behind to neat inn-dwellings. Mafu once more took charge, and I was amazed to find what a pace the lumbering enormousness of his two wains could make. Now we were getting Southward : on the morrow, in a lowering morning, we climbed slowly up a big open loess down, with a very wide prospect over the country, now a panorama of low rolling lines, largely cultivated and largely green in grass, the crinkled yellow desolations of Lanchow being here quite left behind. The air was autumnal, the banks all gay with Asters, amid the gold of Chrysanthemum indicum. Such a queer little blatant common-looking weed to be the mother of so vast and august a race of garden plants, from the Tableaux of Dango Zaka to the mop-heads dipped in anchovy sauce so dear to the English gardener. Dark violet storms now pursued us on a violent gale, and broke in thunder and sharp squalling flaws of cold rain as we lumbered down the steep far descent on the other side, and after a tranquil stretch through a new valley, arrived, under a cleared radiant sky, at Shwa-y-goo, neatest perhaps and cleanest and newest-looking of all these naked, neat and new-looking villages of Kansu.

Mafu and his carts and the smartly saluting soldiers of the Viceroy's guard here parted company with me, on their Eastward way. We struck on Southward, through country still much the same—wide vales of loess, with the crops by now all carried or stacked, but the gao-liang still beautiful in heavy tasselled heads of bronze; and on either side undulating downs of the same, cultivated to the top in long embanked slopes. One sees the loess country, though, very differently from the serene ease of a Shandz'; it wears no such pleasant colours from the jogging back of a pony or the cramped dullness of a sedan. But gradually the downs run higher, at last we were mounting towards big fells that recalled Whernside, in the summery day of blue and haze and soft clouds beginning to grow heavier. And out we ultimately came on the actual grassy crest of the big down-system, billowing far and wide on every hand, and crowned with a chain of low square fortalices away down all the distances. Steeply we descended to the valley, and came at length to Ma-Ing, the biggest place on our road yet. A fair was raging outside, with booths and theatricals. But we held straight on down a street crowded with mats and bamboo-besoms (a symptom of the South) till we turned into a small and ramshackly inn, where I found my quarters in a tiny warm-kanged room, stacked in one corner with Spaghetti, piled up in enormous skeins.

And at Ma-Ing, in that dark and squalid little hole, I was detained by such hopeless floods of rain as made travelling an impossibility for men or mules. In the afternoon it dismally cleared for a while, and I went out to the fair, with Bongie in attendance. The gay street itself was amusing, but even more so was the actual fair, down below by the stream, on the sands and shingles of the river-bed, with all manner of stalls and raree-shows and refreshments and theatricals. But I myself very soon became the greatest raree-show of the lot : and was moving along amid a vast crowd, running before me and behind and on either side, with their feet making a soft din of many waters on the fine loose gravel. It was quite embarrassing, not particularly pleasant, for in China it is generally wisest to avoid such public festivities, where spirits are on the loose and multiplied by multitude, so that one might easily by some indiscretion, either of friendliness or reserve, provoke an outbreak of anti-foreign feeling. However, as I had chosen to come down, I must go through with it : one could only proceed with immovable smile amid the tumultuous laughter all around, showing no sign of supposing the laughter was so pointed and personal as it probably was. Gradually I and my swarms drifted homeward without untoward development, and the swarms by degrees diminished. Quite enough of the cortège, however, accompanied me back to the inn, and crowded into the yard to go on taking their fill of the spectacle. On the whole I was glad to be in foreign clothes that day, and could but hope they were not saying I was as hideous as I felt sure they must be. They were all quite cheery and friendly though, and there was huge fun when the Go-go siphoned them away from time to time. But it was strange to me to be back among the inquisitive mobs of central China, after such long experience of better manners in the North, where, however much one provokes remark, it is rarely obtrusive and never a nuisance. Put it to them reasonably and pleasantly, that the traveller is tired and not on show, and the population of a Northern village at once sees the point : the Southerner takes a different view. He intends to get all the amusement he can out of life, and considers it would be unfair and churlish of you to deny your contribution.

The next day was crowded with incident. In the night, first of all, I had occasion to strike a match. Whereupon the entire box blew up in a blast of flame, and badly burned my hand. Then, in the black of the dawn came Go-go, whispering that it was a very evil day and that the departure must again be put off. But hardly had I composed myself and my burned hand to sleep once more, resigned to yet another day in that mangy hovel, than again came Go-go in grey cock-crow, saying that after all everybody was anxious to get away, *coûte que coûte.* This jumped very much better with my own mood : I alacritously rose and ate and packed ; and soon was heaving out of Ma-Ing, in contemplation of an unrelieved soaker with the little frontal fig-leaf of the litter let down against the wet, so that I could see no more than a glimpse of a hill valley, with boulders and cliffs of immense granite blocks, rounded and glaciated looking.

We toiled over high ground, the rain ceased, the wind blew cold and gusty. It was a mercy to have the sure-footedness of mules to rely on in the copious slime of the track. For, as the day wore down, the rain again descended in deluges, and the loess lanes became like gruel overlying ice. And now the track was skirting the rim of a loess precipice above a river, with deep and very narrow little gullies in its face, most awkward to circumnavigate with the unweildy length of a Shandz', which, by its construction, is not two mules in free movement fore and aft, but one unmanageable invertebrate organism, incapable of bending. These nasty little pitches I bore with philosophic reliance on the mules and men ; till suddenly, at the nastiest of all, where I did not like to look over on the right, straight to the river far below, there came a frantic plunging, slithering, scrambling, scuttering, and there in another moment was I, securely bottled, pensively gazing up at the sky between my feet. Both the mules had fallen and the jao had come off, and was just quivering sidelong on the very verge of the precipice, imperilled every instant by the plunging of the mules to regain their footing. With such dignity as I could muster, and with a desperate tranquillity for fear I should upset the jao into the river, I climbed up like a trap-door spider emerging from the shaft, and floundered down into the mud and the rain. The position was very disconsolate in the pouring wet, with the jao periclitating on the edge, and no sufficient aid at hand to replace it ; pending the arrival of Go-go and the Pai-ren from the latest Yamen, I waddled arduously onwards in the perilous " verglas." Really I could not blame the mules : I only went a hundred yards or so, but it took me a very laborious careful and anxious half-hour.

But now Go-go and the Pai-ren did come along and rescued the jao and got it on to the mules again. I clambered in once more, but with nerve rather shaken, detesting those horrid loess cliffs whose rim we went on skirting and the horrible little ascents and descents in their gullies. Now, however, one of the Yamen escort went before with a mattock, and hacked out a footing in the quaggiest pitches ; with only one more flounder we advanced successfully, and gradually the dark descended and veiled from me the full horror of the depths above which we were proceeding. It was just black night, in a new valley of the hills, when we lumbered into Whitegate Keep (Bei Mun Gwan [1]) and I was escorted through puddles to a decent little room in an inn-yard, undecipherable in the dark.

But Whitegate Keep appeared a squalid, derelict place in

---

[1] Or Bei Ma Gwan ? (White Horse Gate)—not having Mafu during this journey, I was unable to collect the characters for the various place-names, so cannot, as a rule, give them in translation.

the morning, and we moved out early, heartened with the thought of having yesterday achieved the longest stage of the journey. The weather was all a low cloud, raw and cold, with the event long in doubt ; but very gradually the pale sun began to pierce and grew stronger, and, as we soon set to mounting a big fell, finally prevailed. It was very beautiful then, on the high hill-top with the last ravellings of the cloud floating off around us, shot with shafts of sunlight, and the moisture sweeping up from the slopes in white smoky vapours. Our whole day of twenty-three miles or so was spent along the topmost reaches of the down, with remote undulating views, rich in blue and golden colour, of soft sunny valleys full of trees and yellow fields at our feet, and then distance behind distance of expansive high downs like the one we were traversing. Ahead of us up the track there wound the procession of some Mandarin changing his post, with a train of eight mules and a guard of soldiers and mounted attendants in long crimson cloaks, and My Lord a-horseback, and an ark like my own for My Lady, and a very smart pretty little Wa-wa capering about beside his father beneath a big bowler hat of crumpled black tarpaulin. I had seen them indeed earlier, just ahead of me as I left the town, but had been distracted by meeting there a lady of high quality on a mule, veiled in transparent sapphire silk, with a huge duck's-bill coiffure sticking up like a horn at the back of her head, as is the fashion in these parts seemingly, together with the veil, when you take the air. At last, up and down the crests of the fell, we overtook and passed My Lord, and came to a neat little village on a neck, which was our Ban Tien (half-way stage).

Here there was yet another fair going forward. I was glad to alight and withdraw into the inn's one little dark side-room to escape the staring crowds. But now came along the rival train, and its jao disgorged My Lady, a very comely and capable-looking person, clearly of the most decided views and temper, resplendent in a short blue coat, crimson tabard, and tight black trousers. She was accom-

panied by a very fat little semi-demi-palace-dog, which she
sedulously hugged out of harm's way from the mules, holding
it all anyhow as they do, or waving it about by one leg, till
I could not help laughing at its expression of pompous resignation in untoward circumstances.   But the poor lady now
stood fixed in indecision with frowns accumulating beneath
the sleek flat bandeaux that framed her brow.   I had taken
the only room, and she had nowhere to retire to while her
mules ate lunch.   I heard My Lord explaining to her how the
matter stood : there was nothing for it but to emerge from
my seclusion and wave her into it with mutual bows and
smiles and deprecations, while I myself withdrew into my
jao again till it was time to set off once more.

For another two or three hours we crested the down.   The
going was good to-day, and I enjoyed it.   The distances,
too, now showed real hills away in the South and West,
though very, very dim and remote.   Out in the West—real
hills towards the Border !   The thought of Siku, only a
few days' journey now, straight away into the West tugged
my heart constantly like a magnet and every dim cloud
castle on the horizon I madly moulded into Thundercrown
until it melted away.   For the first time, too, I now really
felt as if we were getting to the South, the air was mellower
and the vegetation changed.   Stellera still continued on the
downs, but quite gone were the stately straight Lombardian
poplars of the North, and their place in all the valleys was
taken by rounder dimplier sorts : Prinsepia, Alantus and
Sophora reappear, and the vales were still delightful to
contemplate, lush in green and bronze and crimson of buck-
wheat millet and Gao-Liang very sumptuous with its dense
brown thyrses, ranging up the gently-sloping flanks of russet
brown and loess, ravinated and crumpled.   And then, far
below, appeared a cosy big village, with dark tiles for the
first time replacing the mud gables and flat tops of the North.
Steeply and abruptly we descended the last pitch : it was so
precipitous as to seem almost sheer.   But the sure-footed
mules successfully achieved it, though I had ado, in the

jao, to keep the guns and sticks from sliding out of it as we perpendicularly dropped.

Go-ja-Tsui is a staring place like the rest. There was quite mob enough in the inn, without going forth on the streets for more. But it is wonderful how completely European one gets in time, to see the Chinese I was perpetually thinking that there was surely a foreigner coming to meet me, and then it turned out always to be no such thing. All my own friends, even, I got to see in what proved on closer inspection to be a Chinese Avatar. A touch of brown, for one thing, in the hair is no very rare occurrence hereabouts : near Go-ja-Tsui I actually saw an adult coolie with a full *chevelure* of almost Titian auburn—only just not red. In a very lovely morning, fine to brilliant, we sailed forth again along our road, down and down uneventful valleys, and through empoplared hamlets murmurous with pigeons amid the green. It was delicious going, but I felt I could never quite enjoy coasting the rims of loess precipices over rivers in the abject helplessness of a jao—more especially as the jao itself had a tilt to one side. For the adjustment of a jao is a very nice matter. When properly mounted the litter should be as exquisitely even in its balance as the art of Jane Austen : too often it is lopsided as that of Charlotte Brontë, and one feels all wrong, as if with misyoked buttons and boots like the luckless young man immortalized by the ministrations of Betsey and Sairey. At least until a boulder has been picked up and packed in under the mule's yoke on one side or the other.

Now came a narrowing and a gorge, and then a very picturesque small Hsien, with a beautiful storied tower perched above on a descending spur of the hill that was its Acropolis. This was only Ban Tien ; gaping mobs drove me back from the inn-yard into the deep seclusion of my Shandz', where I dripped with heat and ate the delicious little round pears of Kansu, that melt in the mouth like flowing milk and honey, with the perfect taste of strawberries. But at last I and my ark were hoisted up again,

off we set, leftward, out of the valley ; and mounted on to
the first high down where I did not see Stellera. Along it
and along we wound, up and down for miles. Ahead, in the
forehead of the fell, there unfolded at last a tiny but most
attractive-looking village, which certainly could not be our
stage, since when was ever a stage not in a valley ? But
our stage it actually was, and Geh-Ja-Pu is an entrancing
place indeed, aloft along the high concavity of the fell, with
all the world open before it, and a little fortalice above, and
beneath, a turbulent declension of golden fields over golden
fields in the enormous converging slopes of the down, sinking
away below, with other cosy embowered hamlets nestling in
them here and there at intervals of a mile or so ; and for
distance, an infinite overwhelming succession of diaphanous
blue down-crests, level with our own, dotted along their
eminences, as far as eye could see, with forts. It is a gigantic
prospect from that high place, benign and calm and spacious :
wholly dissimilar in many of its details, it yet recalls the
voluminous luxuriance of Sei am Schlern, as you look down
across its undulations from the Sälegg.

We gutted our goods, and the litter, in an inn, where I
expanded in a big lean-to room at the back, with clean
kangs so new that fires had to be lit in them to dispel the
damp of their mud, and emitted a stinking smoke from the
stokeholes. After which, as the afternoon was still being
golden and gay and glorious, I strolled in beatitude out from
the village along the track which leads, level and broad and
smooth, hemmed with a tight grey-green velvet of the close
turf that clothes the down, along round the curve of the hill
to a high neck about three-quarters of a mile beyond. Here,
abruptly, a new view breaks upon you. Far down below
lies the broad bed of the Wei-Hor, deep in weeping willows,
and away beyond this a renewed succession of hill-ranges,
but more serrated, and with fewer fortresses, at least on the
nearer chain. In a rapture I roamed and sat and lay : it
was one of those golden scenes and circumstances that live
for ever in one's memory, as vivid as in their first moment,

immortally. When at length I rose dazed from my absorption of its happiness and went home, the flies in my room were such a pest, and I so grudged every instant of daylight in that high divine place, that forth I went yet again. The sun was now gorgeously setting, in an undistinguishable tumble of purple cloud-ranges and purple hills. Out into the sumptuous solemn chaos of the West I strained my eyes, in anguished longing for some lost glimpse of the sacred and mysterious Land, still not so very far away out there, but so soon to be lost for ever. But each possible mountain mass that I could dimly discern on the uttermost horizon soon shifted and melted from its first acclaimed solidity, and proved to be only cloud. In all that ruffle of high ranges there was nothing solid : the Sacred and Mysterious Land was finally beyond my sight, and the distances of China all round me held no suggestion of Tibetan heights. Molten in the sorrow of exile I watched the sombre splendour of the sundown, and then, sentimental and low and sad in reaction, I returned to the inn at last, there still to spend more hours patrolling the hard-beaten mud threshing floor of the grain-yard amid stacks of garnered millet, and little cats playing peep-bo in and out behind them. I was too happy for food, too completely occupied and haunted.

Down and down, the next day, steep and far, into the broad plain of the Wei-Hor, full of harvest and tracts of trees. Then, to my surprise, we turned to the right, and up over another enormous fell of loess, all gay with the rose-pink ox-eyes of Chrysanthemum Zawadskyi : only to drop again on the far side into the same valley of the Wei-Hor. And immediately at the foot of the descent lay Tsin Jô, very different from when I first saw it in 1914, for now the bare willows were clothed, and the town was embedded on all sides in profound weeping cascades of green. And the evening, as I strolled the streets till dinner, was deliciously green-aired and hot and balmy. We put up in a less ambitious inn than on our previous visit ; in its narrow stinking darkness I devoted all the next day to articles and letters ;

and on the next morning we resumed the trail, setting our faces towards the new, unknown and already different-looking country that fills the extreme Southerly toe of Kansu.

In a streaky hot day, turning grey and chilly at its close, we drifted out of Tsin-Jô, among the glorious weeping willows, and so gradually to the right and across the Wei-Hor, and then up the flat bed of an affluent. For hours we proceeded, the country quite dull, but very unlike the Northward stretches of the province, being richer, moister, and clothed in vegetation, with the loess now wholly replaced by reddish loam in little low hills, with fortalices on their summits. Our Ban Tien was only 30 li out, with fifty more still to do; always up this valley, which soon became that of a dead stream continuing without break down-hill. The luxuriance increased, and the red hills began to remind me of those about Ga-hoba. Old friends reappeared : the little Berberis, Loniceras and so forth. There were high wild hedges, too, with the Barley Bee Rose in clotted cascades of crimson-fruited clusters. Nor need I have been nervous about that solitary plant of Cratægus crenulata on Thunder-crown, or its occasional appearance at the top end of the Nan-Ho gorges. For evidently those were its very farthest adventures Northward ; now we were entering upon its real territory, and in every hedgerow and coppice it abounded in almost as fierce and unbroken a blaze of scarlet as C. Angusti-folia in its solid hedges along the highways of the Venetian plain about Udine and Gorizia. On and on we luxuriously wended ; and ultimately mounted to the right, over a little col. And now the view ahead was indeed a refresher for sore eyes, weary with the dust-coloured expanses of the North.

Far ahead of us there flowed a sea of hill-ranges, higher, greener, more peaked, more sumptuous with coppice than anything I had set eyes on since leaving Wolvesden ; and all the intervening vales were a surf of verdure. So we wound along down and came at last into Niang-Niang Ba, most charming village, most charmingly snuggled among trees at a convergence of vales. But the only possible room

for me was so very tiny and dark, and so densely occupied by
the family, and so awfully suggestive of bugs, that I could
not face it till I must, and, while the family moved out,
sauntered along the various slopes of down or coppice,
realizing, as I jumped at the barking of a far-off dog or
recoiled with a gasping squawk before a sudden whirr of field-
fares, how thin and worn my nerves were got by now, with
the strain of two seasons' travel, complicated by the defection
of the cat-befriending cook, whose economies by this time
had landed me in a constant loathing for my food and such a
general condition of urticaria, that for long I thought I must
be harbouring all the fleas of Kansu, till every covert had
been thoroughly beaten in vain.

Despite my fears, no enemy came anigh me in the dark,
neither leaping nor crawling. Nevertheless I had but a
dog-sleep of a night, what with expectation of bugs, barkings
outside, and the family close at hand, moved into the next
room indeed, but separated only by a screen, so that, whenever I lay that way, there was its apparently sleepless buzz
of activity or muffled quacks of conversation to contend
with. Rousing in the morning was like coming down in
one's childhood to do penal sums before breakfast in
December : I ate by candlelight in my black little scullery,
crusted with the ebony of many generations' smoke : the
day outside was still solid night, and only lightened to a
sky of level dull grey, with clouds on all the hills foreboding
the worst. Off we set, down towards them, through country
more than ever recalling that of the Nan-Hor, till it grew
richer yet in shrub and coppice, and became like the Mo Ping
slopes accordingly ; and then yet more voluminous and
sumptuous still, like the Fêng San Ling itself. But it
was even more opulent and moist, with superb autumn
colours billowing everywhere ; even in the morning when
powdery drizzles prevailed, I could not refrain from keeping
the curtains open with my feet, to see ahead. Quite
ended now was the reign of loess ; this more vital loam
was jocund as a jungle, and the little crouching villages

among their trees were no longer mud-boxes, but largely
built with poles and wood, and wooden kangs inside.
Whereas, up in the loess lands of the North, wood is as
precious and rare as pearls. Here it can be had abundant,
for the asking, all about. Soakers kept on threatening;
nothing happened, and the wet rich green of the hills came
out more and more beautiful and finally the day decided to
cheer up altogether.

On the cooler cliffs along the glen-sides, I saw dark
mats of tangled green that I thought I knew of old. And
Ophiopogon Kansuensis it was indeed, here, like the
Cratægus and the Rose in the central richness of its distribution.[1] But an even more precious " old and valued "
was now nearing. We wound along indescribably, in and
out amongst the flaming dells and slopes : then, after our
Ban Tien, mounted a little Red Pass. All the gorgeous
shrubbery of the Border now rioted round us, and with a
thrill of joy I saluted the reappearance of Arundinaria
nitida—so far the most lovely, delicate, vigorous and
well-bred of all hardy bamboos, that I can never see it without
feeling an internal thrill of agreement with the old Chinese
poet's exclamation—" How could I live without this
gentleman ? " Not even when battling my way up through
its ice-laden jungles on Thundercrown, or being whipped
with its abundant heavy wetness as I try to plant Rhododendrons in the Ghyll at Ingleborough, can I really mitigate
my enthusiasm for this inimitable loveliness of swaying,
cascading emerald filigree, never more vividly emerald than
in the dead dark of the winter, when all the copse and
woodland is a skeleton, and most of the other bamboos
gone withered and dulled and dingy. So, with a lifted
hat and heart, I hailed its reappearance on the Southern
scene of Kansu.[2]

Now we went up in the woodland to another Pass. Little

[1] It does not seem to thrive or develop very rapidly with us.
[2] A. spathiflora and A. anceps are the only other hardy Bamboos
that even approach A. nitida in plumy elegance.

wild pears had dropped on the path, and I picked them up. And among the tangles of the copse above the road there waved a very beautiful and graceful new Cotoneaster (Micromeles ?), with handsome foliage of silver-grey, and big crimson fruits, gracefully borne. From the top of the pass we had a wilder and finer view than any yet, out over a whole tumbled ocean of ragged forested ranges, higher and higher yet, till lost in cloud. And the depths were all a seething pandemonium of autumn glories, a witch's cauldron of gold and scarlet and orange fire, spilled out in a torrent among the windings of the hills. The Do-fu now brought me and the litter down a short cut. It was appalling—wild, precipitous and sheer, with hardly any track to discern. It seemed a miracle how that cumbersome burden of the jao could be got down it. Yet, with various misadventures and stumblings, down it we did successfully manage to get, lumbering, bumping and crashing awfully, while I gripped on with all my fingers and toes, to prevent being slid out precipitately over the back of the mule, on which I looked perpendicularly down out of my drain-pipe as it battered its way through the sheer fall of the bushes unbelievably like some composite elephant descending a jungle-wall.

A long descent brought us to a pretty village, and yet another stretch to another no less pretty one, which was our stage. Gao Chiao, among flaming slopes of coppice. Up on to the opposite slopes I roamed till dark, sweating mightily in the stuffy twilight as I wrestled my way along, getting seeds of a tiny briar rose, and of Ophiopogon from the ledges of the little broken cliffs that protruded at the top of the copse. But, whereas I had hoped the bridge of Gao Bridge would be a noble span of arches over a noble river, I found it only three stepping-stones over a trickle like an anæmic drain. The next day took us over two small passes, through rich wild scenes like the last, but now wilder and less rich, steeper and not so much cultivated. Finally we got into a long defile, and came to a beautiful little gorge, with a tiny temple perched on a boulder in its throat, and its cool sides all matted with Iris tectorum. Other old friends reappeared. Rosa Banksia; and the copses were full of a Bamboo that looked to be Metake. And then, passing a water-mill in the glen, we emerged at last, to find the hill country now left quite behind us, and in front, a big wide distance of soft and fertile lowlands of reddish loam. And away beyond this, far away, rose new ranges of hills, lower perhaps than the last, but evidently seen even from here, to be much moister, crumpled and Scotch-looking in browns and greens, with at least two much bigger masses of cliff and woodland, masked in clouds from the dense weather raging over there. Those hills were the ranges of the Da-Ba-S'an beginning, and between us lay the open lands of Hwei Hsien, the next considerable town on my route, where I intended to wait, and give Bill a good chance of overtaking us.

I lunched in a Ban Tien, and saw a pious procession go by, with drums and gongs; then was sleepily borne down the uneventful valley, and round a corner, and immediately into the mouldering little walled city of Hwei Hsien. Go-go had gone ahead and got us a good inn, with a good room at the side (the appropriate and honorific end one being occupied by sempsters). But there was no sign or news of Bill; in spite of having told myself that I expected none, I felt flat and depressed in consequence almost to the point of anxiety. Finally, I strolled out in the stifling still heat, and down the long grey dullness of the insignificant streets, to the East Gate: there mounted on to the wall, to the salute of a pleasant little uniformed sentry, and strolled leisurely round by myself to the South Gate, conning the landscape. Vainly will you con it, though, for the environing forests which Bretschneider leads one to expect here—as also at Chebson. For all the lands about Hwei Hsien, up and down, as far as you can see, are plain and open and cultivated. The farther hills are remote, and even on them there is no wood, till your eye reaches their highest inmost recesses. But the Da-Ba-S'an, though really a low little ruffle of ranges, yet has this much of Alpine interest, that it connects, however feebly, the great range of the Tsin Ling running bravely out into the East, across Shensi (the one big Alpine chain that is genuinely in China), with the much greater ranges away in the West, descending from the Tibetan highland. Only quite a few days' journey Eastwards from Hwei Hsien, and those alluring-looking, developing heights would have led us to the Tsin Ling and the foot of Tai Bei S'an, on which we might have snatched a fresh harvest of seeds, known indeed, but precious, Primula Knuthiana, Androsace spinulifera.

Had Bill been to hand, I do not know but that the hope might have galvanized our tired nerves, and strung up our food-sick stomachs to this heroic diversion. But Bill was not there; and though I continued to give him the chance, by waiting on for two more solid days of dullness and hope deferred, still Bill persisted in not being there. And the Loo-yeh crowned my disabilities by sending a message asking me not to go out too much in the streets without an escort as the populace was apparently ill-disposed. Also the Do-fu came fussing and pleading for more cash than had been covenanted, their reasonable plea being that at Hwei Hsien they could buy things and replenish supplies in a way that would be impossible at Eaux Blanches, our next important point.

Abandoning hope of being overtaken at Hwei Hsien, I at last gave orders for starting again. And on the morrow was borne away Southwards, sad in my spirits, feeling like Mrs. Gummidge, lorn and lone, and widowed of my William. We traversed the red undulations of the vale and made straight for the crumpled ranges on the far side. Their moist scotchness proved only the accident of autumnal colouring. In reality they are actually drier than the last, more rocky, more cultivated and less coppiced. Loess had long ceased: here it was all ruddy loam, with outcrops of conglomerate and primary rock, and finally of limestone.

Up and down and in and out of steep complicated pitches
we came and went, steadying ourselves at last down a very
long continuous defile or wide gorges that in a way, though
so different, recalled those of Thundercrown. Vitex
reappeared, Cæsalpinia, Trachycarpus and a Buddleia.
We dropped at length, down and down and down, much
farther than we had mounted, upon our Ban Tien round a
corner, snug and picturesque, deeply folded in the seclusion
of the hills. Here began for me, a herbaceous pretty
Gentian of amethystine pink, suggesting an Incarvillea,
which seems abundant all over central-Southern China.
And now the way became much wilder; often we were
able to follow the actual bed of the now-dwindled beck—
though here, if there is less river, there is also more water
about, in a wider and not so towering gorge. It reminded
me a little of the Bei Shui Jang Gorges below Kiai Jo, and
indeed was so Mediterranean as to suggest the lower reaches
of the Reja. Inured by now to vertiginous edges, I kept
my place and lay placid, feeling now in happier heart,
bucked up with the boldness of having started on again,
on a new section of the journey.

To our left the broadening patches of light and sunshine
on the slopes indicated that the overshadowing hills were
diminishing, and that the range was nearly penetrated.
Nevertheless it was sooner than I expected that we emerged
wholly from the shadow of the gorges, dropped round a
corner, and came into a mule village that I made sure was
our stage—until, a little farther on down, across a much
bigger stream that received ours at a right angle, and then
swept away to the right in a mighty bend, deep among
the hills, I saw the most charming townlet that ever met
my eyes in China emerging on the toe of a wooded hill
behind, with curly-roofed grey temple dominating its
amassment of dark gables, and a many-storied magnificent Gate-tower rising conspicuous. It was Eaux Blanches
—which I so call, not to vaunt a familiarity with French,
but to distinguish this Bei Shui Jang from the entirely

distinct Bei Shui Jang River away in Kansu, at the foot
of the Fêny S'an Ling, which, in the *Eaves of the World*,
I immortalized as Whitewaters. And the river was the
Ja-Ling-Jang, flowing deep from here among wild dark
gorges in the bowels of the main Da-Ba-S'an, away down
out of the last of its hill-ventures towards the leisurely
opulence of North Szechuan, of which, indeed, it is one of
the Four Rivers that give the Four Rivers Province its
name.

And not so very different from the Whitewater River,
after all : if you struggled far away Northward up its
deviosities, you would come to a bifurcation at Biku.
And if you followed one of these, it would be the Whitewater
itself, you would come in yet more time to Wen-Hsien,
snuggled at the foot of the Fing S'an Ling, while, if you
followed the other, it would be the Blackwater, you would
come at last to Siku, tucked into the toes of Thundercrown.
In other words, the Blackwater and the Whitewater coalesce
at Biku, and there become the Min-Hor, which in time
becomes the Ja-Ling-Jang, which in time becomes the
Yang-die-Jang at Chungking, away down in Szechuan,
merging into the Da-Hor, which only foreigners call the
Yang-dze-Jang (and, even so, spell the poor thing Yang-
tze-Kiang, and so pronounce it). And on this old friend
it was our intention, at a favourable point, to take boat and
proceed, to save the labour and strain of further journeyings
down Szechuan to the Da-Hor. I scanned it accordingly
with eagerness at Eaux Blanches. But not yet, evidently,
would it serve our turn, though matted great arks lay
moored at its margin, and my eye longingly followed it to
its disappearance round the corner from Eaux Blanches,
immediately into the clean-cut darkness of the deep Da-
Ba-S'an gorges. But even more longingly, with the ache
of an exile, did my heart's desire track its winding upwards,
till my longings came to Siku again, and Thundercrown
above it, unvisited for evermore, lonely in rain and
shine.

My inn adjoined the tower at Eaux Blanches. It was small and dark and so awfully malodorous that I climbed up out of its stinks into the loft at the end for refuge, fearing the worst. For you never meet the much-talked-of stenches of China in the North, that huge open clean country, roomily populated, with clean bare mud-houses and all the wide earth for humanity's wash-pot, and the sane austere air of the North keeping the world swept and sweet. You only realize the truth of travellers' tales when you have come down South and are merging on Szechuan, coming into a moist, steamy warm climate, bland and clogging, with a very dense population accumulated in wooden houses. Eaux Blanches was my first stink-pot in China. But Eaux Blanches was also very beautiful, and a fanaticism for beauty has always been the real key of my life, and all its happinesses and hindrances. So acute is it that one seems at last to merge into something older still and more universal, standing behind beauty ; it could not be mere *bien être* or adequate secretions that gave me such almost unbearably stimulating delight in a group of silly little trees, on the top of a silly little hill across the river, against an azure sky in the sunlight. In an ecstasy I sat in my loft, and settled down to give Bill ample chance of catching me up in Eaux Blanches.

And then I set out to explore it. Duly escorted by Bongie and a soldier (for the place was reputed of doubtful temper), I went out beyond the town, up the long climb of stone steps that continue the trail. Then with the snug place lying below, I came back along the hill-ridge above to a curly temple half-hidden in green : and down into Eaux Blanches again, by steep stone stairways, visiting *en route* the twin-towered main temple, whose dim arcades of darkness and dust proved to be stacked with coffins. It was a lodging-house of the dead, a guildhall where they lay secure, awaiting the time when their friends should be able or see fit to remove them to a permanent home elsewhere, perhaps far away in their own province. For a while I sat in the grateful cool of its galleries, musty and sombre and obscure, with glints of colour and old gilding on its heavy carvings. And then returned home to the inn down through the fair that was raging in the vast shingle-flat of the river. Goitre had been very evident ever since I left Tsin Jô, and here especially prevailed. Also in an inner yard, I here saw my first Musa (I do not mean any deity addicted to song, I mean a Banana plant).

But Bill did not come, and the stinks plugged up my passages more and more. Also, fusses arose about the jao. It appeared that the farther stages, on to Loyang, were over hills so high and wild that the mule-litter could not hope to accomplish them. Accordingly the litter must be dismantled, and its poles and skeleton packed on one of its mules, while I myself went in a sedan instead. This also meant that I must shell out more money. I felt choused, considering that surely the matter ought to have been declared and settled for in Lanchow, instead of being thus sprung upon me at the eleventh hour. To cool my frets, and in constant hope of seeing Bill approaching at any moment, down the shingles, I went out again at dusk with my Chaperons. A crowd as usual attended, but watched me quite benevolently. However, under a thousand eyes there is no rest. I was driven in at last by a grey dust squall, and on my way my discontents were crowned by an old lady in a shop, who exclaimed as I went by : " Oh, how *fat* the Lord is ! " So now, in feebleness of mood, I allowed myself the luxury of vacillating over whether we should not after all wait yet another day for Bill, seeing that the place was so pleasant, and so ravishingly picturesque. But the problem was settled by the head Do-fu's urging that we should move on at once, to the better quarters and ampler supplies of Loyang, and there definitely wait till Bill arrived.

Thus it was done. My chair proved very comfortable, and serenely I was borne up along the steep high climb

above the river. Then we made away across the top of the
fell and down into a back glen where Zinnias had gone
wild in the shingle, and were looking very much prettier,
in graceful branching stems, and diminished flowers of
blood-coloured velvet, than the dreadful painted-looking
pompoms that you get in gardens. But now all the world
was far-gone in autumn, and even the Zinnias were at their
last flower. At a little eating-shanty under the steep of
the fell we called a halt ; and then, immediately and abruptly,
set to work ascending the brant hill-side, in a succession of
hair-pin coils so short and sharp that assuredly no mule-
litter could ever have got up, or managed their bends. It
was tough work for the sedan ; there were two more halts
for refreshment before the tremendous mass of the hill
was conquered, and the hours of unbroken climbing landed
us on the top. The scene was now very like that of the
Mo Ping Pass, though about 2,000 ft. lower: the same
shrubs reappeared—Cotoneaster and Dipelta—but in much
poorer form and very sparse. Xanthoxylum also resumed,
Ivy occurred and Saxifraga Sarmentosa, and my Grey
Flannel Buddleia was very occasional and sad and sickly
in the rock crevices.

On the crest I alighted to peruse the unfolded world
before me under a forbidding sky of cold grey. And my
perusal plunged me in greyness to match. It was a very
fine view, with tumbled ridges away and away on every
side. But the biggest and peakiest and most promising
now all lay behind me ; and their promise had borne me
such very scanty fruit that what could I expect of the
lower, duller chains ahead ? With sudden dismay I realized
that here I was already more than half-way through the
ranges of the Da-Ba-S'an, without having seen one plant
of any note or newness, or any mountain at all capable of
producing such. Was the Da-Ba-S'an, then, going to play
me the same trick as the Da-Tung Alps, but for the opposite
reason—the one range because it ran too high, but this one
because it ran too low ? Had I come all this way, at such

z

a cost of weariness, for nothing better than these uninteresting fluffy hillocks of 8,000 ft., wadded up in a woodland
of coppice, with nowhere any suggestion of Alpine heights,
or Alpine austerity. I had staked my last throw on some
fertility in the Da-Ba-S'an to counterbalance the disappoint-
ments of the Da-Tung and make them good to my friends
at home, hungry for seeds and more seeds of new species
and genera in an imposing list of names and numbers. But
little should I evidently get in the Da-Ba-S'an to swell that
list. My last throw had failed. My last long adventure
had been undertaken fruitlessly.

Wasted labour, time and weariness are poor condiments
to a grey cold view, under a cold grey sky, under the lash
of a cold grey wind. With a jaundiced eye I contemplated
that world which I could but consider as entirely wasted
as my own efforts in getting there. Why could not
those nasty little cosy mountains have grown only just a
little bit taller—another 2,000 ft. would have done it
—and so developed a flora ? But to expect Alpines at
8,000 ft. in China is like going out to look for Eritri-
chium in Epping Forest. Drearily I followed the track,
silty and black, along the ins and outs of the down-top,
with hard glaciated-looking rocks emerging through the
scalp of dull grass in rounded muffled contours. At the
end a spur jutted out from the ridge, and on it a pretty
little temple perched, embowered in forest. This we did
not enter, but passed straight on beneath the dark of a gate,
and under a hanging wall of woodland beyond, sumptuous
and solemn with autumn. And then down, very steep and
very far by a bad track treacherous with loose shaly stones.
But though this stage is reckoned as 70 li, these can only
be 70 li of difficulty, not 70 li of actual distance. For now
quite soon and only about half a day's journey from Eaux
Blanches and only some 6 miles away, we turned a corner
at the bottom of the drop and there, in a dull defile, were
some derelict-looking buildings. And this was indeed our
stage, though at first I could not believe it, until I saw the

skeleton of the disestablished jao lying unloaded outside the main house. This proved a vast barn-like building, with no accommodation at all except for mules, whose mangers filled the dusty dark of the interior. But a k'ang was curtained off for me in a corner with waterproofing, and in that uneventful place of stoppage we passed the night not unsuccessfully, though my own was broken and haunted by perpetual cock-crowings, and the movements of the mule-men, and the soft monotonous champing of the mules.

The morrow was a miserable day of leaden greyness, with a cold shrilling head-wind. Down the winding way we went on, with walls of Silurian on either hand, yet never attaining to the dignity of a gorge. I saw two stems of what once had been a Brownii-lily, and the first masses of a new Bamboo, tall and lovely and plumy, with stems of bloomy grey when young, and the general Anemone vitifolia was here so vividly red that once I got out of my chair to go and see what it could be. In time we debouched into a wider valley, with a tranquil stream, and turned down it to the right through a little glen. Now came a long vacant stretch, and then ahead of us I saw a tiny perched pagoda, barely distinguishable in the pale grey tones that universally prevailed, against the huge high mass of hill that rose behind. And underneath it gradually unfolded the mouldered little sad Hsien of Loyang. We got into it so early that I was confirmed in my yesterday's conviction that the 70 li of these last two stages was merely a figure of rhetoric. But when I entered the Inn outside the wall, I found all my anticipations falsified, and the Do-fu handsomely justified of their desire to move on here from Eaux Blanches. It was a fine, neat, pleasant place, and my own quarters upstairs quite palatial, after two years of Kansu-Tibet, with everything clean and new as a fresh-minted coin. It was a real human room in fact, up in a loft, with a k'ang built of black brick, and big glass pan s in the window, and even tables with drawers in them, su mounte by a little contrivance like a dresser or a bookshelf. Never had I seen the like in all my Chinese travel.

In high contentment we unfolded and luxuriated. Apart from the comparative luxury, I had a quite definite feeling of relief and achievement in having reached Loyang, and so successfully, with all my flock. For this was the end of my solitary journey. Here, definitely, I would wait for Bill to arrive, no matter how many days it might be before he did so. It was a tedious time, though—nothing to see, and nowhere to go, and only greyness and failure to contemplate. I roamed and meditated and mourned and lay a-bed; a dense dusty ha'ar like a London fog perpetually pervaded all the air, and the whole world was filled with sickly sullen grey. The place itself was cheery and populous, though the Hsien in the midst and its walls were very forlorn : the pageant of life included a funeral procession, and an amazing stout woman in the house opposite with the most ill-tempered face and voice I have ever met who stood on the doorstep all day long, scolding and vociferating incessantly. Then there was the farm-yard below my loft to watch, with a queer-shaped duck, and cocks and hens, and two geese whiter than any white thing in the world, and a sick mule who kept on passing spouts of bright blood.

All the same, the days lagged; I could hardly believe my ears at last, when time had ceased for me, and I lay comatose in a sluggish contentment, when Go-go and the Do-fu came running about 4 in the afternoon of a dead dark day, with joyous cries of "Por Loy lai, Por Loy lai! " I leapt to my feet and forth into the lane with such speed that I forgot my stockings. But up the grey flat wastes of the landscape I could see nothing new, so returned to my room to assume those forgotten attributes of dignity, before sallying out again with more discretion. And there indeed I did see Bill, minute in the distance, making swiftly towards me. And here in a few more moments he actually was beside me, radiant in health and spirits, and heavy-laden with precious seeds from the Ardjeri Alps. But he had not been able to lure either Gomer or the Wa-wa away again from their homes ; and the vivid little brown pony, beloved of the piglet in Wolvesden, had foundered far away in a marsh of Drokwa-land.

We allowed ourselves another day of relaxation after the joy of this reunion, to recuperate and exchange the tales of our respective travels ; and on the morrow resumed our journey, both of us on ponies, the chair having gone home. We traversed gorges and a pass and gorges again ; each day on this track takes you through and across a chain of hills, and brings you out to rest in the intervening valley, before the next. The only incident of this stage was a low-growing rose, conspicuous with very large thick-rounded fruits, like young pomegranates, of flushed golden amber, beset with rare dark bristles. Otherwise the scene and its actors were the same as heretofore. Mah-liu Pa is not a place of note : at grey dawn, and in floods of rain, we quitted it on the morrow. The valley grew wilder and wilder, with big copse-clothed hills, and gorges and ravines of dark rock, that seemed to promise well, but yielded nothing. Bœa reappeared, and Trachycarpus was now native and abundant in the rocks : it looked so odd and inappropriate and attractive, this stately fan-palm playing at being an Alpine of those untropical cliffs. I also saw a Mahonia ; the rosy-headed Clerodendron was expensive-looking as an Ixora along the track ; and by this time Iris tectorum had ceased to occur. And so we emerged from the mountain mass, and saw the next ahead of us, across a wide fertile vale with Tai-an-i sitting on its far verge, at the foot of the hills.

A huge fair was here a-foot ; but I was borne swiftly and sternly indoors, up into a clean wide Inn of quite a new and Southern type, without k'angs. The cold North was evidently left behind and its winters here unknown. We had a happy evening together, toying with the wild and glorious notion of giving up the Yang-dze and striking straight away East to Tai Bei S'ạn, for a desperate grab at the back-end seeds of the Tein-ling. Had we come together again at Hwei Hsien, in fact, or Eaux Blanches, this audacious *volte-face* would probably have taken place ; as it was, we were too far South by now, and the proposed diversion therefore so much more of a strain on our tautened endurance and our slackened digestion. The idea was only good to be played with : in sober fact we had both had our fill of travel and toil by this time, and longed for the moment when we could board a boat on Ja-Ling-Jang, and let ourselves blandly cease.

In thunderous glooms and a stifling Turkish-bath atmosphere, we moved out of Tai-an-i, and up towards our entrance into the hills. The valleys, ever since we left Loyang, had been rich with tillage, and the heights are pricked out with maize to their very tops, on the merest scratches and ledges of the red loam that now universally replaces the loess. It was all very picturesque, with a new characteristic Chinese picture at every turn : not for the first time did I now realize that Chinese paintings, which seem so fantastic in their landscapes, do actually convey a quite accurate generalization of Chinese scenery, though without ever copying any one particular view. Oriental art aims straight at the inner spirit of what it is trying to represent, and now, in the wildest phantasmagoria of peaks and depths, I can see the essential generalization of dozens of pictures that I myself have traversed. In the open lands, meanwhile, there occurred a very lovely tree of heart-shaped foliage drawn out into points, and then the most graceful foot-long bunches, borne in profusion, of bloomy coral-scarlet berries. And it seemed to be capable of bearing fruit even in its tender years : younglings of eight feet or so were weeping their rose-red rain as copiously as their elders. I leapt off my pony to gather it, though in despair of its hardiness. But these Szechuan plants are very surprising : their general level of hardiness is far higher than I could have hoped. Many things in England, from away up in the North, are much more tender than these

children of the equable South : the flora of the hot dry
river—valleys of Kansu—my Buddleia, Convolvulus
tragacanthoides, Oreocharis, the Leptoderms, Androsace
longifolia, all seem hopeless for cultivation in the open
over here, and even Androsace tibetica sulks through our
winter damps. Whereas the Szechuan flora has a more even
temper and a kindlier average of resistance : the red-
fruited tree (F. 753) has so far proved quite equanimous in
our Northern winters.

But the noble races of the rock-garden were long since
extinguished. No more Primulas were possible in these
low-running regions of soft lush vegetation and steamy
warmth. We wound up now into a gorge of rose-grey
limestone, hung with creepers, wild and splendid as a
" schlucht " in the Dolomites. What a wasted life, thought
I, to have such possibilities of Primulas, yet to possess
none. These hard stark walls exactly repeated the stark
hard walls of rosy rock above San Dalmazzo di Tenda, in
which Primula Allionii so closely clings : but where was
there here a repetition of Primula Allionii to round off the
resemblance ? Acidly, in these musings, I scanned the
cliffs, as my pony stumbled along between them, and
disdained the weeds on which they exclusively wasted their
fissures. And then a withered yellowing tag caught my
eye, up on a particularly hot hard face. It was worthy of
closer inquiry ; I got off and climbed up. It *was* a Primula
indeed and, to my eye, nothing else than Primula sinensis
—a discovery that set my tired heart palpitating with all
the old emotions of the hunter, not only in that it was a
Primula, but that it should be P. sinensis, such hundreds
of hard and weary miles away from the Yang-dze Gorges,
hitherto its only recorded habitat. Of course, there was no
trace of flower remaining, and even of seed there was
barely a vestige ; but it crowned my year with a Primula.

Very preciously did Go-go and I explore the cliffs, and
examine each one of the soft baggy capsules, now almost
withered to crisp chaff on their withered brown stems :

the plant abounded in the tightest closest cracks of the hottest, hardest, sheerest cliffs, but the seed was by now so completely shed that only after long agonies of anxious search were we able to glean here and there a stray germ, still clinging round its column. But the small pinch that at length we accumulated was sufficient to introduce the plant. And now it proves to be a quite new species, though close to P. sinensis in a group in which hitherto P. sinensis had been believed to stand alone. Primula rupestris turns out as pretty as the wild forms of P. sinensis, and of a pleasant shade of pink, with variations in depth of tone and amplitude of flower. And it is perceptibly more hardy than P. sinensis, though also a soft thing, and never likely to be trustworthy in the open through the winter, except in very special conditions. These it has, in one dry little overhung niche on the cliff at Ingleborough; and has there accordingly lived happily now through two summers and a winter. P. sinensis would never have been capable of such audacity and endurance; but even so, P. rupestris must be chiefly counted on for the cold greenhouse. These slack-textured fluffy flimsy things will never resist the darkness and raw damp of our winters in the open ground.

Emerging from the gorges, the cobbled track now climbed, very high, to a pass, but though water abounded in these ranges, there is no trace of any moisture-zone vegetation, no big woodland; and culture stretches right up to the crests. Through a stone arch on the top we passed, and then down, endlessly, past a small grave-coppice near the summit, where Aconitum Hemsleyanum towered in solemn sapphire obelisks, very vivid against the dead autumnal brown of decay that now monotonously clothed the whole world. At intervals the descent was so steep that I preferred to light down and walk. The Go-li stage is Go-li indeed, well measured and by distance, and a handsome 30 miles at that. It was quite dusk when we emerged from the mountains and slowly wound across a plain of rice-fields towards what proved to be the big and busy city of Ming

Chiang Jô (where all the old women make match-boxes) lying just like Tai-an-i across the plain, at the foot of the next hill-barrier we had to cross, parallel with our last, and very like them, but that these were rockier, and all tilted up in an odd violent slant of their dark strata, barring their slopes in streaks. A fine and stately Inn received us at Ming Chiang Jô : woodwork, by now, is much more copiously evident in the buildings, and I was further cheered with prospects of getting a chair again.

The chair was got, and in it I was borne away on the morrow up the valley, along beneath the hills. Everything was softly grey. I do not feel to have seen the sun since I left Eaux Blanches : far up in the North were now quite left behind the diamond clearness of Kansu, its blaze of light and heat and cold ; by this time we were well embogged in the gentle muggy gloom of Szechuan, where the sun proverbially shines so rarely that the dogs bark at it in Chung King when it does. Up and down among innumerable foothills we diverged in time from the valley, till, at a dull low point among reddish expansive hills, we crossed the range by a steep ascent, up the steady sharp tilt of the stratum ; and then far down again, with masses of mountains to right and left, very sombre and gorgeous in dark blue violet under the gathering storm clouds that now capped them. They were coppiced and rocky, wilder looking than the last, in the livid savage light. Much traffic was on the road, enormous stacks of matchwood went by in long processions, *en route* for the old ladies of Ming Chiang Jô. Finally we got down into a ghyll that opened out on a soapy blue-green beck, with yet another big dark range across the valley, barring our next day's journey. And then up to the right, by a very long and violent ascent of stone steps in a heaven-high stairway, like that ascent to Saint Somebody's convent, high, high up above Santa Margherita. Through various temple gate-houses we passed, attained the crest, and dropped far down on the other side, in and out, among fields where the population was out a-sowing. They do not plough or scatter. Across the prepared face of the field little holes are scratched in the red loam in orderly succession two feet or a yard apart. Along the rows a woman passes, and drops a pinch of seed into each cavity as she goes ; and then some one else comes after, with a handful of dark and friable-looking manury silt, to pepper in on top.

Seventy long li of travel brought us to our stage at Chiao jang Ba, a very tiny simple village, where the Inn was very small to match, but with enormous accommodation for the mules in barn-like yards, and a walled garden embowered in densely-fruiting trees of a small clustered Tangerine orange—a significant evidence of the climate into which we were now come. Also, being a country place, tiny and clean, it had no such stench as that of the daily-emptied latrine-tanks of the towns and cities of Szechuan, perpetually pestiferous with strings of coolies carrying unsavoury slop-pails slung from each shoulder.

The brooding skies had broken in a sheet of tears when we rose next day to move on. The way was dull at first, up and down among foothills till we reached the beck. But then its course grew wilder, in ascents and descents with a chaos of tumbled boulders all about. We came in face of a huge rosy cliff, with the huge high arch of a dark grotto at its foot, into which the stream disappeared. This, from our high point of vantage across the valley, we duly contemplated ; then wound up the flagged ascent to a wooded neck where a temple nestled. Through arches we went down on the other side ; and there below us was our stream, reappearing from a gorge. But now the track took us away, round and about, mounting high upon the vast flanks of an open down. It was dreary in the streaming wet, a wide-bosomed highland of brown and russet, orcharded here and there with a queer little tree that bore fantastic fruits (Aleurites cordata). Shivering with lowness in my Sedan, I ached yet more for Bill and the servants, splashing unprotected through the deluge, in a sad procession, swelled by

two escort-soldiers from the Yamen at Ming Chiang Jô, a
brace of unbelievable degraded atoms, like the fading ghosts
of two malignant yet imbecile Elementals, chinless and
spidery.

But the enormous circuit of that high bay was at last
accomplished. We curved round to its farther rim, and
there, very deep down below, immediately at our feet,
came into sight again the Ja-Ling-Jang that had lost
itself to our view in the deep labyrinths of the Da-
Ba-S'an ravines, ever since it parted company from us at
Eaux Blanches. And there, too, in a huddle of dark roofs,
lay Bridge-hall, beyond its eponymous Bridge, magnificent
and stately and of many arches, which carries the highway
over the hill-stream there flowing down, tired of gorges and
subterranean adventures, into the candid sweep of the Ja-
Ling-Jang.

It was a tremendous drop to Chao-Tien, down long precipitous flights of stone stairs, like those that descend from
Esino upon Varenna. But the Inn, though narrow, was
good, and any lodging would have rejoiced us after such a
day-long battering of deluges as might have gratified Regan
and Goneril. Fortunately, the next morning, despite the
usual over-night denials, a second chair had been achieved
for Bill. Therefore, in better heart, I was carried out
through the grey drizzle. Almost immediately we mounted
up, and over a big rise and down again to the river on its
other side, where, across an affluent rill, there was a little
limestone bluff, on which, through my blinds, I caught a last
glimpse of Primula rupestris. I had dreaded a long day,
dull and drenching. But gradually the sky lightened and
the rain left off, and the journey turned out beautiful,
following the course of the Ja-Ling-Jang, in and out of
wooded bays, and over ribs of rises, each making a picture,
but one more attractive than all, culminating in a thickly
crowded gate-house, with soldiers and guns, and a dear little
temple beyond, alighted on a pinnacle aloft, with trees
aligned up the stairway that climbed to it. And the way

was wild, too, with stones—although now we were finally emerging from the hill-country, leaving all our hopes irretrievably buried behind us in the Da-Ba-S'an, and drawing out into the many-breasted opulence of the Red Basin of Szechuan. As I undulated along in my chair I scanned the rocks assiduously for the fossils that Richthofen found such a feature of these parts. Not one did I discern, but Bill reported them multitudinous : I only saw a bewildering abundance and diversity of rocks—reddish-dark shales, vast boulders of limestone amazingly *moutonné*, and black enormous blocks parqueted in slopes or tumbled into pandemonium.

Finally we came down out of the hills for good, and away into the open country, with the coal-measures evident, and big arks over-arched in tunnels of matting, plying freely on the swift smooth peasoup-coloured tide of the Ja-Ling-Jang, and often being towed upstream by harnessed leashes of fine jolly fellows, in the well-made, well-featured handsome type that now prevailed (and we said good-bye to goitre at Lo-Yang). Away ahead of us now for a long time lingered Kwang Yuen, out in the flat, embowered in trees. But a sandstone bluff impended over the river, and in its face was a carven gallery of innumerable grottoes and cavities and niches and caves and alcoves, all occupied by scriptured sacred scenes and groups of Buddhas, bodhisattvas, saints, angels, abbots and holy persons. Among several other such rock-carvings in China, the Thousand Buddhas of Kwang Yuen stand high ; and not unreasonably did they delay us. But at length we tore ourselves onward, and in due course arrived down in Kwang Yuen as night was falling. Round the projection of the Northern gate we had to pass, and right away round along the river-front of the wall, above the crowded ranks of barges, till by the West Gate we entered the city, and drew up in a smart Inn, embedded in the usual paralysing stenches from the latrines (so to flatter an unalluring lake) immediately behind our state-apartments. But all the same, it was a huge relief to be here, for this was the end of our trek, the supreme objective towards which we had looked from far-off Lan-chow. Horses, mules and chairs were now done with : nothing remained but to fold our hands in peace, and in the relaxation of complete and well-deserved exhaustion go glassily gliding down the Ja-Ling-Jang through hills of palm and orange to Chung King.

CHAPTER XVI

THE WATERWAYS

It was about 11 before I decided to wake up on the morrow, and found outside my dark room darkness and drizzling damp, corroding as ever. Now it was a case of going out to see our prospective boat. Down a side-alley we went, and descended by a steep and sloppy stone stairway on to the sad mud-flat of the river-shore. And there was the huge matted ark, lying becalmed out on the broad bosom of the Ja-Ling-Jang. A punt was waiting to take us to it, but in between the punt and us intervened a wide stretch of shallow which it was proposed that we should traverse pick-a-back. This was a most perilous and infelicitous proceeding; I cannot feel that I looked my best, with my bulk obliterating the small frail veteran, who yet continued intrepidly staggering on, with slow sure movements and vibrations of his tautened muscles, through the ripples, gripping the mud with his toes at each step. It must have looked like some large blowzy blossom hovering heavily above the water on a quite inadequate stem. My only consolation in this unbecoming conjuncture and Bill's loud laughter at it was the sight of Bill himself horsed likewise in the same undignified position, and similarly periclitating across the straits with the same pinched and haggard expression as I felt sure I was wearing myself. However, we did at last attain the punt without ill-adventure, and so arrived at the barge. This proved full of merchandise and babies. Our landlord was our escort, and now we set to bargaining with the ship-master. But Bill and I, inured to Kansu, proved quite at sea in the dialect of Szechuan:

and the Go-go turned out even more helpless than ourselves, being determined, like all Chinese, not even to make
any attempt at adapting himself to the barbarism of a
different province. He, a Shansi lad, had framed himself
by practice to the tongue of Kansu; but now, neither
could he nor would he condescend to the new little clickings
and neighings and slurred enclitics that alone might have
made his talk pass current in Szechuan. So we giggled and
shouted and squawked at each other with perfect good-
humour but no approach to mutual understanding. Finally
it was decided, in our complete darkness as to stages and fares,
that we should return to the town and there try to find somebody capable of shedding light upon the situation.

So home we went and I wrote letters, while Bill set forth
on his quest. And it so happened that he forgathered with
an elderly lady, whom he ungratefully and ungallantly
described as " a dreadful old doxy in whiskers." But this
forbidding female showed more sense than all her kind.
She advised us to go on again by road, unless we wanted
to run the risk of passing our New Year on the boat, becalmed
and stranded on a mud-flat in the middle of the Ja-Ling-
Jang. The river, in fact, was low, and she did not recom-
mend us to trust to it. This was rather a blow. We did
so want to be at rest. We were so heartily tired out with
the road. And here we had felt so sure of being finally
done with it, and allowed to flop into the lethargy of complete fatigue. But there was no help for it : with mingled
thankfulness and disappointment we acclaimed the old
doxy's counsel, and the rest of the day went by in rapid
readjustments. The mules were chartered on, Bill's shag-
haired little pony sold, and a second chair at last obtained.

It was a notable relief to awake on the morrow to a fine
and eventually a beautiful day. Our first stretch led across
an affluent of the Ja-Ling-Jang, over which we were conveyed
bodily, mules and chairs and all, in a ferry. Now we turned
away from the Ja-Ling-Jang and mounted steeply, up and
up; very high on a big mountain mass that commanded all

the country, and all the silver winding of the Ja-Ling-Jang.
Down into a mere nothing sank the fine pagoda which had
been so conspicuous above the ferry ; and Kwang Yuen
was left behind. Now we were on the highland : at one turn
(only) of the ascent Bill happened on a very attractive
little glossy-leaved evergreen flopping Lonicera, with terminal bunches of bloomy blue-black fruit, well worth collecting for its own sake. The scenery gave our first sample
of the Red Basin. It was very lovely, and quite unlike
anything I had ever seen in China, though reminiscent of
much that I knew in Europe. The Szechuan roads run
over large irregular highlands, with the deep valleys of the
big rivers rarely intersecting them. So now we continued
up and down, among the windings of glens and dips in hills
of tilted reddish sandstone, wonderfully new and picturesque
in effect, suggesting the low vineland hills of the Rhine about
Cologne, with innumerable little red terraces running up
them, dappled with small trees : then, as one descended
into a glen, it was just like passing through some scant
woodland of the Provençal coast, with Pinus maritima here
replaced, over light scrub, by a fine, lovely Cypressus in
the same rich emerald green and fluffiness of effect. The
country, too, flows with abundant water, and the dells and
dips each nurse a beck, with many collateral mossy wood-
rills that mockingly suggested Primulas. Our stage was
short, and ended—for this is only a by-track—in a quite
small village, where I spent the sundown patrolling the
stone-paved threshing-floor below, on the brink of a ghyll,
with a wide vista over low hills of tilted russet strata,
crowded with small cypresses and recalling the foot-hills
approaching Marathon.

The next day still took us on over the highland, but the
scenery steadily grew tamer and duller, with shallower
slants to the strata, and stupid uninteresting profiles to the
distances. As I came down through a slight coppice
towards a village, I saw a spray of silver stars aspiring over
a bush. And it has proved a Clematis of variegated milk-

veined foliage, suggesting Armandi, yet not, I think, identical. Whatever its flower may prove, its branching flight of seed-heads will always have their value, not being fluff-whirls, as usual, but, rather, flattened stars, with rayed achenes glistening. The village was crowded and clamorous with a fair : it lurked in a fold of the fells, and afterwards we had a steep far climb to the very top of the highland, along the crest of which the track then continued up and down for the rest of the 80-li stage. The views were far, the fell-tops wild and brambled like a British common, with a new ramping rose, whose leaves were velvet on their reverse, and a new Viburnum, like a stiff little privet, with black fruit and foliage suggesting an olive's. But the air was now gone all grey and cold, under a cold grey sky, with the distances uglier than ever in a dusty grey ha'ar of dull monotony. It was a relief to arrive at New Hall (Hsin Tang, or Gin-u-Chang), tucked into the bosom of the down, and there to find beautiful quarters up at the end of the inn, very high-pitched in the gable, with pin-new roofing-poles and wainscotting, and beams outlining the white plaster panels of the walls, in the finest simple-life or Garden City style. And here a wet day held us captive throughout the morrow, lying luxuriously abed, though the lofty studio-like room was so a-bluster with draughts from the almost latticed tiling of the roof, that the luxury was strictly tempered to the unshorn lambs.

But a glorious day succeeded, and off we set once more, with a short but lovely stage. First of all we dropped at last off the conclusion of our highland upon a very pretty little towered hamlet standing out on a spur. And then down and down again, and over one of the splendid stone-arched bridges that abound in these parts, and seem so grotesque for the piddling little rills across which they pompously convey such a tuppenny-halfpenny side-road as this is, unusable by anything but foot-traffic and sedans and mules. Then on to the next hill-mass we mounted out of the valley as high as we were on the last. Travellers met us in strings, advancing single file over the down—pedlars and shopmen going North to try their fortunes : each had in one hand a bundle ; and in the other every man of them swung his bird-cage—swaddled in a bandanna to keep its inmate from being frightened. Not that this beautiful and idyllic picture is so purely idyllic as it sounds. The birds are not only objects of sentiment to their owners, they are also important from the point of view of profit. For they are champions of song, and singing matches are arranged, and heavy stakes are won and lost, so that nobody, on however far a journey bound, will willingly abandon his bird ; everywhere in China, the pedestrian on progress is armed with his bird-cage. But, quite apart from profit, the Chinese does also love his bird for itself : of cats he takes no account, and dogs are despised outcasts of the streets, and the universal pig is profit incarnate and more ; but on his bird he lavishes real affection, and all the resources of his love and art are deployed on keeping it well-housed and tended, with the utmost extravagance of exquisite decoration for its perches, and its seed-pot, and its water-pan.

On the very crest of the down, by a steep rise of stone steps, there was an eating-house. We stopped to rest and feed. Papa and mamma were away, and the shop was being run by two minute little pig-tailed maidens of four and five years old, barely as tall as the two gigantic vats on the cooking-range, out of which, straining a-tiptoe, they ladled rice for their customers with complete command of the situation, in a weighty seriousness accepting payment and giving change, and gravely demurring to a halfpenny tip as something excessive and unheard of. Hard by, in an outhouse, was their baby brother's go-cart, a home-made contrivance of wood, which ingeniously combined the functions of a chair, a table, and a tricycle, with a handy little hole in the seat. Having satisfactorily wooed these complete shopkeepers into accepting a few cash for a present, we pursued our way along the down, the air still lovely, but the distances duller and duller, with the innumerable and very shallow strata-lines of the hills now so quieted down as to be almost horizontal. Quite early in the afternoon we drew into Yu-ning-pu, a cosy, fine place along the frontage of the hill, with a noble temple Guild-house in the midst, and a fine raised side-walk of flag-stones heavily arcaded with thatching. Our inn was fine and stately, as last night's, and full of dear old kindly grannies who made much of us. But it was also peopled by a batch of soldiers, returning from very well-known territory up in the far North, having been to Tao-Jo to buy four hundred horses for the troops, and being now on their way South with them to Cheng-tu. And they were a rough, offensive crew, as soldiers proverbially are in China, with no respect for dignities. They soon provoked a row with our own people and, secure that good gentle Go-go could have given them no just cause of offence, we took his side, and ere long had coped successfully with their impudence.

Next day gave us a long 90-li stage. The morning was not so cloudless, but very lovely and pearly and golden, with all the valleys beneath us filled with milky cloud-rolls as we continued along the high-land. And above the milk sea rose the farther hills, away and away, misted and veiled into a perfect Chinese painting. We passed a little village in full fair, and then a charming building tucked into a wooded hill-top. A pine appeared more maritime than even the Cypress ; the springy-turfy " landes " over which we now undulated were more than ever Mediterranean, with their red soil, and their scant herbage, and the tall pines overshadowing them in sparse multitudes, inclining this way and that on naked, spindly shanks. In early afternoon, thanks to our early start, we were borne up a steep slant of stone stairs to the topmost stratum of the fell-neck, beyond which, along the last conclusion of the down, lay out our stage, the comfortable, prosperous village of Hwa-y Su-y.

Here we looked for an inn apart from the soldiers, and at last found one at the far extremity of the village,

presided over by a charming deaf old Manchu, who
yelled at us most affably.   Out along the street-way I
then strolled to the neck, to enjoy the sundown.   And
there away below in its valley reappeared at last, between
the folds of the fell, a silver glimpse of the Ja-Ling-Jang,
just a curved streak of light far down in the grey
depths, in the flat of its vale, striped dimly with emerald
strips of culture, and beyond it, one behind another,
up and up in a disorderly sea of crests like grey waves,
the monotonous hills of Szechuan surged higher and higher
across the whole distance in a monochrome of grey, till they
merged at last into the grey monochrome of the sky, riven
at one point only by a broad flaring rent of clear yellow.
And in the foreground dimly-terraced promontories from
the down loomed out above the depths of the vale, and
immediately before me the converging slopes sank gently
away, ample and voluminous, in broad sweeps of flooded
rice-fields terraced with red-raw ramparts of earth, blinking
up in pale metallic sheen at the sundown like broken cres-
cents of mirror set flat into the fall of the hill, and diversified
by myriads of little cypresses dotted all up the slopes, now
black and attentive-looking, like crowds of hooded gnomes,
in the blurred, dying softness of the twilight.   And in the
shallows the buffaloes were wallowing.

Along and along we went next day, and down a dip,
through a pretty village containing a big tree all hung with
huge citrons like pale-green balloons : and up again, and
still along high ground, with the river only fitfully appearing
below on the right ; till at last we came to a battlemented
piece of wall and a gatehouse, in the beautiful russet free-
stone of which these hills consist (and which therefore is
so handy for the fine building that is so general hereabouts).
And so to an eating-house on a neck, beyond which the down
did definitely diminish and die finally away.   And there,
barring our Southward way, the river came fully into view,
flowing wide in many channels over vast flat beds.   So
now we continued to a crest, crossed over on the right, and

went down and down and down by endless winding flights
of stairs into a gorge, only to mount up out of it again
quite as high up stairways quite as steep and stiff, to continue along the down frontage yet another while before
descending at last once and for all into the valley of the
Ja-Ling-Jang. It was a rippled ocean of grave-hummocks
in enormous expanses. We continued steadily up to the
right, till at length, on a far hill dim and ghostly and grey,
the dim grey shape of a noble tower dawned out of the grey
universal monochrome of the day and the distance ; and
then on a higher mass behind a yet nobler pagoda emerged,
and various stately temples tucked into high folds, above
a now-perceptible level of green tree-tops, which was clearly
to be Bao-ning-fu, though at present undiscoverable. The
lone trail was over. Half an hour more, and we were
traversing the whole breadth of the town, very bustling
and big and busy, with silk greatly in evidence in most of
its shops ; and came at length at its far edge by a little lane,
to a narrow little dark stinking inn, selected because it was
handy to the landing-stage, the conclusion of our labours.

The next day, though gorgeously hot and balmy, and
replete with an almost overpowering sensation of relief and
relaxation, was also one of storm and stress. In the first
place there arrived no passport from the Yamen to protect
our Do-fu on their return journey against the malignity of
the soldiers, from whom the worst was to be expected in the
way of vengeance, now that the protecting sacrosanctity
of foreigners was no longer at hand. In the second there
now appeared a very jumped-up little Jack from the
Governor, with nose and teeth running out ahead of him,
who told us that even our own passport, made out originally
for Honan, Shansi, Shensi and Kansu, had ceased to be
valid on our entering Szechuan, and no longer entitled us
to official recognition and protection. This was a point of
which we had not thought, in starting the new hare of this
Southward journey ; we dealt straitly with the impudent
minion, and yearned for our dear Kansu Viceroy. Then to

get me out of the stenches, Bill manœuvred me away for a stroll in the streets, until it was time to go down to the river and engage our boat. But there was nothing of new interest, and I was delighted at last to go with him to the landing-stage, down flights of stone stairs lined with booths and perpetually sloppy with bucket bearers ascending and descending, to where the fleet lay moored in the river, with perched temple buildings conspicuous on the far side, and crowds incessant, crossing by the ferry, which only plies on certain days. This was a stately and formal descent to the water very different from the sidelong alleys that had sneaked us down to the river at Kwang Yüen : on the " plage " itself it was delicious to stroll down the long stretches of damp sunlit mud, with hulls of big arks lying hawled up here and there for repairs, and ahead, down over the bend of the broad quiet river, the town-pagoda presiding from on high over the scene, upon a hill-top, emerging from a wood of scraggy pines (all town-pagodas, it appears, sit on hill-tops across the river from the town they protect). In the warm sunshine it quite felt like being at the seaside ; and the delight of having finally finished with the road was something inexpressible and now irrecoverable. The first boat we examined was too heavy-laden with stinking pelts to please us. So we adjourned to the next, which proved big and bare and empty, containing nothing except a very brisk and decisive little tidy lady, and a brace of fluffy puppies like baby bears in a basket. This looked likely : we made an appointment with Madam's Mister, and in due course there turned up at the inn a tarred and gaunt old leathern-faced salt in a long blue gown. The rest of the day passed passionately in bargainings. As so often happens, he refused absolutely to capitulate to our proposed (and proper) price, thereby compelling us to appeal to the Yamen, which, as jobbing contractors ought to know by experience, invariably insists on their accepting something even less than the market-price, on pain of breeches down and a good spanking. So it proved, despite the inadequacy of our passport, the Yamen intervened with prompt civility, and secured us the Ark for 80 taels (half of Mr. Noah's demand) all the way down-river to Chung King, for us and all our belongings. The Lao-yeh also sent his belated card, and even promised a passport for the muleteers. But these were now so little concerned for themselves (in contrast to our dutiful and diligent agitations on their behalf), and so keen on achieving fresh trade to take back with them, that I felt discharged of my previous anxieties.

Bargains having been clinched all round, the evening passed in successive interruptions from would-be buyers or would-be payees. On the morrow we were both anxious to get out betimes from the arid, noisome gloom of the inn, with its room floors of mud, trampled and congealed in dank darkness with the unfiltered urine of ages. The promised carriers, however, were as usual non-existent when it came to the point; till suddenly, at the last minute, they all came trooping into the yard in a string, like waiters in a big hotel with a new course at table d'hôte. They were duly saddled with the luggage, and in charge of them I proceeded down to the landing-stage, with two cheery little attentive soldiers from the Yamen so close upon my heels that I felt like a prisoner. Here I found that where the ferry had been plying yesterday there was now a solid bridge of boats, across to the farther shore : and learned that the fashion of Bao-ning is to have ten days of ferry, and then ten days of the boat bridge. Along this, then, we commodiously streamed, until we came to our boat, now lying handy.

The Ark was by this time manned and ready for her journey. Her complement was our two selves, two servants, two attendant soldiers, nine oarsmen, their cook-caterer, the ship-master, his nephew (who was an idiot), his neat little comely lady, his eight-year-old pert small minx of a daughter, and his boat-guard bitch with her brace of black-and-white babies. At one end was the boat's shrine, and the central portion was permanently roofed over with arches of matting, while the oarsmen had an open deck behind to work on, which at night was to be rigged up with its frame, and more arches of matting telescoped out on it above from the central tunnel, till the whole boat was roofed in like the central part. In this I now arranged our quarters and where Go-go was to cook, and where our beds were to be unfolded each night along the central gangway, and how they were to be screened, and how our various arrangements were to be discreetly contrived, with due respect to the square enclosure of mosquito-netting farther down, where Mr. and Mrs. Noah and little Miss Wei-Shang took their rest.

The goods were got aboard, and disposed as best might be, the accommodation being but crowded and scanty for a cruise of fourteen days. All, however, went well, and everybody was in a good temper. Sooner than I had hoped, Bill also rejoined us, having had a very satisfactory wind-up at the inn, with even the mulemen's passport come safe to hand. And sooner than either of us had hoped after this, there was a lighting of candles in the shrine, and to a blare and rattle of crackers flaking away up the water behind us, the good ship Ark drew slowly and solemnly out into mid-channel, and slowly and solemnly set to gliding down the smooth broad face of the Ja-Ling-Jang, to the solemn chanting of its nine oarsmen blithely rowing in the stern, standing each man to his long spliced paddle, corded to its tall rowlock-post.

No words can paint the final languid ecstacy of lying out on our boat, with nothing more to do, and nowhere more to make for, but only to be quiet and be borne onward through the grey day, under the restful grey monotony of the scene with the pagoda gliding by above us on its hill; and then the gradual sliding panorama effortlessly slipping along, with ducks and herons flighting in the wide river shingles as we moved. At dusk we moored to the shore, the prow was rigged up with its temporary arcade of matting, the oarsmen took their last bowlful of rice, and then tumbled immediately to sleep, each in his roll of bedding on the deck aft. Night and rest came down on the Ark ; we prowled the dank mud of the shore awhile, in glory of release, and so came aboard again to bed, unbuttoned and all to pieces with our delight in being at ease at last. There was nothing more to eat ; but there was also nothing more to endure. Our hearts and our stomachs and everything now went flop in the enjoyment of complete exhaustion ; only our tempers, in the reaction, tightened to a quite new but equally delicious complacence. In plain words, we were utterly tired out, nervously, mentally and intestinally ; and now, for the first time, could safely and even pleasurably allow ourselves to acknowledge the fact to ourselves. So kindly night put us to bed.

In black dark of dawn, clamouring, stamping, bumping, shouting roused us to the news that we were casting loose again. Through our broken slumbers I heard the night's arches of matting being pushed back, and the frame being dislocated, and then the slow soft chanting of the oarsmen to their rhythmic stroke lulled me to sleep again in the knowledge that we were once more off, on the face of the river. A lovely monotony filled the next day and all that ensued : I only keep the chronicle to mark the beat of our luxurious lethargy. We woke to a merciless mizzle darkening to deluges. I sat out, under improvised arches of matting, in the bows. Down the successive rapids we adventured, for the Ja-Ling-Jang is full of shoals and rapids ; all the while the oarsmen sweep and bend to their chant of "Ai-oh-ee-oh, ai, ai" as they waft you down the broad face of the river; but when this became broken and dangerous, the beam, propped up on stools, at back of the arcade, from which the idiot nephew, in placider reaches, used to supervise the rowers in front, over the tunnelled arch of the central matting, was now occupied by the skipper in person, awakened from his opium dream under the mosquito net inside, now to preside, tall and gaunt in his blue robe, and impressive in his bad language, over the perils of the passage, and guide in his practised hands, sensitive to each eddy, the vast rudder pole that governed the course of the ship from behind. As the danger-reach grew nearer, turbed and foaming, the song of the oarsmen would accelerate and intensify to the intensified accelerated beat of their oars—Ai-oh, e-oh, *ai, ai, aioh—Eiho*, AI, AI—mounting to a passionate passage of Ai-ai-ai-ai, *staccatissimo fortissimo, prestissimo*, till the actual rapid had been passed; and then expanded, in renewed leisure and relaxation, into " Ai-oh-ee-oh, ai, ai " again.

After which the skipper would come indoors again, and lie down under the mosquito net with his pipe again, while the crew as often as not knocked off for a service of bowlsful of rice out of the barrel from which their stout cookshop-looking caterer was always ready to serve them at intervals of two hours or so (five or six times through the working day). I gathered, in fact, a good notion here, of how and why it is that the Chinese is so famous and willing and indefatigable a workman. His secret lies in many, but very short and complete, intervals of rest. With these, he will work longer and harder, and better than any other race on earth : but these intervals must be frequent, and thorough, and filled with food and fun and complete change ; let him have only ten minutes in every three hours, to lie about. Crack a joke, smoke a pipe and empty a bowl of rice, and he will then buckle to again with redoubled zeal and complete refreshment. What kills him as a labourer is long dull hours and long dull rests. I often wondered, watching our boatmen, whether or no the same results could be got out of European artisans by the same system. To me the Chinese system seems the sane, simple and psychological one ; but in our own scheme of stereotyped hours and mealtimes it is possible that the men could not so safely be trusted to knock off and turn to again. The strength of the Chinese system lies in its lightness and elasticity, and creed of mutually advantageous give and take ; our own cruder theory builds an adamantine unyielding programme of hours and intervals, trusting to nobody's honour and implicating nobody's interest.

Southwick (Nan-Pu) was our midday stage of the morrow, all along a curved bay of stone-built esplanade, where
Louisa could easily have broken her head off the steep,
perilous landing-stairs. It lay in a hollow curve of the hills,
with a pagoda perking behind into the dim soft weeping
greyness of the day. The heavily thatched houses along
the sea-front were pure Cheshire, panelled in broad patches
of whitewashed walls, intersected by lines of black-dark
woodwork. Trees embowered it, and a big palatial tower
rose in the middle like a glorified bandstand, and the roadstead was dense with maltinged arks in rows. Along
beneath an undercliff of the prevailing rounded sandstone ranged Nan-Pu, below a peculiarly dangerous swirl
of the river : huge blocks of the sandstone have fallen in a
chaos to the waterway.

All this course of the river, indeed, grows more and more
definitely hedged with clean-cut straight lines of little cliff,
in which there are tall black rectangular doors of darkness,
squared and stark as anything in Egypt, indicating artificial
caves and galleries inside, excavated so long since that
nobody now knows who by, nor for what. And all the
marge, naked rock and all, is thick set with what look like
amateurish Wireless stations, with wheels and poles and
pulleys. But these are the brine-pits, for which all this
country is famous : from deep in the living stone itself they
haul up their buckets of brine, and the salt-gabelle is one
of the largest items in the incalculable wealth of China.
And in all the stretches of shingle that occurred, the hope-
ful, amid heaps and trenches, were washing for the gold that
the Ja-Ling-Jang brings down from Tibet, like all the other
rivers that have their birth on the golden Roof of the World.

A more delectable method of travelling was certainly never
invented. Balmily we were swept along, through landscape
steadily growing tamer and more silken. The air was like
sweet fragrant oil, and the low sandstone cliffs alongside
universally dripped moisture in dark smears down their bold
bald faces. The river wildly wound and bent, indulging in

many rapids and races and rushes and smooth swelling expanses. And there was nothing more to do, nothing more to say, nothing more to think about. And the pageant of China went smoothly by on either hand, uncannily unfolded like something on a film. Never before had I had leisure or opportunity or detachment to perceive it, but now it came plainly out to view—the blue-clad figures at their work, their rest, their meals, the whole gigantic kindly panorama of this people, so frugal, simple, affectionate and honest, so quietly august in the civilization that they have evolved and maintained through half a dozen thousand years. Through all her troubles and changes China has continued firm in her grasp of essential wisdom : and as you see her unaltering history reeled out before your eyes, it is as if you were getting a glimpse through the veils of European blindness into the elemental simplicity of wisdom, impregnable and immutable, that seeks its happiness in realms beyond the reach of competing telephones or trams.

The heat grew softer and steamier, day by day ; the country slow and flat, and fat and low ; no more cliffs, but terraced little red bare hills. And the river also ran fat and flat and slow, with few rapids for a while. But these were bad ones, and in the night, Mr. Noah being at his pipe under the mosquito netting, the idiot-nephew ran us on a rock, with a shattering concussion. All day we rowed, knocking off at some half a dozen intervals for a quarter of an hour's meal of rice : and at dusk would draw into some village-shore, and there tie up for the night among the other hooded barges in dense rows, with the whitewashed, dark-beamed thatched cottages looming beyond in their ranks, and a curly-roofed temple standing up in the middle and perhaps a pagoda, paternally presiding from a hill across the water. Never before had I so poignantly realized this dear kind land, so colossal in its calm and strength ; and the direct wise people who have made it. Never before had I had time. Glorious bamboos now filled the walled temple-enclosures along the hills with their sumptuous plumage : we passed a particularly famous Temple of Boatmen's Luck, in a fold of the hills ; and then the river abruptly swung in a great bend round shingled miles of " landes " feathery with a big grass-like Pampas, in clumps. And so came to the charming walled town of Peng, lying on a flat behind the shore, embowered deeply in trees, and with a goodly tower. Here we moored to change soldiers. The Laoyeh asked to see our passports ; these we statelily refused him, fearing more fuss, but got our new escort none the less. For we were moving towards trouble : coming events were so near, and their shadow so dark, that already Szechuan was seething with revolt against the President's obvious ambitions, and brigandage, masquerading as civil war, was already agog down the lower reaches of the Ja-Ling-Jang.

I felt calm and comfort spreading like ointment over the raw surface of our nerves. No high events troubled our days ; Bill concocted scones, and the caterer-cook had his tubful of rice perpetually preparing for the rowers, and Mrs. Noah with little Wei-Shang assiduously kept house. It was my first insight into Chinese domestic life, and never in all my experience have I come across a more rigid and unresting housewife than Mrs. Noah. She was for ever at it, scrubbing, scouring, brushing, till the boards of the boat fairly shone with cleanness, and not a grain of dust or dirt was allowed to linger anywhere. She ruled the roost with a rod of iron, and if even I myself cracked a nut, and dropped the shells on deck, down would be brought a little wooden box, with a message, would his Lordship kindly put his nutshells into that. Little Wei-Shang also helped, with a little besom and brush of her own, and frantic squeaks and rushings about whenever the puppies misbehaved. And when the scouring was done, mother and daughter would sit insatiably sewing shoes, and darning and mending. Mrs. Noah was small and neat and trim and comely, with the typical alert build of the born housewife all the world over, and the housewife's tight little hard face and pinched, superficial smile. She never relaxed or became human : her detachment was as inviolable as her courtesy, and we seemed to make no impression on her notice whatever.   Little Wei-Shang was of quite a different kidney, a vivid small butterfly of a child, full of fun and pranks and pusseries, and little quirks of laughter.   She was evidently the darling of her parents, unabashed and candid as a happy kitten.   She played with us, and she played with the puppies ; and what fun it was when the day's work was done, and Little Wei-Shang's best shoes and frock and scarlet ankle-bands were put on and her two pigtails done up with scarlet bows.   Then came bowls of dinner, which she and Mrs. Noah discreetly ate, sitting each on her stool ; and afterwards they crept under the mosquito-netting for the night, where Mr. Noah was already prone with his opium pipe, till the time came for him to resume his place on the bridge. And every evening when we had moored, the tapers would be lit before the shrine, in gratitude for the past day and propitiation for the next.

Quieter grew the country, and broader the river, and blander the warmth.   We had a crate of hens aboard, and one afternoon Bill and I discussed whether hens could swim. I put out a stick to touch one of them, who was sitting on the gunwale.   Whereupon, to my amazement and horror, that misguided fowl rose into the air with loud squawks and flapped heavily away and came down flop in the middle of the Ja-Ling-Jang behind us.   A hubbub arose : the oarsmen easied, contradictory clamours raged : and I then realized that gallant bird was swimming bravely as any duck, chest up and head high, paddling passionately, and evidently meditating abandoning pursuit of the perfidious boat, and making instead for the shore.   But my heart was wrung to see its efforts failing, and its brave head gradually declining, and its hull sinking lower and lower in the water.   But meanwhile the skipper was not idle : to let us lose a hen worth perhaps a full threepence, was not to be thought of : amid shouts the Ark swung back, and put about, and bore down to the rescue of the now sinking hen.   It was almost at its last gasp when the boat-hook caught it, and its head drooped to the water. To general acclamation it was drawn aboard, and hung up to dry and recuperate before the fire. Which it very soon did, and was put back among the other hens, no doubt to tell them the wonderful story. And we issued orders in respect of its courage and skill, that though the other " Ji's " might ultimately all go the destined road of " Ji's," this particular Ji should never be sacrificed to the table, but fill out its full tale of days in laud and honour, as a living legend.

Despite the perpetual expectation of brigands, the scene continued wholly peaceful, and the country continued each day in a diminuendo, wider and flatter, with flatter, wider water, and wider plains of " pampas." We came to a very picturesque place at last, called Nung Mun Chiang, which I regret to have to present to you in so unmanageable a jingle of jargon. There is no help for it though : Mafu was no longer with us to write down, however ill, the characters for the successive place-names, and Go-Go could no more write than fly, so that except for such simple words as were within hold of my own very limited vocabulary, I have been quite at sea for the meanings of names ever since we quitted Lanchow. Nung Mun Chiang had a cheap pagoda on the hill above, and a long bayed frontage of white Kentish-looking houses under the cliff below : a huge fair was being held ; and the blue-clad crowds were dense, with rows behind rows of arks drawn up in the waterway, and quantities of people being borne to and fro on ferries.

We changed escort here, and to my relief had no difficulty in getting four smart soldiers for the next stage, in view of the skipper's increasing anxiety about the brigands. We were now busily on guard ; when we reached Li-Du-Jô (which has a very noble temple, and a low foreshore stacked with reeds, and little screens of reed-matting rigged up all over the place as if it were a camp) we were boarded by big soldiers and a neat polite little man in black satin, who might so easily have been a brigand, except that he wasn't. But the alarm was serious : *in terrorem* we rigged up a camouflage in the prow, with camera-tripod, the rifle, and a cloth thrown over them all—to look like a hooded machine-gun with the barrel protruding. And at Ting Yuon, further down, the Laoyeh sent out, with a new escort, two very elegant and courtly minions, who came, not once, but twice, on purpose to beg us not to go any further yet awhile, since trouble had already broken out down the river the day before.

We held firm, however, in our purpose, and ultimately got our passport to proceed. But then Mr. Noah himself weakened, alarmed by stories of the battle ; and at Ting Yuen we stayed moored all night after all. And really, considering all the perils we had successfully lived through or escaped, it did seem as if it would be a waste to die by some strange bullet in Szechuan, within actual sight of our journey's end. The air was thick, in fact, with drama, as we sat out on deck in the gloaming; plunk, there came a great stone crashing down between us in the soft fragrant stillness. I quite thought it was the opening shot of an engagement, and instinctively assumed my tumbrel-face immediately : but nothing more ensued. It was as well, for none of our staff any longer had any help in them at all ; the strange country and people having deprived them of any small wits they might ever have had and reduced them to a pack of blank baboons.

Meanwhile the country grew richer : rounded bluffs of sandstone reappeared, and the profiles of the hills were castellated in outline with one big phallic cone of rock aspiring, and many a walled temple park of woodland along their tops, and groves of bamboos more and more dense and sumptuous each day, and orchards of tangerine oranges huddled under the cliffs glimmering redly golden in the thick black blocks of their dark foliage. As day dawned we moved out in a milk-white universal fog, that soon cleared to a blinding radiance of light and heat. Various temples, agog with fairs and beanoes, we passed by : Nien Ming is a peculiarly lovely little place, of whitewashed houses piled up among heavy verdure of trees, along the top of cliffs about a creek : a man was pulling up a fishin-gline that seemed to have no end, and the broad face of the river was not more than wide enough for the broad V-shaped rafts of timber that were being floated down, in a plain of spillikins, with a hutch at one end for the raftsmen. Finally the day died down in a consuming glory of orange glow, with the embanking hills and their profiled clumps of bamboo cut out solid in sombre violet, and the swale of the river unctuous in long streaks of alternating black and gold.

Soon after dark we drew into a little cove, and again found soldiers on the watch, to prove to us once more how pressing and general was the apprehension of trouble hereabouts. We had a mischance, too, of our own : for as we edged into our Ark's space in the row of others, the next one bumped us, and a tumbler of the Lord High Keeper of the King's Peace's fell off the table and broke. Pandemonium was loosed : even Mrs. Noah was moved to emotion : everybody talked at once in screams. All, however, got amicably settled, and there came aboard a very comely, pleasant-smiling woman, a gossip of Mrs. Noah's, to sit with her and chat : apparently she habitually ailed, for pussy little Wei-Shang came across to us and prettily asked for medicine for her. And the party was also enriched by two perfectly hideous old Appu's, aunts of the idiot-nephew.

"Ai-oh, EE-oh, Ai-ai—Ai-oh, Ee-oh, ai, ai," calmly, in the calm white misted dawn we were out in mid-river again, long before I had properly woken, so that the rhythmic chanting and soft rhythmic splash of the oars only flickered into my dreams dimly, like a far away half-heard accompaniment. Lower country now, and lower still : a perched village ; narrows ; vast flights of duck, in myriads along all the shingles ; orange groves packed along the under cliffs : and a voluminous glory of bamboos on the slopes ; and now wide-stretching flats of moulded rock, flowing away into backwaters that formed lagoons over the plain. At Ho-Jô a new river, clean and clear as an emerald, flows down into the dun-coloured dirt of the Ja-Ling-Jang, and is immediately obliterated in its filth. Ho-Jô is a very big place, with long and densely crowded quays, and handsome buildings, and a fine pagoda opposite, and an incessant turmoil of ferries and ship-faring in all directions.

It was twelve before our new escort came aboard. I sat on deck to watch the traffic, rejoicing in the strong sharp wind that tempered the blaze of the day. Swirling round the race of the point, the square patch-sailed ships came bravely sailing on its impulse, and the scene was all glad bustle with news of four brigands condignly shot the night before. And as I sat the Queen of Shamakhan went by me, surely shrined in a gauze-curtained sedan, green as grass, with two ancient and dreadful duennas attendant in the prow of the ferry-boat that was conveying her across. Through the green slats she glimmered, in a loveliness almost elfin and unearthly, a lady of very high quality, calm as an image, with face of delicate oval, perfect alike in feature and colour, and high-flung moth-eyebrows that emphasized the immemorial innocence of her mysterious close smile. And so she passed : when a Chinese lady is beautiful, not Cavalieri herself could eclipse her ; she has a finish, a poise, an exquisiteness unsurpassable, of looks, of manner, of movement. But beauty is rare ; and not easy to catch sight of among these barbarous old races who do not care to level the lady with the harlot in a rivalry of half-clad display and advertisement.

The next day hills reappeared, and we entered upon a long passage down between them, in what might almost be called a gorge. High on either side rose wooded, rocky ranges, nursing little whitewashed cottages amid the verdure in their folds. And every one of them had its coal-shoot streaming down to the river in a long smear of darkness. The villages were extraordinarily English in effect, and their scene would have been rurally English too, but that it was bigger and bolder, with much denuded limestone strata uptilted almost perpendicularly to the summit, that made it rather a Provençal picture, taking me back yet again to

the mouth of the Roja; especially as all the long bare hills
have every possible inch of their ground, no matter how tiny
a strip it be, or how un-get-at-able, terraced up for culture
by a bank of rough-walling. And one of the bigger, rounder
hogs'-backs of scar limestone was densely peppered with the
wild Palm.

Stations of the river-police were by this time frequent, and
the face of the river was dense with traffic. Big hulks were
being towed up by teams of thirty or forty towers, almost on
all fours with the strain, bare-legged and bare-bottomed,
glowing rosy on the grey ground of rock and shingle, with
that odd uncanny radiance which the human body possesses
at large in a landscape. Delays by the police-boats brought
us to again and again. Till at a bend of the river, with fine
wooded pinnacles ranging away ahead, we were pulled up
more seriously than before. Bill went ashore to cope with
the authorities, while I filled up the time by exploring the
foreshore, which, from a bluff overhead, descended gradually
in a chaos of enormous tumbled boulders, plumy here and
there with tuffets of grass. I sauntered on: the calm
warmth of the evening was delicious, and conduced to complacent meditation. But then, afar off, I saw Bill hastily
returning from the village : when he noticed where I had
got to he shouted to me to get aboard again as quickly as I
could, feigning debility. Evidently my stroll had been ill-
timed. Languidly I drooped and flopped and stumbled
broken-wingedly down the rocks for the benefit of possible
observers ; and when I came aboard sank swooning into my
deck-chair, there to be histrionically tended by Bill, with
lifting of the arms to Heaven, and convulsive gestures of
anxiety.

It appeared that the police had threatened to keep us
moored here till midday of the morrow, and that Bill had
only dissuaded them by representing me as prostrate in
mortal sickness to be got down into Chung King as soon as
possible. And then, lo and behold, there was I, for all to see,
strolling among the boulders as gay as any grig. However,

the authorities showed no suspicion about my symptoms, and placidly our oarsmen chaunted us out into midstream, and once more downward. But about dusk we were stopped finally and made to moor for the night in a gorge, at what the morning showed me to be a very pretty little coal-wharf, with steep stone stairways down to the water and a cascade above. Then, having loaded up with coke, we made off again, emerging at last into tame country, leaving the beautiful narrows and pinnacled range behind us. Two new-looking great slim pagodas dominated the next town we came to, a buzzing place, where our final police-station worried us. The river now gushed over many wide perilous strata of half-emerged rock, and in the afternoon we came to a much larger town than any yet, with a big foreign factory and chimney-stack and steam-whistle. The journey was almost in sight of its end : in luxuriance, such as the lethargy of fatigue would allow us, we sat on deck to watch the populous scene, and a faceless syphilitic peddling cakes alongside on the shore. I had a moment's unpopularity with Mrs. Noah, too, for after I had been sitting for some time on a bale in the prow there was extracted from beneath it the smaller of the mangy little fluffy black puppies, in so limp a condition that it was long before he showed signs of coming back to life. And then we were off again, and the chaunting of the haulers that we now kept meeting on their way up-stream was a pure joy, no longer a series of high-pitched nasal cat-calls, but deep and solemn and dark as a litany in some old cathedral. So night came down, and in the grey morning of November 16, two months and two days since I rode out of Tien Tang, I woke uneasily, amid rivering clamours, to find ourselves anchored in what seemed the same river, but wider than before, though no less turbid. But we had rounded our last corner, and this was the Great River itself, the Da-Hor, the Yang-dz'-Jang ; and above us hung a steep wharf of houses built of matting, up and up in a wall—the Yang-dz' frontage of Chung King.

COLOPHON

Chung King lies high and up and down above the curve of the river. In due course a brace of chairs came down for us, and we were conveyed dizzily up flights of stairs into the town itself; and thence along its very narrow streets, very crowded, dark and dank and paved, to the narrow dark yard of what proved, however, an inn so foreign as to rightly justify its claim to be an hotel. For here, after two years of exile, I felt myself quite like a child come back to its doll's-house, revelling in the folly of white sheets and spring-mattresses, and tables and chairs and tablecloths and cutlery and glasses.

Out in front was a big wooden loggia looking over the river far below to a range of peaked wooden hills, with temples and pagodas on them, and immediately in front of us, across the river, the name of that great nobleman, Sir Alfred Mond, emblazoned across the frontal of a factory, to bring us once more in touch with the beloved benefits of British enterprise. Not even this happy home-touch, however, not even the spectacle, one night, of raging fire, devouring house after house in its maw, but not Sir Alfred Mond, could cheer the dark of our declining days, in this dark place where the air is almost always suggestive of a London fog. Final disbandings proceeded, and the Ark went back up-river again after farewell visits to the inn from Tanguei, and Little Wei-Shang in her silken bests. We ourselves hesitated long about our next move. My theory had been to take another ark down the river, and alight at South Wu S'an on the chance of getting seed, up in the ranges behind it, of Primula Fargesii and Rhododendron auriculatum. But now the information about the region seemed so vague, and we ourselves were so much the worse for wear, and this fiddling little

373

odd-and-end of a post-final trapese seemed such a bathos, such a contemptible excrescence on the full and perfect round of our travels, that we inclined more and more to abandon the notion of going after a goose so wild with hearts so weary.

And so at last we did, and booked our places on the steamer that now lay moored under the farther bank getting ready for her last downward journey, before the locking up of the Tibetan snows made the river no longer navigable for her. Mr. Chun, our genial landlord, escorted us over to her by ferry, and there we found quarters that seemed palatial, on a vessel of the oddest shape, like two vast trams tied together, side by side. One more night in the inn : we were poled back, quite tremulous, through the awful swirls and whirl-pools of the Yang-dz' heaving all round us in a pale waste of waters, unctuous, vehement and baleful : but the high river-wall and tower of the city in front of us and its piled-up houses of matting, plastered up its sandstone cliff like swal-lows' nests, were all of a lovely picturesqueness in the golden afternoon. And now Mr. Chun would stand us a farewell dinner, and after it, amid general salutations, he and we came away in chairs, and borne down the long stone flights to the river again, the waning moon now glorious in ghastly reflections on its oily expanses. And so we reached the s.s. *Shu-Hun*, and at last our kind landlord had done the last he could to make us comfortable. So it was farewell to him, farewell to Chung King, farewell to the toils and tediums of the track. It was quite with sorrow that I took leave of Mr. Chun, so ingeniously helpful and friendly and full of indefatigable services that never appeared on his modest bill, nor indeed could have been reckoned for in coin. Good luck to the Chung King Hotel !

At daybreak we loosed, so softly that I never knew we had done so till we were already far from Chung King. After a poor night I rose to another brumous day of raw and gusty darkness, whose pearly tones of blue pallor well harmonized with the rapidly-shifting scene. This was precisely that of our last uneventful stages down the Ja-Ling-Jang, but the swiftness of the Yang-dz' is such that even junks going down it make at least double their pace on the Ja-Ling-Jang. As for the steamer, it fairly tore along : the Yang-dz' runs in vast oleaginous swirls and hills and valleys of hideously forceful silent water, with long successions of flats over concealed levels of rock-strata, most perilous and appalling, and least so when emerging. We surged along, however, magnificently tossing the junks along our wake unmercifully, on whitehorse waves against the rocky shores. Then we passed a big mountain of rock, like Sigiri, with temples on it, then came into sight of red ranges, on either hand, very dim and ghostly in cloud.

The next day's journey started out from Nan Hsien in a dense, drizzling brume. We descended in and out amid steepening hills, in a channel dull as the Rhine's but far deeper and finer, the significant note of the Yang-dz' being the appalling depth and volume of it, often confined for miles together to a straight canal-like channel no wider than the Thames at Marlow, down which the incalculable weight of one of the greatest rivers of Asia seethes with a silent intensity of smooth fury that makes you curdle as you watch its bland slow-seeming eddies. At one point the strata on the North bank are quite horizontal, those on the South almost perpendicular : you can see down what a narrow line of cleavage this terrific river has cloven a channel. We anchored placidly at Gui Jô, where wooden combs in bundles (a speciality of the place) were brought on board for sale. After dark there came little dancing-girls (another speciality) and were rowed round the ship in sampans shrilling thinly in the black starless night. And then down came the Lao-yeh of the place, and the dark was shattered with a fury of light and mortars and bombards exploding ; and the shore grew gay with a concourse of torches. And all night long the din continued, with barking of dogs and howling of coolies, and military bands braying and salutes being fired.

Very shortly after leaving Gui Jô, we very abruptly passed

through a Strait Gate of cliffs round a bend, and found ourselves at last in the famous Gorges of the Yang-dz' Jang—
the objectives of all this gigantic journey, because so widely
proclaimed one of the world's marvels. And this indeed
they are ; do not let me discourage those who contemplate
visiting them in ease and comfort and a three days' steam-
trip up from Hangkow. Of this, indeed, they will most
handsomely " repay the trouble and expense." Allowance,
too, must be made for the tired eyes and lowered mood which
was all I had left to apprehend them with by now. Nevertheless, I will boldly premise that to us, who had known the
ravines of Thundercrown and the Gorges of the Nan-Ho,
those of the Yang-dz' proved comparatively tame, and by
no means adequate reward or climax for the length of toil
which we had undertaken to reach them.

Nor need those ambitious of visiting the Yang-dz' gorges
go even so far as Hangkow. You may traverse the Yang-dz'
gorges any day you please (when peace permits) on the
stretch of line between Culoz and Aix-les-Bains, along which
indeed whole scenes of cliffs and narrows and impending
complications of wooded mountains will give you the perfect
picture of every aspect of the Yang-dz's break through its
mountain barrier, substituting, for the line and the stream,
the one monotonous, boiling, mud-coloured Horror of the
Great River, completely filling the valley bottom. In fact,
the most impressive thing in the Yang-dz' gorges is the Yang-
dz' itself, surging along at the rate of an express, in a terrifying concentrated fury of heaves and strivings, so narrow
between the walls as to be an apparent nothing across which
an urchin could chuck a pebble, yet compressed by the
channel into such unplumbed depths that the largest steam-
ship can nose-dive to the bottom and not only utterly dis-
appear and be no more heard of, but even be beyond reach
of plummet. The Da-Hor is no river to jest with, and its
dark bowels digest many a big ship, undiscoverable for evermore.

A flotilla of junks approached to meet us, ahead of the

Great Gate, phantasmal as a floating flight of moths in the grey of dawn against the towering grey of the cliffs behind. But, as day lightened, the Great Gate opened on into a scene of comparative tameness. About seven we passed Wu S'an, and then came into a gorge of twenty-eight miles, astoundingly narrow for so vast a river. You do not need to be told tales of disappearances, to appreciate the rightful profundity of this preposterous channel, that has to be the main drain for all the waters of Eastern Tibet and Western China. For the Hwang-Hor swings up into the far North, while the Mekong and the Salween sweep straight South. In a deep and sombre cutting the gorge winds on, tightly bound by walls of rock, in huge undulating strata of rock, aspiring here and there to peaks. Late as it now was in the season (Nov. 29), hardly a leaf seemed shed, and the rocky limestone hills looked singularly dry for so presumably damp a range. The river receives no tributary : only the merest and rarest rill-runs join it, down lateral chines, above and beyond which there sometimes shows a higher and more rich region. But, noble and splendid as was all the scene, it was on a very small gentle scale to us, after the immeasurably huge austerities of the Tibetan Border : I could not help envying early collectors the fame they acquired so comfortably and easily, boating up the Yang-dz' and mooring here and there, and exploring (often vicariously) these pleasant ravines and chines. And in those far-off golden days too, when everything that every coolie brought home to you, basking over a book in your boat, was either a new species or a new genus ; till you could not step ashore into a back-yard without the merest hideous little weed there being a novelty. Gone, gone are those days for ever, though, and farther and farther away live the Farreris and Purdomiis and Forrestiis of the future, increasingly remote year by year on mountains less and less get-at-able.

At Gui Jô the river widens and passes out of Szechuan into Hupeh. And now comes the finest stretch of the journey. For soon you enter a new set of gorges, far wilder and more glorious than the last—not a titanic railway-cutting but a splendid compilation of cliffs and fantastic peaks and woods, with big high downs and more fantastic peaks tumbling up into the distances on either hand. Then ensues a very dangerous stretch of loose rocks, with one of the river's most fatal and famous rapids, a definite drop already growing visible in the diminution of the water which, ahead of you, is seen in two planes like the double-lake trick at Friar Park. One saw clearly why it is that steamers daren't ply when the river runs low. And now at length we entered into a new and isolated mountain range, and were actually in the I-chang Gorge itself, the last and most famous of all. But the I-chang Gorge is very mild and tame by comparison with its predecessors. It runs meekly between pinnacled tidily-clothed clifflets on either side, neatly arranged all along in horizontal white strata, so regular and obvious that they look as if they were built of white Doulton-ware, a little the worse for use. However, as I say, perhaps my standard was spoiled by greater things seen earlier : and other visitors to the I-chang Gorge will not by any means agree with me, that it makes one feel as if one were passing by waterway down through the ruins of Leicester Railway Station, enormously lengthened and magnified, and so long ago abandoned as now to be stratified in the grass and overgrowth of ages. And the I-changs will certainly arise and slay me, and the dragon issue from his cave to eat me.

For, along these limestone gorges are caverns lurking ; and in them legendary dragons lie sleeping till the moment of their emergence. When we came out from the Gorges, and down a last flat stretch of river, open and dull, to where, in unrelievable monotony I-chang lies flatly sprawling, we found the town agog over the recent discovery of a fossil-dragon in one of the caves. In times so critical this event loomed large for the President-Emperor's future, and an official inquiry was already afoot, and official bulletins were being issued. The Imperialist party argued that the timely revelation of a dragon clearly favoured Imperial claims : the

Republicans with equal plausibility maintained that it
militated as clearly against them.   Yet a third party existed,
which realized that the " dragon " was of course only a fine
large sample of those corrugated scaled-looking barriers of
stalagmite that often get built up in caverns across the lower
rim of their pools, looking, according to their size, like petri-
fied ropes or tree-trunks, or, as in this case, dragons.   But
not even the European population of I-chang was wholly
friendly to this rationalistic interpretation.   They would not
willingly be weaned from belief in their dragon, and only the
crashing political movements of the time, and the eventual
downfall of the Emperor Yuan, at last silenced popular
speculation on the point, by depriving it of popular interest.

The roadstead at I-chang will always be to me the saddest
place on earth.   Round a vast bend of the Yang-dz' it lies,
sad and flat and forbidding-looking, grey under a grey sky,
with nothing but grey flatness filling all the world around,
and the mountains left behind for ever, and even the meek
hills of the gorges now only a dim grey ruffle up the Western
distance.   It may, indeed, be a delightful place to those who
live there, but to me it spells the close of everything.   The
Rainbow Bridge here sinks to its end, and comes back to
earth, fading into the shadows of the nearer shore.   After
I-chang everything grows faint and dim : the past veiled by
apprehensions of the new future, and the future darkened
by sunset flushes from the past behind us.   To my fancy,
the expedition now literally dissolves into cloud.   Out in
the new circumstances ahead the old close-knit realities
fall away like ghosts.   The old bonds were done with and
dissolved : I felt Bill drawing gradually away, and I also,
out of a fairyland, where we both had once belonged, but
from which we were now severally emerging on to different
roads of greyness.   And Bongie and good Go-go were quite
gone.   See how they have faded out of these pages as I
re-lived the past.   They began to vanish when we reached
the Ark, and their essential functions ceased and, as the
journey South continued into increasing civilization, they

grew more and more dithered and dotty every day, more and more unreal ; till now, though both were still with us, they had wholly ceased to be, had become anachronisms first, then lingering evocations out of the past, phantoms as filmy as Faustus' Helen, though in no other point recalling the beauty of the evening air. They had passed, forgotten, in fact, as a dream dies in the opening day. But, better to parallel my own point of view, say, " as a joy dies in the close of dark." Anyhow, they were gone ; though often again in Peking I saw Go-go, and saw Mafu, I never could feel them real or solid. They had passed away ; they belonged elsewhere. I was glad when I no longer saw them. They were less real to me in Peking than the Prior of Cheb-son, and the Gwan-ja of Tien Tang, and Grandmamma Aoo : it is always a jar when things that only belong to the mind's eye persist in obtruding themselves on the body's.

So I bring you no farther. To the rest of my tale belongs only decent uneventful dullness—golden long dull days in a new steamer down the vast dull flats of the river, through country so flat as almost to seem *all* river ; a pause in Hangkow, to learn again, for the first time since leaving London, what a real bath was like, and then the long train-journey up to Peking again, and a dull drab arrival, on December 6, to face the dreadfulness of three months' accumulated correspondence. And here I leave you, reader ; here I no longer know you, nor you me—here for a long time I could not know myself. For we have known each other and belonged to each other away from all this, out in the Radiant Places. And if ever I can return to them, reader, perhaps you will come too ?

BOTANICAL INDEX

Aconitum, 219, 265
  French grey, 279
  Hemsleyanum, 344
  new, 344
Adenophora, china-blue, 248
Adonis, cœrulea, 109, 113, 147
  yellow, 73
Alder, 190, 204
Aleurites cordata, 346
Allium, yellow, 212
Androsace longifolia, 343
  mucronifolia, 146, 188, 206
  spinulifera, 332
  tibetica, 50, 78, 111, 114, 115,
      125, 127, 135, 144, 169,
      183, 193
    late form, 271
Anemone obtusiloba, 142
  vitifolia, 253, 339
Aquilegia viridiflora, 50, 127, 136
Artemisia, 296
Arundinaria anceps, 329
  Metake, 331
  nitida, 329
  spathiflora, 329
  new, 320
Aster, Alpine, 222
  China, 177
  dwarf, pale, 226
  large violet, 197
  new, 148

Berberis, 109
Boea, 341
Buddleia, 333, 337, 343

Cæsalpinia, 333
Caragana, golden, 73, 110, 113,
    131, 250
  pink, 194, 210, 211
Cerastium melandrinum (Chick-
     weed), 285
  white-starred, 205

Cherry, 113, 281
Chrysanthemum Zawadskyi, 326
Clematis, atragonoid, blue, 218
  similar to C. Armandi, 352
Clerodendron, 341
Convolvulus tragacanthoides, 343
Corydalis curviflora, azure, 165,
    260
  melanochlora, 165, 229, 264,
    266
  Purdomii, 266
  scaberula, 246
Cotoneaster Micromeles (?), 330,
    337
Cratægus crenulata, 327
Cremanthodium, 238, 264
Crocus speciosus, purple, 77
Cypress, small aromatic, 83
  copses of, 108, 156, 199
Cypressus, 352

Daphne, 80, 151, 152, 180, 193
  Ivory, 181, 198
Delphinium, pale blue, 293
  purple, 190
  Pylzowi, violet, 239, 246, 254,
    264, 270
  tanguticum, 271
Dianthus squarrosus, 260
Dipelta, 337
Draba, golden, 94, 152, 181

Ephedra, deep rose, 253
Erysimum, purple, 152, 200, 202
  rosy, 207, 212, 285
  white, 217

Fabaria, golden, 109, 127
Fairy Bell, 191, 192
Flora at 10,000 ft., 133

Gagea, 127
Garlic, yellow, 247

381

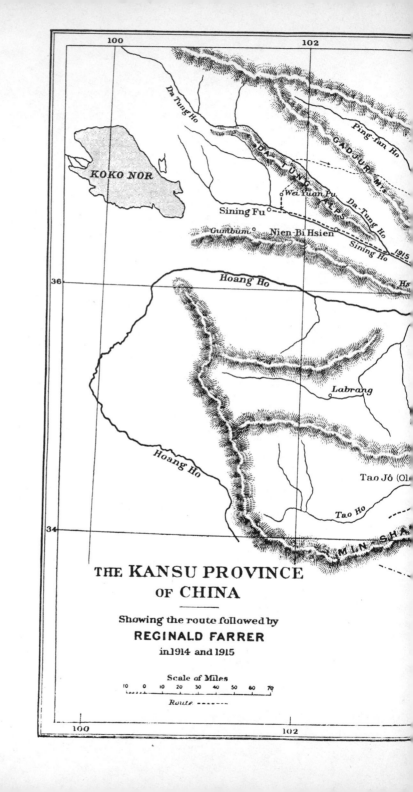

THE **KANSU PROVINCE**
OF **CHINA**

Showing the route followed by

REGINALD FARRER

in 1914 and 1915

Scale of Miles

10   0   10   20   30   40   50   60   70

Route - - - - - -

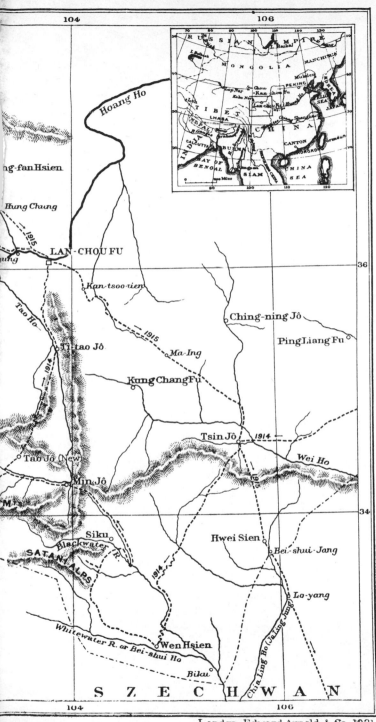

Hoang Ho

ng-fan Hsien

Hung Chung

1915

LAN-CHOU FU

Kan-tsoo-sien

1915

Ching-ning Jô

Ping Liang Fu

Tao Ho

Ti tao Jô

Ma-Ing

1914

Kung Chang Fu

Tsin Jô   1914

Wei Ho

Tao Jô (New)

Min Jô

M'

Siku

Hwei Sien

Bei-shui-Jang

Blackwater R.

SATANI ALPS

1914

Lo-yang

Whitewater R. or Bei-shui Ho

Wen Hsien

Bikú

Chi-a Ling Ho (Ja-Ling-Jang)

36

34

London, Edward Arnold & Co. 1921